9/77

D0857820

364.609   E68

Eriksson, Torsten

The reformers

DATE DUE			
APR 23 '79			
OCT 2 3 '80			
NOV 6 '81			
FEB 15 '84			
MAY 1 2 '86			
MAR 2 8 '88			
NOV 2 2 '89			
OCT. 1 8 1991			
MAY 1 0 '92			
MAY 0 2 2000			
APR 0 7 2001			

Property of
HARRISBURG AREA
COMMUNITY COLLEGE LIBRARY
Harrisburg, Pa.

Torsten Eriksson is a former Director General of the National Swedish Correctional Administration who also served the United Nations as an Interregional Adviser on Crime Prevention and Criminal Justice. He has visited 68 countries on official missions and is a Board member of the International Penal and Penitentiary Foundation and the International Society of Criminology.

PREFACE

The history of the treatment of criminals is primarily the story of man's inhumanity to man. At the same time it contains innumerable examples of his compassion and of his will to lead the offender into a new life as a useful and responsible citizen.

This book traces the development of the treatment of criminals as reflected in the experiments and reforms accomplished by our pioneers. The treatment of criminals through the ages is a fascinating tale, not least when we realize that much of what we think has already been thought by others, that what we say has been said before, and that what we do has already been done and in days when resources were minimal in comparison with our own. Furthermore, the same ideas have been conceived, expressed and executed by reformers who encountered much stronger opposition and were in a much smaller minority than any present-day reformers need experience.

Writing this book has been rather like solving a jigsaw puzzle. Countless pieces of information have been picked up here and there and gradually fitted together to form a whole. For their help in finding the books and documents I needed for this purpose, I am grateful to criminologists and librarians all over the world. In this respect, my principle debt of gratitude is to Professor Thorsten Sellin. I also wish to express special thanks to Mr. Zen Tokoi, Director of the United Nations Asia and Far East Institute for the Prevention of Crime and the Treatment of Offenders (UNAFEI) in Fuchu, Japan, and his deputy, Mr. Minoru Shikita for their support in this work, and to Mrs. Tomoko Itoh for her patience and skill in typing the manuscript.

Stockholm
June, 1976

TORSTEN ERIKSSON

THE
REFORMERS

THE
REFORMERS

*An Historical Survey of
Pioneer Experiments in the
Treatment of Criminals*

TORSTEN ERIKSSON

Translated from the original Swedish text by Catherine Djurklou

ELSEVIER

New York/Oxford/Amsterdam

ELSEVIER SCIENTIFIC PUBLISHING COMPANY, INC.
52 Vanderbilt Avenue, New York, NY 10017

ELSEVIER SCIENTIFIC PUBLISHING COMPANY
335 Jan Van Galenstraat, P.O. Box 211
Amsterdam, The Netherlands

© 1976 by Elsevier Scientific Publishing Company, Inc.

Library of Congress Cataloging in Publication Data

Eriksson, Torsten.
  The reformers: an historical survey of pioneer
  experiments in the treatment of criminals
  Bibliography: p.
  Includes Index.
    1. Corrections—History. 2. Prisons—History.
I. Title.
HV8975.E74   364.6'09   76-25049
ISBN 0-444-99030-5

Manufactured in the United States of America

Designed by Loretta Li

To those who tried, even if they failed

77457

CONTENTS

(portfolio of photographs follows page 180)

THE
REFORMERS

[1] BACKGROUND

Violence and Fear

The history of justice is replete with violence and fear. Ever since the concept of law came into being, the authorities have been convinced that respect for the law mainly depends on the severity of the punishment. Many people, perhaps the majority, hold this conviction, even though history provides ample evidence to the contrary. Fear is effective for a time, but gradually leads to insensitivity. Violence breeds more violence. Regimes that have tried to subjugate foreign peoples have learned this, and whenever brutality by the police, in the courts, and in the prisons has sought to crush lawbreakers, the backlash has been even more brutal.

At the international congress on the Prevention of Crime and the Treatment of Offenders in Berlin in 1935, Joseph Gœbbels, Hitler's Minister of Propaganda, proclaimed that "the criminal shall once again tremble before the State."[1] But crime could not be stamped out by threats and reprisals at that time either. On the contrary, professional criminals flourished as never before in the bitter struggle between the police and the underworld in Nazi Germany.

Thorsten Sellin, the famous criminologist, tells about a woman who was sentenced to death in 1617 after a history of 21 arrests in different towns in Holland. She had already been pilloried 11 times and whipped 7 times. She had also been branded 5 times and had her ears cut off. In addition, she had been banished for life from various towns on 7 occasions. A criminal in Amsterdam was whipped 7 times and branded 7 times between 1603 and 1605. Another man was whipped 7 times and branded 4 times between 1603 and 1606. A third was whipped 8 times, 4 of them during the years 1614-1616, and a fourth was whipped 4 times and branded 3 times in the space of one year, 1616. Still another had a record of 11 whippings and 5 brandings between 1614 and 1618. One man had an eye pierced as a punishment in 1617, and within the next few years he was sentenced to whipping on 6 occasions and to branding on 3.[2]

The most usual sentences were fines, the pillory, death, and corporal punishments. The two last-mentioned sanctions, always carried out in public, were devised with fiendish ingenuity by the authorities and were intended to serve as a warning to the citizenry at large. Consequently many punishments were designed symbolically. Scandal-mongers had their lips sewn together or their tongue cut off; thieves had one hand amputated; and so on. Torture during interrogations to extort the truth became increasingly common during the Middle Ages, particularly after it was sanctioned by a Papal Bull in 1252 in connection with the Inquisition. Korn and McCorkle[3] wrote about capital punishment in the medieval period:

> By the fourteenth century the most common penalty cited in continental records was death. As the number of crimes punishable by death increased, there was a corresponding increase in the ingenuity and variety of techniques of execution. Probably during no other period of Western civilization was there so intensive a search for new ways of making men die. Death by burning, suffocation, drowning, poisoning, impalement, fracture (breaking at the wheel), and burial alive was refined to the point where execution had become a profession combining many characteristics of an art, a science and a public spectacle.
>
> Certain executors achieved a wide reputation for a particular specialty and were numbered among the foremost public entertainers of the day. The city of Hanover developed a specialty in which death was inflicted by wasps. Later this method was refined to provide a slower death by ants and flies—an innovation that increased audience appeal by prolonging the length of the entertainment. The ingenuity and technical skill of the executioners is suggested by the complexity of the instructions they were required to follow. Sometimes the victim had to be kept conscious for a considerable period during which a detailed sequence of tortures and mutilations was carried out. In order to follow these instructions, the executioners were required to master the art of preserving life even while they destroyed it. It was one of the age's ironies that the anatomical knowledge and sheer medical competence of the executioners often rivaled that of the doctors of the day.

In the Forecourts of Humanitarianism

Olaus Petri, who sponsored the Protestant Reformation in Sweden, wrote in the 25th of *The Rules for Judges*, compiled in 1540 and still the preamble to the statutes of Sweden:

As occurs in the case of those who have stolen; they stand on the scaffold, lose their ears and are banished from the community; if such persons go to other lands where no one knows them and wish to reform and conduct themselves well, they are never trusted. The punishment is a hindrance to him who is punished and he becomes desperate and worse than ever before. It might have been better for him to lose his life immediately. The same is done with strumpets, who are put in the stocks and banished from the community, and where they had once committed adultery with one or two they now become every man's whore, which is no amendment. Therefore the judge shall show lenity in these cases so that the evil shall not be compounded for the law always requires amendment and for amendment it shall always be used.

While Olaus Petri was an early advocate for a humane treatment of criminals, he was not the first one. We find traces of understanding of the criminal and his situation as far back in time as we can go. The history of the treatment of criminals is as old as compassion itself. Several of the ancient philosophers were concerned with the problem of punishment, and many of them thought along lines that are in many respects reminiscent of modern ideas of reform. This was true of Plato (427-347 B.C.), who wrote in his "Laws" (Book IX): ". . . for no penalty which the law inflicts is designed for evil, but always makes him who suffers either better or not so much worse as he would have been." Plato saw the criminal as a sick man whose recovery must be a concern.[4] Seneca, a contemporary of Jesus Christ, also believed that punishments should not humiliate the offender. In Sellin's opinion, Seneca anticipated views that have won general acceptance in modern criminology.[5]

The founder of Christianity stated specifically that he had come into the world to redeem sinners and he instructed his disciples to visit the prisons ("I was in prison, and ye came unto me." Matthew 25:26). Since the apostles preached in the same vein, it is clear that prisoners played an important role in Christian charitable works ever since the dawn of the religion. The early Christians themselves had vast first-hand experience of imprisonment and other penalties. Confirmation that Christians were in fact diligent prison visitors is provided by Christian as well as heathen documents of the first two centuries anno Domini. St. Cyprian, Bishop of Carthage in the third century, who died a martyr's death, ordered the clergy to visit and comfort prisoners in accordance with the Gospel of St. Matthew. The Nicene Council in 325 A.D. established *procuratores pauperum*, an organization of prison visitors. As late as the end of the fifth century, we find ample evidence that Christians worked to ameliorate the plight of prisoners. In 529 A.D., Emperor Justinian decreed by law that bishops should visit prisons once a week, on Wednesdays and Fridays; they should determine the reasons why prisoners, freemen and slaves alike, were under arrest; and they should report prison officials if they had neglected their duties. And, at a Church Council in Orleans in 549 A.D., clerics were ordered to visit prisoners on Sundays.[6]

Thereafter little is recorded on the subject for almost ten centuries. In 1488, however, Pope Innocent VIII founded an institute in Rome known as *La prima compagnia della Misericordia di San Giovanni decollato* (The Society of the Mercy of St. John the Beheaded), the purpose of which was to comfort those condemned to death. Several other societies of the same nature were formed in the sixteenth century, e.g., Johann Callier's *Della Pietà de Carcerati* (Compassion for Prisoners), which was mainly concerned with inmates of debtors' prisons. Certain temporal princes also interested themselves in the treatment of prisoners.[7] Emperor Constantine ordered judges to visit prisons each Sunday to make sure that the inmates enjoyed all their rights under the law. And Alfonso X "the Wise," King of Leon and Castille, who came to the throne in 1252 (also a recognised astronomer and philosopher), wrote in his law code *Las Siete Partidas:* "The prisons shall serve to keep in safe custody those incarcerated in them, but shall in no way expose them to spiritual suffering or cause them any harm." These words applied first and foremost to individuals under indictment. But the code, which was never enforced but served more as a guide for judicial practices, also specified that guards who plagued prisoners out of malice would be sentenced to death.[8]

Imprisonment

Although fines, public humiliation, and corporal punishment were the most common penalties in ancient times, incarceration in a prison was also a form of penalty in itself. It is true that the Roman lawyers objected to this, and the famous jurist, Ulpian, decreed in the third century that "prisons should be used for detention only and not for punishment." *(Carcer enim ad continendos homines, non ad puniendos haberi debet.)* By quoting these words in his *Digest*, a collection of sixth century legal opinions, Emperor Justinian transformed them into law. The Roman Republic did not use imprisonment as a penalty. Under the Empire, however, despite the *Digest*, various forms of deprivation of liberty came into use, e.g., forced labor in the mines *(pena metalli)* and other kinds of public work *(opus publicum)*. Legal sources also mention incarceration in a prison *(carcer)* as a sanction. Old German penal law only recognized deprivation of liberty in the form of thralldom.[9] From the beginning of the thirteenth century, we find laws directly stipulating sentences to imprisonment for certain crimes. For example, England's Statute of Westminster in 1275 prescribes two years of imprisonment for rape.[10] It should be recalled that medieval penal systems varied widely from year to year and from one country to another. "It is just as absurd to speak of a 'medieval' penal system as of a 'modern'," according to Hoegel.[11]

The Church also began at an early stage to use monasteries as penal institutions. It was reluctant to put priests and monks at the mercy of temporal justice and found it distasteful that its servants should be submitted to corporal punishment like ordinary people. On the other hand, Ulpian's ruling could scarcely be completely disregarded. Therefore, Pope Boniface VIII (1294-1303) made an interpretation according to which prisons, even though their "purpose is to detain but not punish criminals," could be used for members of the clergy who had confessed to or been found guilty of a crime, either for life or for a fixed period *"in order to do penance."*[12] Special penal cells were equipped for the purpose in numerous monasteries. They were also used for laymen in exceptional cases.

Jonas Hagströmer, a renowned Swedish jurist, wrote on this point in 1875:

> This unassuming character of a purely disciplinary system for the Church's own servants was not retained for any length of time by canonical penal law. During the middle ages, the Church drew into its jurisdiction not only all crimes committed by spiritual persons, but also a growing number of offences by laymen. In this way an ecclesiastical judicial system with power over laymen developed side by side with the temporal, sometimes in competition with it, sometimes excluding it, and sometimes complementing it.[13]

Not all worldly rulers were willing to bow to the Church's claim to judicial authority over its own people. Charlemagne, for example, insisted on the right to confirm sentences. The expansion of the Church's jurisdiction into secular territory was inexplicably rapid in England. As early as 1350, a law was passed to the effect that all scribes, both secular and clerical, should enjoy the "benefit of clergy." Soon, scribes came to be regarded as all who could read. This was usually determined by a judge in the presence of a representative of the bishop. The accused was required to read a well-known psalm that soon came to be known as the "neck verse." After the test, the bishop's representative decided with the words *legit* (can read) or *non legit* (cannot read) whether the accused should be condemned to death or corporal punishment or should be handed over to the Church for sentence.

The Church's punishments were admittedly not "red," as the saying went, i.e., sanguinary, but they could be terrible. Whipping was administered to both young monks and young laymen handed over by the secular courts. The penal cells in the monasteries and bishops' palaces were often dark and damp. A particularly horrible penalty was called *in pace*, which meant total isolation, often for life—in other words, a sentence to death. At the same time, many monastery prisons were aimed at true repentance, and inmates were visited in their cells by father confessors.[14]

The monastery prisons gradually deteriorated until at the end of the eighteenth century they were just as bad as the civilian ones. At that point they went out of existence. Many deserted monasteries were eventually converted into secular prisons, and they are still in use in various parts of Europe.

The fifteenth and sixteenth centuries were characterised by far-reaching economic and social changes. The feudal system started to crumble, cities grew, rural communities began to be decimated. Wars took men from their working environment for long periods, and when peace came the soldiers found themselves unemployed. Many monasteries were closed as a result of the crisis within the Catholic Church and the Reformation, and monks and nuns were compelled to keep themselves alive by begging. Miserable vagrants and beggars, desperately seeking sustenance within or outside the law, created a severe social problem. Professional crime began to flourish, and by the end of the sixteenth century the time was ripe for a new kind of social action. Here England was in the vanguard, in practice if not in theory.

[2] BRIDEWELL, THE LONDON HOUSE OF CORRECTION

In the Spirit of Martin Luther

In sixteenth century England, the law was severe with regard to beggars and vagrants. Cripples could be licensed by magistrates to beg within a specific territory. But other beggars were whipped unmercifully or put in the stocks on bread and water for three days, after which they were banished to their birth-place for three years or, if it were unknown, to the place in which they had most recently lived for three years. The same sentence, plus amputation of one ear, was imposed for a second offense; a third fall from grace resulted in the removal of the other ear. But even these stringent methods were to no avail.[1]

Many religious and social philosophers of the day were concerned with these problems. In 1522, for example, Martin Luther wrote two papers on the care of the poor, which made a strong impression in Europe. Regarding the Church's toleration of begging, he asserted that every individual had a "duty to work." In England, a group of Londoners organized a series of effective measures to take care of the poor who could not manage on their own, as well as the vagrants and beggars who made the streets unsafe. One of these reformers was Bishop Nicolas Ridley, who enjoyed the confidence of Edward VI.[2]

The English reformers wanted to divide the poor and jobless into three categories. The first group was to consist of homeless children, the second of the sick and crippled, and the third of vagrants and lazy harlots. The first two groups were to be put in special institutions provided by the town authorities. For the third group, Bishop Ridley persuaded the King in 1553 to donate Bridewell Palace in London, which became the first known house of correction. The edifice was located between what is now Fleet Street and the Thames. According to some sources, it was opened for its new function in 1555.[3] Detailed rules were drawn up in 1557: inmates were to be disciplined and forced to work to combat sinful living in idleness. Thereafter, discipline and hard work formed the principles on which the treatment of criminals was based for centuries to come. And yet, according to Austin van der Slice, the fathers of the system appear to have been unaware of the reform they had set in motion.[4]

Bridewell was run by sixteen administrators and had facilities for four kinds of employment: a spinning mill, a metal-working and carpentry shop, a flour mill, and a bakery. The prostitutes worked in the spinning mill, while the best of the men were placed in the shop and the worst in the two last-mentioned occupations. Two inmates served as sweepers. All were paid wages for their work and had to pay for their board. The institution was intended to be self-supporting. More and more branches of work were gradually added, and not less than 25 different trades were represented by the end of 1579; apprenticeships in certain fields for young inmates were introduced as early as 1563. (Children of poor parents could even receive permission to be trained together with the Bridewell inmates!)

Ahead of the Times

The innovation in London was so successful that it was soon copied in several other parts of England. This was essential, since a veritable crusade against vagrancy had now been launched. Thousands of people were rounded up and put to work. Those considered to be honest were eligible for the workhouse, but vagrants, prostitutes, and petty criminals were put in houses of correction, or Bridewells as they generally came to be known. In 1576, Elizabeth I promulgated a law according to which houses of correction were to be established in every county of England. Vagrants were collected in these institutions and put to work. The purpose was threefold: inmates would earn their living; they would be reformed through work and discipline; and, finally, their example would deter others from vagrancy and slothfulness.

All went smoothly for many years. However, the initial general enthusiasm for the houses of correction waned with time and funds to maintain them grew scarce. Working conditions for the inmates deteriorated, and eventually all kinds of industrial jobs were abandoned. The judiciary also lost interest in the system. By the end of the seventeenth century the houses of correction had completely lost their reformative character. The Bridewells' principal task was no longer the treatment of vagrants through forced labor. Criminals and vagrants were taken in for corporal punishment, and, in 1720, judges were given the right to condemn criminals either to regular prisons or to houses of correction "as they in their judgement think proper."[5]

Max Grünhut commented: "The whole tendency of the new foundation was fundamentally opposed to contemporary criminal law. It did not involve an exclusion from society by death, mutilation, and branding with permanent degradation. The ultimate aim was to lead back the prisoner into society." But, Grünhut adds, the idea was so advanced for the day that its fate was already sealed at birth.[6]

The original Bridewell institution existed until the middle of the nineteenth century; for long periods it had also held political prisoners and heretics. It was finally demolished in 1863.[7]

[3] AMSTERDAM'S RASPHUIS AND SPINHUIS

Origins of Reform

The word about houses of correction quickly spread to the European continent, and the Dutch, probably influenced by English ideas, opened their first house of correction in Amsterdam in 1596. Nonetheless, Sellin could find no documented evidence that this was the case, and other scholars' research was equally fruitless. However, humanitarian ideas had already appeared in the administration of criminal law in Holland: for example, a religious order had established a house of correction *(Verbeterhuisen)* for young criminals.[1]

Dirck Volckertszoon Coornhert, a versatile and somewhat choleric man, served a sentence for libel. After his release in 1587, he wrote an essay describing a method for combating vagrancy *(Boeventucht, ofte middelen tot mindering der Schadelycke ledighgangers)*. This truly remarkable man, whose name was rescued from oblivion by Sellin, was one of John Howard's predecessors. He outlined a complete plan for the treatment of vagrants in prison. Beggars were to be put to work on public projects or as galley oarsmen. Each province was to have a big prison with cells and a yard in which prisoners could be kept at hard labor; only those inmates who did a fixed amount of work daily would be fed.

Coornhert recommended that capital punishment be abolished and replaced by workhouse sentences. At the same time, the condemned would be branded and have their noses slit so that they could be caught if they ran away. If that happened they would be hung immediately. Petty criminals would have their sentences doubled if they managed to escape. The plan advised the workhouse for some prisoners, public works for others, and galley slavery for the most hardened. While not particularly humanitarian in spirit, it nevertheless is an example of an attempt to achieve a feasible and effective control of crime.[2]

In 1588, an Amsterdam court, consisting of one judge and nine laymen, refused to sentence a 16-year-old thief to death, the normal penalty for stealing. The case was presented to the burgomaster and the members of the city council, "in order to discover and establish some suitable means of maintaining such children of burghers at steady work so that they might be turned from their bad habits and aroused to lead a better life."[3] The next year the matter was taken up by the City Council and became the subject of an animated discussion. The basic principles of what would become Holland's contribution to the continental reform movement of the day were drawn up the same year by Alderman Jan Laurentszoon Spiegel in a memorandum, *Bedenking op de grondvesten vant tuchthuis*. Spiegel's ideas are extremely interesting. The function of houses of correction would not be merely punishment but also reform and correction of the inmates. According to Sellin, this is the first time the term "house of correction" appears in the literature.[4] The German translation, *Zuchthaus*, later came to represent a prison for hardened criminals.

Spiegel's program for the new institution made these points: treatment of the inmates should not be designed to humiliate them but to restore them to health, to teach them moderation in eating and drinking, as well as good work habits, to awaken their interest in finding and retaining respectable employment, and, of course, to instill in them the fear of God. All publicity about inmates would be eliminated. Court proceedings would be held *in camera* and the prisoners taken to prison under cover of darkness. Their escorts and guards would be under oath not to divulge their identity, and prison visits would be prohibited. Spiegel also had plans for leisure-time activities, including competitions and games. But work was of first importance. The recalcitrant would be given simple tasks such as rasping wood, beating hemp, working the treadmill. Cooperative prisoners would be taught a trade. Spiegel further envisaged an institution with a number of different industries. While he did not disregard the problem of security, he believed that the risks varied widely from one prisoner to another. The escape-prone would therefore be kept in cells or even chains, while the majority would be allowed to move relatively freely inside the walls.

Sellin rightly calls this memorandum "one of the most significant documents in the history of penology." Spiegel's project was approved in part. The point about secret court proceedings was struck out, however, and the program of leisure-time activities was not fully accepted. Nor did the plan for industry work out due to lack of funds to invest in equipment. Thus modified, the project was legislated, and the first "rasphuis" for males only was founded in a convent that had previously belonged to the Order of St. Clarissa. Remodeling was completed in 1595, and the first prisoners, 12 in number, were admitted on February 3, 1596.[5]

The Rasphuis

Simon van der Aa described the clientele:

First there were beggars, vagabonds, idlers, capable of working, among the women also prostitutes from the street. *Then* there were other malefactors: at the beginning especially thieves whilst in the earlier years also young persons guilty of minor offences and later older people condemned for more serious crimes were held. As a rule they were confined by virtue of a sentence of the criminal court, but the prison-board was also entitled to seize and lock up able-bodied persons, who were found begging without license. With regard to the latter that board decided as to their discharge according to circumstances. The sentence fixed the term of confinement for the others, but this term could be prolonged because of bad behaviour in the institution. Consequently in such cases as well as in case of confinement by authority of the prison-board the duration of the incarceration was *not fixed* definitely beforehand.[6]

As van der Aa points out, here we have an early, if not the earliest, precursor of the indeterminate sentence.

The prison building was rectangular with a large open yard in the middle. The ground floor surrounding the yard contained a number of cells. The first floor had a few cells, as well as guard-rooms, the warden's apartments, workrooms, and offices. Each cell contained four to twelve inmates. The men worked in their cells, in bad weather at least. The cell walls were paneled in wood. Barred windows overlooked the yard. Each cell had separate toilet facilities. Adult inmates slept two to a bed, boys three. Strict order was maintained in the cells: cleaning was done daily and chamber pots were emptied every morning. Inmates who broke house rules concerning hygiene and order were deprived of breakfast for four days. Flogging and solitary confinement in a dark cell were also resorted to. At the beginning of the seventeenth century, the institution also had a special discipline cell that could be flooded with water. If the inmate wanted to survive, he had to do a superhuman job at the pump. This cell is said to have been done away with after an inmate had refused to save his life by pumping.[7]

There was no heating in the prison. On the other hand, diet and sanitary conditions were unexceptionable. Not a single inmate was a victim of the seventeenth century plague. A physician was available to treat complaints that might prevent inmates from working. Teachers were on hand for the young people, and religious instruction and persuasion were also a part of the pattern of life. But, first and foremost, there was *work*. The foremen saw to it that everyone did his bit. The main occupation of the inmates was rasping brazilwood to produce dyestuff—the institution was granted a monopoly for the process in 1602.[8]

The City Council reached an important decision on November 27, 1600. Respectable and prosperous citizens of the town sometimes had problems with their sons, who wasted their time in slothfulness and escapades instead of working or studying. Thanks to their financial situation and to the protection their unhappy parents always felt compelled to give them, these young men could seldom be convicted of crimes. But, something had to be done. The City Council now decided that a special, completely separate section would be set aside in the rasphuis with single rooms for this category of youths, who could be incarcerated on their parents' request and at their expense for indefinite periods of time. This new section was called "separate" or "secret," and was ready to open in 1603 in an enlarged part of the Clarissa Sisters' convent. It comprised altogether 12 small rooms and one large common room. In the daytime, these well-born young men were allowed to congregate and even take walks in a small yard, but they were isolated in their rooms at night. There was no obligation to work, and in this respect the section differed radically from a true house of correction.[9]

The rasphuis was governed by a board of four men appointed by the burgomaster. They received no pay, but enjoyed certain privileges, including good pews in church. The warden of the rasphuis was responsible to the board members and was strictly forbidden to accept gifts from the prisoners. He was addressed as "housefather," was responsible for the keys to the institution, and was not allowed to relinquish them without special permission. The escape of a prisoner cost the housefather severe punishment. Prayers were read by all the inmates morning and evening and at all meals. Divine service was held every Sunday in a small prison chapel. The board of directors paid a weekly visit as a group, and the magistrates turned up once a year to decide whether each individual inmate's sentence should be prolonged or shortened.

The veto on visits by the public was soon withdrawn. Instead, visitors were required to pay an entrance fee, half of which reverted to the warden. Sellin believes he has found a passage intimating that conjugal visits were permitted. The reason for this might have been official Holland's desire to maintain the population level at almost any price.[10]

The Spinhuis

Toward the end of 1596, when the authorities had several months of experience with the workings of the rasphuis, the Amsterdam City Council decided to create a counterpart for women, which was opened the next year in a former Ursuline convent under the label of a "spinhuis." The new institution was designed for prostitutes, female alcoholics, and wayward girls. Smaller than its male counterpart, it had accommodations for about 40 inmates. It was destroyed by fire in 1643 and rebuilt with a more practical design.

Seventeenth century descriptions tell us that the inmates were classified to avoid overly heterogeneous mixtures of clientele. Since the building was originally a convent, the design was approximately the same as in the rasphuis. There was an open inside yard onto which cells and other rooms faced. The women were usually kept busy at spinning and sewing.[11]

John Howard visited Amsterdam's prisons for the first time in 1776—the last time in 1783. He wrote about the rasphuis, saying there was a relief above the entrance, which depicted a man driving a cart loaded with brazilwood and drawn by lions, wild boars, and tigers. A Latin inscription (quoted from Seneca) read: *Virtutis est domare, quae cuncti pavent.* (It is valor to subdue that of which everyone goes in dread). Above this motto there were two men in chains and a woman carrying a whip in her right hand and the Amsterdam coat-of-arms in the other. The word *Castigatio* (chastisement) was inscribed above her head. The institution had 54 inmates in 1776. As many as 10 to 12 men worked in the same room, in which they also spent their nights. Most of them rasped

[15]

wood from six o'clock in the morning to noon and from one to four. In their free time inmates made small objects, e.g., tobacco boxes, which they sold to visitors who were allowed in for a small admission fee.

Howard tells us that one floor up in the institution for women there was a large work hall, along which ran a narrow corridor designed to allow visitors to watch and converse with the inmates through a wooden balustrade. The hall itself was also divided into two sections by a wooden lattice. Prisoners who had undergone public floggings worked on one side, the rest on the other. The board of directors consisted of two men and two women.

Kitchen, dining hall and three cells, each with 10 double beds for women, were located on the ground floor. The house had 32 inmates at the time of Howard's first visit. He watched them eat the midday meal. First the women sang a hymn in the work hall. Then they marched to the dining hall where they sat at two tables. The food, which Howard thought appetizing, was placed on the table. The housefather, who presided at one of the tables, rapped the table with a hammer. All the women rose to their feet and one of them read a prayer for four or five minutes, after which they all "sat down cheerful." Howard learned that the costs for the spinhuis were defrayed by a special tax on all sales of tobacco, beer and spirits, and a share of fees for public entertainment.[12]

The Amsterdam houses of correction set examples that were soon followed in other places, particularly in the Netherlands but in other parts of Europe also. Many foreigners came to inspect these remarkable prisons. Naturally, Calvinistic views of slothfulness as a grave sin were behind the house of correction concept. Luther, too, regarded begging as a punishable offence. Consequently, the idea was transplanted to many parts of Protestant Europe, e.g., Bremen, Nuremberg, Danzig, Lybeck and Hamburg in Germany; Bern and Basel in Switzerland. But the names varied: *Zucht-, Spinn-, Werk-, Rasp-, Arbeitshaus* in Germany, usually direct translations from the German in other language areas, but always rasphuis and spinhuis in the vernacular. According to von Hippel, the popularity of these sobriquets was confirmed by a Dutch pamphlet printed at the beginning of the seventeenth century and translated into German and French. Entitled *The Story of the Miracle of St. Raspina*, it created a mock patron saint for both institutions who had the power to cure beggars and idlers.[13] According to many contemporary reports, the new institutions were highly effective. The streets were free of beggars and dangerous rogues, and many were brought "to their senses" in the rasphuis and spinhuis.[14]

The Amsterdam house of correction for men was in use as a prison until the 1890s, when it was torn down.[15]

[4] THE OCTAGON IN GHENT

Vilain XIIII

During the 18th century, the country that became Belgium in 1830 was alternated like a challenge trophy between Austria and France. Here as elsewhere, war and economic ruin led to poverty, begging, and crime. The cities could defend themselves to some extent, but country people were often victimized by great bands of roving men, women, and children, forced into crime to avoid starvation. A young well-born Flemish politician, Jean Jacques Philippe Vilain XIIII (1712-1777)[1], Mayor of the town of Alost, was assigned by the minicipal and provincial authorities to persuade the French occupiers to organize a major round-up of vandals in the area. This was carried out in the years 1746 and 1748-49 in the Province of Alost, and about 200 individuals were captured, most of them under 40 years of age. Many were condemned to death or the wheel; others were banished; others were sent to the French galleys. But the situation did not improve, for the French and Austrian armies were demobilized at the end of 1749, leaving the area infested with unemployed soldiers whose depredations made the countryside just as unsafe as before the clean-up operation.

Following this reverse, Vilain XIIII became deeply involved in the problem of the prevention of crime and begging. He came to the conclusion that only strict work-training in special houses of correction would be effective and devoted his energy to the establishment of such an institution in Alost. He submitted a project in 1751, which was rejected. Discouraged by this defeat, he retired from politics the same year and moved from Alost to Ghent.[2] In 1755, however, he was elected *premier échevin de la keure* (corresponding roughly to mayor) in Ghent. In that year he published *Réflections sur les Finances de la Flandre,* an essay attacking the public administration of the day and recommending measures to cure the economic ills afflicting the country. While it only appeared in an edition of 40 copies, the book created a sensation and made many friends for the author, as well as enemies. One whose interest it kindled was Maria Theresa, Empress of Austria and ruler of Flanders. She appointed a commission to carry out the financial reforms proposed by Vilain XIIII, and within a few years, these measures had a beneficial effect on the economic health of the area. Vilain XIIII was elevated to the rank of *vicomte* by the Empress in recognition of his contribution.[3]

Vilain XIIII once again took up the problem of crime early in 1771 when he was invited by the provincial parliament of Flanders to submit a proposal for the prevention of vagrancy and begging. Within two months he responded with a 40 page memorandum, which was worked out in such detail that one is tempted to suspect that the parliamentary invitation was "planted."[4]

As was customary, the memorandum begins with a quotation, *Qui noluerit operari non manducet*, "if any would not work, neither should he eat" (II Thessalonians 3:10). The purpose of the law, Vilain XIIII wrote, was in part to correct criminals and in part to deter others from crime. But moderation should also be exercised. "Excessively stringent laws would lead to their repeal." His earlier experiences had obviously not been forgotten. But, he continued, we already have a law which provides, not only for capital punishment, banishment, flogging, and branding, but also for *forced labor*. Incarceration in an institution, designed to train them to work, would not only have a deterrent effect on the slothful, but would also reduce the costs of crime prevention.[5]

A correctional sanction of this kind tied to a workhouse would prevent beggars and vagrants from becoming serious criminals. Once they had been trained in the institution, they would become useful members of the country's work force, and the citizenry would no longer be victimized by more or less dangerous beggars. At the same time, no action would be taken against individuals who were too old or too sickly to be able to work and were compelled to beg for a living. Vilain XIIII refers in this context to the fact that in 1770 Venice had driven all able-bodied beggars out of the city, forbidding them to return under threat of severe reprisals, while the ill and aged were permitted to beg outside but not inside churches, in the streets, or after dark.

How would the institution be built? It must resemble a fortress, Vilain XIIII wrote, because any vagrant, beggar, or thief who has become accustomed to idleness will try to avoid work that is forced on him. He therefore proposed that the institution be housed in the Ghent citadel, where military guards, walls, and moats would thwart escapes.

Vilain XIIII dwelt at length on the question of discipline. At admission, inmates would be given shaves and haircuts free of charge. From then on they would pay for these services with their earnings. Each inmate would be given his own room which, in addition to a bed, would contain a cabinet with a key in which to store money and other possessions. Everyone would rise at five in the morning, make their ablutions, tidy their room, attend chapel at five-thirty, go from there to breakfast, and then report at work. Soldiers would inspect the rooms while the inmates were at work. At eight o'clock a group of soldiers and prisoners would go to market to buy the day's supply of food. Dinner would be at noon—grace to be said by an inmate. Work would begin again at one-thirty in the afternoon and continue until eight. After supper and evening prayers, all inmates would be locked in their rooms at nine o'clock. Inmates would wear a special prison uniform.

The rules for personal conduct included: smoking would not be allowed in bedrooms or workshops; alcoholic beverages would be totally forbidden; inmates would be penalized if they "wiped their face on the bedlinen,"; inmates were not to be disrespectful to soldiers and officers, not to steal from their comrades; and so on. Most breaches of discipline would be under the jurisdiction of the commandant, but serious offenses would be handled by court martial.

The Octagon

The Flemish provincial parliament approved Vilain XIIII's plan without delay—a few dissenting Catholic voices protested that taking action against begging conflicted with the doctrines of the Church. Empress Maria Theresa gave her consent the next year, and the time had now come to make plans for the new institution. Delegates were sent to inspect institutions in France and Holland. Vilain XIIII himself visited Holland but appears not to have been impressed by the Dutch anti-begging measures, and there is no record of his having looked at the rasphuis and spinhuis in Amsterdam. The Flemish provincial parliament decided in 1772 that the new institution would be located on a site by the canal that connected the town with Bruges, not in the citadel as Vilain

XIIII had proposed. And now comes the interesting statement that the institution "shall be designed not only so as to separate various kinds of prisoners but also so as to isolate each individual at night."[6]

The design was unusual for the times: a large octagonal building with a central octagonal nucleus surrounding a yard. Eight long pavilions radiated from the center to the outside walls. In this way the prison was divided into eight sections between which the various types of offenders could be distributed. Five-eights of the institution were ready to open in May 1775. The architect's name was Malfaison, one of whose advisers was the Jesuit Klukman, who was familiar with the papal prison for boys in Rome (cf. next Chapter).[7]

The same year, Vilain XIIII gave his views on the new institution in a 268-page "Memorandum on the means of correcting criminals and idlers to their own advantage and of making them useful to society." In his introduction, he said:

Man is born to v ..... God Himself decreed this for our progenitor, when He created him. When he was placed in the earthly paradise, it was on condition that he work. . . . Idleness is therefore negligence of the law of nature and the Creator. Each and all of us must work, with brain or hand. This is a universal law and applies equally to the ruler and to his subjects, great and small, rich and poor.

Vilain XIIII described the plan of the institution in detail. One of the "trapeziums" consisted entirely of administrative offices and living quarters for the warden, officers, guards, and work foremen. The entrance to the institution led through this section, from which a gate opened into the central yard. The various sections could be reached through doors leading out of the yard. A detailed description of the guard system is given. Two gates were not permitted to be open at one time, and the outside guards were relieved at short intervals so as not to be over-tired. The cell areas were patrolled at night by guards with dogs. These guards were required to report regularly to a sentry in the central yard, who could quickly summon armed reinforcements by sounding an alarm.

Of the four remaining trapeziums, the one closest to the entrance was designed for serious male criminals, the next one for petty offenders, the third for women, and the last for "volunteers, pensioners, or stipendiaries." Vilain XIIII had thus foreseen that some people who had committed no crime would find it advantageous to enter the institution to learn a trade or that relatives of idlers would manage to have them admitted for the same purpose. He further recommended that the three still unbuilt sections of the institution be reserved for the vocational training of needy children.

The male criminals were locked up at night in sleeping cells with windows overlooking a corridor. As we shall see later, this architectural style was to spread almost like an epidemic to the prisons of the New World and also to be transmitted to other European countries as well. The females were kept in cells for two or more persons. The entire complex consisted of houses of not more than four stories. Most of the workshops were located in the widest part of the trapezium, which also formed the outer wall.

Vilain XIIII was eloquent on the subject of work also. It must, he writes, "be regular, yield a certain income to the prisoner and be carried out so as to interest him, in which case he will be able to continue after his discharge in the trade he has learned in the prison."

The views expressed by Vilain XIIII are relatively modern. He was opposed to heavy, monotonous, futile occupations, particularly the treadmill, work without payment or without consideration for the prisoner's talents or previous occupation or the economic environment in which he would find himself after his discharge. Hitherto, the main purpose of prison work had been to reduce the costs of the inmates' upkeep. Vilain XIIII firmly rejected this approach to the problem.

Vilain XIIII divided the prisoners into two work categories: one comprised foreign vagrants and old prisoners under such long sentences that the chances of their becoming useful members of society later on were more or less non-existent. He thought these people could be put to work exclusively for the benefit of the institution. At the same time, their jobs should not in any way compete with civilian enterprise. Other inmates, whose social rehabilitation was a possibility (to use a present-day expression), should work in shops organized with the idea of teaching a trade that could be pursued after discharge. In selecting a job for an inmate, it should be borne in mind that he would probably return to his home town and that his occupation should fit in with the opportunities available there. Vilain XIIII cited numerous examples of suitable jobs for prisoners from different parts of Flanders.

Like the Dutch institutions for vagrants, the prison in Ghent was also known as a rasphuis. This was inappropriate since wood-rasping was scarcely practised there. The best-known description of the institution was written by John Howard, who visited the Ghent prison on four occasions. In 1776, his first visit, the institution, not yet completed, had about 200 inmates. Howard noted that the cells for men measured 6'10" x 5'4" in area and 7'8" in height. Each cell was furnished with a sleeping bench, a stool, a drop table attached to the door, and a small cupboard built into the wall. Bedding consisted of a pallet, a pillow, a pair of sheets, two blankets in the winter and one in the summer. The prisoners were given a clean shirt once a week. They were strictly forbidden to visit one another. Female inmates, on the other hand, did not have single cells but were accommodated in larger cells.

Howard was impressed by the good order of the place and commented that there was complete silence at meals despite the fact that almost 200 hardened criminals were eating together. He also inspected the eight disciplinary cells, which contained no sleeping benches, but found them empty. The prisoners attended religious services every day. Work was available for all of them. He found the food adequate and emphasized that alcohol in any form was prohibited in the institution. The same was true of all kinds of gambling.

On a second visit in 1778, Howard found that the number of inmates had risen to almost 300, one-third of them women. A third visit in 1781 made an equally good impression. But in 1783, the fourth time he inspected the institution, he found things completely different. Yielding to pressure from industrial and mercantile circles, Austrian Emperor Joseph II had forbidden certain trades in the institution, which led to unemployment for the prisoners with a consequent decline in morale. As a result of this "vile" policy, as Howard called it, the behavior of the prisoners had also changed radically.[8]

A nineteenth century visitor, Sweden's first penal administration director, Carl Axel Löwenhielm, wrote that the prison in Ghent, previously regarded as a model institution, had apparently gone to rack and ruin.

The reason was said to be (and probably is) that the number of criminals rose so steeply when the army was decreased after the prolonged wars that space no longer sufficed to permit single cells, and instead a hammock was suspended above each bed. Consequently, all decency and morality gradually disappeared, solitude (of such great importance) is no longer possible, and the whole system has degenerated into a workhouse instead of a house of correction.

The house was founded in the reign of Empress Maria Teresia and was given from the outset the beehive form for which it is still renowned. It consists of an octagonal central building with eight special prison yards separated by as many wings, with cells facing each yard.

However, only five wings were completed under Austrian rule—and not until the reign of the present Monarch have funds been made available to construct the remainder, the work being done by prison labor. The entire building is surrounded by a wall with a wide moat walkway for night patrols. Four sentries posted in boxes on top of the wall have a view of all the prison yards. The single main exit from the house is guarded by a Concierge and a Corps de Garde, who serve as prison guards and live on the premises. No criticism can be leveled at the construction—it is perfect for its purpose. The diet resembles that in French prisons and the administrative system is the same as under the French regime.

Prison work is designed to meet the needs of the army and is performed directly for the account of the State, which must have lost great sums, since corruption is surely widespread in connection with the purchase of raw materials and their subsequent conversion into finished products.

Wages, small to begin with, are divided up as in France, with the difference that the Institution retains the third that otherwise would revert to the Entrepreneur. The result is the same, however; a prisoner can never save enough to be of real assistance after his discharge, which is not facilitated by special governmental provisions either. Private charity, on the other hand, tends to concern itself with the plight of the freed prisoner.[9]

The Ghent prison represented a new epoch in two respects: its system of classifying inmates and its physical design. Cells faced an inside yard with only one window facing a corridor which made escape exceedingly difficult. Control was further facilitated by having the various sections radiate from a central point. In general, the place reflected the contemporary ideal of a city plan, according to which the ducal palace formed a hub from which the streets emanated like the spokes of a wheel.[10]

But Vilain XIIII may not have been as great an innovator as many claimed. Louis Stroobant pointed out that the idea of work in common and nocturnal solitude had already been tested in the prison citadel in Ghent, as had the use of prison uniforms. Most of the rules for conduct and discipline were also borrowed from the citadel which, in turn, had copied the *tuchthuis* rules in Amsterdam. So, it seems that Vilain XIIII's chief contribution was that of an organiser.[11]

"It was one of Vilain XIIII's illusions, which was perhaps shared by mid-nineteenth century society in general, that vocational skill is all that is needed to find work," according to P. Lenders. But through the years, the same historian wrote, he came to understand that a favorable economic climate is equally important. Vilain XIIII also believed that his institution would be so successful that fear of being committed to it would in itself suffice to inspire many beggars with the desire to work.[12] An unfounded faith in the beneficial effect of punishment that has recurred through the centuries!

[5] ISOLATION IN CASA PIA

Mabillon

England's houses of correction, Holland's rasphuis and spinhuis, the segregated octagon in Flanders, and the various institutions all over Europe that grew up in their wake were designed primarily to deal with vagrants and petty offenders who, if left to their own devices, could turn into "real" criminals, becoming a menace to society.

Two centuries elapsed between the breakthrough of these ideas, which were based primarily on the work-ethic of the Reformation, and the next great step in the history of the treatment of criminals was a prison designed, not only to punish criminals, but also to rehabilitate them and return them to society as useful citizens.

The first to make a serious study of this problem was the Benedictine monk, Pater Jean Mabillion (1632-1707). To begin with, he concentrated on the monastic way of life, for which he listed four rules of conduct: isolation, work, silence, and prayer. This led him to the conclusion that the same strict regimen could be applied to offenders, and in the years from 1690 to 1695 he drafted a plan (not published until 1724) for an institution for the reform and correction of criminals, which reads:

> In this place there would be several cells similar to those of the Carthusian monks, with a workshop to exercise them in some useful labor. One could also add to each cell a little garden which would be open to them at certain hours and where they could be made to work or walk. They would be present at Divine Offices, to begin with, locked in some separate gallery and later united with the rest of the choir, as soon as they have passed the first tests of penance and given signs of amendment. Their food would be simpler and coarser and the fasts more frequent than in other Communities. They should be frequently exhorted and the Superior or some one in his place should take care to visit them separately and console and fortify them from time to time. Laymen and outsiders should not be given entrance in this place, where a strict solitude should be maintained. If this were once established, such a place would appear far from horrible and insupportable, and I am sure that most monks would little regret seeing themselves

shut in there, even if it should be for the rest of their days and that good monks would enjoy dwelling there in order to practice a stricter penance and solitude. I am sure that all this will pass for an idea from a new world but whatever is thought and said about the matter, it will be easy whenever the desire arises, to make these prisons both more useful and more easy to endure.[1]

The Order of the Carthusians mentioned by Mabillon was founded in 1084 by St. Bruno of Cologne. The first monastery was located in the Chartreuse valley near Grenoble, and in 1143 Pope Innocent approved the rules of the order: silence, prayer, manual labor and abstention from meat.[2]

Mabillon was a remarkable man who had many surprisingly progressive ideas about the administration of justice. He recommended the individualization of punishment long before anyone else, urging that due consideration be given to the physical and spiritual needs of the offender in determining penalties. Sellin, who quoted and analysed Mabillon's views expressed in his posthumous work, *Réflexions sur les prisons des ordres religieux*, states that if these ideas had only been known and disseminated at the time they were written "Beccaria's sun might never have risen and John Howard might have been born too late." In reality, however, Mabillon's views on punishment did not become widely known until well into the nineteenth century.[3]

Franci

Contrary to the good Dom Mabillon's belief, the time was ripe for experiments along the lines he recommended. And it is highly probable, though not proven, that he had seen or at least heard of the small institution for young criminals founded in Florence around 1675 by Filippo Franci, a priest and one of the great names in the history of the treatment of criminals. The story began with the foundation of an institution for homeless, mendicant boys—picked up on the streets at night. The place was known as *Spedale* or *Casa Pia di refugio dei poveri fanciulli di San Filippo Neri*. Franci became the director around 1650 and soon achieved renown for his wise and firm leadership. Then came one of those periods when young people seem to be more difficult to handle than usual, and worried, well-situated parents in the town called on Franci to take their delinquent and unmanageable sons in hand. If they were sent to a public prison (a measure their desperate parents sometimes resorted to), they returned to their homes even worse than before, compounding the parents' problems.[4]

In 1677, moved by parents' pleas for help, Franci set up an *Ospizio* or Hospice in his institution, a special section consisting of eight single cells to serve as a "secret place of correction" for these youths. Here the boys were confined night and day and were submitted to "efficacious exhortations" by Franci and his two assistants, or "protectors" as they were called. It is said that the boys were made to cover their faces with a hood when they left their cells to ensure their anonymity. Franci was strongly opposed to coercive methods and advocated compassion and friendliness rather than rigor and severity. Here, therefore, we have the first example of a cellular prison organized on the principle of a combination of severe punishment and positive, character-building personal guidance. The Dutch may be right in their claim that Franci had heard of the "secret house of correction" in the Amsterdam rasphuis. At the same time, Franci unquestionably deserves credit for the pedagogical method used in the Florence Hospice.

San Michele

The same idea was used on a larger scale in 1704 in the papal hospital and poorhouse in Rome, *Ospizio di San Michele*. Here, Pope Clement XI commissioned the architect, Carlo Fontana, to design a cellular prison for delinquent and criminal boys. The Pope announced his intentions with the new institution in 1703:

> It is every day observed how thefts and other crimes are committed, from malice, which exceeds their years, by boys or youths under twenty, for which crimes they are, when they fall into the hands of justice, put into the prisons of our city of Rome. Although kept separated from the others in a place called the *Polledrara*, they nevertheless frequently fall into the same or worse enormities instead of coming out corrected and reformed. Already, at the beginning of our assumption of the pontificate, we thought of remedying this great evil by constructing a suitable place, contiguous to the hospice of St. Michael's in Ripa, to be called a house of correction. This has, in fact, been done, so that at present the building has been finished. It has sixty small rooms, dis-

tinct and separate from each other, all of them united in a vast hall, in the midst of which there is an altar for the celebration of Holy Mass, in addition to rooms for a sacerdote and guards or custodians. There is also an uncovered loggia and under the big room other large rooms have been built, which might serve as shops for the workers in the wool industry or be put to other uses, which may be found necessary or profitable for the said Hospice of St. Michael. Desiring, therefore, to put into operation the institution mentioned, *We command and ordain* that all boys, or minors under twenty years of age, who from now on, on account of errors committed by them, shall be made prisoners by warrants from the courts of the Reverend Cardinal Vicar of the Governor of Rome, of the Auditor of the Chamber, of the Senator of Rome, and of any other judge or tribunal, shall instead of being conducted to the public prisons be sent to the said House of Correction, and the custodians and guards shall inscribe them and register them in the manner used in the public prisons. To the judges mentioned the right shall be reserved of examining them in the said House of Correction and exercise all the privileges they may exercise in the public prisons and to retain them in custody unless the said judges shall otherwise order. And, because there are boys and youths, who are incorrigible and inobedient to parents and others, under whose guardianship they live, and who through an evil character show bad inclinations to vice, *We wish and ordain* that they too be equally guarded, corrected and reformed in the said House of Correction. To bring this about, their parents should turn to Us for an order to detain them in the said new House and to arrange about the monetary fee for their maintenance, payable by such parents, guardians, curators, or administrators to whom is given the power to detain or release them without special mandate or order from the court, since the institution will be recompensed for food and other expenses. In order that the principles of a Christian life, the rules of right living may be taught in this House of Correction, *We ordain* that a sacerdote be appointed by the Reverend Cardinal Protectors of the Hospice. He should not only celebrate the Mass every morning at the altar in the House of Correction but should also teach all the boys and youths there detained the catechism and instruct them in all matters which should be known by all Christians, according to rules to be established by the Reverend Cardinal Protectors of the said Hospice of St. Michael. They should also appoint artisans or masters to teach some mechanical arts in order that idleness may be driven away by industry and that they may learn in fact a new mode of decent living.[5]

The St. Michael House of Correction for boys, opened in 1704, was the first reform and correction institution, according to Mabillon's principles of isolation, work, silence and prayer, regardless of whether his ideas were known to the founder. But they probably were known just as Franci's Casa Pia was known.[6] After all, Mabillon had been in close touch with the Vatican and had been a diplomat in the service of the Pope. St. Michael's looked like an ordinary detention jail. A rectangular structure intersected in the middle by a hall, it consisted of three tiers of ten cells each on either side—a total of sixty cells. A balcony ran along the side of the rows of cells on each floor. The cells measured roughly nine by seven feet. They contained one window in the outer wall and a second facing the balcony beside the cell door, so the prisoners were under constant scrutiny from the balcony. This prison, the first to be built according to the single cell system, has since served as a model for thousands of penal institutions all over the world. The following inscription was printed in gold in the work-hall: *Parum est coercere improbos poena, nisi probos efficias disciplina* (It is of little advantage to restrain the bad by punishment unless you render them good by discipline). These words so impressed John Howard on his visit to the institution that he used them as a motto for his book.

It has been told that at St. Michael's the boys slept alone but worked together at spinning and weaving in the hall. They were chained by one foot to their work-benches. Verbal communication was strictly forbidden, but monks read aloud from religious texts. Breaches of prison rules were punished by whipping. The incorrigible were kept in solitary confinement night and day.[7] A prison for women, according to the single cell method, was added to the St. Michael's complex in 1735. The entire clientele was transferred elsewhere in 1827, by which time numerous modifications in the treatment methods had occurred and humanitarian ideals had fallen by the wayside. In Sellin's words, "Beautiful theories sometimes have a way of turning into ugly practice."[8]

It was John Howard who, more than anyone, spread the word about innovations in the world of prisons. He found the same trend toward isolating prisoners and exploiting solitude in a positive way in many other places. In addition to the institution in Ghent, St. Michael's, and the Amsterdam rasphuis and spinhuis, he was impressed by the Swiss jails, about which he wrote:

> In those of the cantons to which I went, felons have each a room to themselves "that they may not," said the keepers, "tutor one another." None were in irons: they are kept in rooms more or less strong and lightsome, according to the crimes they are charged with. But the

prisons are in general very strong. The rooms are numbered, and the keys marked with the same numbers.[9]

Even those already sentenced were kept in single cells in several places, including Basel. In general, Howard found Switzerland to be the most progressive country in the area of penology other than Holland.

Meanwhile, the single cell system attracted an increasing number of advocates. For example, the English Bishop, Joseph Butler, in his famed "hospital sermons" in 1740, recommended that prisoners be kept in solitary confinement at forced labor and that they be held on short food rations. And in a thesis in 1766, Jonas Hanway, best known for having introduced the umbrella into England, recommended solitude, combined with work and reduced rations, as "the most humane and effectual means of bringing malefactors to a right sense of their condition."[10]

As early as 1766, Empress Maria Theresa of Austria ordered a prison to be built in Milan with 140 cells, including 25 for women and 20 for children.[11] In 1775, the same year the institution in Ghent was opened, the construction of a single-cell detention jail was begun in Horsham, Sussex—not finished until 1779.[12] The new trend was under way, but a man of the stature of John Howard was needed to give it genuine impetus.

[6] JOHN HOWARD—TRAILBLAZER

Background

As late as the outbreak of World War II, there was a gravestone in a country churchyard a mile or so from the Russian town of Kherson at the mouth of the Dnieper River, which bore the following inscription: *Ad sepulchrum stas, quisquis es, amici* ("Whoever thou art, thou standeth at the tomb of thy friend"). Here lay the remains of John Howard, whose significance as a reformer in the treatment of criminals is so great that a relatively detailed account of his life is warranted.[1]

John Howard was born in 1726, the son of a merchant, a Calvinist. His mother died when he was an infant and his father died when he was 16 years old. He inherited a considerable fortune consisting of a house and the sum of £30,000. Like his father, Howard was deeply religious; in his later years he became a Baptist. Because of the legal restrictions on Dissenters, he was barred from attending public school and instead was educated by tutors. He was an indifferent student; he had difficulty with spelling and was considered a poor writer. He was aware of his literary shortcomings and asked friends for help with his manuscripts. He nevertheless became a stylistic innovator. While there is no record of his brilliance as an intellect, we know that he was acutely aware of man's obligations to his fellowman and that he was unable to see more than one side of a problem. In short he was a fanatic.

Howard married twice. His first wife was a woman twice his age, whom he considered was his duty to marry as she had nursed him through a long illness. She died a few years later. He then married a younger woman who bore him a son. Howard is believed to have been an exceptionally stern father. In spite of his moralistic upbringing, or perhaps because of it, the son fell into bad ways at an early age and eventually became insane.

Howard embarked on his career as a social critic, sensational at the time and sharply criticised by contemporaries. He built good dwellings for the laborers on his estate in Cardington, Bedfordshire, and arranged for their children's schooling. He was not unique in this respect, however; his neighbor, a great landowner, did the same on an even larger scale.

After the great earthquake in Lisbon in 1755, which destroyed the homes of thousands of the city's inhabitants, Howard, already an experienced continental traveller, felt called upon to help the victims of the Portuguese catastrophe. At the time, France was at war with England and the ship on which Howard was sailing to Lisbon was seized by a French privateer. Subsequently, he spent a long period as a prisoner of war in three French coastal prisons, but finally managed to arrange for an exchange with a French prisoner in England. He also obtained the release of his English fellow-prisoners. This was Howard's first encounter with prisons. He was shaken by the experience, but 15 years were to pass before he embarked on a lifework that was to give him immortality in the history of the treatment of criminals.

In 1773, when Howard was 47 years of age (a widower for the second time), he was appointed sheriff of Bedford. Rich men were customarily given such positions, but they usually delegated their duties to a deputy. This was not in Howard's character, however. If he accepted a job, he did it himself. His foremost duty was to visit the three local jails in Bedford. John Bunyan had been confined in one of them 100 years earlier and he had written *Pilgrim's Progress* there. Howard was to give it immortality for the second time, according to H.W. Bellows, a biographer.[2]

According to Howard's own account, he was profoundly shocked that arrested persons who were acquitted by the court could be returned to jail if they had not paid fees to the jailer. In those days debtors could be sent to prison by their creditors and sometimes were treated just as badly as real criminals. In general, the laws of England were extremely harsh. Almost 200 crimes were punishable by death. The administration of the jails was delegated by the proprietors (counties or towns) to a manager who in turn was permitted to charge prisoners for extra comforts. All the inmates received free of charge was a minimum of food and a bare floor to sleep on. Payment might be required for a bundle of straw on which to lie. Penniless prisoners often depended on alms from the public. This system was so widely accepted at the time that, in the reign of Elizabeth I, jails were given as a reward to "deserving" individuals, providing them with an income.

If a prisoner or his family could afford to pay, he did not necessarily suffer undue hardship. The well-off could rent single rooms. They could purchase comfortable beds and have their families with them. Liquor was sold by the jailer, and orgies were prevalent in jails where men and women shared the same rooms. Assizes were only held at long intervals, and detention was unduly protracted. In some places, courts met only once a year, and unlucky individuals might be detained for a couple of years before their trial. Work programs were non-existent. Jailers were usually brutal and ignorant with the sole task of holding prisoners in custody. Their methods were often cruel. Prisoners were sometimes chained to walls and floors to prevent escape. There was usually no ventilation in the jails, and jail fever (typhus or a virulent form of dysentery) was one of the most serious diseases in England. Highly contagious, it was known and feared from the beginning of the fifteenth century. Judges were known to catch the disease in the courts and to die of it.[3]

First Tours of Prisons

When Howard had familiarized himself with the wretched state of Bedford's jails, he tried to persuade the bench to request the county to finance improvements. The bench was impressed by his recommendations and promised to carry them out, but on the condition that he could find a precedent in other counties. To this end, Howard set off in 1773 on a year-long tour of inspection of English prisons which was to result in major reforms that gave him lasting fame. But nowhere did he find a prison much better than that in Bedford. He visited one after another, noting what he saw. Howard did not indulge in sensationalism or sentimentality. His accounts of the state of prisons were factual, but he spoke a language that was new, which came to be adopted in future reports on conditions in the prisons of the world. One might even say that his attempts at fact-finding were precursors of the twentieth century sociological approach.

What had Howard seen? He saw underground prisons in many places. In Nottingham, he found three rooms on the ground floor for debtors of a certain social standing and three rooms 25 steps below ground for offenders who could pay. Another 12 steps down he came on damp dungeons cut out of rock which were for prisoners with neither money nor friends.[4] In Gloucester, he saw a dilapidated prison with a nightroom for males "with a floor so ruinous that it cannot be washed." Men and women were separated at night only. He found 20 penniless prisoners who were given no food rations and who were halfnaked and almost dead of starvation.[5] In the Plymouth jail, he found a cell seventeen feet long by eight feet wide and five feet six inches high, in which three men were detained pending transportation to the colonies. Light and air were admitted through an opening measuring five by seven inches, at which the men took turns to breathe. "The door had not been opened for five weeks when I with difficulty entered to see a pale inhabitant. He had been there ten weeks under sentence of transportation, and he had much rather been hanged than confined in that noisome cell."[6] In Exeter, Howard was told by a prison doctor that "he was by contract excused from attending in the dungeons any prisoners that should have the gaol fever."[7] Howard recounts many examples of prison doctors and, of course, prison personnel and their relatives who had died of prison fever. Its consequences were so widely known and feared that they would deter even the most faithful wife, the fondest father from prison visits, according to Howard, who added that in the beginning he always changed his clothes and bathed after every prison inspection. In Taunton, in 1730, according to Howard, a handful of prisoners infected the judges, the prosecutor, the sheriff and several hundred townspeople; all died. And in 1750 the Lord Mayor of London caught the disease and succumbed to it.[8]

But Howard was not the first to observe and to be shocked by the state of England's prisons. Mr. Popham, Member of Parliament for Taunton, had spoken on the subject in the House of Commons, and various official and semi-official studies aimed at improving conditions had been made even earlier. In 1702, for example, a committee appointed by the Society for Promoting Christian Knowledge had examined and submitted reports on certain prisons. Henry Fielding, Jonas Hanway, Joseph Butler, and other prominent men had written and spoken about the need for reforms. But, as Bellows points out, Howard's primary distinction is that he made known his observations at the appropriate time. Through Popham's intermediary, Howard was called to present his case to the House of Commons, a rare honor. His factual reports on the conditions in prisons and his familiarity with a great number of jails made an impression on the House of Commons. To improve his opportunities to advance prison reform, he ran for Parliament but he was defeated by only four votes, a bitter disappointment.[9]

Eager to assemble as much information about prisons as possible, Howard decided to visit the European continent. He began in France in 1775. He saw several prisons in Paris and found them reasonably satisfactory. No prisoners were in irons; the institutions were clean and the air was fresh. He was admitted wherever he went, with the exception of the Bastille. All he had to say was that he intended to give alms to the prisoners, and, of course, to tip the jailer. Later, he took vengeance for the exception, as we will see.

From Paris, Howard proceeded to other institutions in France, Flanders, Holland, and Germany. In Holland he saw the Amsterdam rasphuis and spinhuis. In Mannheim, he found that newly arrived prisoners were received with especial "welcome" by the magistrate. They were fastened by the neck, hands, and feet to a flogging machine and given the great welcome—20 to 30 stripes; the half welcome being 18 to 20 stripes and the small welcome being 12 to 15 stripes. They were then required to kiss the threshold and enter. The same procedure was sometimes repeated when discharged.[10]

State of Prisons

On his return to England, Howard once again toured his country's prisons. Having done this, he went back to the Continent, revisiting the same nations and adding Switzerland to his itinerary. In this way, he saw many continental prisons for the second time in two years. On his return home he collected his notes in a volume entitled *The State of the Prisons in England and Wales, with Preliminary Observations, and an Account of Some Foreign Prisons.* Since he was a poor speller and thought himself to be a mediocre writer, he had his manuscript checked by a friend. This man, the famous Dr. Richard Price, did not yield to the temptation to rewrite the book in the literary style of the day, but left Howard's simple, straightforward text intact. Howard had the work printed at his own expense in 1777, a book of 489 pages with an index and illustrated by three copperplates, one of them a plan of the prison in Ghent.

A brief summary of his observations, partly based on the third edition of the book is given below:

An introduction, in which Howard explains how he came to interest himself in the treatment of prisoners, is followed by two relatively short chapters which give a general review of the distress and abuses in English prisons. The third chapter comprises proposals for improvement. The first point he makes is that imprisonment should not be a disguised sentence of death. Prisons should therefore not be unhealthy, which meant that many decayed English institutions would have to be replaced by new ones. The author dwells at length on prison sanitary conditions, recommending, for example, a bath in which prisoners would be obliged to wash at admission and whenever necessary for personal hygiene. He mentions fire precautions and other safety devices. Furthermore, women should be isolated from men and young offenders from the old and hardened. Each of these three categories should have their own common-room, but they should sleep in single cells. In Howard's words: "If it be difficult to prevent their being together in the daytime, they should by all means be separated at night. Solitude and silence are favorable to reflection, and may possibly lead them to repentance."

It is clear that Howard was not in favor of solitary confinement, of which he had seen a good deal abroad and which he knew was of interest to many reformers. On the contrary, he considered it essential that inmates work in groups. He was directly opposed to solitary confinement "as more than human nature can bear."

Howard stressed that the jailer must be "honest, active and humane. Such was Abel Dagge, who was formerly keeper of Bristol Newgate. I regretted his death and revere his memory. And such is George Smith, keeper of Tothill-fields bridewell." The jailer should be sober, and none of the prison employees should be "suffered to hold the tap" or to profit in any way from the sale of spirits in the prison. No prisoners should be allowed to serve as a guard or be given any other such position of responsibility. (This rule was not put into effect in England until 1865.) "It is the gaoler's duty to inspect the wards himself every day that he may see that they are clean, and not leave this to servants." He should promote cleanliness in every way. "The gaoler should not only reside on the spot, but be constantly at home." The jailer should be paid a decent salary and should be forbidden to ask for reimbursement in any form from the prisoners. The sick should be treated in special hospital wards and be under the care of a doctor. The spiritual needs of the inmates should always be served. Finally: "The care of a prison is too important to be left wholly to a gaoler."

Howard recommended a proper system of inspection. In a special section on bridewells, which at this time were generally used for sentenced prisoners and vagrants although jail and bridewell were frequently housed in the same building, he stated categorically that all who are not ill must work. The need for order and regularity is emphasized. He had definite ideas about diet—no spirits, of course, but a quart of good beer daily! "Persons confined, whose minds are depressed, need more nourishment than such as are at liberty." While work is important, the principal objective is the reform of the prisoner. For the rest, Howard did not believe that prisons could be self-supporting through the inmates' work, but that they could and should contribute in some measure to their own maintenance.

The fourth chapter is the first of several chapters consisting of reports of prisons Howard visited in foreign countries, including, in the latest edition of the book, Holland, Germany, Denmark, Sweden, Russia, Poland, Italy, Switzerland, Flanders, Portugal, Spain, France, Malta, and Turkey.

Then follows a thorough survey of all the institutions Howard visited in England, Scotland, and Ireland. The book concludes with a short chapter: here Howard states that he had striven to present facts, not to gain fame as an author. He only wanted his book to awaken his countrymen's interest in the important national task of alleviating the sufferings of poor debtors and other prisoners.

Montesquieu, Voltaire, Beccaria

Howard's book was favorably received by the press. Its publication came at a propitious time. For half a century, the great philosophers of the Enlightenment had been fiercely attacking cruel penal laws. Montesquieu, Voltaire, and especially Cesare Beccaria, as well as many others, had prepared the ground. In 1764, Beccaria (1738–1794) had anonymously published *Dei delitti e delle Pene* ("Essay on Crime and Punishment"), in which he tackled intelligently and without mincing words the defects in the judicial system of the day and the sometimes horrendous penalties. Proceeding from the natural rights doctrine and Montesquieu's political theory, he arrived at penal principles that would also be based on the concept of the "greatest happiness for the greatest number." He wrote that the purpose of punishment is not to torment or to cause suffering to a human being but to ensure the protection of society.[11]

Beccaria's views emanated from a group of young Italians who supported the periodical, *Il Caffè*, and may actually have originated with the two Verri brothers, one of whom was the governor of a prison in Milan. In any case, the book reflected what young rebels were thinking, not only in Italy, but all over Europe. Five editions of his book were published in as many years. A French translation appeared in 1766 with an introduction by Voltaire, with seven printings in that year.

Voltaire himself was deeply involved in the Calas case, which, due to his intervention, shocked readers everywhere. Jean Calas was a Huguenot merchant in Bordeaux, whose son committed suicide in 1761 by hanging in his parents' home. The boy was melancholy and had been considering converting to Catholicism. Calas was accused of murdering his son to prevent his defection. The judge was a fanatical Catholic, and, with complete disregard for the facts of the case, set out to get Calas convicted. Despite fiendish torture, Calas protested his innocence until the very end. Voltaire eventually managed to clear the family of suspicion, and the judge killed himself from remorse.[12]

The *Il Caffè* group is said to have been deeply impressed by Voltaire's war on prejudice and injustice. Howard certainly was, even though he expressed a poor opinion of Voltaire's character on several occasions.

Beccaria's book was translated into English in 1767 and obviously caused a stir. But he was not interested in prisons, and he explained his anonymity as a desire to "defend the truth without becoming a martyr to it."

Later Voyages

In 1778, Howard made a third trip to Europe, visiting Holland, Germany, Austria, and Italy. It is a surprise and a tribute to Howard's impressive personality that he easily gained access to prisons in different countries; it is also typical of him that he said exactly what he thought wherever he went. He not only encountered cruelty and neglect in prisons, but he found interest in reforming the judicial system. He also saw institutions that he considered worthy of emulation: the rasphuis and spinhuis in Holland, the prison in Ghent, and St. Michael's in Rome. He now began to be interested in medical care and visited hospitals as often as prisons. In 1780, he published an *Appendix*, which included accounts of the trips he had made in 1778. It included a copperplate of the plan of St. Michael's prison. A second edition of *The State of the Prisons* appeared the same year. Howard's reputation was now such that he, together with two others, was commissioned to design a model prison. But the members of the group could not agree, and Howard withdrew in 1781.[13] Instead, he set off on a fourth tour which included Denmark, Sweden, and Russia. One of his comments about Sweden was that, while the country was very clean, the prisons in Stockholm were as dirty and ill-kept as those in London.[14] On his return to England, he added his observations to the third edition of his book, published in 1784. He then went back to the Continent, visiting Spain, Portugal, France and Flanders. In 1785, he was off again, this time on a truly hazardous expedition. He was wanted by the French police. The reason was that in 1779 he had arranged for the publication in England of a book about the Bastille by a French ex-inmate of the dreaded prison, which was banned in France but was available in English translation due to his intervention. Though he was in Paris under an assumed name, he barely escaped arrest. Undaunted, he continued his voyage in disguise, observing prisons in several other French cities, including Marseilles and Toulon.[15] In 1786, he was in Constantinople and Smyrna. While traveling by sea to Venice, his ship was attacked by pirates from the Barbary Coast. Just as the crew was ready to blow up the vessel rather than surrender to the enemy, Howard personally loaded the biggest cannon on the ship with nails and with a single shot killed so many men on the deck of the pirate ship that the captain found it expedient to quit the scene of action. This, at least, is the story that was told, though it was not confirmed by Howard himself.[16]

Howard returned to England in 1787. His son was in a mental hospital and did not recognise his father. A great deal was being written about Howard at the time. He had conferred with heads of state, and new editions of his first book had been published. A second book, mainly about hospitals, appeared in 1789 (*An Account of the Principal Lazarettos in Europe, with Various Papers Relative to the Plague, together with Further Observations on Some Foreign Prisons and Hospitals, and Additional Remarks on the Present State of Those in Great Britain and Ireland*). Here we find a preliminary plan for a model prison, strongly reminiscent of the one in Ghent.[17] Howard also arranged for a translation of the Duke of Tuscany's new penal code, after which, he wrote his will and said farewell to his friends and servants. He did not expect to survive his next voyage, begun in 1789. He traveled via Amsterdam, Hanover, Brunswick, Berlin, Königsberg, and Riga to St. Petersburg where he visited hospitals. He went on to Kherson in the Crimea, where he caught the Asiatic fever and died. It was typical that Howards' last wish was to be buried in the Crimea. But he did not want any monument or fancy inscription to mark his grave. "Lay me quietly in the earth, put a sundial over my grave, and let me be forgotten." This was in the year 1790.[18] An appendix to the account of Lazarettos, based on Howard's notes, was published in 1791.[19]

Evaluation

Howard's health was not good and he exposed himself to much risk when he visited the unhealthy, fever-ridden institutions. He escaped infection for such a long time probably because of his cleanliness and careful eating habits. He was a teetotaler and a vegetarian. During his first illness, he read so much medical literature that he was able to act as a medical expert on his voyages and may have even posed as a physician. At a relatively advanced age, he covered more than 42,000 miles in horsedrawn carriages or on horseback.[20] Howard's friend, John Wesley, wrote: "Nothing but the mighty power of God can enable him to go through his difficult and dangerous employments." Wesley too was a great traveller who never spared himself. According to Bellows, Howard went to visit Wesley in 1789 to present him with his book, but had not found him at home. "Present," said he, "my respects and love to Mr. Wesley; tell him I had hoped to have seen him once more; perhaps we may meet again in this world, but, if not, we shall meet, I trust, in a better."[21]

Howard's many biographers seem to agree that his greatness lay in his single-minded devotion to what he believed to be right. He interpreted the Bible according to the letter: "I was sick and ye visited me. I was in prison and ye came unto me." Man's duty to man was self-evident, in his view. And the demands he sometimes made on other men were equally self-evident. During one of his voyages through the Germany of Frederick the Great, his coach met "the King's courier" in a narrow road. Ordered to retreat to give way to the royal vehicle, Howard refused. The courier was actually entitled to the right of way under all circumstances, but the accepted custom of the day was to blow a horn well in advance of a narrow passage. This the courier had not done and thereby forfeited his right to pass first. There the two gentlemen sat in their coaches, glaring at one another. Finally, it was the courier who had to retreat. John Howard's most critical biographer, D. L. Howard, writes:

> Nevertheless, it was admiration rather than friendship which he had gained. . . . Throughout his life, Howard could not cooperate with others. He was not a friendly man, given to discussion and personal persuasion, but one who, though not impressive physically, liked to dominate in debate. . . . He loved to feel superior, and to be admired for his superiority. Therefore he did not encourage any band of associates to join him in his work.[22]

Nevertheless, no man did more to improve the treatment of prisoners than John Howard. He opened the eyes of his contemporaries to elementary human obligations. Also, despite his oft-expressed dislike of worldly tributes, not only was his grave in Kherson marked by a memorial stone, but his statue by Bacon stands in St. Paul's Cathedral in London. The inscription on the latter reads: "He trod an open but unfrequented Path to Immortality in the Ardent and Uninterrupted Exercise of Christian Charity."

[7] PENANCE IN SOLITARY CONFINEMENT

Experiments with Isolation

At the end of the eighteenth century, it was generally agreed that prisoners should be kept in individual cells at night. If this was not practicable, as in the St. Michael's and Ghent prisons, inmates should at least be divided into small groups, not sleeping in large dormitories. But what arrangements should be made for the daytime? Should solitude be the aim then also? If so, what kind of isolation—complete *(solitary)* or in relation to other prisoners *(separate)*? Should the inmate be put to work alone or was it perhaps better to leave him entirely to his own thoughts, to remorse for his misdeeds—his wicked past? The experts were in disagreement on this question of principle; prisoners were the guinea-pigs.

A new prison with single cells for all inmates had been opened in 1779 in Horsham, Essex. The Duke of Richmond originated the project, praised by Howard in the later editions of his book. This was the first English cell prison. In the same year the Penitentiary Act was passed, the work of Sir William Eden and Sir William Blackstone. The Act ruled that prisoners should be completely isolated from one another, but should be kept at labor of the "hardest and most servile form." The first step in implementing the Act was to be the construction of two penitentiary houses—one for men and one for women. It was intended that the new institutions would be the means "not only of deterring others from the commission of the like crimes, but also of reforming of the individual and inuring them to habits of industry." This Act, together with other pieces of legislation, directed the authorities to build prisons with individual cells at least for inmates found guilty of serious crimes. In 1782, it was decided that a penal institution would be built in Petworth according to the cell system. Three years later a second cell prison was begun, this time in Wymondham, Norfolk. The most famous penitentiary was the one opened in Gloucester in 1791. Its founder was Sir George Onesiphorus

Paul, a contemporary and an admirer of John Howard. The institution comprised a detention jail for 137 people and a prison for 66 inmates.[1] Questioned by a parliamentary committee about this model institution, Paul stated:

> *That prison succeeded beyond* the theory imagined by the original projectors of the system; *far indeed beyond my most sanguine hopes. . . .* During the seventeen years that I particularly attended to the effects of this prison I ever found its inhabitants orderly, obedient to the discipline, and resigned to their situation: *few, if any of them, returned* to a second punishment during that period of my attention.[2]

But even at the time Paul made this statement, the single-cell system in all three English institutions had failed—a result of over-crowding. Nevertheless, the concept was adopted by the New World. The Quakers of Pennsylvania had long been in opposition to the harsh criminal laws brought into the country by the English. Reformers had fought for the abolition of the death penalty and of the many forms of dishonoring punishment and of torture. Benjamin Rush, a zealous propagandist, had made recommendations for prisons that closely resembled Mabillon's ideas, probably never having heard of Mabillon. William Penn himself was one of the prominent men to have been influenced by the new ideas, and he wrote in 1682 that "all prisons shall be workhouses for felons, vagrants, loose and idle persons."[3] The dream of a reform and correctional prison, a prison transformed into a school for disciplinary upbringing, was to become more of a reality in Pennsylvania than elsewhere.

The Prison on Walnut Street

The city of Philadelphia had a prison on Walnut Street. Its construction was begun in 1773, and during the Revolutionary War, it was used for prisoners of war by both sides, according to which army happened to occupy it. After the Declaration of Independence in 1776, it was turned into a common prison in which not even the sexes were segregated and in which the keeper ran a taproom, as was customary in those days. Terror reigned among the prisoners. The newly admitted could choose between treating all the other inmates to a drink or stripping themselves of their clothes, which were then sold to pay for a round or two. This pastime was known as "strip or pay."

In 1776, a Quaker called Richard Wistar founded a prisoners aid society in Philadelphia, the first of its kind in the world. It was disbanded a year later, but was revived in 1787 under the name of the Philadelphia Society for Alleviating the Miseries of Public Prisons, which incidentally, was in contact with John Howard. In 1788, the Society issued a famous memorial in which it declared that, based on their long and careful study of the practice as well as of the theory of the treatment of prisoners, its members had come to the unanimous conclusion that solitary confinement to hard labor and total abstinence from alcoholic beverages would prove to be the most effective means of reforming convicts.[4]

The principle of solitary confinement was legislated in an Act of 1790, which also ruled that a special block of cells of suitable size should be constructed "for the purpose of confining therein the more hardened and atrocious offenders . . . sentenced to hard labor for a . . . term of years."[5] A small block, consisting of sixteen single cells, eight on each of two floors, was erected in the yard of the prison on Walnut Street. It was finished in 1792. At the same time, the entire system of treatment in the prison was changed and soon became the subject of considerable discussion both at home and abroad. The appointment of a female warden, Mrs. Mary Weed, to succeed her husband who died of yellow fever, caused concern.

The new addition to the city jail on Walnut Street was called a penitentiary house, and Americans regard it as the cradle of the reform and correctional system. In reality, of course, as we know, the Quakers had merely copied European theory as well as practice. Nevertheless, the Walnut Street prison was very important to Americans, marking the beginning of a revolution in attitudes to the treatment of offenders. It also revitalized the European debate on the planning of prisons. A significant stimulus in this respect was the enthusiastic account of the American experiment by the French scholar, Larochefoucauld-Liancourt, in 1796, which was translated into several languages.

The most hardened offenders in the prison on Walnut Street were now to be confined in single cells and to be kept strictly isolated from each other and other inmates and at hard labor for a period fixed by the court. Their only contacts with the outside world would consist of visits by prison officials and special visitors representing the Philadelphia society. Less serious offenders would live in unsegregated quarters and work together during the day-time. Silence would be maintained in the workshops and the dining-hall. Inmates would be paid a small sum for their work and reasonable working-hours would be observed. This, at least, was the theory. However, according to Sellin, not many offenders were sentenced to solitary confinement and hard labor. The majority were given hard labor only and were allowed to mingle, at least during working-hours. The cell block in the yard thus appears to have been used mainly for sleeping quarters.[6]

Bentham's Panopticon

The problem of providing every inmate with what one might call a prison of his own continued to puzzle the experts. The English social reformer, Jeremy Bentham, had entered the arena of penal policy in 1791 with his project for a functional prison. It was to be a circular structure (later he envisaged it as a polygon, clearly influenced by the Ghent institution) with an outer ring of cells, each one with a window in the external wall and a barred door to the center facing a circular passageway surrounding an inner tower with the same number of floors as there were tiers of cells. The entire structure was to be covered by a glass roof. The tower would contain apartments for the warden and his family, which should preferably be large since each member would help to keep an eye on the prisoners from the many windows in the tower. A speaking tube would lead from the tower into each cell so that the warden could speak to the inmate whenever he wished. At first, Bentham proposed single cells, but he gave up the idea since "solitude, when it ceases to be necessary, becomes worse than useless." Once he had changed his mind, he said of solitude: "There are ways enough in the world of making men miserable without this expensive one." He thought of cells for six to eight inmates and favored permitting the public to visit prisons to look at the inmates—to talk to them through speaking tubes. Worst of all, he proposed that prison labor be farmed out to the highest bidder. The inmates would be paid a small wage for their work and a certain sum would be set aside against their discharge, but they would have to pay for their own food from their earnings, except for bread and water.

Bentham was obsessed by his "panopticon" or "inspection house," which he also called his monstrous creation. He believed that the plan could be applied to all kinds of structures for which supervision was required, e.g., hospitals including insane asylums, poorhouses, schools, and factories. The point would be to save on personnel without a sacrifice of security, keeping the inmates busy so that they could reduce the government's expense for maintenance. But the English Parliament, which adopted Bentham's project in 1799, finally decided that it would not build a panopticon. In 1812, construction was begun, according to a modified plan that embodied many of Howard's ideas, as well as Bentham's. After nine years of building, there was the Millbank prison for 1100 inmates, all of whom could be observed at once from a single guardroom. Millbank was called a monument to ugliness—one of the most costly buildings in the world since the pyramids. The prison was torn down in 1891.[7]

In the United States, Bentham's concept was adopted in a few places, including the Western Penitentiary in Pennsylvania and, in modern times, the Illinois State Prison at Stateville. In Holland, the prison in Breda was constructed according to a modified panopticon plan in 1901. A small prison in the Swedish town of Luleå is a "pocket edition" of Bentham's idea. According to Gilbert Geis, a Bentham biographer, this was "a story of eccentricity in action."[8]

The international debate was conducted in English, French, and German, and three new words were thus added to the terminology: *penitentiary*, *pénitencier*, and *Buss- und Besserungsanstalt*. The Gloucester prison was the first to be known as a penitentiary, and the concept of deprivation of liberty as a means of reform came to be known as the "penitentiary system" in innumerable papers published in the next few years.

Western Penitentiary

Pennsylvania had reformed its legislation in a humanitarian spirit and had replaced a series of death and torture penalties by prison sentences. In 1818 it was decided to build a prison in

Allegheny, near Pittsburgh, known as Western Penitentiary and intended for the western part of the state. It was designed exclusively for cell treatment and no labor. The architect was William Strickland; he had borrowed many of Bentham's panopticon ideas for his design. The 190 cells were arranged back to back in a semicircular, one-story block. The cells measured nine by seven feet. Outside, there was an exercise yard measuring six by seven feet. The cell block was surrounded by walls. The institution was completed in 1826. From the outset it proved unfit for its purpose, which, of course, was total isolation of the inmates. It soon appeared that the prisoners, particularly if they had nothing to do, found ways of communicating with one another through walls and pipes. The inmates suffered in small dark cells, and, by 1833, it was clear that the place would have to be rebuilt.[9]

New York State maintained a prison in Auburn. The original parts of this institution were built, according to the old system, with large rooms for common habitation. As the population increased (criminality with it), and as corporal punishment decreased, the need for prison space grew, and it was decided to expand Auburn. The cellular system was chosen under the influence of the trend in Pennsylvania. But, instead of emulating St. Michael's with its outside cells as had been done in Western Penitentiary, the Ghent plan with inside cells was adopted. Two rows of stone cells were placed back to back. Outside them were corridors lined with high windows through which the cells received indirect light. The new cellblock, intended to be escape-proof, was built on several floors. The designer of this prison, William Brittin, a carpenter by trade, was its governor. Like John Haviland, whom we shall soon encounter, Brittin attracted a large following as a designer of prisons. But the responsibility for the new form of treatment that now began to be practiced rested on the legislative assembly of New York.

A committee had been appointed to draw up plans for a prison system in Auburn. It recommended that prisoners be classified in three groups. The most hardened criminals would be held in unrelieved solitary confinement; another category would be kept in solitary for three days a week; a third (the youngest) would be permitted to work six days weekly in the shops. The proposal was approved in 1821 and put into effect immediately. On December 25, 1821, 80 men, the worst criminals they had, were put into the new cell block. They were given no work, and they were not allowed to meet or speak with anyone other than the prison chaplain (not even the guards)—unless they were ill. Prisoners were forbidden to leave their cells to relieve themselves, even though there were no toilet facilities in the cells. The air was fetid. The French criminologists, Gustave de Beaumont and Alexis de Tocqueville, who provided this information, described the results:

> This experiment, of which such favourable results had been anticipated, proved fatal for the majority of the prisoners. It devours the victim incessantly and unmercifully; it does not reform, it kills. The unfortunate creatures submitted to this experiment wasted away so obviously that their guards were appalled. Their lives appeared to be in danger if they remained in prison under the same treatment; five of them had already died in one year; their spiritual condition was no less disturbing; one of them went out of his mind; another took advantage of a moment when a guard had brought him something to hurl himself out of his cell, running the almost certain risk of a fatal fall.[10]

This was the death sentence of the system of solitary confinement without labor.

[8] AUBURN AND THE SILENT COMMUNITY SYSTEM

Elam Lynds

William Brittin died in 1821 and he was succeeded by Captain Elam Lynds, who, with his deputy, John D. Cray, invented the new form of treatment known as the Auburn system. The old congregate system had failed, as had the solitary confinement system. Lynds had been partly responsible for the latter and he was anxious to find a compromise between the two. The remaining prisoners in the solitary block were pardoned by the Governor in 1923-24, and Lynds was able to introduce his new method.

He put the prisoners to work in small, strictly supervised units in workshops and out-of-doors during the daytime—to be locked up in individual cells at night. Complete silence was to be observed. A breach of this rule was punished by flogging. Discipline was extremely strict in all other respects. Inmates were required to keep their eyes downcast when walking. The "lock-step" was used when the men walked in groups. Lynds appears to have been convinced that flogging was the most effective and also the most humane of all punishments since it had no ill effects on the offender's physical strength.[1]

Lynds believed that there was little hope of transforming older criminals into religious and law-abiding citizens. He was slightly less pessimistic about the young, who, in his opinion, could learn to work in prison and could be trained to be good craftsmen. If respect for the prison could be instilled in them, they might remain law-abiding in the future, even if their character was not actually changed. He said: "It is the only reform I have ever hoped to accomplish, and I believe it is all that society can expect." It was also his opinion that a warden must despise the prisoners if he is to manage a prison with a firm hand.[2] Lynds's character is well described by a story of which one version is given below:

> A prisoner had sworn to murder Lynds at the first opportunity that offered itself. When Lynds heard about this, he summoned the culprit to his bedroom. Disregarding the man's agitation, Lynds ordered him

to help him get dressed and even shave him. The prisoner dared not carry out his threat. Lynds then dismissed him with the contemptuous words: "I knew you wanted to kill me. But you are too much of a coward ever to dare to do such a thing. Alone and unarmed, I am stronger than all of you together," (quoted from *Actes du Congrés pénitentiaire international de Rome*, 1885).[3]

The views of the advocates of the Auburn or "silent" system are well expressed in the following account by the Reverend Louis Dwight, Secretary of the Boston Prison Discipline Society, which had become a rival of the Philadelphia Society.

The whole establishment from the gate to the sewer is a specimen of neatness. The unremitting industry, the entire subordination and sub-dued feeling of the convicts has probably no parallel among an equal number of criminals. In their solitary cells they spend the night, with no other book than the Bible, and at sunrise they proceed, in military order, under the eye of the turnkeys, in solid column, with the lock march, to their work-shops; thence, in the same order, at the hour of breakfast, to the common hall, where they partake of their wholesome and frugal meal in silence. Not even a whisper is heard through the whole apartment. The convicts are seated in single file, at narrow tables, with their backs towards the centre, so that there can be no interchange of signs. If one has more food than he wants, he raises his left hand; and if another has less, he raises his right hand; and the waiter changes it. When they have done eating, at the ringing of a little bell, of the softest sound, they rise from the table, form the solid columns, and return under the eye of their turnkeys to the work-shops . . . .
    At the close of day, a little before sunset, the work is all laid aside at once, and the convicts return in military order to the solitary cells; where they partake of the frugal meal, which they are permitted to take from the kitchen, where it was furnished for them, as they returned from the shops. After supper they can, if they choose, read the scrip-tures undisturbed, and then reflect in silence on the errors of their lives. They must not disturb their fellows by even a whisper. . . . The men attend to their business from the rising to the setting sun, and spend the night in solitude. (Quoted by Barnes & Teeters from the First Annual Report of the Boston Prison Discipline Society, 1826.)[4]

Sing Sing

Meanwhile, the population of New York State had increased rapidly, accompanied by increased criminality. A new prison was needed and Lynds agreed to build one using prisoners from Auburn. The story of its construction is quite extraordinary and illustrates how a disciplinarian can handle hardened criminals. The project, begun in 1825, was described by Nicholas Heinrich Julius:

Captain Lynds selected about one hundred of his Auburn prisoners who were not only quarriers and stonemasons but also were accustomed to his quick and heavy hand. He took them through the canal in two boats and then down the Hudson River on freighters, chained together by their legs. He put them to work in strict silence the same day they arrived at the site, out-of-doors with no walls and under the scrutiny of guards. The first day they built temporary barracks and then a cookhouse, a smithy and a carpentry shop. True to his severe and silent disciplinary methods, Lynds drove his men to cut stone from the cliffs and build the first block of cells. Within three years, these human beasts of burden had built cells for over five hundred prisoners and a chapel for nine hundred.[5]

The result of these efforts was Sing Sing prison, built on Mount Pleasant, one of the many beautiful names in the history of ugly penal institutions. An Indian phrase meaning "stone on stone," Sing Sing was the name of the nearby village which, to avoid confusion with the soon renowned prison, was renamed Ossining.[6] The same inside cell plan was used as in the latest Auburn building. Large workshops were also constructed. Lynds introduced the same harsh discipline as in the old Auburn prison. Inmates and personnel moved like ghosts in the building. (The guards wore moccasins to muffle the sound of their footsteps.) Obviously Lynds's feat of building Sing Sing with completely disciplined inmates made a deep impression. But a dictator of the magnitude of Lynds was required for the job.[7]

Silent Community

The best account of life in the Auburn and Sing Sing prisons was given by two Frenchmen, Frédéric Auguste Demetz and Guillaume Blouet, who visited the institutions in 1837. Excerpts from their report are paraphrased:

The cell blocks in Auburn have five floors. They contain a total of seven hundred and seventy cells, not including the disciplinary cells which, however, are no longer in use. The surrounding walls are not less than 9.3 meters high. The order is remarkable. The tables in the dining-hall seat 75 men each and are only 30 centimeters wide. The men all sit with their backs in the same direction, and each man's place is marked by two lines painted on the table. The prison in Auburn was begun in 1816. The north wing was finished in 1820 but was devastated by fire and was not ready for occupancy until 1825. The south section was built in 1832.

The plan cannot be used as a model for other institutions, since several sections were built at different times to meet new needs as they arose.[8]

Inmates are conducted to the workshops or their cells the day they arrive. First, however, their hair is cut and they are given a bath in hot water and soap, after which they don the prison uniform.

In summer work begins at five thirty o'clock in the morning and ends at six in the evening. Winter working hours are adjusted so as to ensure that the inmates are constantly occupied during the day.

The cell doors are opened fifteen minutes after reveille and after the officials and guards have arrived at their posts. The men emerge and march in close formation, carrying their chamber pot, water jug, and food bowl which last they deposit in a hall on the way to the courtyard where they empty the chamber pot, wash themselves at a pump, get back into line, march to the workshops and begin work. The breakfast bell is rung between six and seven o'clock, depending on the time of year. The prisoners once again form lines and are led by the guards to the dining-room. When the meal is over they return to the shops in the same order. These transfers from one place to another take no more than twenty to thirty minutes. Dinner is always served at noon and is taken in the same fashion and requires the same length of time as breakfast.

A few minutes before the end of the work-day, fires are extinguished in the shops, the inmates wash their faces and hands, get into line in their usual places, march from the shops to the place where their chamber pots are lined up, empty the water with which the pots are filled into a sewer, and return to their cells. They pass through a hall next to the kitchen. Without slowing down, they pick up their water jug and their bowl of food and continue on their way. When they reach their cells they enter and pull the door to without closing it.

When this procedure has been completed, a guard locks all the cells in the gallery with his key. As he passes, the inmates must knock on the door to indicate that they are present. When this has been done, the guard goes back a second time to make sure that everything is properly closed. On this occasion the inmate must show two fingers through the bars as an extra precaution. This maneuver takes approximately twenty minutes from the time work is finished. The cell keys are then deposited in the guardroom.

The guards spend the night in a vestibule next to the cell block. Now and then a guard inspects the shops and the yards to make sure that the fires are extinguished and that all is in order. Two supervisors and two guards are on duty all night long. Two of them constantly patrol the galleries on the different floors. They wear moccasins and are instructed to move cautiously so as to avoid being seen by the prisoners before they pass by a cell. The corridors are lighted throughout the night and are also heated in wintertime.

The prisoners are divided into squadrons or companies for the movements described above. Each such group occupies a gallery or a part of a gallery. There is a supervisor for each gallery. During all movements the men of each company are kept together and in the same order. They march close together with one hand on the shoulder of the man in front and facing the supervisor. They start walking, turn, increase or decrease speed as ordered by the supervisor and always mark time until told to halt.

The shops are not big enough. They have been built without anticipating the needs of an increasing number of inmates or the introduction of a new trade for one reason or another. The men are placed too close together for effective supervision.

One prisoner in each shop is detailed to keep the place clean, to distribute tools and working material. Supervisors must, to the extent possible, give their orders by signs or at least in whispers in order not to cause a distraction.

For each trade there is at least one supervisor and one foreman who represents both the prison and the contractor. He assigns tasks, supervises their execution and instructs beginners. He is forbidden to speak to prisoners except concerning their work. He is paid by the contractor and may be discharged by the warden of the prison.

The supervisor is responsible for discipline. He alone has the right to give orders to the prisoners and usually sits on a chair on a dais in the middle of the shop. He keeps account of the materials distributed to the prisoners and of the products they manufacture. He also directs the movements of the prisoners to and from the cells, shops, dining-hall and chapel.

In each workroom there is a bucket of clean water from which the prisoners are permitted to quench their thirst. There are toilets on one side of the shops and outside them. Only one prisoner is allowed to enter the toilet at a time. A piece of wood hangs from a rope in the middle of the shop. Every time a man goes to the toilet he removes the wood, replacing it when he returns. No one is permitted to leave the room as long as the piece of wood is not in its place.

To ensure satisfactory supervision of activities, dark wooden galleries have been built the length of the shop wall from which the custodial personnel can watch the men at work without being seen themselves. This precaution is one of the most effective means of checking not only on the prisoners but also on the supervisors. They do not know when they are being watched, and the fear of being taken by surprise is always present and helps to keep them in order.

The dining-hall is in the shape of a parallelogram. The tables are in parallel rows and very close to each other. The prisoners sit with their backs in the same direction so that they do not see the face of those in front of them. A passage permits circulation around the tables. The prison chaplain says grace before and after the meal. The food has already been served when the men reach their places at table, but if they find their helping too small they are permitted to raise their left hand. One of the prisoners who serves the food then brings a second helping. If a man cannot eat up his portion, he raises his right hand and the remaining food is removed. Since the servings are generous, additional helpings are usually balanced out by uneaten portions.

During meals the supervisors sit on a dais beside the tables in such a way that they can see all the prisoners in their group.

The prisoners are awakened at the same time on Sundays as on weekdays. They are permitted to leave their cells to empty and wash their chamber pots. When this has been done, they are locked up again. A clean shirt is issued to each prisoner through the bars. The cells are opened once more at breakfast time and the prisoners are led to the dining-hall. After breakfast they proceed to the chapel to attend Sunday school and divine service, after which they return to their cells where they remain until Monday morning. On Sunday, the prisoners do not eat in the dining-hall. On their way from the chapel to the cells, they pass the kitchen where they pick up their evening meal in a bowl. The prisoners we were able to question told us that Sunday was the longest and most trying day of the week.

On Sunday afternoon the prison chaplain visits as many prisoners as he has time for and talks to them through the cell door. All prisoners do not attend Sunday school, since there are too many of them. The school can only accommodate two to three hundred people. Applications for admission have to be submitted, and the youngest and most ignorant are given priority. The teachers are students in a divinity school in the neighborhood of the prison. Instruction comprises reading and interpretation of the Bible. Writing is not taught since this would provide an opportunity for the prisoners to communicate with one another.

The prisoners are obliged to obey instantly all orders issued by the foremen, to work quickly and efficiently without pause, in silence, and with downcast eyes. When they approach their superiors, they must show deep respect and when they speak to such persons they must do so in the politest terms. They may not speak to one another except when ordered to do so by their supervisors. They are obliged to avoid everything that could cause the least distraction or unrest, may not leave their place without permission from their supervisors; nor may they cover their heads except in the yards or in certain of the shops. They are expressly forbidden to converse with visitors, to destroy or damage their tools or other objects they use, and to speak to their guards about matters that do not concern their work or their needs. The least breach of these rules is punished immediately and sternly. Any misdeed shall be penalized instantly and without mercy by flogging with a whip or a cane on the shoulders or the naked back. Every supervisor has the right to mete out punishment, and there is no fixed limit to the number of stripes that may be given. All that is required of the one who administers the flogging is that he report the name of the prisoner to the Governor, as well as the reason for the punishment and the number of stripes given. Women are subject to the same routine as men, and their days are organised according to the same schedule. They are not subjected to flogging and instead are punished by solitary confinement day and night without work and on reduced food rations or by being forced to sit for a certain length of time in a chastisement chair.

The Auburn prison is governed by a board consisting of five inspectors who live in the town. They are appointed every second year by the Governor of New York State after their names have been approved by the Senate. They receive no compensation for their services and they may have no interests in common with the prison. The administration comprises a warden, a deputy warden, a bookkeeper, a female superintendent for the women, a works superintendent with twenty supervisors, and nineteen guards, or a total of forty-four persons, not counting a chaplain and a doctor. The warden and the chaplain live in the prison.

Demetz and Blouet also visited Sing Sing. They touched on the story of its emergence:

Is it not barbaric to refrain from all the usual precautions against escapes by the prisoners and thus put oneself in the position of being forced to kill men whose only misdeed is that they have not been able to resist the temptation to try to regain their freedom? Twelve years after it was opened, Sing Sing still has no wall around it. Every day prisoners are transported in open vehicles accompanied by a few supervisors, others move in all directions in an open yard and other open territory. In winter the only barrier on one side of the property, a frozen river, offers a possibility for escape, and on the other side guards are posted on the surrounding heights, armed and prepared to kill anyone who tries to shorten his imprisonment by escaping. We repeat: this is immoral and revolting.

Daily life is about the same in Sing Sing as in Auburn, however breakfast and dinner are taken in the cells and not in a dining hall. When the prisoners leave the shops, they march through the yard past a hatch leading to the kitchen through which their rations are passed to each man in turn, after which they proceed to their cells. They are allowed one hour for their meals, during which the supervisors also eat theirs.

Eating in the cells has several advantages. It is more depressing and is therefore good for the prisoners, who must constantly be reminded that they are undergoing punishment. The inevitable conversations between men sitting close together in a crowded dining-hall are prevented. Finally, the period allowed for meals can be prolonged without inconvenience, which permits the prisoners to have some rest, a necessity in a hard work-day.

One objection is that it is difficult to adjust the helpings to suit the individual prisoner's appetite, but we consider this to be of little importance. A prisoner who finds his helping too small may ask the supervisor for more and will receive it. The others leave what they have not eaten in their bowls and the remains are returned to the kitchen. In this connection, we consider that the rations are too abundant in all American penal institutions.

There is no Sunday school but only a divine service on Sundays.

Like Auburn, Sing Sing has a board of inspectors. The influence of the Sing Sing board is much smaller. In fact, since the members all live at long distances from the prison, it may be regarded as almost non-existent. The inspectors appoint the warden, the chaplain and the doctor and also have the power to dismiss them. All other employees are appointed by the warden, who has the same power of dismissal. The entire prison personnel consists of a warden, a deputy warden, a chaplain, a doctor, a bookkeeper, twenty-one supervisors and twenty-five guards. The bookkeeper is appointed by the Governor with the approval of the State legislature for a four-year term. . . .

The functions of the various officials are approximately the same as in Auburn. The only differences are that the warden has more power, since the subordinate personnel is entirely dependent on him and the inspectors are less influential. The authority of the subordinate officials also differs somewhat. We have mentioned that the Auburn supervisors are free to punish the prisoners for errors or misdeeds, but they are obliged to report the incident to the deputy warden. In Sing Sing, they are not required to submit a report; they may mete out penalties at will; and they are accountable to no one.

In Auburn we saw a register in which are recorded day by day the prisoners' misdeeds, the penalties imposed and the names of those administering them. Nothing of the kind exists in Sing Sing. We could not even form a general idea of the kinds of misdeeds and penalties involved. The warden told us that he received oral reports, but other officials appeared to be unaware that this was expected of them.[9]

The authors then compare the administrative systems of the Auburn and Sing Sing prisons:

The Auburn people have great faith in the possibility of reforming prisoners and practically all measures are designed with this in mind. In Sing Sing they believe less in the possibility of reform and therefore neglect measures that might have that effect. Captain Lynds had brought the spirit of severity to the administration of these prisons of which he was the warden for two separate terms. After his resignation, severity was gradually relaxed in Auburn, while Sing Sing, which

Lynds had founded, is more faithful to the tradition established by him.

Mr. Robert Wilste, Lynds's successor, said to us: "The best prison is the one prisoners consider the worst." An apt observation, which is not less true for being overly categorical. A report to the New York State Legislature, which was the basis for the decision to introduce separate confinement as a penalty, contained the following statement: "If we do not introduce a much more severe prison system than the present one, it is generally believed that we will be compelled to revert to the harsh methods of the old penal code."

At Auburn, the cradle of the penitentiary system, they appear to have lost sight of the general principles underlying its adoption. To influence the prisoner more by persuasion than by chastisement, to restore him not only to order and to respect for the law but also to righteousness and virtue through religious instruction: these are the aims of those responsible for this institution. And to achieve these aims, the former severe disciplinary methods have been mitigated. These new dispositions derive from a highly respected gentleman, the Reverend Dr. Smith. Fired by an indomitable zeal and sincere faith, he gave unstintingly of his time and energy to the moral uplift of the prisoners. His self-sacrificing work has won him disciples: The warden and inspectors share his confidence, but in our opinion this confidence is exaggerated. This approach distorts the penitentiary system and will even decrease the likelihood of its success. An enduring change of heart can only be brought about in those who have first been chastized for their crimes and have become convinced that their misdeeds will never remain unpunished.

It is customary in Auburn to pardon each year those prisoners whose behaviour has been exemplary and who are believed to have mended their ways; we could not disagree more strongly with this practice. Anyone who is familiar with prison conditions is also aware of the skill with which prisoners, particularly the most hardened, take advantage of every opportunity to improve their situation and to court the favor of those who may have an influence on their fate. This is precisely what goes on in Auburn. It does not take the prisoners long to understand that the aim of the prison officials is to reform them morally, and they soon learn that they may be pardoned if they give the impression of having seen the error of their ways. As soon as they have grasped this, they have only one thought in mind: to convince the administration that its objectives have been achieved. The hope of success makes it easier to bear the strain; the purposes of the treatment have been defeated. In Sing Sing, on the other hand, they have gone too far in severity, which is no less dangerous. It is true that some satisfactory results are reached with segregation and intimidation, but, as we have already pointed out, they are skeptical about the chances of reforming the prisoners, and the measures available for this purpose are totally neglected.

When we spoke with Mr. Wilste, warden of Sing Sing, about a list published by the Auburn administration of allegedly reformed prisoners, he replied, "I have or have had in this institution two-thirds of these good individuals. And I can assure you that they don't talk religion with me."

No, the Sing Sing prisoners speak a completely different language. They know that no one believes protestations of a change of heart and that an assumption that they have mended their ways will not help to get them a pardon. They have less interest in pretense and they play-act less. They do not claim that the sentence is a blessing; they all complain; they all resent the severity and harshness of their supervisors. They say that instead of leaving the prison as reformed sinners, they leave it with a hatred of society and a desire to avenge themselves with new crimes. [10]

The authors comment further that the harsh methods in Auburn, as well as in Sing Sing and other American prisons with similar treatment methods, had been alleviated under pressure of public opinion. Many wardens known for their severity had been dismissed, and their successors had been forced to bow to public attitudes regarding the degree of severity practiced in prisons.

Wethersfield

In addition to Auburn and Sing Sing, the French visitors saw four other institutions that operated in accord with the silent system. The best known of them was Wethersfield in Connecticut. This prison is especially interesting since only four years before the Frenchmen's visit, it had been studied by William Crawford, head of the English penal administration. While he favored the Pennsylvania system in theory, Crawford feared the high costs of construction and administration and therefore recommended to his Government that it introduce the same system as in Wethersfield. [11]

This institution had adopted all the Auburn methods, with the exception of corporal punishment. An inmate who broke a prison rule was reported by his guard to the warden who, after investigating the case, might order him to be confined in a dark cell with no work and reduced rations. Crawford had noted that this method of chastisement worked satisfactorily and that perfect discipline could be maintained without the cruel corporal punishments inflicted in Auburn and Sing Sing.

The Wethersfield prison was opened in 1826. The man who headed it and introduced the new regime without corporal punishment was Moses Pilsbury. He resigned in 1830, and he was succeeded by his son Amos who, however, was dismissed from his post two years later on a charge of official misconduct, which subsequently proved to be unfounded. After Amos Pilsbury left, discipline slackened; prison labor grew less productive; disorder prevailed in the prison; the guards were no longer obeyed; and the rule of silence was disregarded. Newspapers were smuggled into the prison, a kind of canteen was set up by the inmates, and it became impossible to keep the work going in the shops or even to maintain order. Finally, an extensive escape scheme was engineered by a large group of prisoners who killed one of the guards in the process. Pilsbury was now again the warden, but he was unable to restore discipline without reviving the old forms of corporal punishment. In a statement to the French visitors, Pilsbury said he, too, was convinced that guards must have the right and duty to mete out instant punishment for infringements of prison discipline.[12]

Demetz and Blouet summarized their views of the Auburn system: The first question, they say, is whether chastisement is effective, i.e., can it be sufficiently painful without being cruel to convince the culprit that it is to his advantage to abide by the law? They have no doubt about the answer: The Auburn system of punishment is either cruel or inadequate. The rule of silence can never be totally enforced, and cruel means are required to make it work more or less satisfactorily. The result is that when the power to inflict punishment is unrestricted, the guards will usually be brutal men of questionable morality and cruelty will be rampant. Wherever guards do not have this power, infringements of prison rules go unpunished. The Frenchmen stress the impossibility of preventing prisoners from communicating with one another. A further disadvantage is that equality of punishment cannot be achieved. If the warden is harsh and stern, the prison term will be a difficult and painful experience for the inmate; if he is gentle and tolerant, the punishment will be too lenient. However, the Frenchmen concede that the Auburn system is better than all others from the financial point of view. They further note that under this system certain prisons not only had ceased to draw on public funds for their maintenance but were even contributing revenue to the State coffers. But they wonder what sacrifices are justified to achieve this result. [13]

[9] CHERRY HILL AND THE SEPARATE SYSTEM

Haviland

While Western Penitentiary was still under construction, the Pennsylvania Legislature had already decided to build a prison for the eastern part of the state, later called Eastern Penitentiary and known as Cherry Hill in memory of the cherry orchard that had once occupied the site.

In 1821 the Board of Inspectors of the Walnut Street jail had written of the single cell system:

> To be shut up in a cell for days, weeks, months, and years, alone, to be deprived of converse with a fellow being, to have no friendly voice to minister consolation, no friendly bosom on which to lean or into which to pour our sorrows and complaints, but on the contrary, to count the tedious hours as they pass, a prey to the corrodings of conscience and the pangs of guilt, is almost to become the victim of despair. [1]

Thus, the Board fully recognized the severity of solitary confinement; a year later it proposed that a sentence of one year without labor be the equivalent of three years of solitary confinement with labor.

In 1829, three years after the Western Penitentiary was opened, the Pennsylvania Legislative Assembly ruled that the principle of solitary confinement at labor would apply in the new prison. At this point, however, they had on their hands an almost half-finished prison designed for solitary confinement *without* labor. [2]

Four different architects had submitted plans for Eastern Penitentiary. The serious contenders were William Strickland, designer of Western Penitentiary, and John Haviland. As for his earlier construction, Strickland wanted to use a modified panopticon plan. But, Haviland proposed radiating blocks, reminiscent of the prison in Ghent. In its directives to the competing architects, the Building Commission stated that, "The exterior of a solitary prison should exhibit as much as possible great strength and convey to the mind a cheerless blank indicative of the misery that awaits the unhappy being who enters within its walls."[3] Haviland was asked to submit a plan of a structure that, when it was finished, was described by Theodore Dreiser in his novel, *The Financier*: "The Eastern District Penitentiary . . . was a large, graystone structure, solemn and momentous in its mien, not at all unlike the palace of Sforzas at Milan, although not so distinguished. It stretched its gray length for several blocks along four different streets, and looked as lonely and forbidding as a prison should."[4]

The result of Haviland's work was nevertheless considered by contemporary architects to be esthetically pleasing, a combination of "function and beauty." Furthermore, he later received numerous commissions to build prisons. The ideas for Haviland's plan were derived from various sources. Teeters, for example, found that he was clearly influenced by Fontana's San Michele prison for boys in Rome, in his design of the cells. The radial plan had been used by the English architect, William Blackburn, in both prisons and hospitals, including the Ipswich County Jail in Suffolk, built in 1790. The central rotunda was obviously copied from the prison in Ghent. The idea of individual exercise yards, in turn, was taken from his rival Strickland, a plagiarism that English visitors commented on—acidly. In Teeters' opinion, "it was a sign of genius to combine judiciously all of the practical and successful features of these earlier institutions into one structure."[5] As already mentioned, however, the central rotunda was simply modelled on the ideal town plan of the Baroque.

The forbidding appearance of the building was in itself intended to have a deterrent effect on those who saw it, to replace in some way the gallows as a deterrent symbol, and the bleakness and austerity of life within the walls were also meant to deter the inmates. At the same time, the Building Commission had stated that the treatment was to be aimed at the prisoners' future welfare and moral reform, a penological contradiction. According to Teeters, the prison was originally designed for 252 cells divided into seven blocks of 36 cells each on a single floor. In this first draft the only access to the cells was through the exercise yards outside them and not from the corridor. However, the plan appears to have been modified immediately.[6] The first three cell wings were built as envisaged on one floor but with 19 cells on each side of a central corridor, i.e., 38 cells to each wing, or a total of 114. Each cell measured 11'8" in length, 7'6" in width and 16'6" in height. The connecting exercise yard measured 18' in length and 8' in width. When it was realized during construction that the number of cells would have to be increased substantially, Haviland simply added an extra floor to the remaining four wings. Since the prisoners on the second floor had no exercise yard, they were given double cells in compensation. The cells and exercise yards in the new wings were somewhat smaller in area. The prison came to comprise 582 cells, but since the inmates in the upper floors had two cells each, there were accommodations for a total of only 464 prisoners.[7] Later, Cherry Hill was enlarged to include 14 cell blocks with a total of 900 cells.[8] Today it is no longer used as a prison.

Cell and exercise yard were separated by a double door. Light was admitted through a small opening in the ceiling measuring eight inches in diameter. If a prisoner made a disturbance, this "deadeye" was covered so as to throw the cell into darkness. Food was pushed in to the prisoner in his cell through an aperture in the wall facing the corridor, from which a peephole had been bored for supervision. The entire cell was of stone, but wooden floors for protection from the cold were eventually installed. The bed could be folded against the wall during the day. Other furnishings included a clothes-hanger, a workbench, a stool, a pewter mug, a bowl for food, a mirror, a broom, sheets, blankets, and a straw mattress. Each cell contained a primitive water closet. Demetz & Blouet described their visit in 1837:

> There would be no problem in constructing a third floor, an opinion that is shared by the warden. Behind each cell on the ground floor there is a small exercise yard for the occupant. Some of these small yards are covered by a roof and serve as carpentry shops. The cells on the second floor are double to compensate for the lack of exercise yards.
>
> One might think that the convicts on the ground floor are privileged, but this is not the case. The majority prefer the second floor with the double cells to the ground floor with yards that are cold and damp and are never touched by a ray of sunlight, surrounded as they are by high walls. The sturdiest prisoners may prefer the yards, since they provide better opportunities for exercise. No prisoner is ever compelled to leave his cell. As a rule the cells are hot in the summer and cold and dank during the rest of the year. The explanation of this is the eternally damp walls around the yards which prevent the air from circulating. While their removal has been considered, this has not been done because it would facilitate escape.[9]

The Frenchmen also tell how prisoners had dug tunnels under the exercise yards. The dampness in the ground-floor cells came not only from the faulty ventilation but from the absence of a basement. Floorboards lasted four or five years before they required replacement. To begin with, the cells were heated with hot air piped into the cells from a central heating plant. Nevertheless, some 20 prisoners nearly died from carbon monoxide poisoning, after which the old system was replaced by individual stoves. Standards of cleanliness in the cells were high, and prisoners were required to whitewash their cells twice a year. Daily, one hour was allowed for exercise but, in order to prevent communication between the yards, only every other yard could be used at the same time. Despite this restriction, the warden found that conversations between prisoners could not be prevented. The men communicated through the water closets and ventilators, and communication by rapping was of course also practised. Each supervisor was responsible for 30 to 40 cells. Profound silence reigned in the entire prison.

Treatment

Demetz & Blouet reported that the cells were large, airy, and equipped with a good bed and other essential furniture and utensils. They found fresh water pipes and a good system of ventilation with no odor from the toilets.

On arrival the prisoner is examined by the doctor, after which he is given a hot bath and puts on the prison uniform. His personal effects are placed in a special storeroom to be returned to him when he is discharged. After these preparations, his eyes are covered by a mask or hood and he is received by the warden who exhorts him to strict observance of prison rules, after which he is taken to the cell designated for him. From that time on, his only identity will be the number hung on his door.

When he enters the cell, his eyes are uncovered and he is left alone without work and without books, with only his thoughts. Usually it is not long—rarely more than a day or two—before the prisoner asks for work or books. The period during which a prisoner can abstain voluntarily from occupation varies between four and eight days. The warden decides how long a time shall elapse before labor is permitted, and he reaches his decision on the basis of the man's character and past, the nature of his crime and the degree of his submissiveness. All prisoners agree that the first period of the punishment is the hardest to bear. Thus, they are given work and reading matter, usually the Bible, as a favor and are denied work and books as a chastisement.

If the prisoner is proficient in any of the trades exercised in the prison, he will work at it. If not, he is given an occupation in which he is instructed by a guard. The guards always have adequate skill in the trades represented in the prison.

The prisoners are not permitted any communication whatever with their families or friends, and they are seldom allowed to receive letters. Only the prison inspectors, ministers and priests, the warden, doctor, prison officials and prison visitors may meet with the prisoner. Official visitors are: the Governor of the State, members of the Senate and the House of Representatives, the Secretary of the Commonwealth, the Judges of the Supreme Court, the Attorney-General and his deputies, the President and Associate Judges of all the State courts, the Mayor and certain other city officials, and the members of the board of the prison society.[10]

On the basis of these observations, the Frenchmen thought it not correct to call this prison system isolation or solitary confinement—more accurate to call it a system of separation of one prisoner from another. A visitor who gave to or accepted anything from a prisoner was fined 100 dollars. With the exception of sick prisoners, all were restricted to the food provided by the prison. Tobacco, wine, and other intoxicating liquors were strictly forbidden, and purveyors of the same were punished.

The daily routine was: during the winter, the inmates rose at dawn, in the summer, between four and five o'clock in the morning. Bedtime was between nine and ten o'clock in the evening. In the winter, the prisoners remained at work after dark and were provided with lamps. The exceptions were those who could not earn enough to pay for illumination. Three meals were served daily, breakfast between seven and eight in the morning, dinner between noon and one o'clock, and supper between six and seven in the evening.

The administration at that time consisted of five inspectors, a warden, a doctor, a bookkeeper, one supervisor for each block of cells (38 inmates), and a number of outside guards.

The inspectors were appointed for two-year terms by the Supreme Court. Among themselves, they elected a chairman, a secretary, and a clerk. All of them were to be residents of Philadelphia or its environs. They received no compensation, but were exempt from the obligation to serve in the militia or as jurymen, as well as other public duties.

A prisoner who fell ill was transferred to an infirmary cell. At first, they were put in a common ward, but in addition to the problems that arose from bringing prisoners together in this way, contrary to the principle of keeping them apart, the doctor was convinced by experience that recovery was more rapid in a single sickroom. If a prisoner in a sickroom could not be left alone, the door was left ajar and an orderly looked in at short intervals.

All prisoners were submitted to the same treatment, regardless of their crime or social background. They were required to work at a trade; there was no discrimination between them; bad behavior was punished; good behavior was rewarded by the approval of the foreman. Neither the inspectors nor the warden ever petitioned for pardons, as in the Auburn prison.

The French visitors were convinced that complete isolation from the outside could be achieved within this system. Crawford commented in his report that when he visited Cherry Hill a few months after cholera had raged in Phaladelphia, the prisoners with whom he talked had never heard of the epidemic. In addition, Warden Wood told the Frenchmen that a prisoner, who had been sentenced the same day as his accomplice, had enquired two years later how things had turned out for the latter, even though the accomplice had been occupying a neighboring cell the whole time. The Frenchmen noted that the separate system was simple and easily implemented. True, it was a severe punishment, but it was made less onerous through work and visits by foreman and others. The individual prisoner in his cell had so few opportunities to break the rules of the prison that he neither frightened nor angered his supervisor, who was not afraid to treat him in a kind and humane fashion.

De Beaumont & de Tocqueville had expressed concern that the cellular treatment would have a bad effect on the health of the prisoners. Crawford held the opposite view. Neither Demetz nor Blouet found any evidence that confinement to a single cell had any bad effect on health.[11] In their summation of the advantages of the cell system, the Frenchmen explained:

In the separate system the prisoners cannot become more depraved. They are not under the influence of their fellow prisoners. The false pride in being even worse than ones fellows, the conceit that prevents a prisoner from submitting to his fate, all those feelings that need approval in order to flourish evaporate in solitude. Regardless of his nature, the convict is compelled to look at himself. He is alone with his conscience. It does not take him long to grasp that his punishment is a consequence of his errors and that he has been deprived of his freedom because he has made bad use of it. During the first few days he may only hear the voice of his anger, but what purpose does that serve in the deathly silence of his surroundings. He is defeated. That is the point at which work is given to him. This becomes a distraction for his gloomy thoughts, a solace, and he applies himself eagerly to the task offered him, which is thus not an augmentation of the punishment.

Visits by spiritual counselors are one of the most important elements in the system. They are impatiently awaited by the prisoner who is happy to hear a human voice. It is pointless for the prisoner to play the hypocrite, since pardons are seldom granted under this system. But if the cell prison is beneficial from the moral and religious points of view, it is no less so in the educational sense. The prisoner is eager to master the trade taught him by the foreman. Furthermore, the Pennsylvania system does not require that the prisoners be divided according to social class, category of offense, etc. Still another virtue of the system is that, since all communications between prisoners are prevented, there is no need to speculate on the most suitable size of a prison. Supervision is not difficult, and a thousand prisoners can be kept in the same institution as easily as one.[12]

Demetz and Blouet had this to say about the Pennsylvania system:

The possibility of changing the attitudes of criminals through this system has been doubted. But the purpose of the punishment is not so much to chastise as to set an example to society that is beneficial and moral. If in this process, the criminal can be given the possibility of reforming, no effort should be spared to achieve this twofold result. If the criminal is not completely reformed in solitude, he is at least taught calm and regular habits. He is held in order and discipline; he learns to work and to respect the law.[13]

The objection that it is cruel and barbaric to isolate a human being from his peers is overruled by the Frenchmen with the assertion that isolation alone gives an opportunity for remorse and makes effective the moral and religious influence.

The prison inspectors' opinion of the treatment is quoted by Teeters and Shearer:

We mark, generally, that at first the prisoner indulges in morose or vindictive feelings, and is guilty of turbulent and malicious conduct, but after a few weeks he adopts a more subdued tone, becomes reasonable, and his countenance indicates a more amiable state of mind; is disposed to talk of his past life as one of misery and folly; begins to think that the barrier between him and a good reputation is not impossible; and that there are those in the community, whose prejudices against the condemned are not so strong as to induce the withholding of a friendly countenance to his attempts at restoration. In many, the retrospect of life becomes a horrible and loathsome subject of reflection—the sense of shame and feelings of remorse drive them to some source of consolation and the ordinary means of stifling an actively reproving conscience being denied by reason of their solitariness, the comforts of the Bible and the Peace of religion are eagerly sought for.[14]

Prison Visitors

The 1829 decision of the Pennsylvania Legislature also authorized some of the persons already mentioned, including members of the Philadelphia Society for Alleviating the Miseries of Public Prisons, to visit inmates. This marked the introduction of the *prison-visitors system*. Teeters and Shearer commented on these visitors:

As we look back on those early days of Cherry Hill we are impressed by the large numbers of professional men, citizens of Philadelphia, who voluntarily visited the prisoners, month after month, year after year, in all sorts of weather. They met one or more times each month and made their reports to the Society, commenting on the reactions of their clients. Few types of volunteer work done in modern times can surpass, or perhaps even compare, with the work of this committee in honesty, singleness of purpose, and expenditure of time.[15]

From October, 1829, to December, 1840, all the expenses of the prison, with the exception of the payroll for the personnel, were defrayed by the earnings of the prisoners. In addition, there was a surplus of $400.00.[16]

Dickens, Lafayette, Bremer

Visitors poured into Cherry Hill when it was opened. Some were enthusiastic—others critical. Charles Dickens visited the prison in 1842. He dined in the institution; he was shown around the place; and he talked with prisoners. When he left he expressed himself in complimentary terms, stating that never before had he seen a public institution in which the relations of father and family were so well exemplified as in the Cherry Hill prison. However, he changed his mind later when he had time to digest his impressions:

> In its intention I am well convinced that it is kind, humane and meant for reformation; but I am persuaded that those who devised the system and those benevolent gentlemen who carry it into execution, do not know what it is they are doing. I believe that very few men are capable of estimating the immense amount of torture and agony which this dreadful punishment, prolonged for years, inflicts upon the sufferers; and in guessing at it myself, and from reasoning from what I have seen written upon their faces, and what to my certain knowledge they feel within, I am only the more convinced that there is a depth of terrible endurance in it which none but the sufferers themselves can fathom, and which no man has a right to inflict upon his fellow creatures.
>
> I hold this slow and daily tampering with the mysteries of the brain to be immeasurably worse than any torture of the body; and because its ghastly signs and tokens are not so palpable to the eye and sense of touch as scars upon the flesh, because its wounds are not on the surface, and it extorts few cries that human ears can hear; therefore I denounce it as a secret punishment which slumbering humanity is not roused to stay.[17]

Dickens detailed accounts of the lives of several prisoners, but it turned out that he had misunderstood most of what he had seen and heard. In one cell, he had visited a German prisoner, whose tears and descriptions of the miseries of solitary confinement made a strong impression on him. But, according to William Tallack, the same prisoner was still alive 42 years after the conversation, surviving Dickens. In the last year of his life, returning to the prison, he begged to end his life in his old cell, and this was granted. This strange incident has been explained by the fact that the man had become a "celebrity" (thanks to Dickens) and was constantly bothered by curious visitors and that the prison management regarded it as a good opportunity to retaliate at Dickens.[18]

General Lafayette visited Cherry Hill, and, since he had spent five years in Austrian prisons (three of them in strict solitary confinement in Olmütz), he was able to draw comparisons based on personal experience.

> I am told that they (the prisoners) are to be without the least employment, and are not to be allowed the use of books . . . Another feature chilled me (when) I saw the turrets which flank the corners of the wall,

from which the sentries are to overlook the establishment. I have been subjected to all of this; and of all the sufferings of my life none have exceeded—none have equalled that single oppression of being, for three whole years, exposed to the view of two eyes, watching my every motion, taking from my very thoughts every kind of privacy. [19]

Lafayette preferred the Auburn system. Fredrika Bremer, the Swedish social reformer and feminist, had a different opinion. She wrote on June 23, 1850, about her visit to Cherry Hill:

In the middle of the great rotunda, into which the big corridors lined with cells led like *radii* to a common center, the Quaker Mr. Scattergood, dressed in a light yellow coat and a wide-brimmed hat, was comfortably ensconced in an armchair, looking like a big spider guarding the flies caught in its net. But nay, this simile ill fits the situation and the man, a jovial elderly gentleman with an exceptionally sensible, humane and humorous appearance. It would be hard to imagine a more agreeable guard. He went with us into the cells. Here the prisoners live completely alone, with no contact with their fellows, but they are allowed to work and read. The library was large and contained, in addition to religious books, scientific treatises, travel books and literary works, selected with discrimination. It was with no grudging hand that the seeds of learning were strewn to the prison's children, 'they who sit in darkness.' The spirit of the New World is neither timid nor grudging and does not shun generosity when it desires to do good. It only aspires to choose the right path and then to set to work with unstinting heart and hand.

A young man who had been imprisoned for two years could neither read nor write and was completely unversed in religion when he arrived. He now wrote an admirable hand and reading was his great pleasure. He was soon to leave the prison, and he left it a more knowledgeable and better man than when he entered it. His physiognomy suggested a brutal character, but he now had a very good expression, and his voice and vocabulary revealed innate refinement. Another prisoner had painted his cell in an artistic manner and grown an arbor in the yard in which he was permitted to take the air once a day.

All the prisoners are allowed this daily recreation in yards that radiate from the center of the prison like the spokes of a wheel and are separated from each other by a high wall. As he walks there, the prisoner sees only heaven and earth. The sight of Friend Scattergood was obviously a happy one for all the prisoners. They clearly regarded the Friend as their friend, and his kindly and sensible appearance put them in good spirits. A young woman, who was soon to leave the prison, said she would do so unwillingly since she would no longer be able to see Mr. Scattergood.

In the female prisoners' cells (there were one or two Negro women among them) I saw fresh flowers in vases. These had been given to them by the female guard. They all praised her. I left this prison much more edified than I have many times left church.[20]

The reference to church recurs in many accounts of visits to the institution. Nevertheless, Cherry Hill did not lack scandal. As early as 1843, the place was ripe for grave attacks on the personnel, who were accused of immorality, embezzlement, and brutal chastisement of recalcitrant inmates. For example, one prisoner had been tied to the outside wall of his cell and doused with pails of cold water, partly freezing his body. Later, he was discharged as hopelessly deranged. In another case, an iron bar was driven into a man's mouth and caused his death. It was also proved that prisoners were frequently taken out of their cells to wait on the prison personnel.[21]

However, despite the scandals which at times threatened the reputation of Cherry Hill, there was something about the system that appealed to those who, for religious or humanitarian reasons, looked on prisoners as fellow creatures. Thomas Mott Osborne, an American pioneer in the practical treatment of prisoners, stated that the Pennsylvania system revealed "a touching faith in human nature, although precious little knowledge of it." And, Alexander Paterson, a member of the English prison commission, well known for his writings on the subject, said that the Pennsylvania system resembled "a monastery inhabited by men who do not choose to be monks."[22] The criticism of Cherry Hill may be explained by the fact that many mentally ill individuals were unfortunately sentenced to the prison, and that they were the ones who could not tolerate isolation, reacting with outbursts of desperation and attacking personnel. But, it became clear from experience gained with cell prisons that even normal individuals find it difficult to stand solitude.

Pentonville and Other Imitations

Meanwhile, European countries had begun to take a serious interest in the prison reforms that were being tested in America. In France, François de la Larochefoucauld-Liancourt had written about the Walnut Street jail as early as 1796. In 1827 and in 1830, his jurist countryman, Charles Lucas, published a work in two volumes, the second of which, *Du Système Pénitentiaire en*

Europe et aux États-Unis, contained a detailed account of the Auburn and Pennsylvania systems as he knew them through American reports and with the correspondence of experts, including the Philadelphia Society for Alleviating the Misery of Prisoners. France was the first country to send official representatives to the United States to study the situation, namely, Gustave August de Beaumont and Alexis de Tocqueville, who in 1833 published the results of the investigation of the new American prisons they had begun three years earlier. Their findings can be summarized: In theory, they considered the Pennsylvania system to be the better of the two and its management to be the simpler. But, they were appalled by the building costs with this system and pointed out that, since it had only been in operation for a relatively short period, it was still too early to make a reliable evaluation of the effects of solitude on the mental and physical health of the prisoners. In the case of the Auburn system, there were several years of experience. They considered this system had undoubtedly eliminated many of the drawbacks attributed to the old types of prisons. Demoralization could be prevented in this system, and criminals who were tempted to establish relationships with other inmates could be discouraged from persisting in this respect. Furthermore, the cost of maintaining the prisoners had ceased to be a burden on the state. While they were unwilling to express any difinitive opinion, they favored the Pennsylvania system from the moral point of view. Oddly enough, though, they concluded that the Auburn system offered considerable advantages and that the benefit of experience weighed the scales in its favor. At the same time, de Tocqueville did not hesitate to give his support to the Pennsylvania system in his report to the Chamber of Deputies.[23]

Following an inspection trip to the United States in 1832-34, William Crawford, English Commissioner of Prisons, expressed himself in favor of the Pennsylvania system in principle but, fearing the high costs, he recommended the silent system as evolved in the Wethersfield institution.[24]

In 1834, Dr. Nicolaus Heinrich Julius from Germany visited the United States for a similar comparative study. Before his departure he opposed the Pennsylvania system, but after his return two years later he changed his mind.[25] In 1837, the French jurist, Frédéric Demetz, later superintendent of the famous Mettray training school, and the city architect, Guillaume Blouet (who have already been extensively quoted) had studied the rival systems in greater depth than anyone else. They expressed a strong preference for Cherry Hill. The same was true of a number of others, notably Edouard Ducpetiaux, head of the Belgian penal administration and a prolific author.[26]

Switzerland, too, had been caught up in the wave of prison experiments. In 1825 Geneva acquired a prison known as a *pénitencier*, which Ducpetiaux described:[27]

> The plan was semi-panoptic or radial. Two wings radiated from a central administration structure, each consisting of three floors and separated from one another by a wall to prevent communication between the prisoners by way of windows. The ground floors contained dining-halls and workrooms, the upper floors a total of 54 night cells. The warden of the prison had his private apartment and his office in the central structure, from which he could observe practically everything that went on in the institution and even see the exercise yards. The treatment represented a modified version of the Auburn system. Conversation was not permited at work but was tolerated during recreation periods.

A more stringent regime was introduced in 1833, and a year later the isolation was further intensified. The same process was repeated in the prison in Lausanne. These Swiss experiences were to be of great significance to prison reform in Europe.

A report published in 1847 by Sir Joshua Jebb, head of the English prison administration, caused a sensation.[28] He had been responsible for the planning and contruction of the Pentonville prison and had several years of experience to substantiate his views. Haviland had sent model drawings at the request of the British Government. They were based primarily on the version of Cherry Hill built by Haviland in Trenton, New Jersey. They were used by Jebb with minor modifications. The Pentonville prison was built as a model for solitary cell treatment, completed in 1842. It was intended for convicts between the ages of 18 and 35, selected from the mass of criminals sentenced to transportation. The duration of the cell sentence was fixed at 18 months. Jebb quotes the prison inspectors at Pentonville, who wrote in a report: "We are of opinion that the adoption of Separate Confinement, as established at Pentonville Prison, promises to effect a most salutary change in the treatment of criminals, and that it is well calculated to deter, correct, and reclaim the offender."

Jebb also quoted statements concerning the good behavior of the Pentonville prisoners after this treatment when they had either been discharged or transported to Australia. While civilian passengers on the ships indulged in drunken and riotous living, the Pentonville prisoners were models of propriety. Although the moral results were good, Jebb considered that the health situation was no less satisfactory. The number of deaths was no higher than in the general population, perhaps even lower, and the figures were very low compared with those reported by Eastern Penitentiary and similar cell prisons. This was probably due to the great emphasis on good ventilation, lighting and heating in the Pentonville prison and that the prisoners were given more opportunity to be out in fresh air.[29]

Tuberculosis was the principal cause of death in the prisons. To counter this, Jebb recommended a specific amount of work to improve the inmates' health and also a system of compensation that would stimulate their interest in their labor. But, these ideas encountered strong opposition. In 1838, two Swiss doctors, M. Coindet and L.A. Gosse, attacked the cell system primarily from the point of view of mental hygiene. They claimed that: 1) total isolation has a more harmful effect on mind and body than isolation at night only combined with silence while at work together with others; 2) the number of deaths and of mental disturbances increased in direct relation to the shift of the Swiss institutions in Geneva from the Auburn to the Pennsylvania system; 3) the same was true of the prison in Lausanne; 4) and the feeding method in single cell prisons was bad for the criminals' health.[30] Gosse also proposed that solitary prisoners be provided with a "pedal machine" which would give them exercise in their cells. Indeed, it has been claimed that the treadmill and other devices, with which prisoners were often kept at totally futile work, were worthwhile to maintain good psysical condition, a healthy balance to the sedentary life in a cell.

The strife between these two schools of thought continued many years. According to a report by an 1837 investigating committee in Philadelphia, a comparison between the records in the North American correctional institutions revealed that there were no more, rather fewer, cases of mental illness in the Philadelphia prison than in any other. It further appeared that no matter how greatly one might fear for the prisoners' sanity under the pressure of absolute and continuous solitude without labor, without books, without instruction, without daily association with prison employees and visitors, it was a fact that the inmates, who all were given the comfort and recreation that could to some extent relieve their situation as prisoners, were in no danger of losing their minds due to isolation.

In another report, submitted by the same committee in 1838, it was claimed that not a single case of mental disorder had occurred which could be attributed to the separate system in Philadelphia, although every year cases of madness originating in an earlier "wicked way of life" were observed, but were cured with the help of the system and medical science. The report further cited the case of a prisoner who had been isolated for seven years in succession and had left the prison some time previously in perfect physical and mental health. The man was completely reformed and in good health at the time of the report. At the end of his sentence, he was said to have expressed feelings of the warmest gratitude for the attention he had gotten, adding that he would not forget this kindness.[31]

Europe was ripe for the separate system with labor. "It is one of those strange tricks of history and cultural diffusion that the radial plan, originally developed in English and Continental prisons, was not widely recognised or accepted for large-scale prisons until it had first been transplanted to America by Haviland," writes Norman B. Johnston.[32] However, an unadulterated Pennsylvania system was nowhere adopted; modified versions were used everywhere. Reforms were introduced, accompanied by harsh intellectual and political battles. The new prisons were expensive, and many people with humane attitudes to the treatment of prisoners hesitated, knowing the tremendous costs entailed in the construction of new cell prisons. When one reads what was written in the nineteenth century about penological methods, one is reminded of a witches' dance performed around a mass of grey creatures, the prisoners, by writers, journalists, scientists, jurists, correctional officials and, of course, politicians, as well as representatives of royal houses, including first the Swedish Crown Prince, later King Oscar I.[33]

Reaction

Larouchefoucauld-Liancourt, whose unwarranted praise of Philadelphia's Walnut Street jail in 1796 kindled European interest in the solitary cell, turned against the separate system in his later years. But advocates of the reform were so strong that opposition was largely stifled. Beginning in the middle of the nineteenth century, cell prisons were erected in much of Europe. The press began to pour out annual reports and accounts of how much better things were. Prisoners were quiet and submissive; they paid heed to the prison chaplains; their state of health was no cause for worry, despite their sedentary life.

It was not until the beginning of the twentieth century that there was a strong reaction against the cell prison. John Galsworthy flayed it in his articles and plays.[34] The critics were always influenced by developments in the United States, which took a diametrically opposite course to those in Europe and which gave the victory to Auburn and finally even caught up with Cherry Hill, in which the congregate system was introduced in 1913.[35] However, the defense of the cell was considerably stronger in Europe. After all, here were all these cell prisons which were not suited for any other form of treatment than separate confinement. Once again, English critics played an important role. Sidney and Beatrice Webb wrote a highly critical and widely read book on the English penal system with a foreword by George Bernard Shaw.[36] A book by Stephen Hobhouse & A. Fenner Brockway, in which every aspect of the separate system was condemned outright, made a strong impression in professional circles.[37] Later, a series of articles by Alexander Paterson, Commissioner of British prisons, criticized separate confinement, which was of great importance to later developments. Some of his views, as quoted by S.K. Ruck, were:

> The longest period of solitary confinement in English prisons lasts normally a fortnight. After that spell of comparative silence, a prisoner works alongside his fellows throughout the day and can talk with them, within such limits as are observed in an industrial workshop.
>
> But in a number of European countries, notably Belgium and Holland, prisoners are, for such periods as ten to five years, retained in solitary confinement, speaking only with the officers of the prison. . . .
>
> In Belgium a murderer will spend the first ten years of his sentence in his cell, the Italian will spend seven and the Dutchman five. For but an hour each day he leaves his cell to walk alone round his little walled triangle. Even at chapel, or at school, he must be shut in a box, secure from the sight or conversation of another prisoner.
>
> Yet the figures of Belgium and Holland are clear in their proof that barely as many of these men pass from prison to asylum in a year as is the case in our country. Where a man appears to be suffering mentally

from solitude, he is forthwith put into a prison where association is allowed, but such precautions are not of frequent necessity. . . .

Remains to review the advantages offered by a system of cellular confinement. . .

It is safer, easier and cheaper. . . . There is no fear of a dozen desperados conspiring together to attack an officer and make good their escape. It is easier because the Governor can deal with each man as a separate entity. He need not trouble to study the mass psychology of all his charges, to acquire their corporate goodwill in the observance of the rules. And it is cheaper because a smaller proportion of staff is required when men are safely locked, each in a cell, all the day long.

The second argument in favour of the system is its allowance of time for purposes of reflection. "Know thyself" quotes the kindly Governor and locks up the lad for a few years. But thinking is an occupation requiring practice before it can achieve any useful result. The majority of criminals even under the tuition of Governor and Chaplain at their visits, are not accustomed to periods of continuous thought. Suddenly exposed to such an experience, so far from achieving a state of deep and genuine repentance, they are prone to use the time for weaving explanation and defence of all they have done, emerging with a false perspective of their own merit and importance. It is indeed of primary importance that a man should realize the wrong he has done. There is no other starting-point towards reform. But it is at least open to doubt whether the untutored mind of the highwayman will reach this necessary conclusion after many hours of brooding. He is not naturally introspective. He finds great difficulty in knowing his true self as a single entity abstracted from his surroundings. He is more likely to evolve out of his cogitation a semi-heroic type of individual, praiseworthy but oppressed, in whom he will see himself. Hardened by the growth of his phantasy, he will prove in the end far less accessible to the approach of those who would reform him.

The third contention of those who favour the solitary system is most difficult to counter. They claim that the best way to reform a man who has fallen into evil habits is to place him for some years in such a position that he is screened from all contact with, or suggestion of, evil. They protect him, therefore, from any association with other wicked men, immuring him in a cell where only good influences can play upon him. The Chaplain delivers his message, the teacher draws his mind to follow healthier pursuits, the Governor visits him with good advice. At distant intervals his friends may come and implore him to reconsider his line of life. No evil companion whispers in the other ear, his literature is disinfected, the suggestion of evil is supposedly banished from access. There should result a condition of moral asepsis, in which the man, having absorbed much good and no evil, will lay the foundations of a new and better life.

The advocates of solitude contrast this process with the obvious dangers to which a man is exposed, if, when he has already shown himself to be of weak character, he is thrown daily into free association with men of equal or greater depravity. The conversation of such men may well become a cess-pool of obscenity, their mutual influence a mutual thrusting into lower depths. Those who have watched month by month the hardening mouth, the growing shiftiness of the eye, the crust of suspicion forming, and the sensuality deepening, as men lingered together in penal colonies, appreciate the strength of this contention.

What then is to be said for the other method of association? Can the wicked indeed become good among the wicked; can the sinner turn saint among the sinners?

It is of interest to examine two of the points advanced in both Belgium and Holland in favour of solitude, for on inspection they may prove to be arguments in favour of association. First, it is stated that men who have spent ten years in their cell and then proceed to life in association generally improve steadily during the ten years, but deteriorate markedly on joining the other men. But what else does this signify than that cellular confinement has failed to effect its object? For the business of prison is to train men for freedom, and if on rejoining others men deteriorate, then their improvement has been illusory. Virtue in seclusion is no achievement. Secondly, it is asserted that the majority of men after ten years of solitude reject the offer of association. This, too, can be cited as an argument against cellular confinement. It is not natural for man, good or evil, to wish to live alone, and a system which results in this attitude is asocial in its effect, and is not the right training for a man who shall some time rejoin his fellow citizens outside the walls.

The turning of these two arguments reminds us that for the right answer to our problem we must return once more to the real purpose of a prison, which is to protect society by making the law-breaker fit once again for social freedom. The man must some day return to social life. He must live at peace with his fellows, contributing to the common good and not preying upon his neighbour. It is inconceivable that he should learn the lessons of proper social conduct without practice. He cannot learn to be social in a non-social condition any more than a seaman can be fully trained on land, or an aeronaut upon the sea. It is necessary, therefore, that there should be social life in a prison, that a man should learn to live in a community. He must face temptation inside, hold his own against the tide, practise his virtue and acquit himself as a man of principle before he can be remitted to that freer society whose rules he has flagrantly broken.

But while we recognize that the ideal training for the law-breaker must be in a community rather than a cell, we are not blind to the grave dangers arising from the wanton association of lawless men. A sloppy and unthinking sentiment that revolts from solitary confinement may rush us into forms of association far more injurious to those concerned than any evils of solitude. We are not justified in herding some scores of weak and vicious characters together unless we can take such steps as will ensure that the tone of the whole will be higher than the tone of the individual, so that each man may be raised rather than debased by his membership of the community. This is a stern proviso and involves certain precautions not to be lightly undertaken.

First there must be classification according both to age and degree of criminality. It is obviously loading the dice against the lad to throw him among men, and cramping the chance of the first offender to force him to eat and talk and spend his leisure with the accustomed prisoner.

Secondly, it is idle for us to think that any conversation is better than none. It is within common experience that men whose daily life is devoid of variety or incident will be reduced to two topics only of conversation—their criminal exploits and the indecencies of life. If we are to provide opportunity we must also provide topics of conversation. Hence lectures, classes and debates and a measure of sport.

Thirdly, and most difficult of all, is the necessity to preserve a certain standard in the general sense of prison community. The tone of the whole must be higher than that of the individual member. How easy to write; how hard to secure!

Be it remembered, however, that every virtue as well as every vice is scattered among a prison community. The virtue must be mobilized to fight against the vices. For the good will always beat the bad. . . .[38]

A method of treatment that had been believed to be good, namely, the individual prison in which the convict would only meet good men, the warden, the doctor, the chaplain, other employees and carefully selected prison visitors, all of whom would lead his thoughts into new paths through wise conversations, an exchange of ideas that would completely transform his character, was completely discredited. What was worse was that the mystery surrounding the silent cell prison fortresses, where the public was not admitted (as in the old prisons), bred an unhealthy curiosity. Stories about prisons became fashionable. Not all of them had the quality of Oscar Wilde's *The Ballad of Reading Gaol*, in which he describes how the thoughts of the entire prison are concentrated on the lonely man in the death cell:

> The Governor was strong upon
> The Regulations Act
> The Doctor said that Death was but
> A scientific Fact
>
> And twice a day the Chaplain called
> And left a little Tract.[39]

No sooner had the cell prison system been established in Europe than developments were diverted into new directions.

[10] NORFOLK ISLAND AND
THE TASK SENTENCE

Maconochie

The year 1840 was a red-letter year in the annals of penology. In Sweden, that small and impoverished country in Northern Europe, 1840 saw the publication of a book that pleaded a convincing case for the cell system. The author was the Crown Prince, later King Oscar I, and it led to a decision by the Swedish Parliament to introduce cell prisons for all forms of penal treatment. In addition, the Parliament appropriated funds to construct such prisons, a financial sacrifice by a poor country for the good of convicts that is probably unmatched by any other country. Oscar's interest in the treatment of criminals also led to other European monarchs following suit, and it is fair to say that his little book resulted in many cell prisons being built over much of Europe.

But 1840 was also the year in which one of the most remarkable experiments in the history of penology was initiated on the other side of the globe. Alexander Maconochie was behind this and the place was Norfolk Island, a small island about 930 miles northeast of Sydney, Australia. It was discovered in 1774 by Captain Cook and had been used as a prison colony since the end of the eighteenth century. A village called Kingston had been built on the south side of the island and there prison installations were constructed. Conditions for the prisoners were among the most horrendous in that cruel century. As usual, the reaction to brutal treatment was brutality on the part of the prisoners. Personnel and civilians were attacked at every opportunity. This small island, where violence ruled, was now to become the scene of a remarkable experiment in the treatment of prisoners.[1]

Alexander Maconochie was born in Edinburgh in 1787, the son of a Scottish civil servant. He first had a career in the Royal Navy, receiving several decorations. While in the Navy, Maconochie made a number of interesting experiments with discipline. He tried to avoid the cruel methods usually practiced on warships (flogging and keelhauling); instead he tried to maintain discipline by reasoning with the men. However, he was *too* successful in his methods to please the Admirality, and his newfangled ideas were regarded as dangerous. He attracted special attention for his action in Quebec harbor when he was serving with the British North American naval detachment. To prevent the sailors from deserting, which they were especially inclined to do in North America, commanders were accustomed to forbid them to leave the ship. But, Maconochie informed the crew that shore leave would be permitted under joint responsibility. If there were any desertions, shore leaves would be stopped subsequently. The plan worked—Maconochie's first experiment with "collective responsibility."[2]

When Maconochie left the Navy in 1830, he was made Secretary of the London Geographical Society and, two years later, he became the first professor of geography at London University College. In 1836, he was made a Knight of the Royal Hanoverian Guelphic Order, whose motto was *Nec Aspera Terrent* (Difficulties Cannot Dismay). In his later years, he showed himself to be worthy of this proud motto.[3] In 1837 he accompanied the newly appointed Vice-Governor to Van Diemen's Land (now Tasmania). A large number of transportees had just arrived on the island from England, and it was there that Maconochie's interest in the treatment of prisoners was awakened.

Being an intellectual, Maconochie was obviously familiar with the penological discussions in his homeland, and it can be assumed that he had read Howard's books. However, he had never been interested in the problems of handling convicts until he was faced with them on Van Diemen's Land. He soon pounced on these problems and he formulated his views on how prisoners should be treated in a famous pamphlet, consisting of various representations to the British Parliament, which was printed in Hobart Town in 1838 and in London the following year.[4] The purpose of punishment, he wrote, is to reform the individual if possible, or at least to teach him self-discipline. Before a prisoner is freed, he should prove that he is worthy once more to enjoy the privileges of freedom. Fortunately, the pamphlet did not reveal the full scope of the daring plans being hatched by Maconochie. Also, fortunately, the British Government was somewhat stunned at this point by all the proposals for prison reform that had poured in since Howard's day. Otherwise, Maconochie would scarcely have been in a position to test his theories. However, he was soon able to put his ideas into practice: in 1840, he was granted his request to be superintendent of Norfolk Island prison.

The Concept

Let us first examine the theories. They are best expressed in the series of representations Maconochie made to the Government, condensed in a twenty-page paper entitled *Secondary Punishment, the Mark System*, published in 1848. Two axioms are first presented. Brutality and cruelty not only humiliate those who suffer them, but also a society that deliberately practices or tolerates them. The treatment of the criminal must be aimed at restoring him to society after he has undergone his punishment, delivered from the tendencies that had led him into crime and strengthened in his ability to resist new temptations. In Maconochie's words:

> In administering punishment, we should in every case seek *primarily* to reform the individual criminal, without directly aiming at making an example of him. For this purpose we ought, while endeavouring to gain and direct him, carefully to avoid doing anything calculated to enfeeble him either in body or mind; and on the contrary, we should endeavour by every means, and in every way possible, to invigorate and strengthen him. And lastly, if we act thus judiciously only, and seek to improve him morally and physically (as alone we can hope to do successfully) by properly stimulated exertion and self-restraint, we shall find that the sight of this process, and the known fact that all convicted must pass through it before being again released, will prove more *deterring* than anything we now inflict for the special purpose of deterring. In other words, by making reform our *first* object, and seeking it through properly stimulated industry and self-command (together, of course, with religious and moral instruction, the imparting of which is common to all systems), we shall find that we both *reform* and *deter*; whereas at present, we, for the most part, rather corrupt and allure.[5]

Society's right to punish is self-evident, according to Maconochie, but the convict *shall be punished for the past and trained for the future*. Punishments might be severe, but they should always be planned to strengthen character.

The time required by the prisoner to acquire proper self-discipline cannot be estimated at the time the sentence is imposed. Therefore, in Maconochie's opinion, the sentence should be of indeterminate duration. His chief requirement was that a sentence should consist of a specific "task" to be carried out and not a fixed period of time to be served. The criminal should be sentenced to imprisonment until he had performed a certain amount of work.

To determine the work to be required, Maconochie proposed that the convict be ordered to earn a fixed number of credits, or marks of commendation, through work and generally good behavior, e.g., three thousand or five thousand "marks." His sentence would not be terminated until the marks in question had been earned.

At the beginning of the sentence, the criminal would be kept for a short period in strict confinement, during which he would be exposed to moral and religious influences. This preliminary and unequivocally penal stage would be followed by a program designed to teach the convict good work habits and self-control. He would be given nothing free of charge. He would pay for his lodging, food and clothes with his earnings from labor and by strict observance of prison regulations. These would be translated into marks. By carrying out tasks assigned to him, he would earn a certain number of marks daily, e.g., ten marks. But extra marks could be accumulated through frugal living, extra work, exemplary behavior, etc. Breaches of discipline would be punished only by fines expressed in marks.

When a prisoner had earned a specific number of marks, he would be allowed to work with five or six other prisoners, who would accumulate marks as a team. The team would be responsible for all its members. Bad conduct on the part of one of them would result in a loss of marks for the group as a whole. Restrictions would be lessened with time, and by the end of his sentence, the prisoner's situation would resemble as closely as possible the one he would encounter after his discharge.

The entire system was concentrated on a single objective: the gradual training of the prisoner for his future freedom. The fundamental principle was: nothing for nothing, as everything must be earned. The prisoner should never be humiliated during his term of sentence. The character of a social being must be respected. All brutal and degrading chastisement was to be eliminated. The uniform should not be humiliating, nor should the prisoner be ordered to perform tasks that he himself might regard as degrading.

Of course, these precepts were not new. John Howard had written similarly; Montesquieu, Beccaria, and Bentham had thought along the same lines. But, Maconochie introduced them into practice, and his experimental material could scarcely have been less promising.

Experiments

In reality, Norfolk Island was used for the most hardened criminals, particularly those who had committed new crimes after their transportation to Australia, for which they had been transferred to Norfolk Island. These men were called "doubly convicted." Discipline was merciless, and the prisoners responded in kind. There had been revolts, and guards as well as prisoners had been killed. In the six years before Maconochie arrived in 1840, at least 13 prisoners had been sentenced to death for taking part in riots. The number of prisoners was as high as 1200, and more were added during Maconochie's time. He had received permission to try out his mark system on new arrivals who had only been condemned once, but not with the doubly convicted, whom he himself considered unsuitable for the new experiment. Maconochie discovered, however, that he could not distinguish between the two groups and that his new system must include all. John West, a contemporary clergyman and author of a history of Tasmania, described the first part of Maconochie's governorship:

> On his arrival, Maconochie issued an 'exposition' of his plan: he told the prisoners that punishment would be inflicted, to inspire the thoughtless with reflection and the guilty with repentance. Such would be its object, and such its limits. He exhorted them to a manly endurance and a diligent preparation to acquire the comforts of *honest* bread. He assured them, that while the escape of the incorrigible would be barred for ever, he would delight to hasten the freedom of the worthy. Thus those that earned 6,000 marks would discharge a seven years' sentence, or 7,000 would be required for ten years' servitude: and 8,000 was the composition proposed for a sentence for life. They were, however, to enjoy a portion of their earnings, which they paid in exchange for luxuries, or to reserve the whole to hasten their discharge. Thus it was possible to obtain a ticket-of-leave in one, two, or two and a half years, from a sentence of seven, ten years, or life. He deprecated those lengthened punishments, which deprive men of years of youth, and strengthen and ripen every evil propensity into fatal maturity.[6]

There were three stages in the system: the first stage of the sentence when the inmate was not allowed to use his marks as he wished, the second stage when he was given this privilege, and finally the group treatment period during which each member of a small group of prisoners shared the responsibility for the whole group.

Fortunately the postal service between the island and Australia was slow, for Maconochie's unorthodox methods caused a storm of indignation as soon as they became known on the mainland. Worse was still to come. Maconochie had arrived at Norfolk Island at the end of February 1840. May 24 was Queen Victoria's birthday, and Maconochie decided to honor the sovereign in great style the following day. There were fireworks, theatricals, and other festivities, at which Her Majesty's health was drunk in heavily diluted drams of rum. Maconochie wanted the prisoners to feel like loyal subjects. The prison employees were horrified; the prisoners were impressed. The rum, paid for by Maconochie, was mixed with water and lemon juice. It scarcely smelt of alcohol and it "went, as was intended, to the hearts, and not to the heads, of those who drank it." That Maconochie was courting disaster is obvious in view of a letter of warning he had received from his superiors only a few days earlier. The story caused a great rumpus in Australia, and Maconochie was criticized and ridiculed in the press. By September, it was decided that Sir George Gipps, Governor of New South Wales, might dismiss him if he saw fit. However, the Governor decided to let Maconochie stay on for the time being.[7]

Worried and offended by all the enmity shown him by his critics, who included practically everyone in Australia, Maconochie persisted in his experiment. On his arrival at Norfolk Island, he had found that the daily cost per prisoner was eight pence. He therefore charged each prisoner eight marks at one penny each as a debt to the government. These marks were to be earned according to certain moderate rules that permitted overtime labor. Extra work was reimbursed in marks which could be used to buy goods. Maconochie made extensive use of the shared responsibility principle. Each group consisted of six convicts, who had to earn a total of 12,000 marks.

To deal with the overcrowding of the barracks, Maconochie allowed the prisoners he trusted to build huts with small gardens outside the prison. There they were also expected to take responsibility for less reliable inmates. He built two churches, Protestant and Catholic. Hitherto, only occasional services had been held in dining-halls. He was in general a strong believer in the importance of religious influences. He permitted crosses and tombstones on the graves of prisoners, a "privilege" which until then had only belonged to free men on the island. He brought in musical instruments from Sydney and formed orchestras and choirs. He erected a new prison of his own design, according to the cell system, which was used for the first stage of the sentence. He built schools. He gave every prisoner a small garden plot. He allowed the prisoners to form their own police force under the command of two officials. He conducted interrogations for breaches of discipline like public trials, where the prisoners were allowed to participate. (He complained that he did not have the legal right to use prisoners as jurymen, as in ordinary courts.) He rescinded the rule prohibiting smoking, not to encourage the use of tobacco, but to legalize a habit that had proved impossible to prevent. Prisoners with positions of trust were permitted to wear civilian clothing. He encouraged all prisoners to come to him directly with complaints and problems. To make it easier for them to meet him, he walked and rode about the island, usually alone.

Among the prisoners, Maconochie's system had the success it so well deserved. The island became safe. The detachment of 160 soldiers stationed on it were never needed to intervene during Maconochie's tenure. Civilians could go anywhere without fear. (Maconochie's children moved freely among the prisoners.) But the general public on the mainland still raged against him. Finally, Governor Gipps decided to inspect Norfolk Island. He, too, was unfavorably disposed to Maconochie when he arrived in February, 1843. But he left in an entirely different frame of mind. Even though he was still critical of some aspects, he expressed profound respect for Maconochie's results in a detailed and objective report. The mark system, for example, won his full approval. Not only that: the prisoners discharged under Maconochie had behaved very well, and only a small number had relapsed into crime.[8]

Bitter Ending

Meanwhile, in England it had been decided that Maconochie would be recalled from his position on Norfolk Island. Gipps' favorable report did not reach the British Government until after his successor had been chosen. Undoubtedly, an important factor was the somewhat higher cost of Maconochie's system. In February, 1844, he handed the command over to his successor and left the island. The new man was a strict disciplinarian. The old ways were restored in almost every respect. Torture and flogging were revived for chastisement. By the beginning of 1846, the time was again ripe for a new prison riot.

Maconochie returned to England and for several years campaigned for penal reforms as a writer and a speaker. In 1849, he was appointed governor of a newly opened prison in Birmingham. However, the progressive forces behind this appointment, including Matthew Davenport Hill, known in English social and political history as "The Recorder of Birmingham," could not stand up to the reactionary elements in the city's administration, who soon gained the upper hand and got rid of Maconochie after only two years. Thus, he was dismissed in 1851.[9] Undaunted by defeat, he continued to write and lecture to influence attitudes to the treatment of prisoners. He spent all his own as well as his wife's money on the cause, and in 1860 he died, sick and penniless. John Vincent Barry concludes his excellent biography of Maconochie:

> Alexander Maconochie made his contribution to an extraordinarily difficult social problem, and society repaid him with derision, hostility, and neglect. The significance of his contribution and his great influence in lessening the sum of avoidable human misery cannot be exaggerated. The three universally recognized moral qualities of man are wisdom, compassion, and courage. Maconochie had these three in generous measure and he brought them fully to the service of mankind.[10]

In those days it was indeed courageous to hold such views as these:

> When a man breaks a leg, we have him into a hospital, and cure him as speedily as possible, without even thinking of modifying his treatment so as to make his case a warning to others. *We think of the individual, not of society.* But when a poor fellow-creature becomes morally dislocated, however imperious the circumstances to which he may have fallen a victim, we abandon all thought of his welfare, and seek only to make "an example" of him. *We think of society, not of the individual.* I am persuaded that the more closely and critically we examine this principle, and whether abstractly, and logically, or above all Christianly and politically, the more doubtful it will appear;—Yet it lies at the root of nearly all our Penal Institutions, and the reasoning on which they are founded.[11]

Thus wrote Maconochie in Hobart Town in 1838.

[11] THE IRISH PROGRESSIVE SYSTEM

Transportation

The system of transportation of prisoners was introduced in England as early as the beginning of the seventeenth century. The first indications can be found in a law of 1598, promulgated by Elizabeth I. At that time, England was plagued by unemployment, while the new colonies in America lacked manpower. Thieves and bandits were sentenced to death according to the harsh criminal law of the day, but those who were strong enough were simply shipped to the colonies without further ado. In 1619, James I dispatched 100 immoral females to the colony in Virginia to help to offset the shortage of women. But, until laws were passed in 1678 and 1682, transportation was not included in the penal system as a specific punishment. To begin with, there were no special restrictions established for these transportees of various categories, but since many seized the first opportunity to return to England, it was ruled in the middle of the eighteenth century that pardons would be granted only on condition that the convict remained in the colonies.

During the first few decades, the British Government paid five pounds sterling to a "contractor" for each prisoner he transported to North America, but from 1717 on, the ship's captain instead was given the right to the prisoner's labor for the duration of his sentence. This practice was known as "property in service." The captain could transfer this right to another individual after he reached North America. The authorities had no further interest in the prisoner, unless he violated the condition for pardon and returned to England. When a cargo of prisoners arrived in the colonies, their services were sold to the highest bidder, and in this way the captain passed his "property in service" to a new master.

Transportation to North America did not cease until the North American colonies won independence in 1776. The system was introduced in the Australasian colonies in 1788, when the first infamous cargo reached Botany Bay. But, unlike the system in North America, the convicts now remained prisoners of the state for the duration of their sentence.

Transportation has been judged quite differently. Some regard it as a purely cruel system, but others can prove that it gave thousands of convicts a new lease on life which would have been denied them in the mother country. The attitude of the British officials, of course, had two sides: in the first place, it was a way to get rid of hardened criminals; secondly, it provided the colonies with manpower.

Ticket of Leave

By 1790 the governors of the Australasian colonies had been given the right to remit the sentences of transported prisoners. At first this took the form of absolute pardon, but a system of conditional pardon, known as "ticket of leave," was soon introduced. The ticket of leave contained a statement signed by the governor to the effect that the freed convict was relieved of the obligation to work for the state and was entitled to look for work within a specific district. The system developed fairly freely up until 1811, at which time various rules for the selection of the prisoners were added, and, in 1821, it was decided that those sentenced to seven years at hard labor could be freed after four years, those with fourteen years after six years and those with life after eight years, always subject to good behavior. In 1842, the system had been made even more complex. For example, the convict would first spend a certain part of his sentence, at most 18 months, in the Millbank or Pentonville cell prisons. The next stage would be transportation— lifers to be sent to Norfolk Island and those with shorter sentences to Van Diemen's Land. The latter group, plus lifers who were transferred from Van Diemen's Land after a certain time, would form "probation gangs" working under supervision. Later, if his behavior was good, the convict would be given a "probation pass," which entitled him to limited freedom and to take private employment for pay. The next and final stage was the granting of a ticket of leave.

In 1853, the British Parliament passed new criminal legislation, the Penal Servitude Act, according to which convicts with sentences of up to 14 years were to be put in prisons in their own country, while the judge had the right to decide whether a convict sentenced to more than 14 years would be put in a domestic prison or, after a certain period in an English prison, transported. Those with sentences of seven to ten years could be granted a ticket of leave after four to six years. With a sentence of 10 to 15 years, a ticket of leave could be given after six to eight years. Meantime, the Australian opposition to transportation had increased in intensity, and the practice was finally stopped by law in 1857.

The Act of 1853 had met little resistance in England, but an increase in the crime rate during the next few years was cause for public concern. With the decrease in transportation, a three-stage treatment was gradually evolved for the convicts who now had to be kept in the mother country. The first stage was solitary confinement for a maximum of 18 months. Next came a varying period of public works, during which many prisoners were quartered in laid up ships, or hulks, usually in frightful condition (this practice was already in use in Howard's day) or in special Public Works Prisons. The first of these was opened in Portland in 1848, and the second was the notorious one at Dartmoor, opened in 1850. Prisoners at this stage of their sentences were also sometimes shipped to the fortress prisons in Gibraltar and Bermuda. When the time had come, the prisoner was moved into the third stage, which gave him a ticket of leave, whereupon he was put under police supervision. However, the public complained that this was not sufficiently effective. The freed prisoners, on the other hand, complained that police supervision made it difficult for them to find and keep employment. [1]

Crofton

In 1853, the Englishman Sir Walter Frederick Crofton (1815-1897) was commissioned with three others to investigate conditions in Irish prisons. The following year, Crofton became the director of the Irish prison administration and introduced a system of treatment which not only came to bear his name but also to be known as the "Irish Progressive System."

Crofton was indisputably a good administrator and a man deeply interested in penal questions, as well as social problems in general. In addition, he was a skillful propagandist for his own ideas. He was obviously familiar with what had been written in the field of penology in England and was well informed about Maconochie's experiments on Norfolk Island. In Dublin he had at his disposal a new prison, Mountjoy, which had been designed by Sir Joshua Jebb, architect and later head of the English Prison Commission.

Mountjoy was a cell prison of the same type as Pentonville, Jebb's best known work, an institution which had served as a model for many European prisons.

The cell prison at Mountjoy became the base for the efficient bureaucracy that Crofton was able to organize and put into operation by 1855, one year after his appointment. The entire concept was based on Crofton's belief in the existence of a "criminal class" which had to be controlled and absorbed and gradually reinstated in society as a whole. For the latter to be possible, however, the criminal's physical and mental condition must be such that he is acceptable to law-abiding citizens. In other words, Crofton was thinking along essentially the same lines as Maconochie.

Crofton's views were presented almost more persuasively by his contemporary, Matthew Davenport Hill, famous English jurist and penologist, than by Crofton himself. According to Hill, the foundation on which Crofton's system was based comprised three elements: *application*, *incapacitation*, and *reformation*. Application means that suffering shall be imposed on the convict so that he and others will see "that the profits of crime are overbalanced by its losses." This, of course, is the deterrent principle. Incapacitation, a term coined by Jeremy Bentham, means that as long as the prisoner is incarcerated society need have no fear of him. Equally important is the third element, "reformation," the changing of the criminal during his incarceration so that he will not relapse when freed. According to Hill, no one has expressed this third point better than Maconochie in his declaration of principle published in Hobart Town (see Chapter 10).[2] In addition, Crofton was able to draw on the experiences of Montesino in Spain and Obermaier in Bavaria in developing his method.

Georg Michael von Obermaier became Governor of the prison in Kaiserslautern in Bavaria in 1830 and immediately began to experiment with a humanitarian approach to the treatment of criminals. In 1842, he was made Governor of the Munich prison, which at that time housed six to seven hundred convicts, many of them in chains, guarded by about 100 soldiers. Obermaier freed the prisoners from their chains, dismissed practically all the soldiers and replaced them by humane warders, thereby winning the confidence of the prisoners.[3] Manuel Montesino was a Spanish colonel who became Governor of the prison in Valencia with about 1500 inmates. In 1835, he organized all the prisoners in companies in military fashion, with prisoners as non-commissioned officers. He built a number of workshops and a school in the prison. Well-behaved inmates could be released after completion of two-thirds of their sentence. When this practice was abolished, Montesino resigned his post.[4]

Crofton himself described his new system in a paper which was published in 1862.[5] It should be borne in mind that his system was only applicable to convicts with sentences of at least three years (at that time the term convict meant that the prisoner had been sentenced either to transportation or to penal servitude for at least three years). Crofton's treatment comprised four stages. The first stage consisted of solitary confinement in the Mountjoy prison for eight to nine months, depending on the prisoner's behavior. During this period he was to experience "the full weight of the prison." For the first three months, the prisoner would be on reduced rations and would be allowed no labor whatsoever. After three months without work, even the laziest prisoner longs for something to do, according to Crofton. The time would then be ripe to put him on full rations and allow him to pick oakum or the like. The loss of strength resulting from the first period of the sentence would thus be restored and the prisoner would be fit for normal labor. During the first stage, the prisoner would be exposed to religious influences and would also be instructed in other useful skills, including the art of reading.

At this point the prisoner would be promoted to the second stage, meaning that he would be put to work with other prisoners in a special prison (the Spike Island prison to work on fortifications or the Philipstown prison for skilled workmen). Maconochie's mark system came into the picture in the second stage, since the duration depended entirely on the prisoner's accumulation of marks. In other words, he was the "arbiter of his own fate." This stage was divided into four classes, namely, the third, the second, the first and finally the A-class (an abbreviation for advanced class). Each month the prisoner could earn nine marks under three different headings, including three for diligence. Crofton emphasized that it was not skill but the *will* to achieve something that would decide the number of marks earned. The prisoner could move from the third to the second class with 18 points, i.e., in two months under the best circumstances. A further 54 marks were needed for transfer to the first class, which took at least six months. The move to the A-class required another 108 marks, i.e., at best twelve months. The A-class was likewise graded A-1,

A-2, and so on. If the prisoner was deficient in any respect, he was chastized by a loss of marks. The A-class prisoners were kept entirely separate from the other classes. While instruction was given to the others parallel with labor, A-class convicts studied in the evenings and worked in the daytime.

Lusk—the Intermediate Stage

Next came the third stage, Crofton's one original contribution, which he called the Intermediate Stage. The prisoner was now transferred to a completely open institution. The first of Crofton's open institutions was founded in 1856 in Lusk, a few kilometers from Dublin. It consisted of simple barracks with accommodations for a maximum of 100 inmates. The staff consisted of only six persons. Crofton's open prison caused a great outcry, and, he was not only severely reprimanded, but also threatened by the local citizenry, who feared acts of violence by the convicts.

Crofton laid down two rules of conduct for the guidance of his staff at Lusk: 1) they should convince the prisoner of their faith in him and give him credit for progress that he had achieved and that had been documented by marks earned; and 2) they should convince the public there is good reason to believe that a prisoner who is soon to return to freedom, where he will either succeed or fail, is capable of handling a job. The only rules in this colony were those considered essential for the maintenance of order in any other group of people living under comparable circumstances. Speakers from neighboring towns were invited to lecture on morally uplifting subjects.

In 1863, Crofton wrote that the prisoner's mind was in tune with the minds of those assigned to command him, and that an idea which at first may have appeared impracticable had during the course of the years proved to be a gratifying fact.

In addition to this progressive system, Crofton initiated a special section for the lazy and another one for the dangerous. He was able to report to an official investigating delegation that called on him in 1863 that not one flogging had had to be administered over a period of three and a half years, thanks to his systematic treatment.[6]

The modest installation at Lusk soon became a minor mecca for penologists from all parts of the world. We have, for example, a report on Lusk from a delegate to a congress for the social sciences in Dublin in 1861. He wrote that there were two corrugated iron sheds, each for 50 prisoners. A part of each shed was partitioned off for a guard to sleep in; the rest served both as dormitory and dayroom for the prisoners. In addition, there was a simple building for kitchen and administrative quarters. The whole installation was surrounded by an embankment about one meter high, and there were a few houses where the guards lived. All the characteristics usually associated with a prison were "conspicuous by their absence." Only two prisoners of the 1000 who passed through Lusk escaped.[7]

But, it was at Lusk and other installations of the same kind, notably Smithfield and Fort Camden, that the convict took the final step to freedom when he received his ticket of leave. In a pamphlet in 1863, Crofton established three principles for the treatment of long-term convicts: 1) Long-term prisoners are better and more effectively treated in small groups and by convincing them throughout their stay in prison that any improvement in their situation depends entirely on their own ability to utilize qualities that differ radically from those that landed them in prison. 2) By allowing prisoners to work in a more natural situation before their release than is possible in ordinary prisons, the public can be taught to accept them and thereby lessen the difficulties encountered by ex-convicts. 3) Devices that render professional crime more risky will certainly serve as crime deterrents. Consequently, police supervision, photographing of criminals, and systematic communication with wardens of prisons in the district to keep informed about cases of criminals with past convictions who may deserve longer sentences are all vitally important tools which should constantly be kept in mind.[8]

After-care

If recidivism is to be prevented, however, the convict must have a source of income when he is discharged. This problem was tackled by a teacher at Lusk, a man by the name of Organ, who took upon himself the task of finding work for the conditionally discharged. He went from one employer to the other time after time to persuade them to hire an ex-convict. In an account found among his papers after his death, he recounted:

Some five years ago I went to a gentleman who was a very large employer, and I saw him. I explained to him my mission. I was a long time in inducing him to give me a chance, but after many repeated visits I did succeed. He took one man. I visited that man once a fortnight, although he had removed from Dublin a distance of ten miles, and I visited the employer. That man succeeded in giving the employer satisfaction, and the employer afterwards applied for another, afterwards for another.[9]

Organ also worked closely with the police, whose duty it was under Crofton's system to keep paroled convicts under supervision.

There were too few women prisoners for it to have been practicable to develop as thorough a system as for the men. The first part of a woman's sentence was spent in a special section in the Mountjoy prison, where she also stayed for the second stage. This section of the prison was in charge of a *lady superintendent*, staffed by women only, with the exception of the doorkeeper. An intermediate stage institution was organized for the Catholic women in a house belonging to the Order of the Sisters of Mercy at Golden Bridge, a suburb of Dublin. There the sisters took care of about 50 women, who were kept busy at gardening and housework. There were only two sisters for the supervision of all these women.

After their stay at Golden Bridge, the women were placed as servants with private individuals. Cases of gross maltreatment of women were not unusual. One of them, for example, was badly beaten by her employers, and the Mother Superior of the convent, shocked, wanted to take her back. But, the woman preferred to stick it out until she had served her full time, despite the cruel treatment. Hill regarded this as proof of how "sweet" complete freedom seems to the individual, since he found conditions at Golden Bridge so much better than anything a servant girl in those days could ever hope for. For the Protestant women there was a similar institution, Heytesbury Street Refuge, also in Dublin.[10]

One of the foreign visitors to Mountjoy and Lusk was a Swedish penologist from Uppsala University, Professor Knut Olivecrona. He was very impressed by the treatment methods and described them in his book, *Om orsakerna till återfall till brott* (On the Causes of Recidivism among Criminals), published in 1872. Crofton's system was imitated almost all over the world, particularly in Europe. It was also compared favorably with the predominant system in England. However, the attacks on the system began after Crofton retired in 1862. The first was launched by a Presbyterian chaplain at Lusk. In a virulent pamphlet published in 1863,[11] this minister wrote that the Intermediate State prison was a total mistake, that the good results of Crofton's system resulted from completely different factors than the treatment as such—including the improved economic situation of Ireland, and that Crofton's system was in no way original, only an "English imitation with a French tail." With this comment the author was referring to the intense police supervision, which he found highly offensive. This particular point was, of course, the subject of much discussion in Ireland, as well as in England where it was far from effective. Many claimed in Ireland also that police supervision made it hard for the ex-convict to become adjusted to society. Crofton's situation was exceedingly difficult for a time after Sir Joshua Jebb, head of the English prison administration, who had been criticized for his failure to introduce the same principle as Crofton, publicly condemned the Irish version of the progressive system and the Lord Chief Justice expressed his disapproval of police supervision.[12] However, he was a skillful defender of his system, on paper as well as vocally, and the intense foreign interest in his work brought sympathizers into his fold.[13] From 1866 to 1868, he was one of the commissioners of the English prison administration, and he was among the leaders at the international penitentiary congress in London in 1872. He again served as head of Ireland's prison administration for the period 1877 to 1878, after which he retired. He died in 1897 at the age of eighty-two.[14] By that time, Crofton's system, admittedly in a modified form, had been accepted in England, including police supervision.[15]

By now, there was widespread suspicion of or direct opposition to both the solitary or separate confinement and the silent congregate systems. In 1865, Franz von Holtzendorff, a prominent German jurist, wrote that, "The history of criminal law teaches us that with the advance of civilization milder forms of chastisement are being sought, that progress in public decency is accompanied by similar progress in the concept of justice and in views of the means required to uphold it."[16] He saw Crofton's system as a step in the right direction. And Justinus Jacobus Leonard van der Brugghen, Dutch statesman and jurist, wrote: "We must rid ourselves of the burden of the narrow, pedantic frames of mind that can only envisage the salvation of their fellows in the shape and dimensions of corridors, cells, sewer pipes and padlocks."[17]

Crofton was to have a powerful follower in the United States.

[12] ELMIRA AND THE REFORMATORIES

Brockway in Cincinnati

National discussions on penal problems, as well as the international exchange of ideas, were very lively during the nineteenth century. A number of books and theses were published in the major world languages, and conferences, large and small, succeeded one another. However, the main discussion was between the protagonists of the separate system, on the one hand, and the silent system, on the other. It is true that a few penologists even before Maconochie and Crofton had tried to lead the debate into new directions, e.g., August Zeller, who in 1824, proposed that prisons be true reformatories and described in detail what he had in mind for them.[1] However, a change in penal philosophy did not come about until the first meeting of the American Prison Association in Cincinnati in 1870, when Crofton's skillfully organized Irish progressive system came into the limelight and Maconochie's Australian experiments stirred the imaginations. Also, a new and gifted man of action, Zebulon Reed Brockway, came on the scene.

Maconochie and Crofton had both become penologists and reformers by accident. However, Brockway had been employed in prisons when a young man, and he had worked his way up to the position of warden of a prison in Detroit. He was familiar both with what had been written on penal problems and primarily with the practical possibilities in the field. In a speech at the Cincinnati meeting, his comments were:

> The central aim of a true prison system is the protection of society against crime, not the punishment of the criminals . . . The causes of crime are primarily in the person, secondarily in the circumstances that surround him . . . The change sought in the character of criminals, called reformation, is of a practical nature, and has to do with daily life in ordinary social relations . . . (The reformatory) should contain dormitories. . . . , affording to each prisoner a separate room, such as a respectable citizen might occupy; a dining-hall, upon the plan of a well-regulated restaurant for work-people, where, within due

limits, any desired edible may be supplied; a library building and public hall, suitable for reading-rooms, religious service, scientific and other intellectual exercises of a public nature; suitable industrial apartments for the branches of mechanical business carried on, which, with limited agricultural employment, may constitute the productive industrial occupation of the residents; the whole to be organized substantially upon the cooperative plan. . . .

Sentences should not be determinate, but *indeterminate*. By this is meant that *all persons in a state, who are convicted of crimes or offences before a competent court, shall be deemed wards of the state, and shall be committed to the custody of a board of guardians, until in their judgment they may be returned to society with ordinary safety, and in accord with their own highest welfare.* . . .

The true basis of classification for prisoners is *character*, not conduct. . . .

In administering a prison sentence . . . the *intellectual* education of all classes must take more prominent place. . . .[2]

This was the starting shot for the reformatory movement in the United States. Brockway deserves the honor of having pulled the trigger. His ideas were revolutionary for the time—precursors of what is today called "Social Defence." The revolutionary has always appealed to Americans despite their innate conservatism. Visionaries should be given a chance. This willingness to try new things is probably the main reason why the United States has played such an outstanding role in the history of penology, an otherwise highly conservative field in which every innovation is looked on with suspicion.

Brockway at Elmira

The crime rate, as well as the population, was growing in the State of New York, and more prisons had to be built. A major prison project had been started near a town, called Elmira. The decision to begin construction went back to 1866, but it took time to finish the big, maximum-security institution. It was built according to the same system as Sing Sing, i.e., with sections in which the cells were lighted indirectly and separated from the windows by a corridor. In 1876, it was decided that Brockway should be the warden of Elmira and to dismiss the old building commission. Brockway was given a free hand, and the legislation was amended to fit the ideas he had chosen to interpret, which had fired so many others with enthusiasm.[3]

Brockway was a wise professional, however, and the first thing he did was to build a solid wall around the entire plant. The treatment was planned: a) The inmates were, in principle, to be first offenders, i.e., not previously sentenced to a State prison, and to be in the age group, 16 to 30 years. b) They were to have received an indeterminate sentence, i.e., one with a statutory maximum but no minimum, the latter to be fixed by the institution. c) The treatment should be aimed at changing the inmate's character. d) Final discharge would be preceded by a period of conditional release.

Actually, Brockway was never able to restrict the clientele to first offenders, and at least one-third of the inmates always consisted of recidivists. He held rigidly to the rule that the inmates must be kept occupied at strenuous labor and active leisure-time pursuits throughout their waking hours. ("The various activities of the day must not leave room for a moment's idleness for either hand or head.") Brockway based his system of institutional treatment on the following nine functions:

1. The assumption that prisoners under indeterminate sentences will want to be released as soon as possible and to that end will try to earn as many points as possible.
2. A grading system for the convicts with better conditions and more privileges as they advance from the lowest to the highest grade according to a fixed wage system.
3. A thorough training program for all inmates from the illiterate to the university graduate, using the most advanced methods.
4. The salutary influence of military drill, carried out according to the same logical methods as in a good military academy.
5. Vocational training for every inmate with the specific purpose of putting him in a position to earn an honest living, training that is planned realistically so as to enable him to become an industrious member of free society.
6. Methodical, suitable physical training for those who need it in a well-organized gymnasium with competent instructors and under the guidance of a physician.
7. Occupational therapy suited to those who suffer from anomalous or retarded development.

8. Better nutrition as a result of an increase in the elements in the diet that are good for the health, strengthen the nerves, and produce states of mind and characteristics conducive to industry and endurance.
9. Active moral and religious influence.[4]

Sanborn illustrated the treatment of the inmates with the following example:

Let us now follow the individual convict, between the ages fixed by law of 16 and 30, as he comes from the court which has sentenced him, brought by an officer of the reformatory, not by the ordinary deputy of the court, and enters the office of Mr. Brockway for a first examination. He there reveals to a very searching eye a good part of his history and present capabilities, is assigned to the lower first (numerically second) grade, instructed in the rules of the place, and set to that labor and schooled in that class which seems best fitted for him. By a system as rigid and laboriously recorded as that of a merchant's bookkeeping, he gets a mark for his performance in the shop, the school, and in moral conduct. If he falls below a certain standard he drops into the lowest grade; if he keeps up to the standard for six months he is admitted to the upper first grade, where, if he remains without censure for six months, he becomes a candidate for "parole" or conditional liberation. But before he can go out by this ticket-of-leave system a place must be found for him where he can work at his trade—now usually one which he has learned or practiced at Elmira. This being secured, he goes out, and, after a period of good behavior for six months, he may be, and generally is, discharged from the prison for good. Nor does he very often return thither; out of the 5,000 first paroled, less than 365 were sent back under reformatory authority—not one in ten. Even if he returns he may be again paroled, for more than half of those reported as returning to confinement were again set free. His chance of dying at the reformatory is very small, for only 130 in 8,000 have yet died there.[5]

This was the method of compiling prison statistics at that time. In reality, the figures were not so favorable as they seem in Sanborn's example. Only the prisoners who returned to the Elmira prison were recorded. However, many who received new sentences were sent to other institutions all over the country. Had they been included, the statistics would have been far less favorable, a point that was made years later by Sheldon and Eleanor Glueck in their study of the results of reformatory treatment.

At the same time, as supporters of Elmira did not fail to point out, the institution worked "with nature and not against it"; in other words, the exact reverse of the main complaint leveled at the separate and silent systems by their critics. The prisoner *could* do something to improve his lot.

Elmira became the cradle of the indeterminate sentence, vocational training, and the progressive system in America, according to Cannat.[6] While the institutional administration was legally entitled to release an inmate whenever it wished within the maximum established by law, it usually chose to keep this possibility for individual treatment within the framework of a carefully regulated system which could only be regarded as "fair" by the inmates—whatever else they may have felt about it.

What was really new about the Elmira system was that labor was not performed for the benefit of the government but for the good of the inmate to help him adjust socially. The other ideas were borrowed from Maconochie and Crofton. The institution eventually became very large, the original capacity of about 500 inmates, increasing to about 1700 by the beginning of the twentieth century. At that time, 34 major trades were represented in the institution. However, Brockway, like other American institutional directors, had a hard time defending the prisoners' right to work. The main complaint about prison labor was that "it took the bread from the mouths of honest workmen." A prisoner should not have a job as long as an honest workman is unemployed, according to many Americans then, as well as today. Consequently, Brockway could not afford to allow prison labor to become too blatantly productive. Also, he was obviously compelled to restrict the hours of labor and replace them with military drill. Elmira also appears to have been the first institution to have its own prison newspaper. First printed in 1883, the paper appeared in a weekly edition of 2,500 copies, of which 1,600 were distributed within the institution and the remainder in various parts of the United States and abroad.

For the prisoners, the most important innovation at Elmira was the introduction of an inmate wage system, according to which they were given compensation for their labor, but paid for everything they received, except for the first meal and the first clothing issued after admission. This system was applied to all kinds of labor, even if it was non-productive, e.g., schoolwork. After experimenting with special debit and credit marks, a direct transfer was made to dollars and cents.

A summary of Alexander Winter's description of the system follows:

The prisoner earns one dollar per month for perfect conduct. Deductions are made if he has been reported, fifteen cents for a minor misdeed, thirty cents for a more serious error. Schoolwork marked "perfect" is also rewarded by one dollar per month. If marks drop to seventy-five percent of "perfect," the prisoner earns nothing. If he is marked lower, he is charged as for a debt: one dollar for marks between seventy-five and fifty percent, two dollars for marks between fifty and twenty-five percent, and three dollars for lower than twenty-five percent. For a full eight-hour working day the wage is thirty-five cents in the second, forty-five cents in the lowest first and fifty-five cents in the top first grade. By work is meant all kinds of physical labor. For productive work the prisoner may earn an incentive bonus if he exceeds the prescribed daily quota. He is charged accordingly if he falls short of the prescribed quota. Military service is also rewarded financially more or less under the same system as work. However, if a man is promoted to the rank of corporal he is paid forty-eight cents daily in the lower first grade and fifty-eight cents in the upper first grade. A noncommissioned officer receives sixty cents in the third grade, sixty-three cents in the second grade and sixty-five cents in the first grade. A lieutenant earns sixty-eight cents in the second grade and seventy cents in the first grade, and a captain can earn as much as seventy-five cents a day!

From this wage the prisoner must pay:
1. For food and lodging per day: a) second grade—twenty-five cents; b) lower first grade—thirty-two cents; c) upper first grade—forty cents.
2. For clothes and other goods according to a detailed price list, e.g. ten cents for a hairbrush, five cents for a toothbrush, seventy-five cents for a pair of leather gloves.
3. For visits to the doctor: fifteen cents per visit. [7]

The old credit system was nevertheless maintained side by side with the new system, and one credit was roughly the equivalent of one dollar. When a man was discharged he was given the money that remained to his credit.

In 1894, after visiting Elmira, Major Arthur Griffiths, an English prison inspector, described the regime as one of extreme mildness, "where most of the comforts of a first-class boarding-school, ample diet, military music, the study of Plato, and instruction in interesting handicrafts are utilized in the process of amendment." [8]

The Critics

William Tallack, Secretary of the influential Howard Society in England, held a different view. He wrote in 1889 that the mild discipline resulted in prisoners returning voluntarily to Elmira if they ran into difficulties in the outside world. The claim that 80 per cent of the prisoners were reformed was not, in Tallack's opinion, an adequate defense for the system, since, the deterrent effect had been gravely undermined. He believed that, with this kind of prison system, people would no longer be afraid of committing crimes.[9] It should be noted that Tallack and the Howard Society were at that time fighting for the separate system and regarded all experiments with the congregate system, no matter of what kind, as an obstacle to progress. At the same time, the true picture was not that rosy, as other visitors confirmed. Barnes and Teeters commented:

> The system of discipline was repressive, varying from benevolent despotism to tyrannical cruelty. Little, if anything was done to give the convict any sense of collective responsibility for the conduct of the prison community, and no significant attempt was made to provide any social or political education.[10]

It was discipline that was most important. Vocational training, the modus vivendi of the institution, was never what it should be. Somewhat maliciously, it was said that the motto appears to have been: "Tire out the man with a strict daily routine to the point that he longs to go to bed early." Barnes and Teeters drew the conclusion: "In fact, the reformatory is just another kind of prison."[11]

Borstal

Meantime, many visitors from all over the United States and much of the world came to Elmira. Reformatories sprouted up all over the United States.[12] One of the European visitors was Sir Evelyn Ruggles-Brise, director of the English prison system, who came in 1897. Two years previously, Ruggles-Brise had experimented with the segregation of young offenders in a special section in the prison at Bedford. In 1902, after his trip to the United States, he converted a jail in Rochester, Kent, into a special youth prison, which later was named after the neighboring village of Borstal.[13] Ruggles-Brise had been particularly impressed by the vocational training and after-care programs of the reformatory system. However, he did not want such a wide age span and restricted the clientele at Borstal to boys between the ages of 16 and 21. The legal framework for the Borstal system was provided by the Prevention of Crime Act of 1908. The purpose of the system was to develop the character of the young man, as well as to strengthen his physique and provide him with vocational training under conditions that developed his capacity for responsibility and self-control. The daily routine at Borstal was varied, with time set aside for physical drill, work, individual study, hobby activities, and sports. Ruggles-Brise once said that "the Borstal system is based first and foremost on good discipline, exercised with firmness and kindness."[14]

Later, England established a classification center in a closed institution, Wormwood Scrubs, where preliminary investigations and diagnoses were made. In addition, the age limit for Borstals was raised to twenty-three. The decision where to send the young man was reached after the preliminary investigation. There are now a number of such institutions of various types, open as well as closed.

From England the Borstal system spread to the continent. The Danes adopted it in 1933 under the name of *ungdomsfengsel* (youth prison) at their Söbysögaard institution, and Sweden followed with her youth prison legislation in 1935 for offenders between the ages of 16 and 21 (the Skenäs institution). Since 1902, however, Sweden had a law for compulsory training for offenders between the ages of 15 and 18 (the Bona institution for boys and the Viebäck institution for girls).

In his autobiography, Brockway wrote that as a boy he was expelled from school for disobedience and defiance of his teacher. But, the teacher was entirely to blame, in his opinion. This incident drove Brockway into situations that could only end in open revolt by the strong-willed youth. He came under another teacher, who gained his confidence, after which his schoolwork was eminently satisfactory. Brockway endeavored to apply his own experiences to his reformatory program. Nevertheless, he was fully aware that all members of his clientele were not able to live up to the trust placed in them. Moreover, he suppressed attempted revolts in

[105]

the institution with a resolute hand. He was undoubtedly influenced by Lombroso's theories about the "born criminal," the individual who is immune to any kind of upbringing. In his later years, when to his sorrow, he saw how his lifework at Elmira was destroyed by successors who lacked his stature as a personality, he began to think along new lines. Probation was becoming so common that the prisons were being deprived of their most promising clientele. When this happens, according to Brockway in his autobiography, the prison will inevitably be less a correctional institution,—more a scientific training center for degenerate adults.[15]

[13] RAUHES HAUS AND THE
FAMILY SUBSTITUTES

Wehrli

It had long been recognized that criminal behavior in young people could often be traced to their lack of proper upbringing in the family environment. Thus, the idea was conceived of a *family substitute* for juveniles who, for one reason or another, had been deprived of the guidance and support of a mother and father. To the extent that private homes could not be found for these youngsters, institutions should be devised that would provide to the extent possible the upbringing and affection of a true family.

The first institution of this kind mentioned in the literature appears to be the Wehrli Institution on the Hofwyl estate in Argau, Switzerland. The owner of the estate, Philip Emanuel von Fellenberg, strongly influenced by Johann Heinrich Pestalozzi, had set up a home for delinquents on one of his estates. He opened it in 1810 and put it in the charge of a young school teacher, Johann Jakob Wehrli, who was only twenty years old when he took this assignment, unique for the time. Von Fellenberg described the first group of pupils, which eventually comprised 20 boys:

> The selection of students in this school for paupers had been so to say blindly entrusted to higher authorities. They included beggars taken by the police, scabby, scrofulous, starving, pitiable creatures whose features were marked by unspeakable misery, truculent vagrants who had run away from their previous guardians, filthy street urchins crawling with vermin, lazy and gluttonous, and also children from decent homes, well-behaved but deserted and orphaned. (Cited from Liepmann.)

Wehrli's only training for his new post consisted of a six-week course for rural school teachers and a certain amount of tutoring from his father, who also taught in a rural school. But Wehrli had imagination and passion for his new vocation. He spent his whole time with the boys. He ate with them, worked with them, and shared their sleeping quarters. During the first years, when he was still young, he even wore the same uniform.

The daily routine was approximately the same as for adult workers, except the work schedule was interspersed with study periods. The boys rose at five o'clock in the summer and at six o'clock in the winter. Bedmaking and cleaning were followed by prayers, a thirty-minute study period, breakfast, and finally work until half-past-eleven. Dinner at noon was followed by one hour of lessons, work until six in the evening, supper, games, a thirty-minute lesson, and bed between eight and nine o'clock. Wehrli's talent for teaching was so great that he soon attracted adult disciples. After only a year or so, two young teachers came to work as trainees and, from 1813, a school for country school-teachers was affiliated with the institution, eventually accommodating about 60 students.

According to Wehrli's educational system, both he and the teachers were not to be regarded as some sort of supervisors but as "older brothers." He included the boys in all decision-making and allowed them to take part in all discussions concerning disciplinary matters and the financial situation of the institution. Pestalozzi is said to have been very interested in Wehrli and astonished that he had been able to realize Pestalozzi's own ideas, even though he had never been under the man's personal influence. Wehrli left his school in 1833 to become the principal of a teachers college in Kreuzlingen, in the Canton of Thurgau. He died in 1855.[1]

Wichern

The physically small institution at Hofwyl was an inspiration in many parts of Europe and served as a model for a number of other homes, of which especial mention should be made of *Das Rauhe Haus* (the "rough" house) in Horn, then a suburb and now a section of Hamburg. The founder of this institution was Johann Hinrich Wichern (1808-1881),[2] a self-taught social educator, whom Professor Theodor Heuss, the first President of the Federal Republic of Germany, once called "the greatest son of the Evangelical Church in the nineteenth century."[3]

During Wichern's studies for the priesthood, which he never completed though he was eventually awarded an honorary doctorate in theology, he was passionately interested in the conditions of the poor and was active in the Hamburg Society for Visiting the Poor.[4] He himself knew what it was to live in poverty-stricken circumstances. Left fatherless at the age of 15, Wichern helped to support the family when he was still a schoolboy. In those days he slept only four hours daily. The family was often without food and with difficulty in paying the rent. However, his situation improved later due to the support of kind patrons, and Wichern was able to study in Berlin for a time. There he had the opportunity to attend Professor Nicolaus Heinrich Julius's famous lectures on penology. The Hamburg Society for Visiting the Poor had plans for a saving institution for children and young people who had fallen on evil ways, and one of its leaders, Syndikus (corresponding roughly to undersecretary of state) Johann Peter Sieveking was impressed with Wichern and found him to be a suitable superintendent of the new home.

Sieveking was the proprietor of a country estate called *Das Rauhe Haus*. The origin of the peculiar name is not clear. Wichern himself believed that it meant that the house had earlier been used as a refuge for vagabonds and other homeless individuals. On the other hand, it had once been called *Ruges Haus*, which was believed to have referred to a previous owner. Another theory is that the name derives from the German dialect *Platt-deutsch* and means "the house in the thicket," or even "the humble cottage." However, all these interpretations are merely speculation. At first the name was both a burden and boon for an institution which was in principle intended to exist solely on voluntary contributions and not to accept state subsidy. Wichern and the private individuals sponsoring the project felt this was essential if they were to have complete freedom of action.[5]

Wichern, then twenty-four, and his mother, sister, and a brother took over the dilapidated old house on November 1, 1833. Before that, on September 12, the Visiting Society had listened to a remarkable talk by Wichern and had reached the decision to found the new institution. He had spoken of the "shameful poverty" that was shameful because it deprived the victim of his dignity as a man. The children to be admitted would not get away from their poverty in the new institution, he said, but they would learn that poverty in itself is not bad as long as it is faced in the right spirit. Therefore, in addition to schooling and labor, every effort would be made to give the children a family life filled with happiness and to imbue them with love for the family as such. In those days this was precisely the right appeal to induce the rich to loosen their purse strings.

The first three boys were admitted on November 8. By the end of the year, there were 12, and by the following April, the number had risen to 14 between the ages of 5 and 18. Full capacity had now been reached. In his first annual report, Wichern wrote that "with the exception of one, all of them had been raised in the utmost misery and neglect." All of them were thieves. One of them, 13 years old, had committed 92 thefts. Seven of them had been committed to various forms of reformatory training, including a "penal school" which was set up in a poorhouse in Hamburg after having been housed in a prison. One of them had even succeeded in escaping from chains. Most of them had slept out-of-door for long periods at a time.[6] What happened to them now?

When a boy arrived he was greeted by Wichern: "My child, you have been forgiven for everything. Look around and see what kind of house you have entered. Here there are no walls, no moat around the building, no locks on the doors. We bind you with but one heavy chain, whether you like it or not. Wrench it off if you can! The name of that chain is love, and its yardstick is patience."[7]

The boy had to tell Wichern everything about his life up to the present, his crimes and difficulties, but he also had to promise never to tell anyone else anything about his past. Wichern wanted to avoid discussion between the boys about earlier criminal escapades. The newcomer was then accepted into the family community as if he belonged there. As a member of the family he was to be influenced by "the full force of Christian love," because Wichern believed that a deeply Christian family has all the odds on its side in the struggle with evil. He himself was very hot-tempered and was easily carried away, but he also found it easy to apologize humbly and ask for forgiveness. His character obviously made a remarkably deep impression on the youngsters. His mother was extremely hard-working, and his brother and sister did all they could to occupy and teach the boys. *Ora et labora*, pray and work, was Wichern's motto. The entire family of as many as 20 were constantly at work from early morning until late at night.

One of the main activities was building. Wichern, a gifted writer and speaker, appealed in all quarters for money to expand the institution. While cash and other gifts were donated in a constantly increasing stream, the financial situation was nevertheless too precarious to permit the hiring of outside help. First, they struggled through an epidemic of measles which hit all the children, isolation being impossible. Then a road from the house to the main thoroughfare had to be built. In April, 1834, Wichern employed two helpers *(Gehülfen)* and, through the joint efforts of the entire group, a new family dwelling was completed in the summer of 1834. The new house, which was called *Schweizerhaus* (after its architectural style), became the home for boys, while the old house was taken over by girls.

Reformers usually have a hard time with their contemporaries, and this was true of Wichern. From the beginning, he was attacked in speeches and in print for his ideas, because he was "too young"; because he had accepted the post as leader "to earn money" (his salary was 2400 marks yearly); "to make himself a name"; and so on. The attacks even emanated from clerical circles, this probably the most hurtful for Wichern. But the institution continued to progress under Wichern's wise administration; if he was a great educator, he was an even greater administrator. The nineteen-member administrative council of the foundation did not lead but was led by Wichern.[8]

Wichern married Amanda Böhme in 1833 and moved into a new house called *Mutterhaus* (Mother House), which was later renovated and re-christened *Grüne Tanne* (Green Spruce). From then on, his wife was called *Mutter*, although Wichern himself never agreed to be called *Vater* (Father). In 1836, they began construction of a workshop which came to be called *Goldener Boden* (Golden Ground); a chapel was completed three years later. Thereafter, several more houses were put up, including *Die Schwalbennester* (The Swallows' Nest) for girls, and by the time of Wichern's death at the age of 73, the institution comprised about 25 buildings.[9]

The Brothers

As the institution grew, so did the need for co-workers in the upbringing process, which was based on the principle of dividing the young clients into families of at most twelve members and one leader. For this reason, Wichern established in 1844 a special training school for his assistants, a *Brüderanstalt*, or what later would be called a school for deacons. Wichern wrote that his helpers should be "young men who are proficient in a trade or are otherwise able to make themselves useful in practical ways, but also primarily inclined through their love of God to devote themselves wholeheartedly to the care of our children." He commented that "since the institution offers no salary, they will receive with us a four-year intellectual and practical training as educators of the poor and the like."[10]

Wichern only took children who had either committed crimes or were in danger of becoming criminals because of their family situation or other factors. If practicable, a committee within the administrative council drew up a contract with the father or some close relative of the boy or girl, according to which guardianship was transferred to the institution for as long as the child remained in its care. This was no problem in view of the nature of the clientele. Legal guardians were only too pleased to be rid of the responsibility.[11]

In 1844 Wichern also founded a bookstore and his own periodical, *Fliegende Blätter aus dem Rauhen Hause*, through which information about the institution was disseminated all over Germany and abroad. However, greater responsibilities were soon entrusted to him.

The Home Mission and the Treatment of Prisoners

On September 21, 1848, the German Evangelical Churches gathered for a meeting in Wittenberg. The following day, Wichern held a 75 minute address in which he spoke about the church's duty to help solve the social problems of the day. This masterly speech, which was received with enthusiasm, led to the formation of a central committee for a home mission, of which Wichern later became the director. Urged to summarize the views presented in his lecture, Wichern wrote *Die Innere Mission der Deutschen Evangelischen Kirche, Eine Denkschrift an die Deutsche Nation* (the Home Mission of the German Evangelical Church, a Memorandum to the German Nation). Usually called "Wichern's Denkschrift," it became enormously influential. Wichern now began to travel extensively, sowing the seeds for the societies for home mission and for city mission that came to be.[12]

King Friedrich Wilhelm IV of Prussia had observed Wichern's work with interest. He summoned Wichern and consulted him on various matters. This met with disapproval in many quarters, since Wichern was a "foreigner" from the Prussian point of view. However, the King ignored the critics and commissioned Wichern to initiate a reform of the Prussian prisons. As a result of persistent efforts on the part of Julius and others, it had been decided to adopt the cell prison system, and the great Moabit prison in Berlin was built according to the Pennsylvania and English patterns. Wichern managed to bring about a formal agreement, under which his "brothers" would be employed at Moabit to work for the moral rehabilitation of the prisoners. In 1858, he founded the Evangelical "Johannes Foundation" in Berlin-Spandau for this purpose. According to Wichern's plan, prison personnel, who at the time were usually recruited from army regiments, would be given special training for their task, and a new spirit would thus be infused in the institutional system. To this end, he needed his "brothers" as a sort of avant-garde.

This time, success was denied him. After a period of insanity, the King died and was succeeded by his brother, who became Kaiser Wilhelm I, a man totally disinterested in prison reform. The year, 1861, was full of trouble for Wichern. At that time he had about 60 "brothers" working in Berlin. One of them was attacked by a violent prisoner and, in his desperate situation, ordered a soldier who rushed to his aid to shoot his assailant. Although Wichern repudiated his helper, who was nevertheless acquitted by the court, this did not prevent a storm of criticism in the press. All the enemies of Wichern's Christian reform work exploited the situation. The "Brothers" were the target of every conceivable accusation, primarily their "salvation madness" in their dealings with prisoners. The strongly religious element in their work was criticized by many, including the well-known professor of criminal law, Karl Joseph Anton Mittermaier in Heidelberg, one of the great names in the international history of criminology. The strongest opposition, however, came from Franz von Holtzendorff of Berlin, also a professor of criminal law. Like Mittermaier, Holtzendorff was politically liberal and had no sympathy for the conservative attitudes he believed he found in Wichern. But most important, perhaps, was the fact that Wichern was a "foreigner." The subsidies to his "Brothers" were stopped, and Wichern dropped his work with the reform of prison treatment, on which he had been engaged for several years, spending the summers in *Rauhes*

Haus and the winters in Berlin. He never recovered from this defeat, but he continued to work diligently with *Rauhes Haus* until he was finally broken by bad health. At that time, his son, Johannes, had taken over the responsibility for the ever-growing activity of *Rauhes Haus*. [13]

Daily Life at Rauhes Haus

A somewhat condensed version of Wichern's own description of life at Rauhes Haus in 1845 may be of interest:

At four-thirty in the morning in summertime, the custodian brother mounts the small belfry by the chapel, whereupon the great clock intervenes in the life of the house with a disciplined hand. With twenty--one strokes it now tolls: "For the Lord God is a sun and shield," words from Psalm 84, Verse II, which are cast in the clock. The custodian sees to it that the awakening voice is obeyed in all the twenty-four dormitory houses, and his night duty ends as soon as he sees that all are awake. After a brief morning prayer in each individual family, the first hour of the day is devoted to personal ablutions. The children make their beds in the ten houses in which they sleep. Then, supervised by the brothers, they proceed by families to the pool, bathe and practise swimming. In the winter, when they arise half an hour later, twelve boys at a time wash in great tubs in a room next to the kitchen in the various family houses. Dressing, sweeping and tidying up take almost an hour. Every child has his special task. When his work is finished, he busies himself with reading, writing, or some other quiet occupation, each family of boys or girls in separate groups. The boys are naturally garbed very simply. On weekdays they wear linen work coats and wooden clogs. Only on Sundays do they put on a good suit and proper shoes. The girls are clad likewise. All sleep in simple beds on seaweed mattresses.

The first bell for prayers is rung at ten minutes to six. This is the sign for everyone in the different houses to prepare for devotions in the chapel. At six o'clock the clock tolls twenty-one strokes for prayers. From all the houses the brothers or sisters take the children in their care to the chapel. The children lead the way each one holding a Bible. Those who work in the barns and who have milked the cows and delivered the milk to the kitchen also come to the chapel. The latter is beautifully decorated with greenery the year round and has an organ in the gallery. Devotions last for about one hour. For five or ten minutes after seven o'clock, Wichern holds a "short conference" with the entire personnel in the presence of the children. At this time minor disciplinary cases from the previous day are disposed of and any special arrangements for the coming day are made. The children's cleanliness, their clothes and their Bibles are then checked once again, after which the breakfast bell is rung. Boys and girls are assembled together only at morning and evening prayers.

The children then file out of the chapel by families with the brothers. Under the supervision of a brother, table monitors, selected among the children, two from each family, receive the food from the cooks in large containers for each family. Breakfast consists of a generous helping of porridge, usually with milk. The families eat in their own common room.

When the bell rings, the fifth time for the day, the monitors clear the tables, wash the dishes and put them away. The bell rings once more at seven-thirty, at which time the real work of the day begins. Most of the boys have lessons between seven-thirty and eight-thirty. When the bell rings for the seventh time at eight-thirty, all assemble by families in front of the work building. A staff member hands out various work assignments, which are carried out in groups but not by families. Each boy is given the task for which he is best suited. At ten o'clock each child is allowed a ration of home-made bread, which the brothers and sisters distribute to the children at their places of work. The eighth bell signifies that the bread baskets are on their way.

For the girls there is no morning lesson period. Instead they begin after breakfast at half-past-seven to attend to the various household chores of an institution. The girls learn by heart chapters from the Bible or songs which they sing cheerfully as they do their needlework. Those who require it are helped to learn to read by the sisters.

The bell rings again at ten minutes to twelve, and young and old prepare themselves for the main meal of the day. All work ceases. The children are separated from their work groups. The kitchen maids put the food for each family in a locked room. While this is being done, the dining-room monitors gather outside the locked door, which is opened at the stroke of noon. The children eat with their family and its head in a friendly and cozy atmosphere. Each family consists of twelve children. The food is simple, frequently only rice, bean or barley broth and, of course, potatoes. A welcome addition in the summer is the produce of the kitchen garden. Meat is served twice a week. The children eat as much as they want, but seldom overeat.

Those brothers who are not in charge of a family eat with the Wichern family. At the beginning Wichern used to invite a family of children to his table, but this became more difficult as his own family grew.

After dinner the children are allowed to play until one o'clock. Then boys, girls and adults return to work. The bell calls them to the working house and the distribution of tasks is begun anew. Everyone works until half-past-four. Just before that, the thirteenth ringing of the bell announces that the time has come to get ready for the evening meal, which is doled out at the fourteenth ringing. The children eat supper with their families. This meal consists of a slice of bread baked in the institution and beer three times a week. Sometimes warmed-up leftovers from the main meal are served instead of the slice of bread. On their birthdays the children visit Mrs. Wichern who gives them sandwiches and coffee. After supper the children may play until five o'clock. In summer the boys work between five and seven o'clock, but those in need of instruction have lessons for part of this period. In winter there is always school work between five and seven, since it is not light enough for manual labor. The bookbinders and printers are the only ones who work the whole time. The hour from seven to eight o'clock is for recreation and is spent by each family in its playground. Bread is distributed now also, but many are not hungry enough to eat it. In the winter before the institution was so large, Wichern used to bring everybody together in the hall of his house. During this friendly gathering in which Wichern's family also took part, people sang, read aloud or told stories. At eight o'clock there was a ten-minute service in the chapel with hymns, prayers and a short reading from the Scriptures. Then the families retired to their apartments, where they remained quietly, and by nine o'clock all the young inmates of the house were safely in bed.

In the winter the first night watchman goes on duty at eight o'clock, in the summer at ten. All lights must be out by eleven o'clock. Only the duty brother is awake and ushers out the last hour of the day at midnight with a verse from an old poem from the South of Germany:

> Hear ye men and harken well;
> Twelve o'clock hath tolled our bell.
> Twelve, O Man, it is time's goal;
> Think on thine eternal soul.

He then awakens a brother to replace him and to take the second watch. At four o'clock, the latter calls out the hour with the last verses of this old poem.[14]

The institution aroused great interest at home and abroad. It was visited by several royal personages, including, of course, Friedrich Wilhelm IV of Prussia and a number of other German princes, and Danish Queen Karoline Amalie.[15] Elizabeth Fry came with her brother in 1841 and described it in a letter as a good institution. "They looked so happy, and altho' in fact it may be said to be a sort of Prison, yet they are so ruled by love and attention to their wants that there are no walls, nothing at all to keep them from leaving the place."[16]

A Swedish Critic

Wichern wrote that Rauhes Haus could have as many as 4000 visitors during the summer.[17] He did not want his institute to be either a "reformatory barracks" or a "penal institution," but he was not spared criticism of certain elements in his educational methods.[18] One of his critics was the Reverend J. Holmgren, the first director of the Child Saving Institution, *Råby Räddnings-institut*, in Lund, Sweden. During his visit in 1840, the latter wrote in a letter to the Board Chairman, Baron Gustaf Gyllen-krok, who had earlier paid a visit to Rauhes Haus:

You, Sir, expressed the belief that what would strike me on my arrival at *das Rauhe Haus* would be the miserable clothing of the children. This was indeed the case, but the poorness of their nourishment is truly no less than that of their dress. Added to this, they are exposed to the effects of the cold, which are clearly evident from frostbite of the hands and feet from which boys as well as girls suffer. The girls wear sleeveless garments and their blue and red arms are sad to see. It is only natural that the children are frost-bitten. They are poorly clothed, must sit still for an hour at a time several times a day in unheated rooms and listen to sermons or lectures, known here as *Haus-andacht*, and even sleep in cold rooms. Here, in my opinion, is much to be criticized, much that could never be tolerated at *Råby*. To observe these errors with ones own eyes is relatively useful, since one can thereby become aware of how things should be, although they are not. . . . But before I conclude, I would nevertheless like to say a few words about the instruction itself. It consists almost entirely of devotions, which naturally are not without great value, but it seemed to me that it would not be out of place to give some thought to such things as are useful to individuals in the world of today. It is self-evident that the first and noblest task must be to try to awaken and nurture a religious belief in the children. But I do not believe that the only way to elevate the human spirit is to devote the hours intended for true education to reading one or another unrelated chapter of the Bible. The manner in which the devotional hours are conducted is, I find, very reminiscent of that of the non-conformist pastors in Sweden. And I do not know if that is the best way to proceed with errant children. Instead of arousing their hate of the evil within them and their love of good, I believe it breeds in them a pernicious self-satisfaction and self-love generated by this kind of divine service.

The devotions, which are long and frequent here, contain much that is elevating in itself, but consist mainly of exclamations and gesticulations, without any real substance. They are attended faithfully by all the children, including those who cannot read. It would not be out of place to see to it that the children learned something else than to sit and listen hour after hour to expositions on subjects of which they do not know the fundamentals. The ways of this place are considered to be the best by those in charge. It is therefore advisable not to say one word that might imply disapproval, because the people here, no matter how good they may be, are slaves under narrow-minded opinions; they are conceited, stubborn and intolerant. No sooner has one entered into conversation with them than one becomes aware of these traits. *Gehülfen*, who have been artisans and also serve in this capacity here, are those who actually teach the children, while the director himself seldom takes any part in this activity. The devotions are conducted by him and seem to interest him greatly.

. . . . But it does not seem right that the primary obligations of children whose upbringing has been neglected and who therefore should here enjoy a more careful upbringing is to attend numerous devotions and to listen to lectures of which many of them are incapable of understanding. They cannot grasp the essence of Christianity, they must be content with the outer trappings; they acquire an aura of Godliness with no inner understanding of what their outer appearance suggests. There is therefore good reason to fear that the training system followed here will easily breed dissimulators and hypocrites. One case may serve as an example: The boy who two or three years ago set fire to one of the buildings here was able, both before and after this dastardly deed, to conceal the wickedness of his heart under a mask of dissimulation and hypocrisy.

The *Gehülfen* here, thirteen in all, are primarily romantics with a strong admixture of ignorance. Regarding themselves as close to heaven, they believe that all those who do not resemble them have little chance of ever reaching that blessed goal and are bold enough to pronounce their damnation. Moreover, these *Gehülfen* are the supervisors of the children in the families. They say prayers with the children morning and evening. Their prayers consist mainly of a series of exclamations and there is often no sense in what they say. Occasionally, when the spirit moves them, these *Gehülfen* let the small families listen to their pious reflections for as long as three hours at a stretch. This happened the other day in the infirmary. The duty *Gehülf* compelled the patients to sit and listen to his lecture for all of three hours. (Cited from Ekelin.) [19]

It might sound as if life at Wichern's institution with its strictly regimented routine was dreary. But the Swedish visitor neglected to mention an important point. While Wichern made everyday life as dreary as it is, in fact, he regularly interspersed the monotony with pleasant activities. People should have fun in between their boring chores, sing, dance, and be merry to the extent permissible according to the Christian view of life. Not only the usual festivals were celebrated at Rauhes Haus, but special ones were invented. Furthermore, both sexes were represented, which is of vital importance to create a harmonious existence—reminiscent of the outside world. Wichern made this point repeatedly in his innumerable publications. Co-education is essential, *but* it must be supervised. He also stressed in his annual reports that "carryings-on" between boys and girls never occurred, even though the latter in particular were usually "morally ruined" before they came to the institution.[20]

After Wichern

What results were achieved with this treatment? While the statistics of those days are not particularly reliable, it is stated in the thirty-fourth annual report that 5.1 per cent of the pupils discharged from Rauhes Haus in the period 1833-1845 were convicted of crimes and 3.9 per cent of the graduates in the years 1846-1867 were lost to penal institutions. These figures do not include individuals removed from the institution by their parents during the treatment period or runaways who were not taken back in.[21]

Wichern's wife, "Die Mutter," survived him by a few years. His son, Johannes, retired in 1901, and after him came a series of successful leaders who consolidated the undertaking which, however, gradually was turned into a training school for deacons. The institution was ravaged by fire on two occasions, and runaway pupils sometimes committed crimes that shook public confidence in its work. Then came Hitler and World War II. The Nazis had long had their eye on the institution, but took no action until January, 1943, when it was expropriated by SS, i.e., *Schutz Staffel*, the Nazi Party police force. On July 27 of the same year, however, the entire installation was almost completely destroyed by the great bombing attack that set fire to all of Hamburg.

After the war, the institution was doggedly built up again. The present leader, the Reverend Wolfgang Prehn, bases the program on four different activities: a boarding-school for 180 boys from unhappy family backgrounds; a state-subsidized school (*Wichern Schule*) for delinquent boys and between 100 and 200 "normal" youths with a total student body of 650; an old people's home with 65 single rooms; and a school for deacons and social workers with accommodations for 90 students.

While state subsidies are now accepted, the institution depends heavily on private contributions and Prehn is one of Germany's most assiduous beggars. He must collect about one million marks a year to make ends meet, and he does this through a "circle of friends" of more than 30,000 people who donate varying sums of money fairly regularly.

On the occasion of the 120th jubilee of Rauhes Haus, the President of the Federal Republic of Germany, Theodor Heuss, stated: "Wichern never had the time to become a good theologian, because in his eyes it was so important to be a good Christian."[22]

Mettray

An institution similar to Rauhes Haus was the French reformatory, *Mettray*, near Tours, founded by the jurist, Frédéric Auguste Demetz, whom we met earlier as a student of American institutions, and Vicomte de Brétignières de Courteilles.[23] Demetz had been deeply impressed by an American reformatory in Boston (discussed later) and an English one at Parkhurst on the Isle of Wight which eventually came to accommodate as many as six to seven hundred boys. But his own institution more closely resembled Rauhes Haus, which he had visited.

Before the institution was begun, Demetz trained 27 assistants for a period of seven months.[24] Opened in 1840, the new institution became widely known. Among the visitors were the Swedish Supreme Court judge, Knut Olivecrona, and the head of the prisons administration in Sweden, Gustaf Fredrik Almquist. The latter commented about a visit he made in 1874:

> The methods used at Mettray for the training and reforming of children are as simple as they are natural. Children who have been deprived of parental care during infancy need a decent home and a good family life. This is given them in the company of contemporaries whose morals and attitudes have been somewhat ameliorated under the direction of an educated, loving family head *(chef de famille)* and his experienced deputy *(souschef de famille)*. These heads and a group of at most forty children each form a family, which has its own residence entirely separate from the other families.
> The children, who work during the day and rest at night under the eyes of the family father, are under constant supervision and attend divine services morning and evening. They appoint two older brothers *(frères aînés)* from the group who, if they are approved by the director, are permitted to help with the supervision. The family has joint responsibility for sins of omission and commission, as a result of which all

[120]

members of each family share happiness and sorrow alike. Everything is designed to foster good traits and a sense of honor and to accustom the children to obedience and truthfulness, industry and decency; but they are also given happiness and innocent diversions.

Everything at Mettray reveals that both director and teachers know how to win the children's devotion and complete confidence. As a result of the treatment, which is serious, even severe, but loving and healthy, bad habits and tendencies gradually fade away as of their own accord. All is imbued with a religious spirit, and the upbringing is purely Christian with no nonsense. Hypocrisy and false humility are not tolerated; truth and frankness shall prevail in all situations. The children are taught devotion to duty, as well as respect for the law and for the demands of decent behavior and good morals. Their time is devoted to study and work, mainly farming. The moral superiority of the heads of family and the teachers generally suffices to steer the misguided youths without resort to physical force or threats of beatings.[25]

Olivecrona's description of the special section of Mettray is of interest:

While the farm colony is intended to be a reformatory for delinquent boys who either lack every kind of moral guidance or whose parents or guardians, belonging to the dregs of society, are incapable of bringing them up properly, *La Maison Paternelle* is for delinquent boys whose parents belong to the well-situated classes, who have the means to give their children a good upbringing but whose efforts to make them obey and to keep to the path of truth and virtue have failed. How often does it not happen that parents belonging to generally respected families have a son who, while still at school, has begun to live wastefully and extravagantly and, when he lacks money, to steal from others, to commit swindles and forgeries and, under the best of circumstances, is spared worse consequences than expulsion from school? Has it not happened that sons of respectable parents have exhibited such unruliness and defiance that parents and teachers alike have despaired of ever being able to bring them to heel?

What is to be done with such a delinquent boy by parents who have neglected to correct their son's errors from early childhood? Hitherto the only solution has been to send him to sea or to America. Only rarely have such experiments been successful, with the son returning to his home reformed after having undergone all kinds of trials and tribulations. In most cases he has been irretrievably lost to his family and society.

M. Demetz has taken to heart these tragic situations. When it has proved impossible in the home and at school to bring uncontrollable boys to their senses and to teach them obedience, another method should be adopted, and that method, he believes, is isolation. They must, according to M. Demetz, be taken from their homes, where they are accustomed to have their own way, removed from the influence of their comrades and restricted to the company of their teachers. This is the principle on which *la Maison Paternelle* is based. This institution is therefore to be regarded as a sort of full-time boarding-school for delinquent boys from the more prosperous social classes, but where the pupils are neither acquainted with nor know anything about each other and associate only with their teachers.

After I had inspected the farm colony, M. Demetz took me to *la Maison Paternelle*, situated a short distance away in the beautiful park that encloses the colony. Surrounded by tall trees and luxuriant shrubbery, we find a number of small houses with many separate entrances, each house being separated from the other by pretty flower beds. Each pupil has two rooms, one of them a bedroom and the other a study, both well-furnished and lighted by a skylight. The teachers occupy adjoining rooms. The boys are completely cut off from all association with one another. They take their meals in their rooms. The boys' family names are known but to M. Demetz, for within the institution they have only numbers, not names. During study periods, a teacher comes to the pupil's room and gives him instruction, and during the hours of recreation, when the pupil may take walks, ride, fence, do gymnastics or, in summer, practise swimming, he is constantly accompanied by a teacher. The pupil is never left alone outside his room, and walks outdoors, always with a teacher, are planned so that the pupils do not have a chance to meet or to speak with each other. All encounters with other pupils are so completely shut off that, according to M. Demetz, two brothers had spent two years in the institution without being aware of one another's presence and did not learn until later that they had been in *la Maison Paternelle* at the same time. When a pupil is in his room, he is shut in as if in a jail and cannot get out until the teacher comes. In this way isolation forces rebellious temperaments to obedience; and studies soon become an agreeable pastime for those who, if left to themselves and to their egotistical ways, would throw their books aside. In the long run, the association with serious men, who remonstrate with them like a father, cannot but exert a beneficial influence and bring to their senses these youths who previously were led into trouble by bad examples or were guilty of vicious or reckless pranks through thoughtlessness.

When I visited Mettray there were twenty-two boys and youths between the ages of twelve and eighteen incarcerated in *la Maison Paternelle*. They usually remain for only six months to two years or until M. Demetz considers that they have changed their ways to the point that they can be returned to the care of their parents or guardians. While they are in *la Maison Paternelle*, they receive instruction in religion, philosophy, physics, chemistry, mathematics, French, Latin, Greek, German, English, writing, book-keeping, drawing and music, according to the wishes of their guardians. Twice a month M. Demetz sends the pupil's guardians a printed bulletin concerning the boy's health, behavior, industry, studies and progress during the past two weeks. The guardians are thus in a position to judge for themselves how the boy's situation has been and whether there is hope of his improving his ways.

La Maison Paternelle is somewhat newer than the farm colony at Mettray. Since it was opened, more than nine hundred delinquent boys from more or less wealthy social backgrounds have left it reformed. This is in truth no small gain to society, at the same time as the happy results of M. Demetz's humanitarian endeavors have been a boon to hundreds of families, whose members had earlier been in the depths of despondency from the bad conduct of a young relative.

It is self-evident that an institution like *la Maison Paternelle* is expensive to operate, since a large teaching staff must be lodged and salaried. The isolation system in itself also contributes to the high cost of construction and maintenance of the buildings, equipment, etc. Each pupil is charged a fee of 300 francs monthly, or 3,600 francs a year; but this cannot be called unreasonably expensive, bearing in mind the large outlay for the salaries of the administrative and teaching staffs, etc., in such an institution. Those fathers who, in their worry about a delinquent son, have turned to M. Demetz for help have willingly paid the fees charged and later, when they have had the joy of welcoming to the bosom of the family a reformed and settled youth previously regarded as a prodigal son, have not seldom expressed their gratitude to M. Demetz by means of generous donations to the farm colony at Mettray. [26]

By the turn of the century, the regime at Mettray had become almost military. At that time the institutional population consisted of 325 boys sentenced for crimes, 99 who had been remanded for reformative treatment (*correction paternelle*), and 25 who had been handed over to *la Maison Paternelle* by affluent parents. After one year, each inmate who was not under sentence was given a "one-year stripe" and so on up to a "three-year stripe." Each stripe was accompanied by a reward of five francs. Certain positions of trust, e.g., *frère aînés, moniteurs de gymnastique,* were worth one franc monthly. The best pupils were given a gold sprig to wear on their sleeve at the year-end examinations, and a ten-franc bank deposit was the prize for those who passed the finals. Each week the "families" had a good conduct competition, the winner being the one with the fewest penalties. The reward was an extra meal with meat and the best placing at institutional festivities. Fourteen different trades could be practiced, but the majority of pupils (a total of 253) did farm work. [27]

Val d'Yèvre

Rauhes Haus in particular but Mettray also were relatively costly installations with separate houses for each "family unit," which at Rauhes Haus comprised 12 children. A less expensive version came into being in 1847 in the *Colonie agricole pénitentiaire du Val d'Yèvre* near Bourges in France, built by Charles Lucas. It was also large, having accommodations for 460 boys. Olivecrona described it in 1868, commenting:

All the boys admitted to the colony are divided into two main categories: the older boys and the younger boys, who are further divided into smaller units of sixteen in each group or company. Each one of the two main sections has its separate dining-hall, dormitories and playground. Each dormitory is occupied by fifty boys, and there is a sleeping area for the guard at one end of the room so that he can keep his eye on all the boys. The latter sleep in hammocks like seamen, and during the day when the room is aired the hammocks are rolled up and fastened to the walls.

Immediately under the director there is a supervisor of the guards (*gardien-chef*), who receives his orders directly from the director concerning all matters of discipline within the institution, and a head foreman (*chef du service agricole or chef pratique*) who also executes the director's orders with regard to the work of the pupils. Next in line come a certain number of guards (*contremaitres*), who are charged with the direct care of the boys, supervise their morals, conduct and industry, instruct them in their work, and counsel and admonish them. The entire personnel, for which wise instructions are issued by M. Lucas Sr., is comprised of married men whose families live in the colony. M. Lucas follows the principle of allowing only fathers of families to associate closely with the youths, since such men can be expected to treat with greater paternal understanding, greater paternal gravity the misguided children whom they are to lead toward righteous conduct and useful activity. This principle is unquestionably correct. At the same time I would comment that an even more favorable result would be attained if mature, married women, who themselves were mothers, were to take part in the supervision of the younger boys' section. A man can never handle children with the patience of a woman, a mother. A woman can appeal to the hearts of the young much better than a man, arouse their better feelings and in all respects make herself understood by children; a man can never win the love of children in the way that a woman can—and it is always the power of love that is such an important element in the upbringing of children. At *la Colonie du Val d'Yèvre* there are boys between the ages of seven and eighteen to nineteen years old, and those sent there have been sentenced to an average of six years in a reformatory. Unquestionably, all these boys under the age of twelve years are in need of maternal care—advice, warnings, admonitions, that only a mother is fully qualified to give. It is for this reason that I express the opinion that M. Lucas's excellent reformatory would undoubtedly benefit from employing women also for the supervision and guidance of the younger boys or those under twelve years of age.

Monitors (surveillants) of the first, second and third class are selected among the boys who have distinguished themselves by good conduct to assist the guards (surveillants). They wear special badges. One first-class and two second-class monitors are always assigned to each of the two main sections. Each sub-section or company of sixteen boys also has one third-class monitor.

One of the distinctive principles for the maintenance of discipline in the colony is that of solidarity established by M. Lucas. The boys in each main section and especially in each company are in a certain sense jointly responsible for each other's conduct. In addition to the rewards which may fall to the individual in competition with his peers, others also are made to the entire section or company. Just as the admirable conduct of an individual benefits all the members of his company, bad behavior on the part of a single boy results in a demerit or withdrawal of a privilege for the whole company. The solidarity principle is a wise idea, and experience has proved the value of its use. Since all the boys in the company know that bad behavior or laziness on the part of one of them will reflect on all of them, they will all be on the lookout for each other's mistakes and eager that they be corrected. The principle in question is also intended to inhibit egoism in the young men and to teach them that good should not be done for personal gain only but also for the benefit of others. This basic rule of solidarity, added to the wise system of appointing monitors (surveillants) among the boys—an appointment that they themselves must regard as a distinction—has unquestionably contributed to the creation of an esprit de corps in the group, which must be very helpful in maintaining truly good order among such a large number of boys who already have a record of criminality. The fact that each boy is aware that through good behavior he can achieve the distinction of becoming a monitor for the other boys in the company or even a second or first-class monitor is an effective stimulus for good conduct, at the same time as his sense of honor is awakened.

Rewards are always for the individual's good behavior on the whole, and for this reason no special rewards are given for industry and skill alone; for many may work well and even diligently under the strict supervision required by the penitentiary treatment, but still leave much to be desired in other respects.

Spying and informing are forbidden. Misdemeanors are reported publicly at the general meetings held by the director each Tuesday, Friday and Sunday in the chapel. On these occasions the director conducts an enquiry in the presence of all the boys. He hears reports submitted by guards or monitors, as well as the defense offered by the accused, after which he gives his verdict. Those found guilty are sentenced to various disciplinary sanctions, including a public reprimand, a notation of misconduct on a bulletin board in the chapel and, in more serious cases, a beating on the palm of the hand with a leather strip. No member of the staff may mete out punishment of his own accord. This may only be done by order of the director following the enquiry concerning the misdemeanor and in the presence of all the guilty's boys comrades. I was present at one of these general meetings conducted by the director and was therefore able to observe the gravity and the fairness shown by the director, which clearly made a profound impression on the youths.

The entire institution being an exclusively agricultural colony, all the boys work at agricultural jobs and related tasks and crafts. In proportion to their age and physical development, the boys therefore take part in all kinds of labor in the fields, ditch-digging, tilling the soil, harvesting, haymaking, viticulture, gardening, etc. The boys also learn to care for horses, oxen, pigs, etc., as well as bricklaying, building, carpentry, and smithery in order to be able to repair their agricultural implements or to do the basic construction work required in the country or on a farm. They also participate in all the household chores of the institution, learn to bake their bread and cook their meals, in addition to which they do all the washing and housecleaning. Furthermore, they are taught to sew bed linen and clothes. As a consequence, all bedding and the boys' clothes, as well as their shoes (wooden clogs), are made in the colony. In this way the boys become proficient in all the domestic skills, which can be of help to them on many occasions in the future.

A priest is in charge of religious instruction in the institution. The boys are also taught reading, writing, arithmetic, singing and gymnastics certain afternoons each week in the autumn and winter months from September 16 to April 15. During the rest of the year when the boys are busy in the fields, schoolwork is confined to Sunday afternoons. The institution has a small library of good books, which provides useful and pleasant reading material for the entire personnel and from which the boys may also borrow books to study during their free time.

The boys enjoy a healthy and plentiful diet (meat three times weekly) and are given practical clothing adapted to the season of the year. These circumstances, combined with well-ventilated dormitories, have undoubtedly contributed to the excellent health of the colony's inhabitants. The robust and vigorous appearance of the boys confirms this impression. Even more impressive is the fact that only two pupils died in 1865, one in 1866 and four in 1867, i.e., a death rate of 0.37 per cent in 1865, 0.32 in 1866 and 1.15 in 1867.

The boys remain in the colony for three to six years. When they are discharged they are given new clothes and a small sum of money to help with their most basic needs. Excellent behavior may even lead to an extra sum which in exceptional cases may be as much as one hundred francs. Through the good offices of the director, employment is always found as a farm, vineyard, or garden worker, or in the army or navy as an enlisted soldier or sailor. In this way the future of the discharged boy is always provided for in the best of ways. Moreover, since they are under the supervision of a *société de patronage* (benevolent society) for the first three years after their release, they have a further spur to continue their good behavior. The results achieved by M. Lucas and confirmed by twenty-one years of experience must be considered exceptionally gratifying in all respects. . . .

The twofold objective has been reached. The marshy, barren land which he (Lucas) began to cultivate twenty-one years ago has been transformed into the most fertile fields, the best cared for garden one could hope to see, where they have even constructed a small movable railway about two thousand meters long to transport goods within the colony. More important, however, is that in the process of cultivating the soil, he (Lucas) has restored to society as good and useful citizens hundreds of young reformed criminals who, without the good upbringing they received at *la Colonie du Val d'Yèvre*, would presumably have continued their criminal career and populated the State prisons with the same number of villains. According to the records maintained, only seven to eight per cent of the youths discharged from the colony relapsed into crime—a truly remarkable result. To have done so much good, to have rendered such services to mankind as M. Lucas has done, must give a satisfaction that is beautiful to possess. The blessings of the young men rescued, the respect of all good citizens are also rewards that will always belong to M. Lucas and his memory. The experience acquired at *la Colonie du Val d'Yèvre* is a priceless asset to the treatment of young criminals from which all countries could benefit.[28]

Wichern was naturally interested in the institutions that grew up using his work as a model. But, he was critical of them. He wrote about Mettray, for example, that an institutional section consisting of 40 boys could scarcely be called a "family." Another difference he mentioned was that Mettray only took boys from prisons to which they could be returned if they proved too difficult to manage. Furthermore, Mettray subsisted primarily on state funds.[29]

Nevertheless, it was Mettray and Val d'Yèvre that were copied, not Rauhes Haus where the costs involved in the small-group system were considered to be prohibitive. The attempts to find the same principles in Mettray and Val d'Yèvre as those on which Rauhes Haus was based are almost pathetic, for they simply did not exist. Nor did the two French institutions have the vitality of

Rauhes Haus. They became the focus of increasingly bitter public criticism and were finally closed, the last of them, Mettray, in 1937.[30]

Bellefaire Home

A latter-day American successor to Rauhes Haus is *Bellefaire Home* in Cleveland, Ohio. The pedagogic point of departure is very similar, but the program can be carried out on another scale thanks to the greater resources available to the American institution. The clientele consists of youngsters admitted between the ages of six and sixteen. Most of them belong to one of two categories: *dependent* (homeless, penniless, cannot receive proper care) and *neglected* (deserted, neglected, found in company or in places that endanger the child's moral development). At the same time, others categorized by the juvenile court as *delinquent* are also accepted. A visitor to the institution described it:

> Bellefaire Home is a private institution which is owned and operated by *the Jewish Agency* in Cleveland and accepts only children of Jewish parentage. The area served is very large, almost half the United States. I would make it clear from the outset that the restriction to Jews was not the choice of the owners and managers of the institution, who in fact greatly regret the resultant homogenization of the clientele. But due to the non-partisan policy of the United States regarding religion and to the myriad of different religious denominations and schools of thought, it is almost inevitable that private institutions have had to restrict themselves to a single faith. The state-supported institutions must always employ a number of chaplains of different faiths in order not to jeopardize the principle of religious freedom. In fact, the diversity in religious matters appears to cause almost as much difficulty as racial differences.
>
> Physically the installation is designed like a resident college. There is a large and handsome administration building with a colonnade. This building contains offices for the staff, a conference room and a large library with a fine reading-room for the pupils. Behind it are the other buildings spread over a large, flat area that gives the impression of one great lawn with narrow paths between the houses. One of the latter is an auditorium and gymnasium with a swimming pool in the basement, another is a circular synagogue containing a large number of classrooms, a third is an infirmary with a day-home for children at the back, and lastly there are eight residential "cottages" for the students.
>
> Each cottage consists of two student residences, one for boys and one

for girls, separated by a common kitchen. About a dozen pupils and two house parents live in each residence. The houses have two stories. On the ground floor there is a large sunroom containing a piano, a television set and a radio, a reading room, a dishwashing room and a kitchen. The other side of the house, which can be reached through the kitchen, is arranged in the same way. The second floor of each residence consists of two single rooms with bathrooms for the house parents, a large washroom with showers and toilets, two dormitories and one single room. The children are placed in the residences according to age.

The daily schedule when I was there was as follows: The children rose at six-thirty in the morning. Breakfast was between seven and seven-thirty. Beds were then made and rooms tidied until eight o'clock, when a bus picked up the children and took them to school. Back again from school at about four o'clock in the afternoon and dinner at five. Thereafter a social gathering in the student residence until six o'clock, when homework was begun. The day ended with various kinds of recreation between seven and nine o'clock, which was bedtime for the children. Lights were put out at half past nine. The older youngsters were given half an hour longer recreation. In general, the treatment was based on the following principles:

Ordinary schooling was not provided at Bellefaire. Instead the students were placed in not less than fifteen different schools in the city. Special teachers were employed for pupils with learning problems. In addition, all pupils received special instruction in Hebrew. One cottage was in a sense an institution in itself and comprised two residences in which the pupils, in accordance with their parents' wishes, were brought up in the orthodox Jewish manner. This small special institution was the source of some irritation, since its students could not help but feel that they were treated more strictly than the others—were not allowed to go to the auditorium on Friday evening, could not ride their bicycles on Saturday, etc.

The basic work of upbringing was the responsibility of the house parents. The latter were usually university graduates, and a great deal of effort was spent on training them in the art of child guidance. The husband was usually employed outside Bellefaire during the daytime and only worked mornings and evenings in the institution. The wife was always employed full-time. Approximately half of the house parents had children of their own, which was generally regarded as unsuitable. "Our children either feel deprived of parental love, become jealous and difficult when their parents busy themselves with the other young children, or they are spoiled in the residences for the older youngsters." The five-day week applied to the house parents, who spent their two free days in a special apartment and were substituted by *relief parents*.

The house parents had nothing to do with cooking, which was the responsibility of a special cook for each cottage, but were expected to serve the food and clear the tables. Their duty was to keep order in their group of pupils, to teach them good manners and habits, to arrange parties and other social events and, most important of all, to occupy themselves as intensively as possible with each individual child. Every corner of the soul was to be explored. Nothing should be left to routine or chance. The objective was to turn every pupil into a harmonious individual, prepared to manage on his own when the time came to leave the institution and possibly also to assume responsibility for others.

The hours when the pupils were at school were devoted primarily to staff conferences. The house mothers had joint sessions and individual conversations with case workers and with the psychologists, each of whom served as superintendent of a group of student residences and was directly responsible for training the house parents.

The seven case workers had a psychologist at their disposition for conducting tests. Each pupil was assigned to a case worker, who met with him once a week, or more if necessary. The institution also had a staff of three psychiatrists, two of them psychoanalysts. In addition, it employed a physician and a dentist on a part-time basis and three full-time nurses.

Recreational activities were managed by a psychologist with special training for this type of work. He had a large staff of voluntary as well as paid assistants, who were in charge of various activities such as carpentry, model construction, athletics, and theatricals. Extra counsellors trained as teachers or recreational leaders were employed during vacations in order to keep the children occupied during the hours when they would otherwise have been in school.

A large number of volunteers helped with the social training aspect of the program. Their recruitment and instruction were the responsibility of the supervisor of the volunteer department and his two or three assistants. Some of the voluntary workers served as individual Big Brothers and Big Sisters each with one pupil whom they met with at least once a week, visited at school and invited to their homes. About twenty pupils had "Bigs." The assignment of a Big to a child was taken very seriously. The man or woman selected had to be suitable for the particular boy or girl in question and had to agree to maintain the relationship for a full year. On the other hand, it might be decided that a certain pupil was not suited to the kind of personal involvement that inevitably develops in the relationship between a Big and his protégé. If it was considered that he would not derive any real benefit from his association with a Big, the idea was dropped.

Another type of volunteer workers were the "Sunday Bigs," who took three or four pupils out on Sundays for a drive or to a ball-game, or the like. Other volunteers visited the institution one evening a week and led working groups, directed plays, conducted chamber music or served as athletics coaches.

A staff conference was held once a week, at which several cases were discussed with a case worker. Contact with discharged pupils was maintained as long as possible, at least three or four years, and special members of the staff travelled all over the United States for meetings with former pupils. During my visit a small research section was being set up in which one or two psychologists were to study the causes of maladjustment, as well as the results of different therapeutic methods.

Bellefaire Home is one of the most elaborate institutions of its kind in the world. It is regarded as one of the most modern in the United States, and the two men at its head, Leon H. Richman, administrative director, and Fritz M. Mayer, director of studies, are considered to belong to the elite among institutional educators. The question usually arises in such cases whether it is reasonable to invest so heavily in such a small number of individuals who are not particularly maladjusted or perhaps not even maladjusted at all. To my questions on this point, Bellefaire's leaders replied that children who run the risk of becoming maladjusted are precisely the ones in whom an investment should be made and for whom no preventive efforts should be left untried. They underscored the difficulty of finding qualified foster parents even for relatively uncomplicated cases and pointed out that under the Bellefaire system the foster parents are 'brought into the institution, where they can be guided and supported in a way that is impossible when the children are spread out among a number of different foster homes.[31]

The Boston House of Reformation

In America, the State of Massachusetts decided in 1826 to remand young criminals to a special institution, rather than a penitentiary, which became the Boston House of Reformation. The place was built and a seven-member board of directors was appointed. The educational director was the young Reverend E.M.P. Wells. His only staff consisted of a school-teacher and a supervisor. The number of pupils soon increased to almost 100, about one-tenth of them girls. The majority of the inmates had been convicted of theft or arrested for vagrancy. After a few years' experience, Wells concluded: "No matter how bad a boy is judged to be, he can always be reformed if he is under fifteen years of age and very often if he is over that age also. He who has been regarded and treated as incorrigible can become worthy of the utmost confidence." (Quoted from Liepmann.)

Wells devised a daily schedule consisting of five and a half hours of work, four hours of schooling, two and a quarter hours of recreation, one hour and a half for meals, and one hour and a quarter for devotions. He was firmly convinced of the educational value of games, in which he participated.

Wells set up three "bad" grades and three "good" grades. Those who were believed to have a definite tendency to behave badly were put in the first bad grade. They were not allowed to participate in any games or entertainment arranged at the institution; they were forbidden to enter the teachers' room; and they were denied the right to vote. Next was the second bad grade for even more problematic pupils. The same restrictions applied as in the first bad grade, but in addition the pupils were not permitted to talk to other inmates unless it was absolutely necessary, nor could they address teachers without express permission. They might not sleep in their own bed; they were under constant supervision outside the dormitory; and they were forbidden to receive any extra food rations. In the third bad grade, finally, all the previously mentioned restrictions applied and, in addition, the diet was limited to bread and water. These pupils were kept in solitary confinement.

Next came the three good grades. Good grade No. 3 was for those who had shown a positive attitude in their behavior. These pupils were permitted to go into town with a "responsible person" once they had earned 25 behavior credits; they were allowed to move freely within the institutional grounds; to go to the gymnasium and reading-room; and to read books and periodicals in the auditorium. Other privileges were added in the second good grade, including the right to visit the town for an annual festive occasion without escort; the right to carry certain unimportant keys; the right to be appointed to certain "offices"; the right to borrow books from the reading-room; and so on. The first good grade was the best and yielded further privileges, namely, to take walks outside the institution; to go to one's own room or to the dining-room unescorted; to leave the auditorium without special permission; and, most important of all, to wear civilian clothing.

Wells's system was so arranged that a pupil might move up from the lowest grades relatively quickly, but promotion was increasingly slow, the higher he rose. We recognize this system from Crofton's Irish progressive system. To move from the third to the second bad grade took at least one day, from the second to the first bad grade also at least one day, from the first bad to the third good grade one week, from the third good to the second good grade two weeks, and finally from the second to the first good grade not less than four weeks. Informing on another pupil was forbidden except in so-called matters of conscience. Wells set up a court consisting of 12 members and established positions for a chief of police and his deputies. The so-called responsible persons, or monitors, were elected once a month by a council of pupils.

On arrival, the newcomer was given a medical examination, bathed, clothed, and introduced to the other students. Next, he was informed in detail about the house rules and made to understand that it was entirely up to him how fast he would be able to rise in the ranks. The first week, however, was always spent in the second or third bad grade. Transfer to a higher grade was voted on by the student council. The number of votes required for transfer to a higher or a lower grade was carefully specified. A boy who behaved especially badly could be excluded from the community and could lose his vote for a period of time, after which time he would be reinstated.

The institution attracted many American as well as European visitors. Among the latter were de Beaumont, de Tocqueville, and Julius. By 1832, however, the Boston House was in trouble. At that time, a commission appointed by the municipal authorities inspected the place. The religious instruction was found to be unexceptionable, but the general schooling program was judged to be poor. The commission complained that the children were not compelled to work harder to contribute to the expenses of the institution. The entire institution was said to be characterized by excessive recreation and entertainment instead of by strict moral and physical discipline and correction. The children were kept in the institution too long, which made the whole operation too costly. Wells did not bother to stand up to his bigoted critics. He resigned, and the fate of this pioneer institution was sealed.[1]

The George Junior Republic

It was not until 1895 that the Boston institution acquired a worthy successor. This was the George Junior Republic in Freeville, New York, which was named after its founder, William R. George.[2] This remarkable man defined his objectives: In the first place, the delinquent children in his care should be considered to have the *right* to a happy childhood and a good upbringing; secondly, with an eye to the future, they should be taught a trade and trained to be good citizens. He had 350 acres of land at his disposal, and a clientele consisting of 100 boys and half as many girls between the ages of 14 and 21 years, some of whom had been labeled incorrigible by courts and parents alike. He proceeded to create a small "republic," which was actually modeled on the United States government. His guiding principle was that nothing should be free of charge—everything should be paid for in work. After a few years of experimentation, George entrusted almost the entire responsibility for his republic to the boys and girls. It has been claimed that this marked the end of the originally high rate of escapes. George himself took a "back seat" as a senior adviser.

The government of the republic had three branches: legislative, executive, and judicial. The legislative authority was exercised by the town meeting, which was comprised of all citizens over the age of 16 years, convening once a month. Each year, the town meeting elected a government consisting of a president, vice-president (usually a girl), town clerk, and treasurer. The constitution gave the right of veto to the director on questions of bills and laws, but he practically never exercised this privilege. The government appointed the other office-holders of the Republic, including judges, attorney general, police, and prison officials. Through special legislation, the young citizens also established a female judgeship, as well as a prison for girls. Jurisdiction belonged to the youngsters, but the adult employees were entitled to serve as assessors in court proceedings. The court met once a week, in open session, of course. It was empowered to hand down sentences to fines and to deprivation of liberty for up to six months. Visitors at that time reported that the sentences to deprivation of liberty were harsh and remarkably old-fashioned. The "convicts" were put at farm or construction work that comprised six hours more than normal working hours and paid less. The prison diet was meager and the rule of silence was applied. Convicts had the right to appeal to the town meeting and the institutional director, which rarely happened.

The economic structure was based entirely on George's principle of nothing for nothing. The citizens themselves must build up their Republic and construct new houses when the old ones were obsolete, learn crafts and other trades. As a result, a long series of occupations gradually developed, and eventually the institution was able to operate its own bakery, dairy, laundry, carpentry shop, printing establishment, and even a department store. The inhabitants lived in small houses spread all over the territory of the Republic. Each house was in charge of adult employees, always including a matron. The co-educational principle sometimes caused problems, but the moral tone of the institution was considered to be sound and healthy, and no good or justifiable reason to remove the girls could be found.

Since the youngsters were unskilled in the workshops, they soon decided that they needed good instructors. These teachers, however, created problems from the point of view of competence, and a clear demarcation line had therefore to be drawn between the areas of authority of adults, on the one hand, and youngsters, on the other.

After a few years, a supreme court consisting of three institutional officials was constituted. In the event of a conflict between a so-called collaborator, or official, and a citizen, the matter was taken to the citizens court if the former was the plaintiff and to the supreme court if he was the accused. Otherwise, individual freedom was as complete as possible. Visitors at the time observed that some of the young citizens were very shabbily clothed since they did not want to work and therefore could not earn enough money. However, if the assets of one of these citizens dropped below five dollars, he was sentenced to "imprisonment" and to hard labor for the Republic until he decided to look for regular employment. Competitive sports, theatricals, and music were very important in the life of the tiny Republic.

In summarizing his experiences toward the end of his days, George wrote that people can be divided into two categories: those who do right because it is right and those who only do right if it suits their convenience and believe in and obey the law only to the extent that it seems to be politically opportune. And, he considered that he had proved this theory in his children's republic.[3]

The Boys Republic

While George never craved publicity, his work nevertheless was widely noted and he soon acquired disciples all over the United States. In 1908, a number of similar institutions joined together in the National Association of Junior Republics.[4] Among these was the Boys Republic in Detroit, which will be described in some detail on the basis of notes made by a visitor in 1949:

> On the outskirts of the great automobile city of Detroit there is a small but remarkable institution for boys, Boys Republic. The exterior is far from impressive: A few old, dilapidated houses on a relatively small lot, with private homes on one side and a couple of acres of open ground on the other.
>
> About 70 boys live here, remanded by juvenile courts for various crimes or because the court found some other reason to sentence them to this kind of training. The range of offenses is wide. Some of the boys have been guilty of armed robbery, while others have never harmed a fly but have not been able to adapt themselves to an ordered way of life. The age of admission is from 14 to 17 years and the average period in the institution is about one year.
>
> The boys live in two houses containing large, dreary dormitories. There is a common and equally dreary dining-hall. The personnel eat in an adjoining dining-room. The entrance to both dining-rooms is through the kitchen. In other words, the place is far from elegant. A separate building contains schoolrooms for theoretical instruction,

while one or two other buildings accommodate handicraft and repair shops. Then there is a gymnasium for basketball, boxing and weight-lifting, which also serves as an auditorium. There is also a small infirmary building and another little house with office space for the clerical and other personnel. A third structure contains a modest general store, which plays an important part in the educational program of the institution.

The underlying theme can be summed up as follows: The road to rehabilitation is through *training in citizenship*. The boys shall learn about society and their place in it by living in Boys Republic, which is constituted along the same lines as a miniature American community. In other words, the principle of self-government is the foundation on which the institution has been based during the more than forty years of its existence. It was founded in 1907, at which time it was called Ford's republic (it was Henry Ford, Sr., who donated the initial capital). The same principle still applies, even though many modifications have been introduced through the years.

The self-government program now has the following structure: Each new boy must wait for ten days before he acquires "citizenship." When this point is reached he may vote and take part in the *Citizens' Court*. The officials elected by the boys comprise the president, vice-president, judges, assistant judges, recording clerk, assistant recording clerk, sheriff, health inspector, and grounds supervisor. Elections are held every six months. Every other month the boys meet in the general assembly, which has the power to pass, amend and abrogate laws. The powers of the boys to regulate their lives are very far-reaching. The institutional management has the veto power in certain matters, particularly those pertaining to finance. The idea is thus to allow the boys to learn from experience how important it is to appoint good leaders and how unpleasant life can be if laws are not wise. Now and again incidents occur that shake the small republic in its very foundation and the whole system collapses temporarily: if, for example, the president and the judge run away, commit a crime or otherwise make a mess of things, or if revolutionary ideas among the inmates lead to unwise legislation. Under such circumstances, all management can do is to introduce a dictatorship until stable conditions are restored. And then life again proceeds according to the established pattern.

The citizens' court meets twice a week to deal with complaints by officials and boys about citizens of the republic. Officials are also present in court. Proceedings are usually rather solemn, although they are occasionally enlivened by repartee, which can happen in ordinary American courts also. Nowadays the only sentences that can be imposed are fines, ranging between 25 cents and 25 dollars. The court used to have greater powers, but the consequences were so often undesirable that the system was abandoned once and for all.

I participated in three such sessions. Complaints were submitted on printed forms and distributed to the persons involved in the case beforehand. The plaintiff pleaded his own case. Witnesses were heard by the judge himself. The judge was addressed as "Your Honor" by the officials also, who were just as polite as the boys and considerably less aggressive.

The offenses under the jurisdiction of the court were tardiness, absence without leave, irresponsible behavior (this included running away), disobedience, neglect of duty, destructiveness, insolence, undesirable behavior, and dishonesty (theft). Relapses were punished more severely than first offences. The judge had one scale to go by—still another lesson learned from years of bitter experience—but a certain amount of freedom within this framework. The fine for tardiness (late arrival at lessons, drill, meetings, meals, etc.) was a minimum of 25 cents for the first offence, 50 cents for the second and 75 cents for the third, but the judge could take the one dollar maximum for each offence if he wished. For irresponsible behavior in leaving the institution without permission (according to a law established by the boys themselves, it mattered not where the boy went or how long he stayed away), the minimum fine was five, ten and twenty dollars, respectively, with an absolute maximum of 25 dollars. As an extra sanction imposed by the institutional administration, the offender lost "merit points," which will be discussed more fully later on.

But where did the money for the fines come from? The answer is: from the boys' wages. And this brings us to the *financial training* in Boys Republic. On his arrival, each boy was informed that he would be paid for everything he did, for school work, vocational work, and administrative duties, but he would also have to pay his own way. Money for food, lodging, clothes, recreation, sweets would all be paid from his own pocket. All that he would be given free of charge was board and lodging for the first week.

The minimum hourly wage was 40 cents, which could gradually be raised to 50 cents. The president received an extra two dollars weekly for his services. Income was booked every week, and the boy was always aware of his financial status. He could either bank his money or receive it in the Republic's aluminum currency, as he preferred. His number was stamped on the coins—a precaution born of experience in order to prevent the boys from doing each other out of their earnings in games of chance, etc. Nobody was allowed to buy anything with other than his own money, but for the rest he could spend it as he saw fit. He was allowed to decide on the quality of his shoes and clothes. Foolish spending and breaking of the law were heavy drains on his pocket. If he was in the red for more than 30 dollars he was put on welfare, i.e., the welfare service became responsible for him and all the other boys had to raise the money for his living expenses. There was, of course, a special Public Welfare Committee for this purpose.

I assume that many readers wonder if the boys really "ratted" on each other to the court. They did, indeed. This may sound unpleasant and contrary to a boy's natural instincts, but all these boys appreciated the function of the court in the right way, as an instrument for their own self-discipline. President Burry explained to me that only very rarely did a boy seek revenge for a complaint made against him. A complaint was dropped if there was good reason to believe that it had been lodged as an act of vengeance.

In addition to the self-government program and the financial training method, there was a third guiding principle in the Boys Republic's educational system, the so-called *merit points.* The sum of fifty earned merit points entitled the boy to probation. One point monthly could be earned in each of the branches of work, in financial management, in attendance at the institution, in participation in recreational activities, as well as one to three points in general adjustment. Extra points could be earned for good progress in school or vocational training and for judicious use of money. In reality, the merit point system was highly complex. The final total had to be distributed over all the areas in which points were awarded. These points were set by a committee of officials, on which the boys themselves were not represented. They had been previously, but the system was changed at their own request. After attending a merit evaluation meeting, I had the impression that points were adjusted with an eye to their suitability from the standpoint of discharge. When a boy had reached the stage where he should be discharged, the requisite points were arranged for him, which makes one wonder what purpose was served by the whole procedure.

What, indeed, was the purpose of this whole system? It entailed a lot of work. Two and a half employees were required to manage the boys' bank accounts and run the store. Was it worth it? The boys themselves were in favor of self-government and the economic system. The director of the institution, Mr. M.A. Saltzgaber, a psychologist trained in modern methods and with a long experience of varying types of reformatory work, was somewhat hesitant when I pressed him for his views. The merit system had outlived its usefulness, in his opinion. And the guiding principles should not be over-estimated. He had greater confidence in the institution's new psychiatric department, which consisted of a psychiatrist, a psychologist and three case-workers. This department was to be expanded in order to provide better service.[5]

Osborne

It was obviously more difficult to introduce into true penal institutions the principle of joint responsibility for the management of an institution and for the treatment of its inmates. A perverted form that had long existed in the criminals' own system of justice was the Kangaroo Court, according to which prisoners were permitted to maintain order among themselves in exchange for certain privileges. However, this administration of justice by the prisoners themselves had served no positive ends. Oddly enough, the first experiment of the kind was made in the old prison at Auburn, which thus once more came to play a pioneer role in the history of penology. A well-to-do man, Thomas Mott Osborne, had for several years been the chairman of the board of the George Junior Republic. George had mentioned to him on several occasions that a considerable degree of self-administration could probably be introduced into prisons. Osborne was skeptical at first, but gradually became more and more fascinated with the idea of conducting an experiment.[6]

The opportunity came in 1913 when Osborne was appointed chairman of a commission for the reform of the prison system in the State of New York. Considerable manipulation was needed to wangle the appointment for himself. He first studied Auburn, among other institutions, and found that it still applied the silent system and extremely strict discipline, but nevertheless had problems with maintaining order and, first and foremost, found it difficult to achieve contact with the prisoners. In order to gain true insight into prison problems, Osborne became an "amateur prisoner" for eight days. He took the experience so seriously that he even refused to work in order to be chastized by twelve hours in a dark cell. He originally planned to make this experiment under cover of complete anonymity, but he was advised against this both by the warden and a prisoner in whom he had confided, who both assured him that the unerring instinct of the other prisoners would reveal the maneuver. There was therefore no secret about the true identity of "Tom Brown," and both personnel and inmates knew what was going on. At the same time, he appears not to have obeyed the rule of silence himself, for he had many meetings with various prisoners, including Jack Murphy, a recidivist under sentence "twenty years to life," who came to have great influence on the reform program he decided to set up. As a motto for this program he borrowed Gladstone's basis thesis: "It is Liberty alone that fits men for liberty."[7]

A prison should permit the greatest possible measure of freedom to its inmates, according to Osborne. Outside the walls, a man has to choose between honesty and crime, so why not teach him the advantages and disadvantages of these alternatives while he is in prison? Experience is the best teacher, and consequently there should be both laws and courts within the walls to protect the industrious from the lazy, those who have the will and the interest to make a new future for themselves as law-abiding citizens from those who do not. He criticised the Auburn system on the following grounds: The constant confinement in small cells for long hours on end, interrupted only by daytime work with other inmates in complete silence, creates tensions that are released by frequent fights. The situation is particularly trying on Sundays when the men are isolated for as long as sixteen hours. Overcrowding, with several men in cells intended for one man only, further compounds the problem. The system encourages immorality (in Osborne's view, masturbation rather than homosexuality). Inmates become addicted to drugs, not seldom provided by corrupt officials. The entire institution suffers from the disorganized and unproductive works program, which cannot pay the inmates enough to stimulate their interest in working. The rule of silence creates hypocrisy and constant attempts to circumvent it. The dreary monotony of prison life produces hypersensitivity and stultifies the men's will power. Finally, the custom of using inmates as spies creates mutual distrust between the prisoners, leading to nervous tension and brutality. The officials are infected by the inmates' nervousness. The inmates' initiative and sense of responsibility are lost.[8]

The Mutual Welfare League

Osborne received permission to try to get the Auburn prisoners to work with him to obtain better conditions in the institution. Osborne's guiding principle was that a privilege should never be accorded without demanding something in return from the prisoners, i.e., an individual and a collective responsibility for the privilege. The management and personnel at Auburn agreed to take part in a far-reaching experiment with increased participation of the inmates in planning treatment. Osborne then formed his famous Mutual Welfare League. Everyone could in principle belong to this league, and exclusion was regarded as chastisement by one's peers. He began by convincing the warden of the institution to allow Auburn's 1400 prisoners to have a meeting, which he planned with the greatest care through a committee of 49 prisoners appointed by secret ballot by all inmates.

The guards carried the ballot boxes from workshop to workshop. The prisoners were allowed 30 minutes to themselves to select representatives, in proportion to their number. The 49 met alone with Osborne without any guard—for the first time in more than

100 years. A nine-member working committee was appointed. The remaining 40 men were divided into five grievance committees, which would take turns in dealing with complaints. The members of these committees would also serve as sergeants-at-arms. Appointments would be for six months. The first general election for the "forty-niners" was held on January 11, 1914. The winners were installed seven days later. On February 12, 1914, fourteen hundred men marched unescorted, in dead silence, and in perfect order to the prison church where they listened to a concert. The guards consisted of prisoners! (Afterwards the personnel had to admit that they would never have been able to keep such good order.) Later on the committee of forty-nine organized football games, also without guards.

Everything ran smoothly in the first wave of enthusiasm, but trouble gradually developed among the forty-niners. Undesirable elements had managed to work their way into the group, which resulted in a number of irregularities. However, since privileges were immediately withdrawn, the prisoners discovered that it was in their own interest to elect the best possible representation in the committee of forty-nine and to abide faithfully by agreements reached concerning order. So the system worked relatively well on the whole.

Osborne took another step when he set up a special grievance court handled entirely by prisoners, the function of which was to deal with all minor offenses, particularly those committed by prisoners against each other. Eventually these inmate courts were given full jurisdiction over all disciplinary offenses on the part of prisoners with the exception of the following five, regarded as major crimes: (1) attack on a prison employee, (2) dangerous attack on another prisoner, (3) refusal to work, (4) instigating a strike, (5) and an attempt to escape.

Osborne's reforms were emulated in some places, but, in general, they were not overly successful. Sing Sing failed, for example, and put a stop to inmate participation in decision-making until Osborne himself was persuaded to take on the wardenship of this giant institution on December 1, 1914. He immediately succeeded in putting things right.

As at Auburn, the prisoners elected a committee of 60 delegates to serve as the board of the newly constituted *Golden Rule Brotherhood*. The committee appointed a sergeant-at-arms, a "chief of police," and a working committee. The secretary of the working committee became the key man in the system, spent his entire time at the job, had his own office and assistants, received and answered correspondence. A large number of sub-committees were appointed for various functions and, as at Auburn, one of them handled certain cases of infractions of discipline. The severest sanction was suspension from the Brotherhood, which entailed withdrawal of the privileges common to all inmates with regard to correspondence, visits, recreation, etc.

Music and drama were important elements in the Brotherhood program at this time.[9] Performances were given in other institutions, including relatively remote ones. The following incident is told about one of these excursions, which might have led to catastrophe for the whole system. It should be recalled that American opinion is adamant on the subject of this kind of experiment. Success is all-important; failure is unacceptable.

In nine automobiles with no accompanying guards, Osborne and a troupe of actors and musicians—all prisoners—drove to Manchester, New Hampshire, to give a performance. On the trip home, which was made at night, a bad snowstorm blew up, and seven of the cars took the wrong road at an intersection. Finally, six of them made their way back to Sing Sing. The seventh ran into all kinds of trouble, including running out of gas and a punctured tire. The tour leaders had to wake up a farmer and enquire the way to the nearest prison where they could spend the night. They lost their way again, but finally arrived at a small town from which there was a bus route to the vicinity of Sing Sing. They had to borrow money to pay for their bus tickets. Fortunately, they all finally arrived back at home base. One of the group was a lifer; another was under a twenty-year sentence. Questioned later as to why they had not taken the chance to make a getaway, they all replied that they had to think of their responsibility for their comrades in the prison.

Nevertheless, Osborne ran into opposition of the most despicable nature. He was a Democrat, and the State of New York was run by Republicans. Only a year after his appointment, he was accused of having made homosexual advances to several prisoners, among other irregularities. He agreed to resign temporarily, but after a six-month investigation the charge was dropped and Osborne was reinstated in his office. However, he resigned voluntarily three months later due to opposition of the governor and the head of the prisons administration of New York State.[10] Osborne was appointed warden of the naval prison in Portsmouth, New Hampshire, in 1920, but resigned after new accusations of homosexuality had made his position untenable.[11]

A Norwegian Critic

Once Osborne was gone, the self-government system lost its inner strength and changed character. In 1922, the warden of the Opstad penitentiary in Norway, Arne Omsted, described his impressions of the situation following a visit the previous year:

> The self-government system still exists at both Auburn and Sing Sing, but on a very reduced scale. What remains is: 1) The prisoners are unguarded in the dining-hall, while they take the air or play games, in church during services and at moving pictures or other performances. 2) The prisoners elect representatives among themselves who act as a kind of foremen in the workshops; these delegates, in turn, elect a "sergeant-at-arms," who calls meetings, etc., and also five judges, who pass sentence on infractions of the League's regulations. As sanctions they can suspend the offender from the League or forbid him access to the recreation yard. Infractions of prison rules, on the other hand, are punished by the prison administration.
>
> There was a wide divergence of opinion concerning the system. Leaders of the League, with whom I spoke at length at Auburn, were enthusiastic about it and had nothing but good to say of it. But it should be borne in mind that the prisoners who held positions of confidence in the League were in an enviable situation. These men (according to the printed report for 1917-18, there were 35 of them at Sing Sing at the end of the year) had no work except to sit in the League's office, side by side with the administrative offices, and correspond with film distributors and theatrical troupes, prepare posters and programs, and so forth. So it is no wonder that these men were pleased with the system.
>
> Opinions differed among the other prisoners. A Norwegian prisoner in Sing Sing told me that the men in charge at the League were incompetent fellows who, in his view, would soon lead the League to collapse. He further stated that the friends of the League are not telling the truth when they claim that the earlier abuses came to an end after the League was formed. Many things were going on of which the officials knew nothing, for example, sodomy, smuggling of drugs like opium and morphine into the institution. There was a lot of money in the hands of prisoners—he believed as much as several thousand dollars—which had been smuggled in by visitors. As I myself saw, there was practically no control of visits. A Norwegian-born prisoner in Auburn told me that it was a matter of indifference to most prisoners

whether the League existed or not. Also, there were two parties in Auburn, the New Yorkers, who had the leadership at the time, and the others who claimed that the New Yorkers only cared about themselves and their own people and paid no attention to the other group. At Great Meadow I had a long conversation with a Norwegian and a Swedish convict, both of whom had been in Sing Sing. Neither of them liked the League; the leaders were mainly interested in what they could get for themselves; if they knew they could use a man they would do him all sorts of favors. Behind the League there were outsiders with plenty of money who kept it going.

A man whose judgment I trust is the physician at Auburn, Dr. Frank Heacox, a highly regarded individual who was deeply committed to his work. He was no admirer of the self-government system. In his view, conditions in the prison have not improved, disciplinary prob lems are about the same, and escapes are just as frequent as before—in 1919-20, for example, twenty-four men escaped, most of them from the gangs sent out to work on the roads. Most prisoners do not approve of the League, and only those who can benefit from it personally are in favor of the system. The work standard is not better, rather worse than it used to be. The uncontrolled mingling of the prisoners Dr. Heacox considered to be wrong since the bad elements have a pernicious influence on the others. In his opinion, more men were reformed under the old system. The reformative effect of a prison sentence depends on the influences to which the convict is exposed. With free association between prisoners, it is not the best men that make their influence felt. In the seven years the system has been in operation at Auburn, it has not proved itself to have increased the prisoners' self-discipline, their sense of honor or their will to do the right thing.

At all the institutions I visited that did not have self-government, I discussed the system with the warden and other officials. They all, without exception, held approximately the same views as Dr. Heacox.

My personal impressions of conditions at Sing Sing and Auburn were not good. The behavior of the prisoners verged on defiance. During working hours in the shops, one heard whistling and loud talk and saw prisoners taking it easy with their feet on benches and tables, unconcerned even when officials entered the room. Groups of prisoners who were not working wandered about the place, smoking and reading newspapers. The atmosphere was very disorderly, the prisoners ignoring the most elementary rules of conduct. When I was shown around by the chaplain, no one thought of standing up or taking off his cap. An occasional prisoner gave us a nod and a "morning, chaplain!" I spent a Saturday, Sunday and Monday at Auburn. There was no work on Saturday afternoon, but all the prisoners (1,254) were out in the recreation yard watching a baseball game between their own team and one from the town. Those who were not playing wandered about in the most uninhibited fellowship. Most of them were watching the players and followed the game with raucous comments, yells and whistles. In one corner of the yard, some of the men lit a fire and cooked various victuals they had gotten hold of. On Sunday morning I attended the Protestant service. The preacher had no pulpit, but strolled around on the stage. He behaved in a much more relaxed fashion than is customary in our churches. His sermon was frequently interrupted by laughs from the congregation and was followed by thunderous applause. At two o'clock in the afternoon there was a performance by a third or fourth class touring theatrical troupe, consisting of twenty-odd actors, about half of them males and the rest females, most of them colored. For almost two and a half hours, they performed a series of the craziest, most licentious skits, with songs, cancan, negro slapstick. All this went on in the church. In the semi-darkness of the hall, actresses in short skirts and plunging necklines wandered among the prisoners. At the end of the show, the sergeant-at-arms came onto the stage with the manager of the troupe, harangued him in a well-phrased address, bestowed on him honorary membership in the Mutual Welfare League and decorated him with the League's medal of honor. A couple of hours later, several films were shown in the same locale. These, too, were of the craziest variety, with the actors chasing each other over the most unlikely obstacles, upsetting shelves and cartons over themselves, and so on. This performance also lasted about two hours. As a matter of fact, movies were shown every evening.

In our prisons we have done too little to entertain the prisoners. Here they have gone to the opposite extreme. This was *panem et circenses*. The Mutual Welfare League was primarily occupied with arranging distractions for the prisoners. The quality of the programs is indicated by what has just been related. During their stay at Auburn or Sing Sing, prisoners might gain the impression that amusement is the content and meaning of life. When one recalls that it is these very burlesque shows and similar distractions offered in the cities that have been the downfall of so many, it hardly seems logical to provide still more of the same fare in the prisons. The only justification would be if the prisoners were to acquire an aversion for distractions from over-indulgence. As the situation is here, with ball-games all Saturday afternoon, entertainment all day Sunday, and movies every evening, there is little opportunity for intelligent and uplifting distractions like reading, etc. As Dr. Heacox said, it is not difficult to understand why more prisoners were reformed under the old regime.

The fact that the self-government method has turned Auburn and Sing Sing into caricatures of prisons does not mean that it would be incompatible with good order in a prison to give the prisoners a somewhat greater opportunity for self-control and self-discipline—self-government seems to me an unfortunate term. The leadership and administration of the prison can only be exercised by those who are responsible for finances, who determine the daily schedule, the regulations, the fare, etc., who decide on work programs, purchases of equipment, and so on. It is a fact that a freer treatment of convicts, which leaves more to their sense of honor and of responsibility, makes greater demands on the warden than the old authoritarian system.

Osborne, who initiated the self-government system at Auburn and Sing Sing undoubtedly lacks some of the most important qualities needed for such a difficult task. The individual who occupies such a position must first and foremost be a healthy, normal male. The more experienced reader of Osborne's book, *Society and Prisons*, will understand that he in fact lacks the qualities in question. This impression was confirmed by men who knew Osborne well.[12]

Alexander Paterson, the prominent English penologist, was of a different opinion. Like Omsted, he had made a study of the system on the spot, and he wrote about Osborne:

His was a brave experiment, but for its success it demands someone who has exceptional personality. It is easier to find a hundred good wardens who will control their prison by the usual weapons of authority, with the inevitable resort in the last instance to force, than it is to find a single man who can maintain not merely order but a healthy morale in a democratic prison governed by a representative body of prisoners. As in all forms of democratic government, there is always a danger that the worst men will become interested in prison politics from the worst possible motives. . . .[13]

Osborne started two associations for reformative activity in the penal system. They merged in 1933 and took the name of the Osborne Association with headquarters in New York, which was a delayed rehabilitation of the great penologist, after his death, as is customary. The Osborne Association sponsors studies of the conditions in penitentiaries and institutions for juveniles. Meantime, the Mutual Welfare League at Auburn was disbanded in 1929 following a prison uprising which, according to the testimony of the warden of the prison, could not be blamed on the League.[14] The prominent penologist, Lewis E. Lawes, also found it necessary to dissolve its counterpart at Sing Sing.[15] The whole concept had lost touch with reality. What once had been a treasured privilege had been turned into a self-evident right, liberated from the responsibility that goes with a privilege.

Makarenko

Since Communist ideology based on the writings of Marx and Lenin builds on collective responsibility, cooperation, and training, it is natural that something like "self-government" would play a significant part in various kinds of institutions in the Soviet Union. This became the case soon after the revolution in both penal and particularly juvenile institutions. The foremost exponent of the training methods used on young criminals in the Soviet Union is Anton Semjonovitch Makarenko.[16] He was a pupil and a great admirer of Maxim Gorki. In 1920, he was entrusted with the responsibility for a small reformatory for homeless, so-called wild children (besprisorniki), near Poltava in the Ukraine. For a long time he tried using kindness and understanding, but the hard-boiled and experienced young criminals, responded with arrogant scorn, until one day he lost his patience and reacted to an insolence with a sharp blow. The boy burst into tears and was comforted by Makarenko, who at the same time informed the whole group in a loud clear voice that from now on a beating could be expected by anyone who disobeyed him. The youngsters realized that Makarenko had their best interests at heart, but that he was not going to coddle them and that he also knew how to use his fists—personal qualities that usually command respect and obedience in youth institutions. From that time on, Makarenko maintained firm, but at the same time understanding and well-intentioned discipline. He named the institution the Maxim Gorki Work Colony. There over a period of five years he evolved the principles for the treatment of unmanageable children that he further refined in the Kuryasch reformatory (five miles from Kharkov in the Ukraine), to which he moved with his wards in 1926 (which also bore Maxim Gorki's name).

Makarenko used to say that if a child starts misbehaving, it is not the fault of the child but of the methods used in his upbringing. He did not believe that such things existed as morally defective individuals. He was convinced that, if you place them in a normal environment, make normal demands on them, and give them normal opportunities to live up to these demands, they will turn into ordinary people. At the same time, Makarenko excepted "organically" handicapped individuals from his theory.[17]

It was not until Makarenko took over his third institution that he embarked on his experiments with self-government in earnest. This institution was for youngsters in need of vocational training—located near Kharkov. By this time, Makarenko had come to the attention of the Commission set up by the Central Committee of the Communist Party in 1921 under the direction of Felix Djershinski, father of the Soviet police system, for the purpose of establishing and supporting institutions for children and young people. Makarenko's new institution was called the Djershinski Commune. It was organized in the following manner:

The pupils—boys and girls—were divided into a kind of family groups *(otrjad)* of seven to fifteen members. Each group had a superintendent *(kommandir)*, who at first was appointed by the institutional management but later, when the group had achieved sufficient maturity to take part in the self-government program, by the pupils themselves. Under Makarenko's system, the groups were kept together during working hours as well as leisure time and at night in a common dormitory. Twice a month all the pupils gathered for a meeting *(obsjtsjeje dobranie)* in order to elect a Presidium and various committees responsible for administrative matters, order, hygiene, etc. Day-to-day business was handled by a council *(soviet kommandirov)*, consisting of all group leaders. All these citizenly activities were supervised by institutional officials. The entire clientele consisted of up to 500 inmates.

Bolchevo

The extent to which Makarenko had access to publications dealing with comparable experiments is not known. In any case, no mention of this is made in his writings. During the eight years of his wardenship of the last-mentioned institution, his reputation as a skillful educator and administrator became firmly established. His methods were copied in other parts of the Soviet Union, including Bolchevo, the institution for homeless young delinquents near Moscow. After a modest beginning with about ten youngsters between the ages of sixteen and twenty, the colony grew to the point that in 1935 it had more than 1500 inmates and was one of the largest open institutions in the history of penology.

The activity of the colony became stabilized during the 1930s. Its clientele came from institutions within the Russian Soviet Federated Socialist Republic but could be remanded directly by the courts. The interesting feature of this colony is that it specialised in habitual criminals. While beginners in the ways of crime were also accepted, an investigation in 1933 revealed that the average number of sentences per inmate was at least nine. It is relevant that the R.S.F.S.R. also maintained certain open institutions exclusively for first offenders. The consensus was, however, that many recidivists really wanted to mend their ways but needed help to do so.

But how could one know who was sincere in his desire to give up crime? Decisions on applications for admission to Bolchevo were made in meetings of the general soviet, in which all the inmates participated. Among this great mass of young criminals who had all lived for varying periods of time in what is called the "underworld," there was always at least one who knew what manner of man or woman the applicant was, whether he or she had the character required to become a good citizen of Bolchevo.

Yes, man or woman. The institution was designed like a large village with a number of houses, mostly of barracks type, in which most of the inmates slept in large dormitories, but also some dwellings for families. There was also a special section for women with about 250 beds. Marriages between inmates were allowed, but only with the permission of the general soviet. Before reaching its decision, the soviet would determine whether the parties had advanced far enough in their vocational training to be able to take on the financial burden of a family and whether they were sufficiently "morally mature" to assume the responsibility for a family. Eventually there were so many married couples with so many children, almost 1000 in the 1930s, that special schools and various other children's facilities had to be built to accommodate them.

In principle, the administration of the colony was managed by the prisoners themselves, various boards and committees for different purposes being appointed by the soviet. Officials were few; in addition to the warden, there were a few physicians, teachers, and engineers to run the workshops. The latter were concentrated on the manufacture of special products, particularly sporting goods, including skiis, sleds, rackets, footwear, and gymnasium equipment, for which Bolchevo received prizes. Beginning with only a few primitive workshops, Bolchevo had built up large modern factories by the 1930s. All working prisoners were paid the same wages as civilian workers. They paid their own way and contributed to the common expenses of the colony from their earnings. According to an official report, the institution was self-supporting as of 1930 and had begun to amortize the initial expenditures by annual payments to the government.

After six months of faultless behavior at Bolchevo, the "colonist" was entitled to a one-day leave. This privilege could then be repeated every third week, and free time was usually spent in Moscow. It was forbidden to possess or drink alcoholic beverages in the institution, and card-playing was not permitted. Chess was a popular pastime, and billiards was allowed. Like all the great civilian manufacturing enterprises, Bolchevo had an extensive recreational program primarily of an educational and cultural nature. Lectures, concerts, and theatricals succeeded each other; courses in general studies or special studies in drama; dance and voice were available; and extensive sports activities were naturally a part of the program since the majority of the inmates were relatively young.

Obviously, infractions of regulations and other offences occurred. These matters were brought to the attention of the general soviet meetings, which could cancel leaves, impose fines or isolation for up to one month, and even decide that the offender should be excluded from the community, which meant transfer to an ordinary prison.

Discharge was also decided on by the soviet—regardless of the duration of the sentence which might have been fixed by the court. If he wished, the dischargee could remain at Bolchevo as a free worker, something that very rarely happened in the 1930s. The rate of recidivism was believed to be approximately ten per cent, but the information on this point is vague. Only under exceptionally extenuating circumstances could a recidivist Bolchevo colonist be re-admitted to the institution.

Bolchevo was closed soon after the outbreak of World War II, as was the case with a large number of "Makarenko colonies." By that time, conditions in the Soviet Union had been stabilised to the point where the problems of the "homeless" were considered to be non-existent. Moreover, these colonies had gradually been de populated. [18]

[15] PROBATION

Thacher

As far back as records go, we find many examples of sentences not being executed, either because the convict was pardoned by the monarch or by decision of the court. In the latter case, the courts usually attached some condition to the sentence, a proviso that "he mend his ways." As the great German jurist, Franz von Liszt, pointed out, *liberatio conditionalis* (conditional release) from jails was very common as far back as the Middle Ages, particularly in Italy and in the German city, Augsburg.[1]

In its regular form, this meant that the court first established guilt, i.e., conviction, and then pronounced the sentence deserved by the convict, but added a clause postponing its execution. If the convict committed a new crime, the first sentence also went into effect automatically.

In England, with its judicial system based as much on precedent, *common law*, as on written law, *statute law*, a number of different ways by which the convict could get out of the sentence he actually deserved were devised through the years. For example, there was the *benefit of clergy*, the privilege of the clerical estate, which gradually was extended to all citizens.[2] However, this rule of exception was mainly used to lighten sentences, primarily the death penalty, but not to cancel them entirely. Another example is *judicial reprieve*, which means that for some reason, often because the prosecution appears to have little basis in fact, the court postponed passing sentence. Then we have *recognizance*, an obligation binding the accused to behave himself in the future, in default of which he would be summoned to appear in court once again. *Binding-over*, a term that came into use much later, was approximately the same as recognizance. All the three sanctions mentioned could be associated with bail determined by the court, which was paid by the accused himself or by someone who was willing to act as his guarantor. The bail was forfeited if the accused failed to discharge the obligation. Finally we have the term *filing*, which meant that because of extenuating circumstances or some other legitimate reason, the court filed its findings in a register or the archives without handing down any definitive decision. In principle, the documents could be retrieved at any time thereafter and the suit carried through to completion.[3]

In England, as in the United States, private individuals had frequently paid bail for the release of friends and relatives with no sentence or only a minor one, when in the years 1823-43 Peter Oxenbridge Thacher, a district judge in Boston, Massachusetts, introduced the method of allowing young offenders, in particular, the privilege of recognizance. In the annals of the day, there was special interest in the Chase case, which Thacher described in a book about his court decisions. Young Terusha Chase was tried in 1830 and found guilty of crime on her own admission:

> . . . but upon the application of her friends, and with the consent of the attorney of the commonwealth, she was permitted, upon her recognizance for her appearance in this court whenever she should be called for, to go at large. It has sometimes been practiced in this court, in cases of peculiar interest, and in the hope that the party would avoid the commission of any offense afterwards, to discharge him on a recognizance of this description. The effect is that no sentence will ever be pronounced against him, if he shall behave himself well afterwards, and avoid any further violation of the law.[4]

Thacher's method was sanctioned by law in Massachusetts in 1836, but its application was specifically restricted to petty criminals:

> This alteration consists in the discretionary power proposed to be given to the courts and magistrates, before whom this class of offenders may be brought, to discharge them, if they have any friends who will give satisfactory security for their future behaviour, for a reasonable time. When such securities can be obtained, it can hardly fail to operate as a powerful check upon the conduct of the party, who is thus put upon his good behaviour.[5]

John Augustus

The next scene is also set in Boston, this time in the police court in August, 1841.

> I was in court one morning, when the door communicating with the lock-room was opened and an officer entered, followed by a ragged and

wretched looking man, who took his seat upon the bench allotted to prisoners. I imagined from the man's appearance, that his offence was that of yielding to his appetite for intoxicating drinks, and in a few moments I found that my suspicions were correct, for the clerk read the complaint, in which the man was charged with being a common drunkard. The case was clearly made out, but before sentence had been passed, I conversed with him for a few moments, and found that he was not yet past all hope of reformation, although his appearance and his looks precluded a belief in the minds of others that he would ever become a *man* again. He told me that if he could be saved from the House of Correction, he never again would taste intoxicating liquors; there was such an earnestness in that tone, and a look expressive of firm resolve, that I determined to aid him; I bailed him, by permission of the Court. He was ordered to appear for sentence in three weeks from that time. He signed the pledge and became a sober man; at the expiration of this period of probation, I accompanied him into the court room; his whole appearance was changed and no one, not even the scrutinizing officers, could have believed that he was the same person who less than a month before, had stood trembling on the prisoner's stand.—The Judge expressed himself much pleased with the account we gave of the man, and instead of the usual penalty,—imprisonment in the House of Correction,—he fined him one *cent* and costs, amounting in all to $3.76, which was immediately paid. The man continued industrious and sober, and without doubt has been by this treatment, saved from a drunkard's grave.[6]

The narrator, John Augustus, a prosperous shoemaker in Boston, has been called the world's first probation officer. He was born in 1784 and died in 1859. At the time of his death he had bailed and supervised 1,152 male and 794 female probationers, the majority of whom remained on "the straight and narrow path." Augustus's interest in social problems extended over wide areas. He obtained permission to visit prisons, and there, too, he often was able to lend a helping hand financially so that prisoners could be released. He was particularly concerned with alcoholics, but he did a great deal for neglected children and immigrants. He sometimes had as many as 15 persons living in his home, and he established a special shelter for the young women in his charge.[7] Augustus must be recognized as a great reformer; and, as is the fate of reformers, he also encountered strong opposition. In the eyes of many, his activity was considered to be dangerous to public respect for the law, and he was always in trouble trying to defend himself against those who believed that all criminals must be severely punished for their misdeeds.

Fortunately, Augustus was on a good footing with the Boston judges, who appreciated his interest and were happy to allow him to carry on his benevolent activities:

In 1847, I bailed 19 boys, from seven to fifteen years of age, and in bailing them it was understood, and agreed by the court, that their cases should be continued from term to term for several months, as a season of probation; thus each month at the calling of the docket, I would appear in court, make my report, and thus the cases would pass on for five or six months. At the expiration of this term, twelve of the boys were brought into court at one time, and the scene formed a striking and highly pleasing contrast with their appearance when first arraigned. The judge expressed much pleasure as well as surprise, at their appearance, and remarked, that the object of the law had been accomplished, and expressed his cordial approval of my plan to save and reform. Seven of the number were too poor to pay a fine, although the court fixed the amount at *ten cents* each, and of course I paid it for them; the parents of the other boys were able to pay the cost, and thus the penalty of the law was answered. The sequel thus far shows, that not one of this number has proved false to the promises of reform they made while on probation. This incident proved conclusively, that this class of boys could be saved from crime and punishment, by the plan which I had marked out, and this was admitted by the judges in both courts. [8]

Fortunately, there were people willing to continue Augustus's work, among them the prison chaplain Rufus R. Cook and several members of the Boston Children's Aid Society. On the whole, these successors to Augustus based their activities on the methods he had developed in his 18 years of experience. Augustus had come to the conclusion that efforts should be concentrated on first offenders "whose hearts were not wholly depraved, but gave promise of better things." [9] He often made exeptions to this rule, but never took a criminal under his protection who did not expressly request it or without having carefully studied the case and without familiarising himself with the background and the personality of the individual in question. [10]

The duties Augustus set up for himself were to watch over his protégés' general behavior and to make certain that they attended school regularly or found a respectable job. He often gave them a roof over their head either in his own home or with someone else. [11]

It is to the credit of the effective work done by Augustus and his followers that a law was passed in Massachusetts in 1869, according to which a State official would be charged with investigating all cases of children brought to court. The official was to be present at the hearing and was to arrange for the placement of the child in a foster home or elsewhere, if the court so decided. In 1878, the State legislature ruled that Boston was to have a probation officer. The former chief of police, E.H. Savage, was chosen for the assignment, thus becoming the world's first full time government-employed probation officer. The probationary period varied between three months and one year. In 1880, the legislature went the whole way and gave all the cities in Massachusetts the right to appoint probation officers. Not until 1891, however, did probation become a regular practice in all of Massachusetts with the passage of a law permitting lower courts to appoint probation officers. In 1898, the higher courts were also given the same authority.

It was not until 1897 that another American state, Missouri, followed the example of Massachusetts. Things moved faster from then on, and at the turn of the century, six states in addition to Massachusetts had introduced probation.

From the judicial point of view, probation in Massachusetts meant that the *final verdict was postponed*. Not until the probationary period had elapsed did the court determine the sanction, which, if the offender had behaved well, would usually consist of a small fine. Missouri took a different approach. Sentence was pronounced but its *execution was postponed* and could be annulled at the end of probation. Probation was intended primarily for younger criminals, and some states reserved it for that category only. After the first American juvenile court was established in Chicago, the probation system developed at a much faster pace, and, by about 1912, practically all the states had legislation providing for juvenile courts and probation. However, it took a much longer time to extend probation to adult criminals also.[12]

Developments in England

England had more or less kept apace with the United States. As early as 1820, the Warwickshire Quarter Sessions had introduced a practice whereby children accused of crimes could be sentenced to one day in prison on the condition that the parents or employer promised to exercise better supervision over the child in the future. Matthew Davenport Hill, whose name has already been mentioned on several occasions and who had served as a lawyer in Warwickshire as a young man, introduced the same method when he was appointed Recorder in Birmingham in early 1841. Young criminals brought to court for the first time were frequently remanded by Hill to the care of their parents or other guardians. With the cooperation of the local chief of police, Hill then exercised supervision through delegates who visited the released children in their homes. The results of the investigations were carefully entered into a special register which was begun in 1842.[13]

Another judge also, Edward William Cox in Portsmouth, was widely known for his use of conditional sentences. He employed a person to supervise the behavior of those given conditional sentences. Cox's interest was mainly concentrated on first offenders and juvenile criminals.

In the course of the nineteenth century, various associations had been formed by individuals and by social and religious groups with the purpose of preventing crime, especially among young people. In 1756, the blind, humanitarian London judge, Sir John Fielding, and Jonas Hanway (mentioned before) had formed the Marine Society, which persuaded the courts to hand young boys over to it rather than to send them to jail. In other words, the formation of the Police Court Mission by the Church of England Temperance Society in 1876 was not a revolutionary innovation. The most important task of these missionaries was to reform individuals who had been arrested for drunkenness and were to be tried in a police court. This activity was soon extended to include the placement of women and young girls in suitable homes and to help both adults and juveniles arrested for misdemeanors to find employment. The missionaries were also charged with the supervision of criminals released on probation. This work was mainly confined to London and other large cities. The London judges also adopted a different method than the one used by the Warwickshire judges and Matthew Davenport Hill. Instead of imposing sentences of one day in prison, they began to release offenders without any formal sentence on the condition that a police court missionary took the responsibility for them. In other words, the recognizance method.

It was not until 1879 that the first British law regulating conditional sentences was passed. It was called the Summary Jurisdiction Act and stipulated specifically that the courts for misdemeanors, i.e., Courts of Summary Jurisdiction, were to grant conditional release to the offender on the condition that he could be recalled to the court if necessary and that he behaved well. Although this law said nothing about supervision, it is nevertheless regarded as the original statute for legal supervision of convicts. The year before, Massachusetts had passed its law, which was made known in England through the efforts of the Howard Society, later better known as the Howard League for Penal Reform, which exerted all its influence to bring about an elaboration of the existing British legislation. The principal objective was to establish a regular system of supervision by paid employees. An amended law came about in the Probation of First Offenders Act in 1887, but it, too, contained no rules for supervision. It was not until the Probation of Offenders Act was passed in 1907 that a true organization of state-employed probation officers was founded. The same Act made it possible to use probation for recidivists.[14]

Probation on the March

The conditional sentence was now going ahead full steam in all countries with civilized judicial systems. In 1884, the French Senator, René Bérenger, recommended *sursis*, i.e., postponement of execution of sentence, which came to be the most usual form in Europe. Belgium passed a law in 1888 based on Bérenger's proposal; France not until 1891. In neither case, however, was any provision made for supervision. This seems to have been due to the aversion caused by earlier police supervision of persons sentenced for political crimes.[15]

In Prussia, a royal decree in 1825 provided for the pardon of two young boys sentenced to hard labor for one and two years, respectively, on the condition that they were taken care of by an association for the care of neglected children (*verwahrloste Kinder*) and that the sentence would be enforced if they did not reform. The decree also authorized the courts to follow the same procedure "in exceptional cases." Conditional pardon by decision of the sovereign on the recommendation of his minister of justice became the legal device preferred by the German states in general, beginning with Saxony in 1895.[16] Denmark and Italy also used conditional pardon to begin with. The Danes adopted postponement of execution by decision of the court in 1905, at which time Norway had been using the system ever since 1894.[17] Sweden followed suit in 1906.

True probation, with personal supervision and individual assistance to the offender, had greater difficulty in gaining general acceptance. However, the question of short prison sentences had now become a subject for discussion between jurists and others interested in penological problems, as had the question of special courts for juvenile offenders.

Probation in its various forms is now firmly anchored in the legal systems of the majority of economically and socially advanced nations, and the scope of its use is increasing steadily. In a thesis published in 1948, the Danish Knut Waaben's explanation of this was: "We have seen ample proof that severity promotes criminality. All we can do is to put our hope in special forms of reprimands and upbringing." [18]

Meanwhile, if conditional sentence becomes so common and is administered so automatically that it is generally regarded as merely a warning, then a reaction can be anticipated. The latter did, in fact, come about, as will be shown later.

[16] THE NORWEGIAN GUARDIANSHIP COUNCIL

Getz

Americans are generally given credit for having created the first juvenile court, established in Chicago in 1899. However, similar arrangements were in existence in Australia in 1890.[1] In reality, Norway deserves the honor of having been the first country in the world to organize a true judicial apparatus for determining the treatment of juvenile offenders. This came about on the initiative of the great Norwegian jurist, Attorney General Bernhard Getz. Getz was the chairman of the Criminal Law Commission, and his draft of a law on the treatment of destitute and neglected children was published in 1892.

In this draft, he discussed the question of which organ should have the power to decide the treatment of young offenders in a reformative setting. Getz did not believe that such decisions should be in the hands of the ordinary courts. In his opinion, it was not so much a question of examining evidence and evaluating specific actions as of the living conditions and the character of both child and parents. Such matters, he pointed out, are often ill-suited as evidence in a court, but should be understood at first hand, which cannot be expected of a court composed of a magistrate and two lay-judges. At the same time, Getz did not want to put these cases under the jurisdiction of a municipal organ such as the local school board or welfare agency. In his opinion, it would be reprehensible to transfer decisions of such import as the separation of children from their parents from the state, where they rightly belong, to local agencies. He then presented the Committee's findings:

> On the basis of these considerations, the Committee recommends the establishment of a corporation, which would represent both local personal and professional expertise, the community as well as society at large, and the members of which would mainly be recruited among individuals whose occupations bring them into contact with the lower classes.

This corporation would not function as a court with normal legal procedures. On the other hand, the present system, under which decisions can be made without any firm foundation on which to build, is equally unsatisfactory. It is also peculiarly Norwegian to discard, even in the most important cases, all established forms as soon as a decision is to be reached administratively rather than in a court of law. It is therefore proposed that meetings be called by the corporation, to which all the interested parties should be summoned and at which they would all have an opportunity to be heard. It is likewise unconditionally recommended that an investigation be made of the child involved and of his home. This would make it possible for the parents to be in contact with the highest executive authority, which would alone be responsible for any action taken, except in certain exceptional cases.[2]

The new organ, which Getz modestly called the "Corporation," was named the Guardianship Council (vergeråd) by the Criminal Law Commission. The name of the law was also changed to "Law on Compulsory Upbringing." According to the bill drafted by the Commission, there was to be a Guardianship Council in every commune. It would consist of the local magistrate as chairman, a minister, a physician, one member of the school board and two members of the welfare board. The law was to apply to all children under the age of sixteen. But the age of criminal responsibility—eligibility for indictment and sentence according to the penal code—was to continue to be fourteen years. Thus, two alternatives were available to the fourteen to sixteen-year-olds, namely, punishment or training. The Commission's recommendations were presented in 1892.[3]

Court or Not

By 1893, a bill was introduced into the Storting (the Norwegian Parliament) by Minister of Justice Ole Anton Qvam (The title had now been changed to "Law on the Treatment of Neglected Children.") However, not until 1896 did the Parliament finally reach a decision on what at that time was a very remarkable concept. The bill of 1893 was revolutionary in the sense that the "mandatory woman" was brought into the picture. The two members of the welfare board proposed by the Commission were reduced to one, and a "Woman Resident in the Commune and Willing to accept the Task" was added.[4] Finally, in 1896, the bill was brought up for debate. This time, the spokesman for the government was Prime Minister Francis Hagerup, a prominent jurist. The number of mandatory women had now been increased to two.

The argument in the parliament concerned primarily the position of the judge and the connection with the penal system. A strong faction advocated associating the Guardianship Council Law and the exercise of its functions with the school. The children also had to be educated and, it was claimed, the school board would be the logical agency to administer the Guardianship Council Law. Some members insisted that judges should play no part whatever. The school board should either exercise the functions of the Guardianship Council or elect a purely municipal committee for the purpose. Others favored including a judge, but not as chairman. The reason given for excluding the judge, or at least for not giving him the chairmanship as a matter of course, was usually that the heart of the matter was to reform delinquent children, not to punish them. According to this school of thought, it was essential to avoid as far as possible the atmosphere of criminal court proceedings. The claim that it would be difficult to ensure a fair evaluation of the circumstances by a group consisting solely of municipal officials was also disputed. These officials had proved themselves quite capable of handling comparable matters in other contexts.

A very interesting statement was made in the course of the debate by Qvam, who, as already mentioned, had introduced the bill in 1893. He said in part:

It appears from the paragraphs of the first chapter of the Law which have been adopted so far that the Guardianship Council will have the following function: To determine whether a child has committed a crime or whether the parents or guardian of the child have shown such depravity or neglect that the child might become morally depraved; or to determine whether such circumstances exist that the child's morals will suffer if the authorities do not intervene. Further, it shall determine whether the parents' relationship is such that the child should be taken from them. These are questions of such decisive importance to the entire future of individuals and also of such great significance to society that every precaution must be taken to ensure their wise solution. As far as I know, such cases are handled in court in all other countries except our own. . . . As I have said, they must be handled under the most trustworthy circumstances. If one reads the rest of the proposition, it is clear that they must be resolved only after thorough preparation and after a final hearing has been held, which in principle coincides with existing court procedures. This final hearing should be conducted in accordance with our most recent procedures, which are based on the principles of direct encounter and oral reports. In short, a hearing at which the decision-making authority has an opportunity to see as well as to hear the witnesses and also the individuals whose fates are to be decided. How, then, should we organize the court that is to have this authority? It has been found impractical to hand these cases over to the *lagmandsret* (district court), the *meddomsret* (ordinary court of the first instance with one judge and two lay-judges), or to a single *underdommer* (judge of the court of the first instance). The *lagmandsret* is certainly sufficiently well organized, but it would involve an overly complicated procedure. The *meddomsret* is too weakly constructed to be trusted with the final decision, and this is naturally even more true of the single judge. Were such a weak court to be utilized, it would be necessary to establish a strong and reliably constituted supervisory court. But that would entail the entire proceedings being repeated before this court; one could also transfer the oral proceedings into written reports, but nowadays this is considered completely undependable. Consequently, all that remains is to try to establish a justiciary body strong enough and varied enough in its composition to be completely trustworthy. It is on the basis of these considerations that the Guardianship Council institution is founded. It seems self-evident that a judge should be included among the members of the Guardianship Council. It seems equally self-evident that the chairman of the board should be a judge. We know of no court where the chairman is not himself a judge, and to us, who were involved in the preparation of this proposal, it seemed unnatural to establish a court where the judge would not be the chairman.

Qvam stressed repeatedly that the Guardianship Council was in fact a court of law. However, his views were countered by the following arguments:

The decision to take a delinquent child from its parents and put it in a rescue institution is not a matter for the courts. It should be a decision made by the members of the school board, the men who have been entrusted with the child's future. There is nothing about a judge that makes him more qualified to arrive at the correct decision. In fact, the school board is better equipped to reach the right judgment. It is, after all, the school board that has handled these matters hitherto. Why does it suddenly become a risk to allow it to retain its authority under even more fixed, correct and safe rules than previously?

This view was expressed by Cabinet Minister Wollert Konow. Another speaker, Prime Minister Johannes Steen, found it absurd to remove the category of juvenile criminals from the jurisdiction of the criminal courts by fixing the age of criminal responsibility at 14 years, as proposed, and at the same time to continue to claim that decisions should be reached in the same way as at an ordinary trial.

> In my opinion, this is contradictory to what is said to be the intention: On the one hand, decisions have been made to cover certain age groups, i.e., the years when children are in school and those immediately thereafter, and, on the other hand, to treat children in a fashion or at least according to procedures and rules from which they have been exempted. [5]

The argument ended in a compromise: the judge was included, but not automatically as chairman. At the same time, he was to conduct proceedings as far as hearing sworn witnesses, etc., was concerned.

Theory versus Practice

The law was put into force and the Guardianship Council began to be tested in practice. The first major discussion of the workings of the system was generated in late 1907 in a novel by Björn Evje, a former teacher and house-father in a reform school for boys, who wrote under the pseudonym, Mikael Stolpe. The book follows the young boy Jan Vik from the day when the Guardianship Council decides to place him in a "school home" until he is discharged, a total wreck, several years later. Stolpe's attack was primarily aimed at the big reform schools. Since he claimed to be describing unvarnished reality, his book gave rise to heated discussions in the press and to official investigations (which partly substantiated his accusations), and to the formation in 1908 of what was known as the School Home Committee. The Guardianship Council was also the subject of debates in the Norwegian Parliament.

Stolpe's description of the Guardianship Council is highly malicious. Here we see the authoritarian judge acting as chairman, conducting the proceedings with a strong hand. Some of the members agreed slavishly to everything he said, the most typical of these being the mandatory female member, the wife of a bank manager. Others held their tongues, until finally the judge ran into opposition from the typesetter Rode, who is portrayed as the one who is actually in the right. He objected both to the handling of the case and to the decision, but encountered an almost solid wall of opposition from the others.

The majority of Guardianship Councils were naturally outraged at Stolpe's grotesque and prejudiced description of their activities. In a parliamentary debate on the Councils in 1912, however, he was partly supported by the Socialist clergyman, Alfred Eriksen, who expressed himself:

I have been a member of the Kristiania Guardianship Council since the beginning of the year. We meet about once a fortnight. I am a member of the section which includes . . . . the entire east end of the city, where there is most to do. I joined the Council without any exaggerated belief in the kind of treatment they administer. By now I have attended many meetings. Usually the meetings have a very tight schedule to follow. We start at five o'clock in the afternoon and can spend fifteen minutes on each case—that is how precisely we are regulated. We get going around five to five-thirty, and in the course of the evening, from about five to eight o'clock, we go through twelve to sixteen cases, deciding whether a child should be taken from its parents, considering where children might be placed far out in the country in strange environments, reaching judgments on their offences, or considering placement in a reform school. It is easy to imagine the quality of this kind of deliberations. As I have mentioned, I did not join the Council with any great expectations or believing that it would be an enviable position. At this point, I will not treat in any detail what I will be saying in my views of the various paragraphs. Let me say, however, that during my time on the board, I have been surprised at the way the Guardianship Council has functioned. At meeting after meeting I have felt more and more intensely that the law must be changed and that the changes must be in the two directions already pointed out by the majority of the social council. We must establish more satisfactory rules for deciding whether a child shall be removed from its home. Today these rules are not precise enough. I have already mentioned several examples of how easily the Guardianship Council changes its decision when someone with authority intervenes in a case.[6]

The Guardianship Councils themselves made a number of statements that recommended changes. It seems clear that they found their task to be relatively tricky. The work load was always heavy and working conditions were unsatisfactory. A child welfare committee was appointed in 1915 to continue the reform of the system. After studying all the problems involved, the committee reported that the principles on which the new system was based appeared to be correct and that no evidence to the contrary could be found during the period the law had been enforced. It was then considered unnecessary to examine in detail the questions that had been raised concerning the introduction of an agency of a more judiciary character, e.g., special juvenile courts.

Tove Stang Dahl, a research scholar at the Institute for Criminology and Criminal Law at the University of Oslo who had been given a fellowship to investigate Norway's child welfare system, reported:

> It is thus clear that the Guardianship Councils were *not* intended to be courts of law. The subsequent discussion also proves that there was a fear of giving the Councils a too obvious judicial appearance. Consequently, several spokesmen in the debate on the Guardianship Law were opposed to having a judge serve on Councils. It is another matter that the Guardianship Councils were regarded as judiciary bodies in the eyes of the general public, as well as of the administration. In reality, it can be claimed that the Councils functioned as a kind of juvenile court. For example, some of the rules of criminal court proceedings were applied in the handling of Council cases. In its treatment of delinquent children, the Councils actually functioned as a court. I therefore find it appropriate to compare our system to the Chicago juvenile court.
>
> The aversion to the similarity between the Council and a regular court was continually expressed in certain circles, and in the law of 1953 concerning the protection of children, which superseded the Guardianship Council Law, a judge was not included as a permanent member of the Child Welfare Board. This also was in line with the opinion of the Committee on Child Welfare that the number of mandatory members of the Council should be decreased. The Committee felt that the presence of a judge was not needed to ensure correct and wise treatment of a case. At the same time, his presence might be required in certain controversial cases (including those in which a child was placed in a foster home against the wishes of the parents). Therefore, it was felt that a judge should be at the disposal of the Council for advice when required. The Committee justified the change by arguing that it would diminish the work load of the judges and by recalling the objections to the presence of a judge in the old Guardianship Councils.[7]

Sweden followed suit in 1902 with its *child welfare boards*, Denmark in 1905. Child Welfare Board also became the new name for the Norwegian Guardianship Councils. The Scandinavian system of boards operated by the municipal government acquired a special character. In other countries, the juvenile court institution developed along varying lines, sometimes as a responsibility of lay judges (always assisted by a legal adviser), as was to a great extent the case in England, sometimes as a section of the regular court in Germany and France, or as an independent court in some of the American States. Probation became a special form of treatment in these boards and courts, not a suspended sentence. Instead, the latter evolved within the framework of penological policies designed for adult criminals and the older category of young offenders. [8]

[17] THE SHORT, SHARP SHOCK

Wigram

During the second half of the nineteenth century, strong forces were at work to eliminate short prison sentences on the grounds that they did not act as crime deterrents, but instead accustomed criminals to prison life and removed the fear of this form of punishment. Franz von Liszt and many other great names in the International Union of Penal Law, which was founded in 1889 and which held the view that sociological as well as juridical considerations should be applied to crime and punishment, were strong advocates of this theory. [1]

The English Howard Society also was propagating for the increased use of the conditional sentence, but some of its influential members clearly regarded this as dangerous. One of the latter was the Secretary General, William Tallack, who, in a book published in 1889, made a strong case for the advantage of confinement to a cell even for petty criminals. He wrote that "Penal deterrence, so essential to tame the ruffian, and to warn the dangerous elements in the community, must be rendered *more* penal than hitherto, instead of less, by means of an intenser and therefore necessarily shorter, application, of strict and hated cellular separation."[2]

The Gloucester prison once more comes into the picture at this point. In the 1880s, the courts in that country regularly punished all crimes of theft, regardless of the amount of property stolen, with severe cellular treatment for one to two months, "after which the impressions of prison life remained vivid and disagreeable." For a second offense the thief was sentenced either to two months in a cell followed by two years of police supervision or to six months in a cell plus four years of police supervision. A third offense gave a long period of hard labor. The Gloucester authorities took excellent care of released convicts, found them work with employers who were first told of the prison sentence by the man himself or, if the latter preferred, by the local chief of police. Tallack claimed that both sides were satisfied with the system. Having nothing to hide, the ex-convict need not fear exposure and perhaps dismissal from his job. The employer, in turn, had not been kept in the dark.[3]

Speculating on the problem, Tallack came to the conclusion that deterrence and resocialization cannot be combined with any great hope of success. To illustrate his point, he related a story about a slaveholder who was flogging a slave and at the same time submitting him to religious harangues, causing the victim to protest: "Massa, if floggee, floggee; and if preachee, preachee; but not floggee and preachee too!"[4]

Tallack then proceeds to the question of the short prison sentence for juveniles. He refers to a Judge Knox Wigram, who protested in a book against affixing the prison stigma on young criminals and also questioned the wisdom of protracted treatment in a reformatory setting for petty criminals. Wigram wrote:

> It would be an immense boon if there were some legitimate way of ordering a boy or girl to be locked up, in solitude, for twenty-four hours, either at a police-station, or at some other place, perhaps still more suitable. There would be no romance about it; nothing heroic, no prison experiences to boast of. The "obstreperous" boy or board-school truant, locked up alone for twenty-four hours or so, with nothing in the world to do, bread and water in extreme moderation, and a plank for the night, would have tasted punishment in its purest form. He would understand that he had been treated as a child. He would not have liked the treatment, nor the being delivered at his father's door next morning—like a parcel—with one shilling to pay. (Quoted from Tallack.)[5]

This was an idea worth thinking about, according to Tallack, who goes on to describe the Dayfeeding Schools in Aberdeen, introduced in 1841 and actually intended for poor children who came voluntarily, but also with a "special class" for thieving children remanded by the authorities.[6]

Jugendarrest

The ideas expressed by Wigram were germinating in the minds of many others. It was generally agreed that prison sentences should be avoided for the youngest offenders. But it was also believed in many quarters that a suspended sentence or referral to a child welfare institution was not always a suitable reaction to an offense committed by a young person. The German educator, F.W. Foerster, had in several contexts, including a book published in 1911, *Schuld und Sühne (Crime and Expiation)*, advocated *Jugendarrest*, juvenile detention, combined with hard work.

> It is because of the demand for a gradation of punishment that in some cases, e.g., grossly unbridled behavior or insubordination, we resort to deprivation of liberty. Then, the function of the punishment is to bring the culprit to his senses *(Besinnungsstrafe)*. In not a few cases, even harsher detention combined with fasting would be called for. Complete fasting on one or two days a week, but adequate nourishment on the other days, is in no way harmful to health, may in fact be beneficial, and such chastisement is extremely painful and thus suitable for the young—particularly in cases of brutality. Why not adopt this simple method in such cases rather than always resort to the brutalizing system of flogging? [7]

Foerster's views with roots in the ancient Christian concept of chastisement as a *"medicamentum spirituale"* [8] were taken up in German legal circles on several occasions and finally were incorporated in a proposal for *Jugendarrest*, which was presented by the professor of criminal law, K.F. Schaffstein, in 1936. The idea interested the Nazi rulers of Germany, particularly the then undersecretary in the Department of Justice, Roland Freisler, and a law on the subject was passed in 1940. However, the formulation in Nazi terms was far removed from the intentions of a man who fathered the idea. "Foerster's sublime concept of a punishment designed to bring the victim to his senses was degraded by Freisler into a method of inflicting suffering through a psychic shock, an approach that to this very day in a misleading fashion haunts German juvenile justice and the discussion about *Jugendarrest*," according to Professor Rudolf Sieverts. [9]

The Nazis used *Jugendarrest* as one means of keeping an eye on young people who tried to shirk their duty to their country's industry during the war. When the war was over, however, and the Germans began to rebuild their country, *Jugendarrest* was dropped by East Germany on the grounds that it was a Fascist-capitalist invention. The West Germans, on the other hand, retained the system.

Jugendarrest was an important element in the law on juvenile courts passed in West Germany in 1953. It consists of three different varieties:

1. *Freizeitarrest* (Leisure-time arrest) from Saturday afternoon until Monday morning, for one to four week-ends.

2. *Kurzarrest* (Short-term arrest) for young people who do not normally have their week-ends free. Two days of short-term arrest are considered to correspond to one week-end of leisure-time arrest. This form of arrest may not exceed six days.
3. *Dauerarrest* (Long-term arrest) for at least one week and at most four weeks.

The German juvenile court legislation differentiates between three age groups: children under 14 years *(Kinder)*, youngsters between the ages of 14 and 18 years *(Jugendliche)*, and "pre-adults" *(Heranwachsende)*, i.e. young people between 18 and 21. The youngest group cannot be held responsible for criminal offences but, if necessary, may be handed over to the child welfare authorities. The intermediate group comes under the jurisdiction of the juvenile courts, while the oldest youth category *may* be treated in the same way as the intermediate group under 18 years.

Three types of sanctions can be applied to young criminals in the age group 14 to 18 and, to a certain extent, young people up to the age of 21, namely:

1. *Erziehungsmassnahmen* (Training sanctions), which may consist of rules of conduct that must be observed, of supervision, or of special educative arrangements.
2. *Zuchtmittel* (Correctives), meaning either a warning or an order to undertake certain duties, or a sentence to *Jugendarrest*.
3. *Jugendstrafe* (Youth prison), for at least six months and at most five years.

Thus, *Jugendarrest* is not a penalty from the legal point of view. The young person sentenced to it is not legally condemned. He is not listed as having a criminal record, but his name is merely inscribed in the court register, from which it is removed when he reaches the age of 25. In this way, the social stigma of a prison sentence is avoided.

According to the legislation, the treatment during *Jugendarrest* is intended to awaken the youngster's "sense of honor" *(soll das Ehrgefühl des Jugendlichen wecken)* and to make him understand that he must take the consequences of the illegal deeds of which he is guilty. Persons sentenced to leisure-time detention shall be confined to a cell for the entire period and may not encounter their peers. On the other hand, complete isolation is not necessarily the rule for those sentenced to long-term arrest. Old jails, frequently adjacent to the courthouse, are usually used for leisure-time and short-term arrest. The young people sentenced to leisure-time arrest turn up at these jails on Saturday afternoon at the hour determined. They are admitted and locked up in their cells where they remain, often without any attention, until they are let out on Monday morning. Long-term arrest is usually better organized. The youngsters are kept occupied and spend certain hours of the day together at games and other recreational activities and also at work. Visits to the institution are also permitted in some cases. Special institutions for clientele sentenced to long-term arrest are also being considered.[10]

A Swedish penal official who studied the treatment of young criminals in Germany wrote in *Kriminalvården*, the journal of the Correctional Administration of Sweden:

The persons under arrest are locked for the duration into single cells, where they are occupied with assembling industrial products, etc. The treatment also includes an element that to us is peculiar and unknown. According to the law, every prisoner may be submitted to "strict days," when the diet is reduced and the prisoner is compelled to sleep on a wooden bench with a slightly elevated head-rest. He is allowed no pillow and the bedding consists of a blanket only. In one of the custodial places I visited, the only food provided on these days was a small loaf of bread plus a "water soup" for dinner, while at the other one the only difference in the food was that the bread was served dry and dinner was less filling than usual. The number of "strict days" varies, but as a rule includes the first and last days of the sentence.

Opinions differ widely concerning the treatment as a whole. At the first detention institution—in Remscheid/Westphalia—the judge of the juvenile court appeared to feel that he should do everything in his power to exert a positive influence on the inmates. For example, each youngster had to write an essay after his admission. The theme is set by the judge and varies from case to case. One may be asked to write about his crime, another about a play he has seen, a third about some special experience. After work the inmates are permitted to borrow books dealing with their fields of interest or other serious literature. Thrillers and light fiction are forbidden. Each inmate may only have one book at a time, and a new one may not be borrowed until he has written down his thoughts or reflections about the previous one. The treatment also includes private conversations with the youngsters under arrest. On some evenings the inmates gather together to listen to a lecturer or to discuss political and other problems under the leadership of the judge or a teacher. The judge of the juvenile court in Remscheid was of the opinion that enough could not be done during the institutional period to exert a positive influence on the inmates. The judge regretted deeply that treatment could not be continued after discharge from the institution. The reason for this was that *Jugendarrest*, unlike *Jugendstrafe*, is not a criminal sanction, and juveniles under *Jugendarrest* may not be subject to any kind of after-care once they are discharged. During *Jugendarrest* the offender shall be made to understand that he has behaved wrongly, but after he is released he shall once more regard himself as a free and irreproachable citizen.

In contrast to the treatment at Remscheid, we have the method applied in the detention institution in Hamburg. It is noteworthy that the latter institution has been regarded as a model for *Jugendarrest*. There it is believed that each individual treatment should be adapted to fit the purpose of *Jugendarrest*. Thus, books, lectures, etc., are only rarely permitted in Hamburg. While they are under arrest, the young people are kept in complete isolation, and the solitude—and perhaps also the lack of occupation—is intended to force them to concentrate their thoughts on their predicament, the effect of which, according to the judge of the Hamburg juvenile court, will be lost if the inmates are submitted to too much "treatment." All kinds of treatment, it was claimed, no matter how well thought out, soon comes to be regarded by the inmates as a kind of diversion with the result that the entire juvenile arrest system finally becomes watered-down and meaningless. (Quoted from Augustin.)[11]

Although originally intended as a harsh warning to the young offender and in no way planned for rehabilitation, it is obvious that treatment efforts have, in some institutions, been added to such an extent that the original idea is almost completely replaced by a quite opposite one, as exemplified by the following anecdote:

A couple of years ago, I incidentally broke a journey in a small German town. It was Sunday. While waiting for a train, I strolled around in the quiet streets and happened to pass by the provincial court house. I entered and saw a sign, *Jugendarrestlokale*. I asked an attendant if I could see the inmates. Yes, he said, but there is nobody inside during the day. "We have one boy, but as usual he is with the judge's family." I asked to see the judge, who lived in the court house, and was admitted to a garden. There I found not only the judge and members of his family but also the juvenile offender. The judge explained to me that he always used the *Jugendarrest* legislation this way. The juvenile came on Friday night and slept in his cell. On Saturday morning he was brought out to converse with the judge and his wife and children, as well as with "useful friends of the judge," called in to talk with the boy. At night the boy returned to his cell to sleep. His cell was not even locked. "We eat together, the boy plays games with my children and their friends, sometimes they even go out together to a football game or some other event. We have several talks, about serious as well as trivial things, the boy, myself, my wife, and my visitors, among whom I can count upon the assistance of specialists in medicine, psychology, education, social welfare. I always sentence the young culprits to four weekend arrests. At the end of the fourth time we know each other rather well. The boy usually gains confidence in me, and I am myself better advised on how he should be helped than when I first saw him in the court room." [12]

This little story is quite significant of what always happens when educated people (and those with a keen interest in others) become responsible for the treatment of delinquents.

The German juvenile arrest system is based entirely on the assumption that it will serve as a kind of warning signal to the youth that he had better abstain from illegal activities in the future. It should be, as it was expressed, "a shot fired in front of the prow" to check the vessel's dangerous course. In 1955, the ministers of justice of all the states of the Federal Republic of Germany issued joint directives concerning the application of *Jugendarrest* to all prosecutors in juvenile cases. Certain of these directives are quoted below:

1. *Jugendarrest* is an appropriate disciplinary measure in cases of relatively innocuous offenses by otherwise well-behaved young people, who it is believed can still be reformed through a brief but severe period of incarceration, during which they are compelled to reflect on their situation, and through the restrictions placed on them while they are under detention.
2. This form of discipline does not appear to be suited to young individuals who are truly delinquent or so mentally retarded that they do not understand the purpose of *Jugendarrest*.
3. It is not compatible with the objectives of *Jugendarrest* to apply this sanction indiscriminately to all juveniles brought to court for the first time.
4. Particular attention must be paid to the question of sentencing a young offender who has already undergone *Jugendarrest* to the same sanction for a new offense. It may well be advisable to impose a longer period of arrest following a sentence to leisure-time arrest. On the other hand, it probably usually serves no good purpose to resort to *Jugendarrest* in the case of a young individual who has already undergone a longer period of such detention and shortly thereafter commits a new offense. Unless a real juvenile penalty appears to be indicated in a case of this kind, it is advisable to choose some other type of sanction, which will have a more permanent reformative influence on the young offender.

. . . .

7. If a sentence to *Jugendarrest* is imposed, it must not be formulated so as to give the wrong impression that it constitutes a true penalty.

The use of the terms "penalty" and "punishment" must be avoided in connection with *Jugendarrest*.

8. If there is reason to fear that the young person will be discharged from his job or expelled from vocational training because he has been sentenced to *Jugendarrest*, the judge or, at his request, the case worker should contact the employer or the one in charge of the vocational training in question to explain the legal character and reformative intent of *Jugendarrest*. The same applies to cases in which the youngster, if he is a schoolchild, is threatened by reprisals on the part of the school resulting from the sentence. (Quoted from Sieverts.)[13]

The outcome of a system of treatment depends in the highest degree on the nature of the clientele selected. The Germans admit readily that juvenile court judges have not always understood how to make a good selection. According to a paper submitted to the Committee on Crime Problems of the Council of Europe, *Jugendarrest* is considered to be particularly suited to the following categories of offenders:

1. Offenses in which the youth has acted irresponsibly;
2. Offenses due to youthful arrogance or ruthlessness (physical assault, damage to property, libel, etc.);
3. Offenses connected with activities of particular interest to young people (driving without a licence, theft of technical articles);
4. Offenses deriving from youthful defiance (resisting a police officer or some other official, unjustified absence from school);
5. Offenses resulting from youthful adventurousness;
6. Offenses due to the youth having been misled;
7. Minor accidental misdemeanors. [14]

The attitude to *Jugendarrest* varies widely in Germany. It happens that juvenile court judges are accused in social welfare circles of using *Jugendarrest* as a kind of "convenience." It is an easy way out for a judge who feels he must react in some way to a juvenile offender, it does him no great harm, and possibly complicated extra-institutional measures that would otherwise be called for can be avoided. From the point of view of the penal administration, leisure-time arrest is a troublesome form of treatment, since most of the clients come in for the week-ends, leaving the institution empty for the rest of the week. The personnel hangs around with little to do on weekdays but overworked on Saturdays and Sundays. Modern penologists also have very little interest in the purely afflictive sanctions, preferring a form of deprivation of liberty that permits them to use their therapeutic methods. Furthermore, it is obvious that the German version of juvenile detention is in no sense innovative, despite the myriad of publications that have tried to make it seem so. On the contrary, it represents a return to the penal methods tested as long ago as in the San Michele prison for boys in the eighteenth century.

The majority of the youngsters themselves seem to be favorably disposed to *Jugendarrest*, and the system has been copied in other countries, e.g., the Netherlands.

Detention Centre

In the course of the discussions in England that preceded the 1947 Criminal Justice Bill, the desirability of abolishing short sentences to deprivation of liberty for juveniles was emphasized. It was agreed that the system of treatment should, in principle, be split up, in the first place into forms under which the youth need not be removed from his home and, in the second place, into forms which required care in an institution. It was soon agreed that the former would consist of fines, probation, absolute or conditional discharge, and a new variety, i.e., treatment in an *attendance centre*. The last-mentioned meant that the youngster would be ordered to spend a few hours on a specified day in an institution, usually headed by the police, where he would be put to work or occupied in some way. This order might be imposed for a sequence of days. With regard to the treatment that was to be given to institutionalized young people, it was agreed that there should be supervisory homes, e.g., probation hostels and remand homes, designed for relatively short stays and usually combined with an investigation of the offender's need for treatment, as well as approved schools, borstal training, and prisons for long-term treatment. But some form of short-term treatment was also required for young offenders who needed a thorough "shake-up."

The discussion ended in agreement concerning what was called a *detention centre*, a jail-like place but not a real jail, in which the youngster would be submitted to what was given the catchy name of "short, sharp shock" treatment. The idea was that young people who were believed would benefit from this "jolting" treatment would not have to be housed in local jails, in which little could be done to help them. The Advisory Council on the Treatment of Young Offenders undoubtedly considered that its main task was to remove young criminals from ordinary prisons and, in order not to provoke needless opposition from the advocates of the so-called tough line, chose to make the proposed short-term treatment prison-like. The Advisory Council's proposal was adopted and incorporated in the penal legislation of 1948. Since then, the detention centre has put down such firm roots in the British penal system that the 1961 Criminal Justice Act states that the objective is to abolish prison sentences for criminals below the age of 21. As we will see, however, the entire dispute is a matter of terminology. One might say that jail has been replaced by a jail with another name. The first institution, which was opened in Kidlington, near Oxford, received many visitors and was long the focus of a lively discussion on the forms of treatment of young offenders. Many asserted that it represented an ominous step backward. Others were pleased with the strict discipline in the institution, and a few considered that prison sentences were still the best medicine for such scoundrels.[15]

A Swedish visitor gave the following report in the periodical, "Kriminalvården":

This form of penalty has already become very popular in the courts and a sharp increase in its use has probably been checked primarily by the limited number of places available. The fact that the inmates are given effective physical training in the space of a short period is said to be one of the advantages of the system. Contamination of inmates by other inmates is claimed to be prevented through intensive activity. Youths who have got into trouble through mischief are deterred from further crime. The institutional period also provides intensive training in personal behavior and hygiene. At present, sentences to a detention center may be imposed for between three and six months. The law is being amended to raise the maximum period to nine months. Up to one-sixth of the institutional period may be remitted for good behavior. The former inmate is not put under supervision, but previous conditional sentences are not abrogated by the sanction, and many inmates are nevertheless under supervision after discharge. The introduction of aftercare is being considered. There are currently twelve detention centers in England with a total population of approximately nine hundred. The institutions are of two kinds: Junior Centres for the age group fourteen to seventeen and Senior Centres for the age group seventeen to twenty-one. Each institution serves its own district, and the court is obliged to contact the institution before imposing a sentence to make sure that the youth in question can be accommodated. Only one sentence to a detention centre is permitted.

In view of the low recidivist rate shown by studies hitherto (approximately 27 per cent), it is considered to be probable that the detention centre is the right answer for those juvenile offenders in whom the causes of their criminal behavior is not to be sought in serious psychical defects or environmental damage. But I encountered strong suspicion of this form of punishment, particularly of a more general use of it, in many quarters. It was pointed out that only a very small number of juvenile offenders are completely free from hereditary or environmental defects and that the great majority of those who would be sentenced to detention centre if the use of the sanction were expanded would certainly be young people who could not be expected to be resocialized by a treatment designed purely to deter them from committing crimes, without taking into account the factors causing the criminal behavior. It was also pointed out that the detention centers were being compelled little by little to discard their purely repressive methods and to adopt the positive borstal forms of treatment. Thus evening courses have recently been started in detention centres also and, as already mentioned, it is intended to introduce a system of after-care.

The daily schedule in a detention center is very strictly regulated, almost in military fashion. Discipline is severe, there is strong emphasis on physical training, and exemplary behavior is required of the inmates. The pace is fast, and recesses are few and far between. The compulsory evening courses were one exception to the military routine. They were given by civilian teachers, in what appeared to be a relaxed and pleasant atmosphere. The inmates' privileges are extremely restricted. Smoking is forbidden, only one visitor a month is permitted, only one letter may be sent and one received weekly. All personal belongings are forbidden, including rings, photographs, etc., and furloughs are obviously not permitted. Personal relationships between staff and inmates are presumably non-existent. On the other hand, the standards of behavior required of the personnel appear to be very high, and great care is taken in the recruitment of staff members in order to avoid sadistic or domineering tendencies. The following daily schedule at one senior center is probably typical:

06.00:   Morning call
06.15-06.35: Calisthenics
06.35-07.00: Bedmaking and tidying of rooms
07.00:   Breakfast; change to work clothes
08.00:   Assembly for inspection and departure
                  for place to work
08.15-11.50: Work
11.50-12.10: Change for lunch

```
12.10-13.00:  Lunch followed by change back
                  to work clothes
13.00-16.45:  Work
                  —interrupted by a one-hour break
                  for calisthenics
16.45-17.00:  Change for tea
17.00:        Tea followed by social period until 18.15
18.15-19.45:  Evening courses
20.00:        Supper
20.30-21.00:  Social period
21.00:        Bedtime
21.30:        Lights out.
```

In the junior centers, where many inmates have still not completed their compulsory schooling, work is exchanged for lessons during the school terms. (Quoted from Karlström.)[16]

The British penal administration wrote in a report to the Council of Europe:

Detention centres are places of security but they are not comparable with prisons as regards the normal security arrangements of the latter. In the majority of cases there are wire perimeter fences, locked doors and window mesh, but a prison atmosphere is avoided as far as possible. Security is attained by the supervision and vigilance of the staff, careful organisation and by the cooperation of the inmates. From the beginning the centres have been smart and brisk places with a strict and firm regime. In every respect of life at a centre the highest possible standard is required at the highest possible tempo. The boys are required to be alert, well-mannered, punctual, clean and tidy. The community in which they live is one in which the second best is not accepted.

Formally, the attitude of the staff may be sharp and exacting: no nonsense is tolerated. But this is not regarded as the whole of their duty. They are expected to be as much concerned with the character and quality of their boys as they are with the outward standards of discipline, and a considerable amount of moral and civic training is achieved by staff during the day and evening apart from the periods of direct instruction arranged for this purpose.[17]

The last point is significant and, as already mentioned, things have developed along the usual lines. Since the selection of personnel has been careful, those chosen have gradually put ever-greater emphasis on "moral influence," as it is called in England. The outward disciplinary framework has come to play a subordinate role, without being entirely discarded. Or, as the head of the section for detention centers in the British prisons administration stated in a discussion in the Committee on Crime Problems of the Council of Europe: "about all that remains of the short, sharp shock is that it is short!"[18]

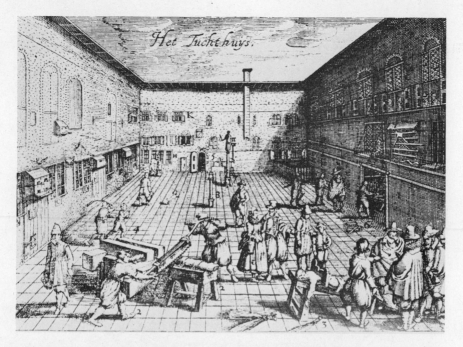

1. Amsterdam's Rasphuis in 1614. (From Thorsten Sellin, *Pioneering in Penology*, Philadelphia: University of Pennsylvania Press, 1944)

2. Workroom of the Spinhuis in 1783. (From Thorsten Sellin, *Pioneering in Penology*, Philadelphia: University of Pennsylvania Press, 1944)

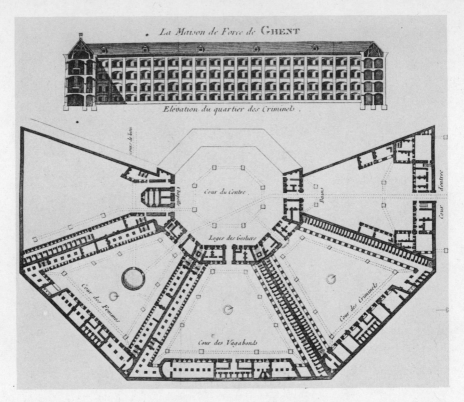

3. Architect Malfaison's sketch for the octagonal prison in Ghent. (Vilain XIIII, *Mémoire* etc., Gand: Pierre de Goesin, 1775)

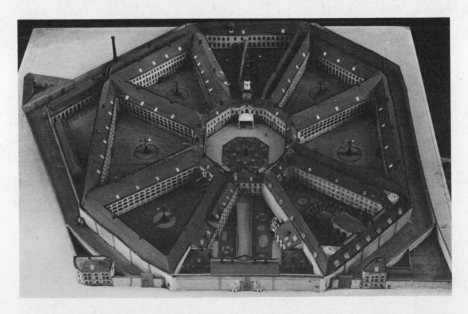

4. A model of the finished octagonal Ghent prison. (Photo taken with the permission of the Belgian Prison Administration)

5. An English jail in the 18th century. (From Joseph Adshead, *Prisons and Prisoners*, London: Longman, Brown, Green and Longmans, 1845)

6. Single cell, occupied by a man sentenced to life imprisonment in chains, in 1847, at the Swedish Carlsten's fortress prison. (Photo owned by the Nordic Museum, Stockholm)

7. The still existing San Michele prison in Rome. Exterior view.

8. Interior of San Michele prison. (Both photos owned by the Italian Prison Administration and taken in 1970)

9. **Cherry Hill prison.** (From G. de Beaumont and A. de Tocqueville, *Du Système pénitentiaire aux États-Unis* etc., Paris: Fournier, 1833)

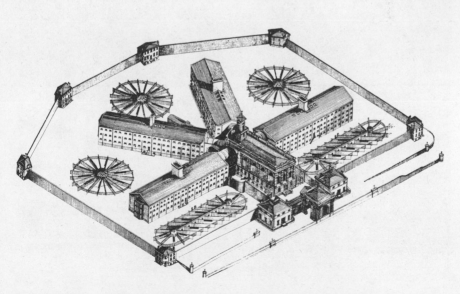

10. **Architect's sketch of the Pentonville Model Prison in London.** (From Joseph Adshead, *Prisons and Prisoners*, London: Longman, Brown, Green and Longmans, 1845)

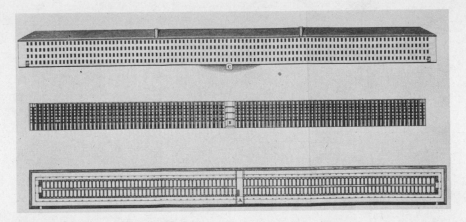

11. **Sing Sing's first cell block.** (From G. de Beaumont and A. de Tocqueville, *Du Système pénitentiaire aux États-Unis* etc., Paris: Fournier, 1833)

12. **The panoptical prison at Stateville, Illinois.** (Federal Bureau of Prisons, Handbook of Correctional Institution Design and Construction, Washington: Government Printing Office, 1949)

13. The Karlskrona prison in Sweden, built 1851, and model for a small cellular prison with less than 100 inmates. (Author's photo)

14. Inside view from top floor and cell at the Karlskrona prison. (Author's photo)

15. Exercise yards at the Karlskrona prison. (Author's photo)

16. Individual boxes in a Swedish prison church. (Photo owned by the Swedish Correctional Administration)

17. **Parade at Elmira.** (From S.J. Barrows, *The Reformatory System in the United States*, Washington; Government Printing Office, 1900)

18. **The original "Rauhes Haus".** (Photo owned by the Rauhes Haus)

19. The Mettray reformatory. (From M. Bertin, *Colonie Agricole et Maison Paternelle de Mettray*, Paris: Rue Cherubini, undated)

20. Highfields. (From Lloyd W. McCorkle, Albert Elias and F. Lovell Bixby, *The Highfields Story*, New York: Henry Holt and Company, 1958)

21. Various views of the Roxtuna Psychiatric Institution for Young Adult Offenders are shown in the following five photographs. (Photos owned by the Swedish Correctional Administration)

(a) An aerial view.

(b) Exterior view of medium security cottage for nine inmates at Roxtuna Psychiatric Treatment Center for Young Adult Offenders.

(c) Interior view of living room of medium security cottage with individual rooms in background.

(d) and (e) Interior view of individual rooms in medium *(above)* and minimum *(below)* security cottages. All inmates at Roxtuna have individual rooms.

22. Open institution for 120 inmates at Skänninge, Sweden. (Photo owned by Remnes Foto, Mjölby, Sweden)

23. Inmate's single room at Tillberga, a modern open institution in Sweden. (Photo owned by the Swedish Correctional Administration)

24. Individual cell at the Stockholm jail for prisoners awaiting trial. Every prisoner has an individual cell. (Photo owned by the Swedish Correctional Administration)

[18] WITZWIL AND THE OPEN INSTITUTIONS

Kellerhals

The Swiss had long been using convicts for all kinds of outdoor work under strict supervision—street-cleaning, road construction, ditch-digging—when in 1895 they built the institutional complex, Witzwil, in the canton of Bern, which with its numerous open sections was the signal for a new approach to the treatment of convicts. Like so many other experiments, this too was based on the personal belief of the institutional director that he was on the right track and also on his ability not only to operate his institution in such a way as to convince both inmates and personnel that he was right, but also to persuade the authorities and the general public of the practicability of his ideas. This Swiss innovator was Otto Kellerhals. He was an assistant to the governor in a conventional penitentiary when, at the age of 25, he was entrusted with the task of building with prison labor a new closed institution to replace the Bern jail, which was to be torn down to make room for the city post office. Two different schools of thought had been arguing about how the new institution should be planned. One side favored an ordinary cell prison with the separate system for the majority of the inmates and handicrafts in work cells. Opposed to this were representatives of the handicrafts who did not want competition from prison labor. Since the majority of prisoners were countryfolk, they should do farm work, according to this group, which also naturally exploited the old argument that outdoor work is good for criminals who have fallen into evil ways as a result of their over-indulgence in alcoholic beverages. The victory went to the second school of thought but, because of Kellerhals, the institution turned out much differently to what had been anticipated.[1]

In 1893, Kellerhals settled on a large farm, which not only accommodated him and his family but also the other employees and their families and the working team of convicts. The area was called *le Grand Marais* (the great swamp) and was quite barren. Some of the working group built roads; drained the soil which was then cultivated and planted; and bred livestock. Others built a jail of the conventional type with one hundred cells, kitchen, dining hall, and chapel. The work had progressed at a surprisingly fast speed; the order and atmosphere of the colony had been excellent and in 1895 it was established as an independent institution, Witzwil, with Kellerhals as its first governor.[2] In the same year, Kellerhals wrote a brochure in which he presented his views on the kind of treatment that should characterize the new institution. "Idleness is the mother of all vices," he gave as his motto and continued:

> Three things are important. First, that the work assigned to the convict suits as far as possible his capabilities and also makes him better equipped to earn his living after discharge. Second, that work in the institution is arranged so as to have a reformatory influence on the convicts. Third, that the work is organized in a practical fashion from the point of view of the institution itself and that it is reasonably profitable without, however, competing with the civilian market.[3]

These were hard conditions to fulfill, as Kellerhals was to discover. The fact that he had the support of the canton administration probably did not depend solely on their interest in reforming penal methods but also, as pointed out by the internationally recognized criminologist and professor of criminal law, François Clerc, that institutional costs could be reduced with Kellerhal's method.[4] At the end of 1895, the institution had 95 inmates and 14 employees.

A Danish Observer

In 1899 Witzwil was visited by the Danish prison official Adolf Goos, who commented:

> At the time of my visit, the institution had 104 inmates, most of whom were doing farm labor. A few, however, were working in shops as shoemakers, tailors, etc., but everything they produced was used within the institution.
>   It is only first offenders who are sent to the Witzwil Penal Institution and only men with sentences up to three years. They spend the first three months in cells and work together during the day, although they are confined in single cells at night. When half the sentence has been served, they are promoted to Class 2, where their earnings are larger,

where they are not under constant supervision at work, and where they are also eligible for more responsible positions, e.g., in the kitchens and stables. In the third stage of the sentence, they move up to sections of the institution where they live with the personnel and are treated almost as free laborers. In general the treatment is based on encouraging the inmates' self-respect by showing as much confidence in them as possible, on the condition that they do not abuse this. Means of chastisement are confinement to a punishment cell, demotion to a lower class and withdrawal of permission to work in the fields. The last-mentioned punishment is highly effective, according to the governor. The diet was the same as in the Neuchâtel Prison. During the three months the convicts spend in single cells, the institutional officials are supposed to get to know them but the governor assured me that he can only become genuinely acquainted with them when he gets them out in the fields. To my objection that working together with others entailed a danger that they would take up with bad company, the governor replied that they had no time to get into trouble, since they were kept at hard work without interruption and were then locked up in their separate cells. That the work was in fact strenuous is clear from the results achieved with the help of such a relatively small number of convicts. Nor should it be forgotten that the institution was spared the worst elements, since the clientele at the institution is confined to individuals under their first sentence to hard labor. Here, as at the Neuchâtel penitentiary, the inmates are comprised of both *"correctionels"* and *"criminels."*

No matter what one may think of the contrast between this treatment and generally accepted penitentiary principles, it cannot be denied that when one observes these men at work they make an excellent impression, physically at least. It was a pleasure to see them suntanned and vigorous in contrast to the pale and unhealthy appearance that always characterizes convicts who have spent a long period inside a prison. It was likewise a pleasure to observe the energy which the work was performed. They worked in columns, each one led by an employee, whose appearance differed so little from the convicts that at first glance it was difficult to distinguish him from them.

That escapes cannot be avoided in an institution which allows the inmates such a large measure of freedom as Witzwil is understandable. Last year six inmates escaped, but four of them were caught the following day. They were punished with the dark cell and did not try to escape again. There is a colony attached to the institution to which released convicts may go and where they are employed in the same way as the inmates.

Witzwil was unquestionably the most interesting penal institution I inspected, and it is impossible not to pay tribute to Kellerhals for the great and admirable work being done under his direction during recent years, which has led to the cultivation of large tracts of land that have now become very fertile. [5]

By the time of its 60th anniversary, the institution had grown to accommodate 400 convicts, three-quarters of them in open sections, and 91 employees. Over the years they had cultivated more than 6,000 acres of swampland and constructed 124 of the existing 152 buildings. The institution comprised five sections at the time it was shown to the delegates at the First United Nations Congress for the Prevention of Crime and the Treatment of Criminals in Geneva in 1955.

The oldest section, the Witzwil cell prison, was called the "barracks" and it was used for ordinary convicts who had not been sentenced during the past ten years and whose sentence did not exceed three years. There was also a large house, *Lindenhof*, for inmates sentenced to work training, with accommodations for approximately 200 young vagrants interned for one to three years, a clientele whom it is difficult to teach a liking for work and the patience to persevere at it. These inmates could be discharged when they had "learned to work." In addition, there was *Eschenhof*, a home for a total of 32 alcoholics who had been sentenced to deprivation of liberty during the past ten years or who resembled this unregenerate category "in character." Most of these men were not only alcoholics but also work-shy.

A story was related about a prisoner who begged Otto Kellerhals on the eve of his discharge to let him stay, since he had nowhere to go. Kellerhals arranged this and later on founded the work-home, *Nusshof*, which gradually came to accommodate 45 "colonists." Eventually, the clientele changed from unconditionally discharged men to mainly probationers who could not find employment and a place to live in the outside world. In 1955, these men could earn, in addition to free board and lodging, from one to three francs a day for their work and thereby save a little money. Many *Nusshof* inmates were found jobs with farmers and small businessmen in the neighborhood. Finally, there was the mountain colony, *Kiley*, which could accommodate 20 men who had shown themselves to be especially trustworthy and well-behaved, under conditions that were exactly the same as that of civilian life. [6]

Witzwil still looks the same today. Except for the closed section, it is the rule that all prisoners are employed at the many occupations represented in the institution as if they were free men. More than one-third work independently. When Kellerhals began, there were not many who believed that he would be able to get as much work out of the kind of inmates the institution had to deal with, most of them physically run-down and many mentally defective. However, with a simple kind of occupational therapy, Kellerhals and his coworkers managed to activate cases that appeared hopeless at the outset, starting off with easy and undemanding tasks and proceeding gradually to a completely normal work-load. On the whole, this pioneer institution has been successful. It had been estimated that it would take more than a hundred years to cultivate the extensive lands owned by the institution, but in reality it took less than thirty.

During the first few years, Kellerhals hoped that it would be possible to build dwelling-houses on the *Grand Marais* for discharged men who had become skilled farmers, able to settle down and support their families. However, this project proved to be impracticable. At the same time, serious efforts have been made, particularly while Kellerhals and later his successor and son Hans Kellerhals were in charge, to help the discharged to a new start in life.

After having spent some time in his home community in Neuenburger Jura, ex-inmate F. leased a piece of out-of-the-way land. But he lacked the necessary capital. In agreement with the social welfare authorities, we sold him a few cows on credit. We have visited him and observed how he and his family are struggling to keep the livestock and grazing ground in good condition. It took him years to pay off his debt to us. This year, however, we were able to buy a bull calf from him in final settlement of his debt. Thanks to wise cooperation between the institution and the social welfare authorities, a family could remain united in this way and a farm could be kept in operation. (Quoted from Hans Kellerhals.)[7]

No major disciplinary problems appear to have beset the institution. Minor incidents have inevitably occurred and inevitably have caused critical voices to be raised. Alcohol has been smuggled in; there has been the occasional fight; and employees have now and then been exposed to violence on the part of the inmates. Homosexual problems have arisen. But, it can be proved that escapees who have been caught and brought back have turned into elite prisoners.

It is not surprising that eighteen-year-old R. also sought relief from his worry by trying to escape, that he cut up his clothes in the tailoring shop and that he was difficult to manage for a long time. The son of divorced parents who remarried and then divorced again, he was sent first to foster parents and later to a children's home. After that he was sent to three homes for boys, one after another, then to three youth institutions and two reformatories for the unruly, and to six district jails before he was finally put into our hands. Gradually he also became a trusted inmate. (Quoted from Hans Kellerhals.)[8]

This is just one of thousand examples to prove that, given time and patience, something can be done with even the most hopeless cases. Furloughs from the institution were granted in 160 cases in 1962.

The men have returned from furlough with practically no exception. If someone happened to miss a train while he was having a beer in the station bar and later received a dressing-down from his immediate superior in the institution, the message sank in much better than if the governor himself had lectured him. (Quoted from Hans Kellerhals.)[9]

Followers

Witzwil soon awakened the interest of other Swiss cantons, which started similar institutions, and also abroad. The head of the Swedish Prisons Administration, Victor Almquist, visited *Witzwil* in 1907 and later organized the work training institution at *Svartsjö* along the same lines. As usual, however, it was first and foremost the Americans who quickly adopted the Swiss idea and developed it further. A Professor Fetter at Princeton University had written several articles in the journal, "The Survey," about *Witzwil*, and news of the institution had also come to the attention of the Americans through a book by Edmond Kelly in 1907. And, in 1915, the American penologist, Amos Butler, was able to open Indiana State Farm, which was closely patterned along the ideas on which Kellerhals' *Witzwil* was based.

Chino

The Americans introduced the new idea on a large scale almost immediately. In general, they organized camps or colonies for dependable convicts who usually worked in the forest or on farms, but a number of very large open institutions were also established at a rapid rate. One of them with a rather dramatic history is the Chino institution in southern California, a few miles from Los Angeles. It was opened in June, 1941, a strange phenomenon for those times.

From the beginning it was intended that Chino would be a completely ordinary maximum security institution for southern California, which would function with approximately the same kind of clientele as the San Quentin penitentiary outside San Francisco. An administrative building, one or two cell blocks for prisoners and a number of gun towers for armed guards had been completed and work on a wall had begun when the progressive and dynamic man who was to be the first warden of Chino, Kenyon J. Scudder, called a halt to all construction and requested permission to revise the treatment methods planned for the institution. (Scudder had previously been chief probation officer in Los Angeles and was convinced that he could manage Chino as a primarily open institution.) Being an exceptionally persuasive man, he was able to obtain a half-hearted promise from the California prison administration and the Governor of the state to try out his idea. If things went wrong, construction could proceed according as planned— and Scudder could be fired. [10]

The convicts were to be selected among inmates in the San Quentin prison, which Scudder visited to pick up the first group.

The men are brought down by Greyhound Bus, and I rode the first bus myself with two other Supervisors. We brought the men right out of the Jute Mill and the Main Line Mess and other places in the prison. There were many of them not having been outside the inner walls for many months. We had no handcuffs, guns or even locks on the bus. We took them out five or six times during the trip to enter the public washrooms in bus stations or in the gas stations on the way down. At six o'clock that night they came singing through the gate of the California Institution for Men. Since that day a fine spirit has prevailed.

We said to the men: "A cell is a cell if you make it a cell, or it's a single room. These are cells that we have to put you in, but we consider them as single rooms and do not lock the door. Six months from now we'd like to say that we've never had to turn a key in this institution. There are gun towers here that can be manned if you make it necessary. The gun towers are evidence of what the public thought we needed here. It's up to you as to whether we have to use them. The same applies to stringent regulations. We have no rigid regulations so far but can make them if the necessity arises." (Quoted from Handbook of American Prisons and Reformatories.)[11]

Scudder reported on his results in July, 1942, when the institution had been in operation for a year. Six hundred thirty-three men had been transferred from San Quentin. Of these, 11 had escaped but had been apprehended by the police and returned to San Quentin. There had been no disturbances in the new institution, and its inmates had made admirable contributions to the defense industry, which was of such vital importance in those days. The institution was now well established, and Scudder was allowed to continue to expand it with several new minimum security sections, but with a maximum security section also. A Swedish observer in 1950 reported on Chino:

It now comprises a main institution, entirely open, for 1,500 inmates, a few minimum security camps for a total of 400 men, and a maximum security observation institution for 300. The buildings are spread out and in general very handsome. Chino is a complete community with schools, a library, a hospital, factories, farms, a chapel and athletic facilities.

The closed section at Chino is used as a Reception Guidance Center, or observation center, for Southern California. All prisoners with sentences of more than one year are put through a period of observation by a team consisting of a psychiatrist, a psychologist, a sociologist, a social case worker, and a teacher. The inmate's life history and personal characteristics are compiled in a report on which decisions concerning his treatment are based (see below in connection with Adult Authority). During the observation period, the inmate is occupied with school work and a certain amount of vocational training, but primarily with a form of group therapy known as social living. Special problem films are extensively used in the group therapy sessions. ("You and Your Family." "Act Your Age," "The Feeling of Rejection," "Shy Guy," "The Feeling of Hostility," "The Feeling of Depression," "Problem Drinker," for example.) After the men have seen the film they discuss its contents. The group leader must be much more active in this form of group therapy than is usually the case.

The clientele in the open section of Chino consists primarily of men who are regarded as "good risks" for minimum security treatment, and most of them are first offenders. The institutional program is based on the following principles: The inmate shall not be treated as an ordinary convict but as a member of the Chino community. He shall be treated politely and with consideration for his feelings. He shall be encouraged to maintain close contact with his family and friends. The visiting rooms are attractively furnished, and there is a large and exceptionally beautiful park for visitors. The inmates are allowed to act as guides for visitors to the institution and to share responsibility for formulating the rules of everyday life. A special effort is made to foster religion in the institution.

The recreational program is very extensive. All kinds of educational and hobby activities are available. The industrial and agricultural projects provide jobs for the majority of the inmates, who also perform the routine tasks of the institution.

The Chino principles have unquestionably been successful as far as the calm and orderly operation of the installations is concerned. The convicts have been completely won over by the drive for courtesy, and it is hard to imagine a place where outward behavior among such a large group of men is so impeccable. The escape rate is very low, usually at most one per month. The camps, on the other hand, have a higher rate of escapes, i.e., six per month. (Quoted from Eriksson.)

The following comments on Adult Authority, quoted from the same source, may be of interest:

Since 1917, California belongs to the States that apply the system of relatively indeterminate sentences. This means that, when a court has adjudicated a case and imposed neither a conditional sentence nor a prison sentence of very short duration, the convict is put under the jurisdiction of what is known as the Adult Authority, an internment board which is on the whole free to decide when he shall be given his freedom. Judging by available reports, this indeterminate sentence appears to work satisfactorily. Far from wishing to restrict it, there are campaigns every year to have it extended to short prison sentences and to the area of conditional sentences.

The procedure with the Adult Authority begins with a thorough investigation carried out at a Reception Guidance Center (one at Chino, one at San Quentin). Six months later the convict appears before the Adult Authority for the first time. All five members of the board are State employees. They usually work in sections of two or three members. The first consultation with the Adult Authority lasts for an average of fifteen to twenty minutes. At that time the members of the board have already read the report from the observation institution.

The convict then meets with the Adult Authority at intervals during his imprisonment: when the board wants to review earlier decisions with the possibility of revision in mind, for example, the question of the institution in which the man should serve his sentence. In the case of convicted murderers, this review does not take place until seven years have been served. The same interval is required for convicts sentenced to life imprisonment. In the case of recidivists the period is one year before the completion of the minimum sentence fixed by the court. For others the usual interval is one year.

The Adult Authority has grown remarkably severe in the exercise of its function. It retains recidivists for long periods and establishes very precise rules for conditional discharge and also requires that these rules be meticulously observed. [12]

Natural Bridge

Another form of open institution in which the Americans have been pioneers is located near Natural Bridge, the well-known tourist attraction in Virginia, and is a good example of new approaches to the treatment of young offenders under minimum security conditions. The following passage is quoted from a Swedish report:

A large part of the American experiments take place in various kinds of camps. One example is the camp operated by the Federal Bureau of Prisons close to Natural Bridge, Virginia. It has accommodations for sixty young men, who are lodged in two relatively primitive barracks. The inmates are former pupils of the Federal Reformatory in Washington, D.C., who have applied voluntarily for admission to the camp. Pupils who are considered to be suitable for the special treatment at Natural Bridge are then selected from among those whose names are on the waiting list. The installation has been in operation since 1944. It works according to the counselor system. The treatment follows a highly consistent pattern and is based on the following main principles:

The entire staff consists of twenty-three persons, of whom fourteen belong to the counselor group. The chief counselor is in charge of the group. The camp director is a university graduate with experience as a case worker, and the same is true of the chief counselor. As of September 1949, eleven of the thirteen counselors held university degrees. Several of them were good athletes. All had a background of practical experience. One had been a teacher in a vocational school, one a chemist, a third a minister, a fourth a construction engineer, a fifth a professional baseball player, etc. Five were veterans of World War II. None of the counselors had prior experience of work in a correctional institution at the time of their employment. The Federal Bureau of Prisons therefore arranged for them to take several months of special training, during which the treatment program to be used at the institution was evolved in discussions. It is now patterned as follows:

The sixty boys are divided into six teams, each with one counselor as a leader and another as an assistant leader. The teams with their counselors develop a group spirit and compete with one another according to a rather complex system of grading for different kinds of accomplishment. The winners are acclaimed once a month and rewarded by excursions, etc. The work bonuses are low.

The counselors also serve as case workers for their own teams, but are not expected to have more than a superficial understanding of the other inmates. Each week the team has a session with its counselors during which everyone is free to speak his mind. The counselors also have frequent informal conversations with their teams about all sorts of problems. These conversations are intended to comprise the most important part of the life-training aspect of the program. The counselors work along with the boys rather than over them.

The boys in each team themselves select junior team leaders. The latter, in turn, constitute a Boys Council, which meets once a week with the personnel. The Boys Council has the special task of helping newcomers to adjust to life in the camp and of organizing recreational activities.

The daily schedule is as follows: 06.30: morning call; 07.00: breakfast; 07.30: work; 11.30: dinner; 12.15: work; 16.00: work ends; 16.30: supper; 17.00: recreational activities; 19.00-21.00: school work in classes; 21.30: bedtime. The day starts half an hour earlier in the summer. There is no real work on Saturday, but the inmates tidy the place, smarten up their appearance and organize a program for the evening. Movies are shown once a week.

At first a psychiatrist made regular visits, but this is no longer considered necessary, since all the boys have been thoroughly studied before their transfer to Natural Bridge and those who appear to need psychiatric help are instead moved to another institution.

Escapes are relatively frequent, about one in four inmates making a getaway. Escapees are usually re-admitted if they return voluntarily. Those who do not come back on their own accord may be taken in again on the condition that they have not committed a crime while they were out. Those who escape a second time are normally not re-admitted. (Quoted from Eriksson.)[13]

Things progressed more cautiously in Europe. The English opened their first minimum security institution in 1936 in New Hall Camp at the Wakesfield Prison. They began with 20 convicts, carefully selected from a prison for a select clientele, and gradually increased the number to about 80 with a staff of only six.[14] Not until 1947 was a second open institution inaugurated at Maidstone.[15] The Dutch experimented with an open institution at Veenhuizen (Norg) as early as 1918.[16] By the time of the Twelfth International Penal and Penitentiary Congress in the Hague in 1950, the Europeans still had little to report about experiments with minimum security institutions, with the exception of the Scandinavian countries.[17] But, things began to move faster as a result of the rapid increase in the number of prisoners that occurred in most countries during the 1950s. By the time of the First

United Nations Congress on the Prevention of Crime and the Treatment of Offenders in Geneva in 1955, a number of countries reported a strong interest in and experiments with open treatment, and a resolution was adopted at this Congress recommending expansion of this form of treatment. [18]

Helsinki Work Camp

One of the open institutions that aroused special interest after the Hague conference was the relatively new Finnish installation, the *Sjöskogs* Work Camp, which since 1958 has been known as the Helsinki Work Camp. What primarily astounded all visitors was, first, the large number of convicts (between 200 and 400)— and the small number of employees (only about a dozen, apart from foremen and administrative personnel) and, second, the fact that the inmates were paid the same wages as free workers.

Arvo Simula has described the camp in the periodical published by the Finnish penal administration. A summary of his two articles is given below:

The Helsinki work camp was founded on March 1, 1950, in the immediate neighbourhood of the Helsinki airport, and the Highways and Waterways Administration anticipates that, since the airfield and the closest housing area are still only thirty per cent completed, its operations will continue at least until 1970. The inmates are housed in simple barrack-like buildings. The administrative quarters are so small and provisional that it is impossible to convince some visitors that they have been used for years as the offices of the camp. There is no fence around the camp, nor are the doors to the houses locked. On the other hand, the inmates' range of movement is strictly regulated. It is therefore obvious that the small personnel must be constantly on the alert. It should also be noted that the girls who work in the canteen live in the camp area, as do the civilian workers employed by the Highways and Waterways Administration, which sometimes causes problems. Firmness as well as tact are required of the personnel to handle this delicate situation.

The inmates wear their own civilian clothes and hire work clothes from the camp for a moderate sum. Housing, bedding and other essentials are provided by the camp, but are paid for with twenty-five per cent of the daily earnings, calculated according to the average hourly wage. The inmates must pay for their own food, which is purveyed by the camp. In addition, deductions from the inmate's wage are withheld to cover income tax, family payments, forced savings, etc. The destitute inmate is given an advance, which is later deducted from his pay.

The responsibility for the camp is divided: the penal side is under the Ministry of Justice, the work side under the Highways and Waterways Administration. It cannot be denied that the camp personnel frequently run into knotty negotiation situations, in which they have to defend penal considerations against an apparently almighty employer. Questions of prestige and other petty interests naturally also come into the picture, and the results of discussions are frequently rather meager—as is often the case in labor relations. Cooperation with management on both sides is a peace-keeping strategy in which, as is true in the civilian market in our country, the stronger side is the victor. Nevertheless, a more positive aspect of continuing negotiations is that they give the representatives of management what we might call an invisible lesson in penal care and the handling of people.

The Helsinki work camp is the biggest one of its kind in the country. It is a kind of miniature society, for it comprises convicted men from various parts of Finland and all categories of individuals, including physicians, architects, engineers, judges, teachers, business leaders, artists, technicians, contractors and, of course, a majority of ordinary workmen. Seventy per cent are serving sentences for drunk driving. In addition, there are both fine defaulters and recidivists under prison sentences.

The foremost condition for success in running a work camp is the maintenance of order and discipline, but, because of the special conditions, different methods from those in closed institutions must be used to achieve this objective. Unexpected roll calls are frequent as one means of keeping inmates on the premises. Other practical devices have also proved helpful in supervision. For example, we often summon a man by loudspeaker to the office on some pretext or another. At the same time we can check whether he is in a normal condition, i.e., sober and clear-headed. If he does not appear at the office immediately, we find out whether he is up to mischief or if there is another reason for the delay. Since constant supervision is difficult, careful records are kept of everyone who is on shift work, is sick, or is engaged in some hobby outside his lodging. At the same time, all inmates are required to report at the office when they arrive and in connection with furloughs. Through these supervisory measures, the inmates learn order and discipline without even being aware of it. After all, their deficiencies in these respects have often been the cause of their criminal behavior. The supervisory system may appear to be weak in one sense, or even capricious, but this is not the case. On the contrary, it is highly effective, which was substantiated by the superintendent of a home for boys who recently served a sentence in the camp. He intimated that a prisoner could feel freer behind a high wall than here, where everyone voluntarily put himself in the neighborhood of a loudspeaker, since one could never know when one might be called to the office, which would entail an interrogation if one did not appear immediately.

If we examine the activity at the work camp and the life training we endeavor to provide, it is not difficult to find many problems, the handling of which requires a high degree of responsibility and unselfishness on the part of the small staff.

Fine defaulters and recidivists often return to prison as if they were coming home to rest. First offenders, on the other hand, arrive at the camp's provisional installations in a state of great confusion and insecurity and with preconceived notions, for many of them have lost their jobs and find themselves in an extremely precarious financial situation. Many of them are convinced that their marriage will break up. They have lost their self-confidence and all that remain are hate and a desire for revenge. Some of them do not understand how they got into such a predicament, against whom or what they must struggle. It has been claimed in numerous reports and committee findings that sentences to deprivation of liberty should be long enough to allow the institution's life training program to have a reformative effect on the inmate. This view is probably correct with regard to recidivists, but long sentences appear to have only undesirable and negative effects on first offenders. For example, long sentences easily lead to the severance of remaining family ties. Men remanded to a work camp are frequently under short-term prison or fine-conversion sentences, and public opinion unfortunately appears to be that no life-training work is required in these cases, that the loss of freedom in itself will be a sufficient deterrent. Personally, I cannot agree with this attitude after having observed these conditions at first hand. In my opinion, it is on these men that attention should be concentrated in order that their criminal tendencies do not continue to develop and thus lead to increased recidivism.

An individual who has presented himself to serve a sentence at the work camp is received with friendliness. He is given the camp regulations to read, and he is carefully instructed in how important it is that he become thoroughly familiar with them, because they protect him from misunderstandings and guarantee his legal rights. In addition, it is made clear to him that the fact that he has been accepted in a work camp is a sign of confidence which presupposes self-discipline, for the only individuals regarded as suited to a work camp are those who do not have a criminal character, who can subordinate themselves to the regulations without argument, and who are diligent workers. Finally, the hope is expressed that he will turn to an official if he has questions and not ask the advice of "experts" among his co-inmates, which will only confuse him. Through these frank and simple introductory conversations, we try from the very first day to get the inmate to understand that society and its servants are not fighting anybody, that the same hand that chastises also guarantees legal rights, whether we are at liberty or confined in a work camp. I have never failed to give my full attention to these introductory conversations, but I have also never seen their efficacy so clearly revealed as in this camp, where many have expressed special thanks at their discharge for the words they heard in the introductory conversations. The impressions made on the inmates in their initial contacts with the personnel appear to be of decisive importance for their positive development, for one accepts with confidence and frankness officials in whom one has confidence. This is the first objective, after which we can begin the requisite life-training work, the inmate having been brought to understand what is needed for his own good.

The selection of lodging is also of decisive importance to subsequent attempts to exert a good influence. While the placement of fine-defaulters seldom presents any great problem, since most of them are already known when they arrive at the camp, the placement of prison convicts is often difficult. The point of departure, of course, is that all inmates are equal. In practice, however, they must be lodged so that they have a chance to get on with their room-mates. If a physician and a workman who is neither intellectual nor interested in the world around him are lodged together in the same cottage, both of them will feel very lonely because their mental development and their experience of reality differ too widely. But the great problem in placement is caused by the recidivists. They often try to disseminate unfounded suspicion of the personnel and of society in general, for that matter. It is unfortunately also true that they frequently act as inveiglers, but at the same time are careful not to get into trouble by breaking rules themselves. For this reason, they should serve their sentences in ordinary prisons, but this is no solution either, because they write from prison to their sympathizers in the work camps and in that way exert such strong pressure that none of the inmates dare say a word for fear of reprisals even after discharge. In addition, they exploit accomplices in the out-side world who, for some reason, are dependent on them as agents and who try to make trouble by constantly spreading malicious gossip. In my opinion, these categories do not belong in work camps.

The outcome of life-training work is highly dependent on the in-mates' state of mind. Mistakes on the part of the personnel or in the regulations can make even a calm individual nervous and irritable. Considerable good will, selfless and interested work, firmness and a belief that one can succeed are required of the personnel. Meaningful recreation must be arranged for the inmates and organized in a coordi-nated program suited to different age groups, so that everyone can find an outlet for his particular interests and need for activity. In accordance with these principles, we try to arrange all kinds of leisure-time occupa-tions in order to bring the inmates together in groups and in that way exchange stupefying and negative pastimes for something that is posi-tive and constructive. This is the safety valve which, in addition to many other means, can be used to influence the men's minds. Our various activities include choirs, drama groups, orchestras, elocution courses, lecture series, language courses, occupational therapy groups, quiz programs, games and athletics, as circumstances and the availabil-ity of local talent permit. Different entertainment with programs, de-pending on the season of the year, are arranged once or twice monthly, and family type movies are shown every other week or so. Outside teachers have been used for only a few courses. In addition, artists from Helsinki have visited the camp and encouraged us in our recreational activities. Spiritual needs have been cared for primarily by representatives of the Pentecostal Church who visit us every Thursday or Friday evening. If we add to this the fact that members of Alcoholics Anonymous make a fine contribution to the inmates' training, we can appreciate the many-sided and rich nature of the work with the inmates, which is essential if anything is to be achieved with the life-training program.

I often have discussions with inmates in the evenings, but usually they do not talk about their problems on their first visit. Instead, they very often open up completely at the second meeting, and their stories are frequently heart-rending. Fear of divorce and concern for their children's future often seems to bring them to the brink of nervous collapse. Failure is already a fact, and the inmate therefore finds it difficult to adjust to the knowledge of his wife's recriminations, whether silent or voiced. He often feels that he alone bears the guilt for the situation that has arisen. The wife, on the other hand, has given up the struggle in desperation at her husband's continued abuse of alcohol and, for that reason, wants to use the opportunity for revenge and to bring him to his knees. In this situation she forgets that she is also unwittingly ruining things for her herself and for the future of the family. It appears to be difficult for quarreling spouses to settle their differences alone without the help of a third party, for neither of them can bring themselves to swallow his or her pride to the point of taking the first step rather than waiting for the other one to do so. There seems to be one exception to the rule that if a third person interferes in the affairs of a couple he will be rewarded with a box on the ears: in the work camp one can be unwittingly involved in a situation where both man and wife beg for help in resolving their unhappy dilemma. Many a father also visits the camp to talk about his son, a brother about his brother, a fiancée about her fiancé, and so on. How can they be transformed into decent citizens now that they have shamed their families and betrayed their confidence, a transgression that people often find it difficult to forgive. For the families usually take on great financial burdens as a result of the miscreant's crime. At the same time, one sometimes can note with joy that these conversations have led to a happy ending, which gives one strength to continue the work.

Many of the inmates of a work camp are accustomed to intellectual work but have no experience of heavy outdoor labor. As a result, the sentence is a much greater burden for them than for men whose former employment required physical fitness. During the latter part of the sentence, however, this imbalance usually evens itself out as the physical condition of the intellectuals improves. In this connection, we should recall that the intellectuals in a work camp are also generally in a rundown condition, a good remedy for which is manual labor. [19]

The Helsinki Work Camp was probably one of the best administered, requiring the smallest staff of any of the prison camps in the world.

[19] HERSTEDVESTER AND THE PSYCHIATRIC CORRECTIONAL INSTITUTIONS

The Insane Criminal

The insane or mentally deficient offenders have been exempt from penal sanctions for a very long time. But while this principle has prevailed, the definition of insanity and feeble-mindedness has nevertheless been a bone of contention. Even in the days of the Roman Empire the jurists were struggling with this problem. The **Emperors Marcus Aurelius and Commodus, co-regents from 175 to 180 A.D.**, issued the rescript quoted below to Scapula Tertullus concerning one Aelius Priscus, who had killed his mother and was suspected of being insane:

If you have clearly ascertained that Aelius Priscus is in such a state of insanity that he is permanently out of his mind and so entirely incapable of reasoning, and no suspicion is left that he was simulating insanity when he killed his mother, you need not concern yourself with the question how he should be punished, as his insanity itself is punishment enough. At the same time he must be closely confined, and, if you think it advisable, even kept in chains; this need not be done by way of punishment so much as for his own protection and the security of his neighbors. If, however, as is very often the case, he has intervals of sounder mind *(lucida intervalla)*, you must carefully investigate the question whether he may not have committed the crime on one of these occasions, and so have no claim to mercy on the ground of mental infirmity; and, if you should find that anything of this kind is the fact you must refer the case to us, so that we may consider, supposing he committed the act at a moment when he could be held to know what he was doing, whether he ought not to be visited with punishment corresponding to the enormity of his crime. But when we learn by a letter from you that his position in respect of place and treatment is such that he is in the hands of his friends, even if confined to his own house, your proper course will be, in our opinion, to summon the persons who had the charge of him at the time and ascertain how they came to be so remiss, and then pronounce upon the case of each separately, according as you see anything to excuse or aggravate his negligence. The object of providing keepers for lunatics is to keep them not merely from doing harm to themselves, but from bringing destruction upon others; and if this last-mentioned mischief should come to pass, it may well be set down to the negligence of any who were not sufficiently assiduous in the discharge of their office. (Quoted from Monro.)[1]

"This letter is of the greatest interest, since it takes up all the penological problems still being discussed by forensic psychiatrists," according to Torsten Sondén's analysis of this remarkable document.[2] Nevertheless, attitudes toward the insane changed during the Middle Ages: insanity was often believed to be due to the victim being "possessed" by an evil spirit and the insane criminal should therefore be treated brutally. Even as late as the eighteenth century, the theory that the insane could be deterred by punishment still had its advocates. By the nineteenth century, however, the old Roman attitude had once more become generally accepted.[3]

Thus, the insane or feeble-minded criminal should not be punished, regardless of the enormity of his offense. The problem was relatively simple in the case of those who were clearly out of their mind or *furiosi* (possessed by furies), as the Romans expressed it. But, with increasing understanding of a sick mind and its manifestations, as well as the efforts by the medical experts to have all the mentally sick made exempt from penal treatment, conflicts arose between the medical profession and public opinion. The latter strongly objected to apparently "sane" individuals being relieved of responsibility for their crimes, and the courts frequently found themselves in a dilemma. In cases in which the public did not understand the background, medical certifications of insanity were often believed to be a threat to law and order. Sondén reported on a case of this kind, which was also reviewed in Naumann's Journal in 1866.[4] A farm hand charged with arson was found exempt from criminal responsibility on the basis of a medical certificate. The prosecutor, a sheriff, took the case to a higher court, claiming:

It is not difficult to foresee what will happen in the long run if this procedure with criminals is applied consistently. Thieves and robbers, poisoners and murderers, the whole range of criminals, serious and petty alike, will not hesitate to deny or to produce obscure and devious excuses for their crimes if they see that, with the assistance of the Royal Board of Health, such tricks will help them to avoid punishment and will instead get them into asylums where, in accordance with current theories of the treatment of the insane, they will be treated as completely healthy individuals and kept occupied at various pleasant diversions until it suits them to regain their sanity and be returned to society as fully recovered. (Quoted from Naumann.)[5]

As we have seen from the foregoing, insane convicts had found it difficult to tolerate confinement in a cell, and many prisoners became insane under the new forms of solitary confinement introduced during the nineteenth century. In 1844, the British Government decided to intern 235 insane criminals in a private mental hospital, Fisherton House. This was the first measure of its kind ever adopted. However, as the number of convicts in need of psychiatric care, as well as the number of the certified insane increased, the British opened several similar special institutions, which were a sort of midway between a prison and a mental hospital. One was built in Dundrum in Ireland in 1850; another in Scotland was attached to the Perth prison in 1858, and a large institution in England was opened at Broadmoor in 1863. The clientele was mixed, comprising both offenders exempt from criminal responsibility and insane convicts unfitted for ordinary prison discipline. The Broadmoor Criminal Lunatic Asylum became widely known in Europe as a result of Lombroso's complimentary description of its activities.[6]

With a law of 1850, the Belgians had embarked in another direction, namely, to establish special sections for insane and feeble-minded criminals in the general mental hospitals. However, inasmuch as it became clear that special measures were required to deal with insane and feeble-minded criminals, most other European countries soon followed the British example and established psychiatric wards in certain prisons, whose psychiatrists usually were used by the courts for opinions of the psychiatric status of persons awaiting trial.

In 1878 an international psychiatric conference was held in Paris, where an attempt was made to determine which method was preferable: to remove the insane and with them the psychiatrists from the prisons or to affiliate the treatment of insane criminals with the penal system. The majority of the delegates favored the system with mental wards in the prisons, although it was generally agreed that there should also be special psychiatric institutions for criminals or at least special wards for them in certain mental hospitals.[7]

In Sweden, the Royal Serafimer Order Society proposed to the Government in 1873 that special sections for the mentally ill be established in two of the country's prisons. The penal administration followed suit and two years later requested permission to set up sections for the purpose at the prisons in Varberg and Norrköping. The Royal Board of Health approved of this proposal, but emphasized that persons who had committed crimes under the influence of insanity should be treated like all other insane and be confined to mental hospitals. At the same time the Board was in agreement with the penal administration concerning the "true" criminal patients, i.e., convicts who had become insane during their sentence.[8]

The Right or Wrong Test

The more restrictive the administration of justice concerning exemption from criminal responsibility due to insanity, the more urgent it became to set up special sections for the insane within the existing penal structure. This was true, for example, in the Anglo-American sphere, where the M'Naghten case in 1843 had "set the pace." The same year, a certain Daniel M'Naghten killed Prime Minister Sir Robert Peel's secretary by mistake, his intended victim being Peel himself. M'Naghten was acquitted on the ground of insanity. The verdict caused such an outcry that the House of Lords summoned the judges to interrogate them about the principles on which exemption from criminal responsibility was founded. The answers to these questions became known as the M'Naghten Rules. Fourteen of the 15 members of England's highest court explained in this case that, if insanity was pleaded as a reason for exemption from criminal responsibility, "it must be clearly proven that, at the time of the committing of the act, the party accused was labouring under such a defect of reason, from disease of the mind, as not to know the nature and quality of the act he was doing, or, if he did know it, that he did not know he was doing what was wrong." This has been called "the right or wrong test." Later court verdicts have established that wrong does not mean an illegal act but one that is morally reprehensible.[9]

As a result of this restrictive interpretation, the number of insane convicts in countries applying the M'Naghten Rules naturally has been disproportionately much higher than in countries with a broader concept of lack of criminal responsibility. In addition to the patently insane and clearly mentally deficient, others, particularly cases in which temporary insanity can be proven, have been included in the category of those exempt from criminal responsibility.

In addition to the insane and the mentally deficient, individuals whose personalities were such that they could not be regarded as normal began to be the subject of study toward the end of the nineteenth century. This category of people came to be known as psychopaths, a highly controversial term that has frequently been labeled as unsuitable. Several countries passed special legislation for this type of clientele. Mainly, it became the practice in the twentieth century to separate them from the ordinary convict category and to refer them to special institutions, usually under medical supervision.

The courts frequently found it difficult to arrange for a psychiatric examination by a competent doctor. The accused obviously could bring in a doctor if he could afford the cost and believed it would help his case. The prosecutor could do likewise, and many tragicomic battles were waged in various countries with medical experts contradicting one another in the courtroom. (In countries with the Anglo-Saxon legal system, this was known as the "battle of experts.") On the other hand, many judges did not bother to request a medical opinion of the mental condition of a defendant, either because of indifference or because it was difficult to arrange for such an examination. In the United States it was not until 1921 that a prominent Boston psychiatrist, Dr. L. Vernon Briggs, wrote a widely read book, *The Manner of Man that Kills*, about the need for a mandatory psychiatric examination of those guilty of capital crimes and of recidivists to determine their mental condition and imputability. He even drafted a bill on the subject, which was passed the same year in Massachusetts and came to be known as the Briggs Law. What was remarkable was that all the psychiatrists in Massachusetts pledged themselves to perform examinations free of charge until such time as the state could pay for them. It was not until 1938 that another state followed the Massachusetts example, and many American states still are without comparable legislation.[10]

In England, psychiatric examinations by court order became increasingly common during the 1930s. The English courts had the power to request prison physicians to submit reports on the mental status of all indicted persons. This system is still in force. The opinions are usually very brief and are written on the basis of a cursory examination; a physician attached to a local jail may be required to submit several hundred opinions a year. Not until the Criminal Justice Act of 1948 was passed were the courts empowered to tailor their sentences to fit the mental status of the defendant, including cases in which the latter had not been relieved of criminal responsibility because of insanity. Since that time the courts may impose probation on the condition that the defendant puts himself under medical care.[11]

Vervaeck

Belgium was the European country to organize the best system. There, in 1921, Dr. Louis Varvaeck set up psychiatric annexes in ten penal institutions in which not only the indicted were given examinations but convicts also were put under observation to determine whether their mental condition could be deemed abnormal. In France the first psychiatric annex was established in 1927. Today the majority of European countries have access to psychiatric expertise for their convicts.[12]

Not only has the medical examination system been expanded to help the courts' investigations of defendants' mental state at the time of the crime and in the current situation, as well as for advice as to the best way to treat the offender to prevent future criminal behavior, but psychiatry has come to occupy an increasingly strong position within the penal system itself, with responsibility for convicts unsuited for ordinary penal treatment and also for consultation regarding the treatment of normal cases.

Classification

The introduction of the new element of psychiatry was sometimes an extremely painful process, and battles were waged between representatives of the penal systems and psychiatrists in all countries. With increasing experience on both sides, however,

[203]

psychiatry now has a firm footing as an indispensable and fully accepted supportive science in the treatment of criminals. This is especially true in the area of treatment planning, or classification, which all countries now try to apply to the extent possible to every offender committed to a penal institution. Classification means that the newly admitted convict is submitted to a more or less exhaustive study of his personal background, to psychological tests to determine his traits and abilities, and to a medical examination to evaluate his mental and physical state of health. The purpose is to decide how the convict should be treated in the future, the kind of work he should be given, the recreational activities that might stimulate him, the institution to which he will be assigned, how persons close to him can be used in his resocialization, etc.

The number of diagnostic centers for treatment planning by psychiatrists and sociologists is steadily increasing in most countries. Expansion would unquestionably be explosive were it not for the general shortage of qualified personnel, primarily psychiatrists. In Sweden, for example, the Parliament several years ago approved a "regional psychiatry" plan, according to which psychiatrists would be appointed to serve specific groups of institutions. This plan was never fully implemented due to lack of psychiatrists.

Of particular interest in this connection is the work being done in institutions for non-insane offenders headed by psychiatrists. The clientele of these institutions consists mainly of convicts who need special treatment because of their abnormal personality, primarily those whose particular abnormality renders them dangerous. Three such institutions, one for adults and two for juveniles, are described:

Herstedvester

In April, 1935, the Danes opened an instituion for psychopaths in Herstedvester, fourteen kilometers from Copenhagen. The function of the institution was described in the official directive governing its activity:

The purpose of the institution is to protect society from the dangers to law and order that the individuals held in it would represent if they were at large and, within the framework defined, to submit them to treatment designed for their individual needs in order to fit them to return to freedom. During confinement, which is not a penalty but a precautionary measure, the objective shall be to adapt the treatment to suit the internee's personality. [13]

The first director of the institution, Georg K. Stürup, a psychiatrist of outstanding repute in international penological history, commented:

Simple custody, or a "closeting function," was out of the question. Humanitarian considerations required that, within the limits defined for public safety, an opportunity for treatment be provided that would lead at least to some of the internees being discharged in such a condition that they could be restored to society as responsible citizens. [14]

In 1967, the physical appearance of the installation was described:

The various buildings are surrounded by a high wall with a gatehouse on the south side. Immediately inside the gates we see two cell blocks, one containing 40 cells divided into four sections of 10 cells each, the other with 60 cells divided into four 15-cell sections. Farther back in the grounds there is a workshop building with a gymnasium in the middle. Still farther back there is a sick bay with doctors' offices, laboratories and an operating theater. Farther north there is a 40-bed section, divided into four units, and a playing field. The institution also includes two wooden barracks, one of which serves as an open section for 18 inmates, while the other is used as a warehouse for the workshops. There is thus a total of twelve general sections, with capacity for 10 or 15 inmates, a barracks section, a sick bay and, finally, an isolation section, comprising altogether about 200 beds, with spacious grounds between the buildings.

The administrative personnel consists of four doctors, one psychologist, three nurses, one superintendent, three welfare secretaries, four case workers, and 18 clerks, or a total of 34 persons. The works foremen are 18 in number. The supervisory personnel comprises one supervisor-in-chief, four supervisors, 28 assistant supervisors, 65 keepers and 10 extra keepers for daytime work, or altogether 108 persons. The total personnel thus amounts to 160. The institution shares some of the facilities of the nearby Vridsløselille prison, including catering.

The inmates may either eat at small tables in their own section or take their food into their cells, as they prefer. A small hobby workshop is attached to each section.

The works building contains a well-equipped printing shop, as well as facilities for cabinet-making and for rough carpentry. There are also shops for tailoring, painting, bookbinding, etc.

The institution began to be crowded in 1943, and the following summer an open section with accommodations for up to 20 inmates was added in nearby *Kastanienborg*. By 1951 it was found necessary to expand still further, and a nearby estate, *Lysholmsgård*, was purchased and converted into a home for 15 inmates, who worked at farming and gardening. The two estates are jointly administered by a chief supervisor, a supervisor and nine keepers.[15]

Dr. Stürup described the therapeutic methods:

The purpose of the treatment at Herstedvester is to influence the mentally abnormal offender in such a way that he becomes aware of his own behavioral pattern to the point that he can find self-expression in a socially acceptable fashion. We thus try to make him aim at reasonable goals. To achieve this we try to give him confidence in himself and trust in other people. In this way he can reach a stage where he can find a job that will permit him to feel like a normal, responsible citizen and perhaps one day to become a part of a family group. For this reason the treatment is based on a combination of educational psychology, psychiatry-psychology, and social training. The prerequisite for an intelligent treatment is a thorough clinical study of the offender, and the treatment itself has two phases, a re-educative and maturing phase and a more socio-therapeutic phase, often of an analytical nature. The latter depends on the confidence of the individual and therefore can usually not be initiated until considerable time has elapsed. Individual psychotherapy forms the nucleus of this treatment, but in some cases a form of group therapy can be used accompanied by narcosynthesis. Lobotomy has been found indicated in exceptional cases. For alcoholics we use a special sociopsychiatric method with disulfiram as a supportive measure. The most important element in the "social" treatment is close cooperation between the other members of the team and the continuity of the program in the institution and after discharge on parole. We try to establish a close relationship with the inmate's family while he is still in the institution through, for example, escorted furloughs. This contact with the outside world is often of great importance to the post-discharge treatment. The latter is planned entirely at the institution and is carried out by the welfare secretary or one of the case workers. We rely on frequent contact by telephone and mail and personal visits, more frequent for the more difficult clients, who generally live in the neighborhood of the institution. Local supervision is seldom exercised. As a rule, an official of the institution who lives within easy distance of the parolee volunteers to visit him several times a week during his free time. All welfare work with the approximately 300 individuals currently on parole is carried out in constant consultation with an institutional psychiatrist who is thoroughly familiar with the background of the parolee in question.

It is still too early to give any reliable statistics concerning the results of the treatment, since too short a time has elapsed since the method has been more or less firmly defined, which was not really the case until approximately 1940. Meanwhile, of the 113 non-sexual offenders in the institution in the period 1939-45, 3 died during their first term and 5 have still not been discharged. Of the remainder, 2 died after discharge, while 50 have not relapsed, most of them over a long period. Fifty-three have been re-admitted. One of the latter, a former arsonist, was under a short sentence for a petty theft, and 24 were still in the institution. Thus, the final result is that 29 were still in the institution, either for the first or the second time. It can therefore be claimed that a relatively large number were resocialized. Exactly how many and how permanent resocialization proves to be cannot yet be established.[16]

Roxtuna

A law on youth prison was passed in Sweden in 1938, modeled on the Danish youth prison and the English Borstal legislation. The idea was that youth prison would be a punishment for boys without serious character defects or treatment needs. But, reality turned out to be quite different. An open institution had been built at Skenäs near Norrköping. Meantime, the courts began also to impose youth prison sentences on juveniles with psychopathic traits, apparent developmental defects, or other psychic anomalies, a practice that had not been anticipated when the legislation was formulated. Nevertheless, the practice was sanctioned by the Supreme Court and approved by the Government. It created a need for entirely new therapeutic resources than originally had been foreseen. Psychopaths and other young people with mental problems were not receptive to the form of training that was hoped would be effective in the open Skenäs institution, causing problems for the treatment of their peers; they started fights, organized escapes, and so forth. A more secure institution with appropriate treatment methods was needed, and in late 1949 the Government ordered an investigation of the problem by a committee composed by representatives of the Penal Administration and other experts. The results of this study were submitted on December 15, 1950, in a report entitled, "An Institution for the Recalcitrant" (SOU 1950:47). The committee had examined the clientele at penal institutions for persons sentenced to youth prison, made studies of a number of foreign experimental institutions, particularly in the

United States, and, with this background, proposed that an institution be built that would respond to what appeared to be the treatment needs of this difficult category of young offenders. This was the origin of Roxtuna, which represented a revolution in Swedish, as well as international institutional thinking, but which also brought about an outcry because of the high building costs and of the large staff needed to maintain the institution. Had it not been for the wholehearted support of Herman Zetterberg, then Minister of Justice, Roxtuna would never have materialized. Nevertheless, the plan had to be redesigned to reduce costs, but not to the point of changing the basic concept of treatment. (Incidentally, Zetterberg is probably the only minister of justice in the world to have insisted on the construction of a certain type of correctional institution as a condition for remaining a member of his country's cabinet.)

Roxtuna was opened in 1955. It provided immediate relief for the strained resources of the penal system, but suffered from the initial difficulties encountered by this type of institution.[17] With the appointment of Dr. Ulla Bergkvist, psychiatrist, in charge of Roxtuna, the organization worked more smoothly. Excerpts from a brief report submitted by Dr. Bergkvist about her institution in 1962 are:

> Roxtuna is designed according to the small-group principle. It comprises a combined sick bay and admissions section with five sickrooms and four rooms for the newly admitted, respectively; four semi-open sections with capacity for nine in each; two closed sections with seven beds each, four of these rooms being "strongbox" cells used only for extra-judicial punishment. Thus the institution actually has ten maximum security cells. In addition there is a completely open section with capacity for nine pupils. All the rooms are single, with the exception of the sickrooms which contain two beds and can be used for two patients if necessary.
>
> In accordance with the small-group principle, the personnel is permanently assigned to the various sections and there is thus no rotation of staff. There are four keepers in the admissions section, one of whom is chief keeper; the semi-open sections have twelve keepers, two of them chief keepers; the closed sections have a total of eleven keepers and two occupational therapists; the open section has no personnel. The institution is designed for the most mentally problematic juvenile offenders; according to the committee's recommendation, it was to be an institution for "difficult" cases. All juveniles sentenced to youth prison are sent first to the reception center in Uppsala, where the plan for execution of sentence is drawn up and the classification process

carried out. Roxtuna also accepts pupils from other institutions in the youth group in the event that they show nervous tendencies, or the like. Transfer to Roxtuna from another institution depends on various factors, e.g., a temporary depression, acute tension, a more or less dramatic emotional outburst, attempted suicide, or because the boy in question is too sensitive to tolerate a large community and is better suited for a small group.

On his arrival at Roxtuna the youth is placed in the admissions section, where he spends the first few days locked up for what is known as isolation observation. This is done so that the pupils can grow accustomed to the institution gradually and become acquainted with some of the staff before they join their comrades. During this initial period the superintendent, who is a psychiatrist, the psychologist, the social workers and one of the keepers have talks with the pupil and try to become familiar with his personality, interests, vocational background, etc. The treatment team, consisting of the aforementioned plus a representative of the vocational teaching staff, meets every Monday. On these occasions the team discusses the new pupil, whose views it also listens to, and decides where he will be placed and where he will work, whether he should be allowed to study by correspondence, etc.

In the absence of counter-indications, all pupils are transferred directly from admissions to a semi-open section. Some degree of differentiation is exercized in this connection. For example, the more extrovert, active, sports-minded "tough" pupils are put in one section, the more sensitive "underdog" type in another. The classification principles vary according to the nature of the clientele, but the point is that the pupils in the same section shall learn to adjust to one another and to some extent live "socially" in a group. Obviously we take into consideration the personality of the keepers attached to the different sections in order to achieve a degree of harmony between them and the pupils.

The pupils are put to work as soon as they have been transferred to a semi-open section. Roxtuna has four different vocational streams consisting of a machine shop, a carpentry shop, an automobile repair shop, and a greenhouse, nursery and garden. Some of the pupils work as helpers in the boiler room and the central kitchen. For the last few years, the institution has also had a group working in the neighboring forest.

All the housework in the sections is done by the pupils, and each boy is responsible for keeping his own room in order. The pupils take weekly turns helping the keeper to clean the common rooms and the area around the section, to fetch the food from the central kitchen, to lay the tables, wash dishes, etc. Pupils and keepers eat all their meals together in their section.

In the event of misbehavior, escape, abuse of furlough, etc., or if he himself requests it, a pupil is transferred to a closed section. Following an escape compounded by a crime, the offender is kept in a closed section, usually until the question of prosecution for the crime has been settled. Pupils in closed sections work in the section occupational therapy shops and have no contact whatever with other inmates.

Free time at Roxtuna is devoted primarily to sports, and the pupils compete in inter-club soccer, handball, table tennis, etc. All sections have had television sets since 1960. There is a loud-speaker in every cell, and radio broadcasts can be heard from the central receiver during leisure time. Television programs are shown on weekends and on two evenings during the week chosen by representatives of pupils and staff. Other entertainment, including jazz concerts and amateur theatricals, is occasionally offered.

The pupils' contacts with the outside world, planning of furloughs, discharge, job-hunting, etc., are handled by three social workers, each of them responsible for two or three sections.

The treatment practised at the institution is environmental-therapeutic in nature, based on the small-group principle. A prerequisite for this type of treatment is that the institutional climate is good and that each staff member feels obliged to have a positive approach to the pupils, to make them to the extent possible feel accepted by the adult authorities with whom they are in contact and at the same time to maintain discipline and a certain distance. In addition to the therapeutic work by the keeper in each section, weekly one-hour discussion sessions are held under the direction of the superintendent-psychiatrist, the psychologist, the assistant superintendent-psychiatrist and the social workers. Individual psychotherapy is also practised extensively. Medication does not play a prominent role in the treatment. Pupils with drinking and stimulants problems or with depressive or restless tendencies, as well as those who are physically run-down, are treated with insulin in intermediate dosage over a period of about four to six weeks. Tranquilizing and somnifacient medication is used sparingly, while treatment with tonics, vitamins, etc., is generous.

The clientele is extremely heterogeneous. The level of intelligence varies between clearly retarded and highly gifted. Psychic deviations range from mild neurotic symptoms to serious brain injuries and even psychoses. Every year one or two pupils become acutely psychotic, necessitating transfer to a mental hospital. In many cases the psychic abnormality is so severe that it will lead to exemption from criminal responsibility later in life. In fact, several inmates have already been declared unimputable as the result of medicolegal psychiatric examination.

The great majority of the pupils are mentally disturbed, primarily emotionally. What we hope to achieve with treatment in these cases is to establish an emotional contact and, through positive environmental therapy, among other things, to influence the immature developmental level of the majority in a positive direction.

The most significant difference between Roxtuna and most other institutions is that it is based on the small-group principle, which allows relatively efficient utilization of the staff. The tensions between personnel and inmates are reduced with the small group system, and the pressure of the institutional community presumably is less burdensome for the inmates. Pupils who have had severe problems with their peers in other institutions often feel more secure in a small group, and others with domineering tendencies have less opportunity to assert themselves.

The first stormy years of Roxtuna's existence now seem to have been weathered. The institution runs relatively smoothly, and a therapeutic climate has begun to make itself felt. But this is not enough. We hope that, when the personnel reaches full complement, we shall be able to embark on more active treatment programs. The spirit that now prevails in the institution at least promises a positive point of departure. [18]

Like the Danish Herstedvester, the Swedish Roxtuna aroused world-wide interest and has served as a pattern and a source of ideas for therapeutic innovations in other countries.

Hawthorne

Hawthorne Cedar Knolls School, near New York City, is an example of an advanced institutional treatment of neurotic juvenile offenders. A Swedish visitor's impressions of the School from the year 1950 are cited:

The School is in Hawthorne, a suburban community about one hour by train from New York City. The institution itself, which is about fifteen minutes by car from the railway station, is located in an attractive rural area. Many of the officials live in New York City and are picked up and delivered at the station by the institution's automobiles.

This institution is about three times the size of the Boys Republic[19] and thus has a population of around two hundred youngsters, approximately one-third of them girls. The clientele comprises the age group eight to eighteen years with the majority in the older brackets. All have been remanded to the School by the juvenile courts. The average stay is about two years. Hawthorne specializes in psychopaths and other cases that are particularly difficult for psychological reasons. The pupils live in cottages accommodating fifteen to twenty, some of them relatively primitive, some new and spruce, but all of them very homelike in appearance. The cottages are usually divided into a number of small rooms, unlike the usual pattern in the United States. In one or two of them the pupils even have their own rooms. Then, of course, there are common areas, notably a large living-room, but no dining-room since meals are served in a separate building.

The clientele was about the same as in the Swedish approved school for boys at *Lövsta* and for girls at *Skarvik-Tallåsen*. There is another interesting parallel with the Swedish institutions: At one time Hawthorne consisted of two institutions at about the same distance from one another as Lövsta and Skarvik-Tallåsen. Hawthorne was for boys and Cedar Knolls was for girls. A couple of years ago the auditors of the Swedish Parliament commented on the "unnatural attraction" between the young people at Lövsta and Skarvik. It is true that this attraction caused a great deal of trouble in the training program. Exactly the same phenomenon occurred in the American institutions. Finally the situation became untenable, and radical measures were called for. The Swedes, who faced an identical problem, moved one of the two schools to another community. The Americans did the exact opposite and moved Cedar Knolls to Hawthorne, which explains the long name of the school. The move solved the problem. "We've had only one pregnancy in ten years, and we can put up with that—things were worse in the old days," I was told by Norman V. Lourie, Director of the Hawthorne Installation.

Lourie would not even consider giving up the coeducational principle. This natural framework for upbringing provides more support than it creates problems, in his opinion. The relationship between boys and girls is far more natural when they meet daily. The sexual drive is not so repressed and eruptive and can be kept within bounds much more easily.

The director's opinion was shared by his colleagues, as I learned when I moved around the place and spoke frankly and at length with members of the staff, many of whom had experience in segregated institutions.

Because of its size, the institution also included a large number of buildings for different purposes: an auditorium, a gymnasium, a schoolhouse and workshops. The psychiatric clinic dominates the scene both in size and as the core of the therapeutic program.

In addition to this thumbnail sketch of the external aspects of the Hawthorne School, it should be noted that it is owned and operated by a Jewish organization in New York, the Jewish Board of Guardians. In the United States, Federal and State institutions are compelled by law to make provision for the exercise of the Protestant, Catholic and Jewish faiths. Private institutions may be restricted to one or another religion, but in that case the courts must see to it that the convict is placed in an institution corresponding to his religious affiliation. Thus, Gentile children may not in principle be remanded to Hawthorne, but I encountered many exceptions to this rule. In these cases the parents themselves had requested the placement. Mr. Lourie claimed, as might be expected of an institutional director of his stature, that segregation by religion in private institutions was a drawback, as was racial segregation when it existed.

The goal of the Hawthorne institution was to render its young wards "fit for society by providing good living, psychotherapy, work education, pay and satisfying relationships with healthy, accepting adults." A large staff, as well as a great number of volunteers, worked together toward this end.

Meantime, the means used to achieve this goal were different from those at the Boys Republic. There was no form of self-government at Hawthorne. The pupils were not taught how to handle money through a system of financial reward. Pocket money and bonuses for industry were doled out very sparingly. "We don't believe that our pupils' problems are superficial," Mr. Lourie replied to my questions on the subject. He did not deny that institutions of the Boys Republic type may be good. "But we believe that we accomplish more by concentrating on the children's inner conflicts."

The main features of the therapeutic program are most easily described by beginning with the cottage activity. Each cottage was headed by a married couple. Usually the husband had a job or was a student. In one case the wife was the student and the husband the homebody. On the other hand, both man and wife were on full time duty in some cottages. These cottage parents had no cooking responsibilities. They were expected to keep the house in order with the help of their charges and to care for the latter to the best of their ability, to occupy themselves with them, and to try to understand them. But they were to act and react as ordinary parents, not as psychotherapists. "The cottage parent is not either a group worker, recreation worker or group therapist. He is a person who lives warmly and ruggedly with children." To avoid overly long working hours, the regular cottage parents were relieved once a week by substitute parents.

The children were assigned to their cottage according to age and sex—boys and girls did not live in the same house—but the most important basis for placement was to put the right child with the right cottage parents and to compose the group as wisely as possible. For example, it might be found advisable to put a new, unadjusted youngster in a group that was adjusted and had achieved a degree of stability in order to exploit the social strength represented by such a group. Or it might be considered inadvisable to place a new pupil in a group that was on its way to achieving balance. In the differentiation process, utmost consideration is given to the tensions within the group and to the possibilities of exploiting the group members' influences on one another. It is customary in American institutions with the cottage group system to place new arrivals in a special reception cottage for a time before final assignment. At Hawthorne the newly admitted was temporarily assigned to a suitable cottage on the basis of the recommendations of an admissions-committee consisting of the director, the head of the clinical section and the superintendent of the educational department. In this way they avoid what they consider to be the undesirable atmosphere of separate reception cottages.

There were altogether eleven cottages administered by a Homelife Department headed by a special superintendent with a staff of assistants, whose job it was to act as training advisers to cottage parents. The latter all met a couple of times a week with the superintendent and his assistants to discuss the children's problems—and to a great extent their own personal problems also. In Mr. Lourie's words: "There is no limit to the effort that should be put into understanding the cottage parents and helping them with their problems." He added: "There is scarcely any aspect of institutional work that is more important than the welfare of the personnel." (This concern for "integration of staff" is characteristic of progressive American institutions.)

The new pupil's first association with the Hawthorne training program is thus the Homelife Department. The second is what Americans mean by the term "education" (vocational work, school and free time activities). The Homelife Department had a staff of thirty, the Educational Department nineteen.

The entire difficult work of psychological adjustment was directed and checked from the Clinical Department, which had a director, a psychologist, four psychiatrists and fourteen psychiatric case workers. Two of the latter served as supervisors of the others. The procedure in this department was as follows:

Each new pupil was assigned to a case worker after having been tested by the psychologist and examined by one of the psychiatrists. If necessary, the psychiatrists also acted as case workers. The pupil then began to meet regularly with his case worker, usually two or three times a week. No case worker had a load of more than thirty cases, of which ten to fifteen were generally parolees. The principal function of the case worker was to listen, to function as the object of the pupil's abreaction. As a rule he was not supposed to interfere in the daily life of his cases, to contact the cottage parents, or to show himself in the cottage under any circumstances. The youngster should be able to talk to his case worker with complete confidence in his discretion. In this way the case worker to a great extent acted the part of a psychoanalyst. The entire program of the department was based on psychoanalytical principles, and the four psychiatrists were also practising analysts. However, the case worker's role was not limited to that of listener and psychotherapist; he also had various other responsibilities as a social worker. If he considered that some special action was required on behalf of a pupil or if he felt a need to discuss a particular case, he was expected to turn to a supervisor. The latter was not permitted to have any direct personal contact with the pupil in question, in order to be able to remain completely objective in any conflict that had to be resolved. It was assumed that the case worker would be deeply involved on the pupil's side and thus incapable of a completely nonpartisan attitude to the problem. In addition to their main duties, the two supervisors acted as case workers with a few pupils so as not to lose touch with the practical side of the treatment.

The Homelife, Educational and Clinical Departments thus cooperated to form the field of force in which the institution with its 150 employees endeavored to teach their young charges how to cope effectively with social reality. A very important function was also handled by two groups of volunteers, "Volunteers" and "Big Brothers and Sisters."

The Volunteers were a group of outsiders who directed or merely participated in various recreational activities. Two assistants, under the supervision of the deputy director, were responsible for recruiting suitable people for this work. The "Bigs" had their own organization, chaired by a woman. They arranged for a volunteer to visit each boy and girl regularly in the institution and also to take each one out regularly for home visits or entertainment in the community. I learned that it was easy to find Bigs and that more people applied for membership than could be utilized.

Volunteers and Bigs had a total enrollment of about 200, while the number of employees amounted to approximately 150. A very large organization was thus involved in the 200 cases that could be accommodated in the institution. Did the results warrant the investment of financial and human resources?

I could not obtain a completely dependable statistical reply to this question. However, the number of "lost cases" seemed to amount to approximately twenty to twenty-five per cent which, bearing in mind the nature of the clientele, is an excellent result. I also had the impression that the so-called lost cases were largely comprised of pupils who had improved to a considerable degree during their stay at Hawthorne. (Quoted from Eriksson.)[20]

The three institutions described in the foregoing, all of which can be regarded as unique, obviously have continued to develop in the intervening years. The distinguishing feature of this type of institution, of course, is that they are not static, but are constantly evolving to reflect changes in society or the disciplines (psychiatry, psychology, pedagogy) on whose findings their programs are based.

[20] HIGHFIELDS AND THE
PSYCHOLOGICAL INSTITUTIONS

Psychoanalysis and the Criminal

The Highfields experiment is one of the most interesting programs to improve therapeutic methods for criminals that has been
undertaken so far in the twentieth century. The background is interesting.

The breakthrough of psychoanalysis in the first part of the century, with Freud's, Adler's, and Jung's methods of interpreting and
treating behavioral deviations, resulted in several attempts to apply
these methods to the treatment of criminals. The Freudian view of
the causes of criminality was presented by Franz Alexander and
Hugo Staub in the book *Der Verbrecher und seine Richter* (The
Criminal and His Judges), Vienna: 1929. About the same time,
trained psychoanalysts began to work with institutionalized
juvenile delinquents. During the period, 1918-1922, August Aich-
horn operated the *Oberhollabrunn* and *St. Andra* reformatories
near Vienna, where, in collaboration with the psychiatrist, Erwin
Lazer, he experimented with treatment of small, differentiated
groups. He described his methods in the book, *Verwahrloste
Jugend (Wayward Youth)*, which was widely read, translated into
several other languages, and came to exert a strong influence on
future developments.[1]

In England, the Quakers financed the therapeutic experiment
described in David Wills's book, *The Hawkspur Experiment*.
Wills later embarked on a similar project, *The Barns Experiment*.
Disciplinary punishment was taboo in both of these small institutions. Wills wrote, "As soon as the boys began to suspect that this
was our intention, they naturally began to put it to the test." They
had not before encountered people whose instructions were not
accompanied by overt or implied threats. The first months at Barns
were a hideous strain on the staff. The boys rushed about the
building, yelling, shouting, and slamming every door. No games
could be organized; meals were nightmarish; and playing hooky
was the rule. "This is a funny place," said one little boy. "You

never get the belt!" But all of a sudden, after four months had passed, everything calmed down. From that time on, all children worked well in school and behaved "normally."[2]

Group Therapy

Common to these and a number of other experiments was that treatment was based on the principles of individual therapy. However, the need for trained therapists and the attendant costs were so great that the experiments could only be carried out on a small scale. Naturally, therefore, the next step was to try to apply psychoanalytical methods to several individuals at the same time. Group therapy was the name given to this form of treatment. A pioneer in group therapeutic methods in the United States was the physician, J. H. Pratt, who published a paper on the subject in the *Journal of the American Medical Association* in 1907.[3]

It was not until World War II that group therapy began to be used on a larger scale. What was to do be done with all the soldiers who could not adjust to the harsh conditions of war, sentenced for disobeying orders and other offenses making them dangerous to their comrades with a lack of discipline? Many American soldiers in this category were sent to a rehabilitation center in Fort Knox, Kentucky, where they were treated by a team of physicians and psychologists. One of the latter was Dr. Lloyd W. McCorkle, whose original training was in sociology.

McCorkle at Highfields

After the war was ended, the sociologist, F. Lovell Bixby, became head of the penal administration of the state of New Jersey. Bixby was a progressive man, willing to try new approaches. He decided to introduce group therapy methods in his institutions and called in McCorkle. For the next few years group therapy was given in some of the institutions. At first the staff was skeptical and openly hostile to the method, but they soon offered support. It quickly became apparent that the group therapy methods introduced at Fort Knox were successful in prisons.

Three years later (June, 1950) the time was ripe to begin a full-scale experiment with group therapy. The site was Highfields (previously owned by Charles Lindbergh, who made the first solo flight across the Atlantic), a few miles from Trenton, New Jersey.

A Swedish visitor who had observed the progress of the High-fields project since its inception wrote about the institution in 1967:

The house is an old two-story structure. Its fourteen rooms and kitchen include living quarters for the director and his family, a sociologist trainee, and two house parents, situated on one side of the second floor. The inmates have the use of two large rooms on the second floor of the other side. The ground floor is taken up by the director's office, the dining-room, kitchen and bathroom, as well as a room for the trainee. Thus, Highfields is neither a well-planned nor a well-equipped institution.

There are no rooms for recreational activities. For most of the year the boys spend their free time out of doors, where there is a small playing field. The garage has space for weight-lifting, boxing and wrestling, but it is difficult to keep the boys occupied on rainy days in the winter, when about all they can do is to play cards and chess indoors.

Twenty boys can be squeezed into the two dormitories. All of them are in their teens and have been sentenced to probation with the condition that they spend a period of time at Highfields. They are brought to the institution by the probation officers. They remain for three months, and the purpose of the stay is to bring them to a better understanding of themselves and of the reasons for their criminal offenses. This self-insight comes from the group therapy sessions held every day in the week except Thursday and Saturday. The sessions are held in the director's office and led by the director and the sociologist trainee. Also present are the house parents, a foreman and a secretary, or a total of six officials.

A typical day's schedule at Highfields is as follows:

6 a.m.:	Arise
6.30 a.m.:	Breakfast
7 a.m.:	Clean up rooms and make beds
7.30 a.m.:	Depart by bus for a hospital in the neighborhood
8 a.m.-12 noon:	Various kinds of work in the garden, laundry, etc. of the hospital
12 noon:	Lunch
1 p.m.-4.30 p.m.:	Work assignments at hospital
4.30 p.m.:	Return to Highfields
5.00 p.m.-5.30:	Prepare for dinner
5.30 p.m.-6.30:	Dinner
7.30 p.m.:	Guided group interaction session for the first group

8.30 p.m.:	Guided group interaction session for the second group
10 p.m.:	Bedtime
10.15 p.m.:	Lights out.

The boys are paid fifty cents a day for their work at the hospital. One of them stays at home to help with odd jobs around the house.

Highfields has only two firm regulations: no boy is allowed to leave the institutional grounds unaccompanied by an adult. The other is that the boys are not allowed to seek out or even speak to female patients in the hospital. In addition to these fixed rules, a number of other practical, though flexible regulations are worked out in cooperation with the boys themselves. The fixed rules are necessary for the maintenance of institutional control, the flexible, which of course are often broken, are useful in the group sessions.

During his stay at Highfields, each boy is allowed two or more three-day furloughs from Friday morning until Sunday evening to visit his family and meet with his probation officer. Several hundred furloughs were successful during the first five years. Breaches of furlough regulations occurred in only four cases. Everyone is given a three or four-day furlough for Christmas, Thanksgiving and Easter. Extra furloughs are granted for exceptional reasons. There are no restrictions to the number of visits a boy may receive from close relatives and friends. There is no censorship of mail, newspapers or books.

But punishments do exist, usually decided on by the house parents and generally consisting of one or more hours of extra work without compensation at disagreeable jobs, such as garbage disposal. In exceptional cases the boy may be penalized in this way for several days at a stretch.

The courts decide which boys are to be remanded to Highfields. In the beginning, it was found that the courts sometimes tried to force Highfields to take cases which were completely unsuited for its form of treatment. Later, however, selections began to be made in consultation with the director-therapist. Three types of boys are definitely unsuited: hardened young criminals with firm roots in an anti-social way of life, boys with serious psychiatric problems, and habitual truants. For the rest, Highfields is prepared to accept roughly the same kinds of clientele that normally are sent to the ordinary institutions for juvenile delinquents.

The group therapy method at Highfields, known as guided group interaction, is based on the same principles as those later introduced in Sweden—to a great extent influenced by the experiences at Highfields. [4]

The Americans were extremely interested in the Highfields experiment, and several investigations have been made to determine whether the new treatment method yielded better results than the traditional reformatory system. All these studies have been favorable to Highfields. The Highfields recidivism rate is about half that of ordinary youth prisons for the same type of cases. Nevertheless, it has been reported to be as high as 27 per cent with a one-year risk zone. However, it may still be too soon to come to any final conclusion as to the end-results. (The history of criminology is littered with experiments that began well and ended badly.) Albert F. Axelrod succeeded McCorkle and Elias as director of Highfields. To the original program he added a "house meeting," held on Sunday evenings. In a detailed report, which confirms that the initial program has been retained more or less intact, Axelrod wrote, "In contrast to the regular group meetings, the house meeting is not for the purpose of discussing individual members of the program, but rather the program itself."[5]

During its experimental years, Highfields has had the good fortune to be run by very skillful therapists. (Skillful therapists are few and hard to come by!) Meantime, New Jersey has established several Highfields institutions, and other states have followed the example. (Kentucky made an exact copy of Highfields in its Southfields Center.) The same principles as those at Highfields, but in another form, were the basis of the Provo, Utah, experiment. There a group of boys on probation lived at home, attending a center five days a week, during which they worked for several hours, taking part in group discussions.[6]

Fenton and Group Counselling

The institutional group therapy described hitherto has been of very high quality. Its practitioners have been well trained and their work has been skillfully planned and carefully thought out.

At the end of the 1950s, however, California boldly decided to involve the great majority of its prison clientele in group therapy. At that time the California prisons had a total population of almost 25,000 inmates. Group therapy had already been practised for several years in certain institutions, including the California State Prison at Folsom, a maximum security institution for recidivists, and the Vacaville medical institution, in which the majority of the inmates were involved in this form of treatment. It was also given on a small scale in other institutions, but the number of groups was limited due to the scarcity of trained therapists.

Dr. Norman Fenton, Chief Psychologist in the California Department of Corrections, proposed a daring innovation: to involve all inmates and to use laymen as leaders of therapy groups. This resulted in a terminological dilemma. Group psychotherapy was the term that the psychiatrists preferred to reserve for their own activities and possibly also for groups not led by but under the supervision of a psychiatrist. In New Jersey the program was named "guided group interaction," since psychologists and sociologists were in charge. Fenton now introduced the concept of group counseling for the activity directed by clinically untrained leaders and defined the objectives under the points summarized here:

1. To develop a group setting for the inmates to study their own and each other's feelings and attitudes under the helpful and accepting auspices of the group leader.
2. To assist inmates to recognize that their own problems are not unique. Others have the same distortions of feelings. Thereafter, they may profit from seeing how others strive to face and deal with their problems. In some instances, the feelings expressed by others in the group may arouse an awareness in the listeners of similar but hitherto unrecognized feelings in themselves. Some inmates have great difficulty in the acceptance of the concept that, if they return to prison, their lack of control of the impulses to behavior originating in their feelings may be largely responsible for their criminal behavior. In other words, they are resistive to the idea that people do not always consciously and knowingly control their own actions. They are confused or misled by the older concepts of will and will power.
3. To help inmates to adjust to the frustrations, which are an unalterable part of prison life, as a prelude to better adjustment after release to society. This may be done by patient and calm discussions among the group of the conditions of institutional living and of the reasons for various rules and regulations which are imposed by the prison authorities. Or there may be group discussions with expressions of strong hostile feelings about the conditions of life in prison. The need may be understood by the inmates, as they grow in maturity through these frank discussions, for the tolerance of the certain-to-be frustrations of prison life related as this may be to similar need for self-control in the face of unpleasant circumstances after release from prison.

Inmates are permitted to tell about their grievances or to express hostilities toward perhaps seemingly unnecessary frustrations in prison life with diminishing fear or anxiety as they become more secure in the presence of the accepting, non-punishing group leader. Those who do not talk may also profit from the effects upon them of being present while other inmates in the group are permitted to express their hostilities. The group leaders' permissiveness toward their expressions of hostility toward him or the administration of the prison or toward authority elsewhere serves as a model of permissiveness for the inmates when they begin their own criticisms of each other.

4. To help the inmates recognize the possible significance in their cases of emotional conflicts as underlying the different kinds of criminality, such as robbery, burglary, forgery, or the other offenses. An inmate previously unaware of the emotional basis of his crimes or unwilling even to recognize feeling as causative, may be helped to achieve this insight by observations of others in the group. The inmate may also appreciate the significance of repressed feelings concerning his disturbances toward authority figures, such as parents, employers, or law enforcement officials as possibly a partial explanation of why he is in prison. The examination of his own emotional disturbances or those of others and their relationship to criminal behavior may also lead to better understanding of criminal behavior. The inmate has to accept himself as someone with a costly disturbance of feeling. He should gradually after weeks of group counseling become at least open-minded to the above belief that the release and examination of his inner feelings in the group are likely to be helpful for his future well being and happiness in society.

5. To permit the inmate to learn about his social personality (how he affects others) as it is presented to those about him. He can learn the effects upon others of his personality in the permissive setting of group counseling wherein he is told frankly about his shortcomings by his fellow inmates—not by those in authority. Incidentally, this type of spontaneous group appraisal of each other is carried on in other groups who assemble sometimes socially, as in the college dormitory, and who agree to be frank in their appraisal of each other as persons. Both good traits and undesirable ones are reported by the group to the individual. This experience may be very helpful for their growth in self-understanding.

6. To help the inmate understand the world of make-believe, of phantasy, and how costly a part it may play in his social adjustment. Any disturbed unhappy individual may find relief in day-dreaming. The inmate's day-dreaming is more costly to him because it may lead to criminal behavior and to prison. Control of action arising from day-dreaming, which is founded in disturbed feeling, as pointed out in Chapter I of the textbook, *What Will Be*

Your Life?, is a problem which faces the inmate who wants "to get out and stay out."

7. To try in the reality situation of prison and the planning for life on parole to be as helpful to the inmates as group leaders as individual counselors are expected to be. When inmates come to them with practical problems, group leaders answer their questions or obtain the assistance of the staff members most likely to be helpful. The group leader should have the names of the institutional correctional classification officers for each of his counselees since help with many practical problems can most often be obtained from them. Other members of the staff may also be involved, however, since these problems may involve such diversified matters as vocational ambitions, welfare of relatives, the hobby program or religious matters.

8. Finally as mentioned earlier, a basic goal of group counseling is the improvement of the emotional climate of the institution, the transformation of the prison to a therapeutic community. The training and treatment program in the prison to be most effective must find support in the attitudes of the entire staff. There should be a sympathetic desire on the part of all personnel to help the inmates in their efforts at self-understanding and self-control.[7]

While Fenton recommended that laymen should be used to a great extent in the new program, he naturally took it for granted that they would receive instruction in the techniques of group counselling. The plan was approved by the great prison reformer, Richard McGee, Director of the State Department of Corrections, and was put into effect with characteristic American speed. It is relevant that the California institutions were grossly over-crowded at the time, due to the population explosion in the state and the resultant increase in the number of criminals. While it was hard to find group leaders, it was even more difficult to produce quarters in which group activities could be held. The working conditions for a project of this kind could scarcely have been less favorable, but the idea was a good one and the enthusiasm of the institutional personnel was tremendous.

All kinds of personnel were received with open arms. Courses for group leaders were organized, periodical reports were submitted by them from the time they began their work, and a special periodical for group counseling was published. In full awareness of the program's deficiencies, the slogan was: "Let's do our best; any treatment is better than no treatment at all."

Enthusiasm and innovation are eventually succeeded by formalism and decay, according to Joseph W. Eaton in his book on the California prison reform. When group therapy came into fashion, it also attracted numerous officials who saw in it a means of earning overtime pay and acquiring credits for promotion. "Quantity hates quality." Some group leaders took their responsibility rather lightly. The term "treatment" became a catchword. "Treatment is an empty symbol if it is used to designate actions which lack in substance, such as diagnostic skill and leadership ability to influence individuals or a group to accomplish a specified objective," according to Eaton.[8]

The same author noted that it did not take the inmates long to learn the vernacular, even though this did not necessarily reflect a change in personality or behavior after discharge. Inmates appeared to be interested in order to ingratiate themselves with the prison officials. Many of them entered the program shortly before their applications for parole were to come up for consideration, but dropped out as soon as a decision was reached. According to reports from the Adult Authority (the parole board), inmates who previously tended to claim that they were more or less innocent of their crimes had begun to use such phrases as: "I didn't understand myself, but now I have gained insight about my personality." Other phrases have been used but with the same intent, namely, to try to fool the parole board. Furthermore, a rather small minority of the personnel engaged in group therapy believed in what they were doing. According to Eaton, one study revealed that five psychotherapists (eight percent of the total) and 156 laymen group leaders (24 percent) had faith in the method.

But Eaton concluded: "Formalism occurs in every social movement as it becomes stabilized, when the spark of innovators becomes the substance of a job description, on the basis of which many men have to be recruited. The crucial element is not that formalism occurs, but how much it pervades the organization."[9]

It is nevertheless a fact that the great group therapy project in the California prisons led to a marked change in the institutional climate. Escapes and disturbances decreased in frequency, relations between personnel and inmates improved, and it is believed that recidivism may have declined.

As often in the past, Europe followed in the footsteps of the Americans. England and Sweden were first, but group therapy in various forms is now firmly established in the world of penology in the other Nordic countries and on the Continent as well. It was the topic treated at a meeting of experts in Geneva in 1961 (organized by the United Nations) and a European colloquium on the subject (organized by the International Penal and Penitentiary Foundation), was held in Brussels the following year.[10]

[21] THE THERAPEUTIC COMMUNITY

Alcoholics Anonymous

In 1939, *Alcoholics Anonymous* was published in the United States, written in a confession style by several alcohol addicts who had managed to cure themselves of their drinking habit through mutual support. What was later to become a world-wide movement numbered at that time scarcely 100 former alcoholics, loosely bound together in an association of three groups. It all began with a conversation between a New York stockbroker and an Akron (Ohio) physician, both addicted to alcohol and both desperately trying to rid themselves of the habit. In 1935, as a result of their conversation, these two men brought together in Akron a group of alcoholics who wanted to be cured. They were advised and supported in this effort by Dr. William D. Silkworth, a New York specialist on alcoholism. (A second group was formed in New York and a third in Cleveland.)

The book made an enormous impact. From all over the United States people asked for information about how to contact existing groups and how new ones might be organized. In 1940, John D. Rockefeller Jr. helped the movement to gain publicity through a special dinner to which he invited some alcoholics as guest speakers. By March, 1941, the membership in what from then on were simply called *AA-groups* had increased to 2,000 and, at the end of the year, to 8,000. In 1962 there were over 9,000 groups in more than 80 countries.

The movement was founded on principles which have become known as "the Twelve Traditions," early formulated by the first members of the movement and later confirmed at the First International AA Conference at Cleveland, Ohio, in 1950. These "traditions" are listed below:

1. Common welfare comes first. Personal recovery depends on AA unity.
2. We believe in a loving God, as He may express himself in our group conscience. We have no leaders, only trusted servants who do not govern.

3. The only requirement for AA membership is a desire to stop drinking.
4. Each group is autonomous, except in matters affecting other groups or the AA as a whole.
5. One primary purpose is recognized, to carry the AA message to the alcoholics who still suffer.
6. There should be no commercialization. An AA group should never endorse, finance or lend the AA name to any related facility or outside enterprise.
7. Every AA group is fully self-supporting.
8. The movement is non-professional in character, but service centers may employ special workers.
9. AA as such should not form national or international organizations, but service boards may be created, or committees, directly responsible to those they serve.
10. AA should not express any opinion concerning outside issues and the AA name should never be drawn into public controversy.
11. Public relations should be based on attraction rather than on promotion. Personal anonymity should be observed at the level of press, radio, TV and films.
12. Principles should always be placed before personalities.

The principles were summarized as follows:

It was thought that no alcoholic man or woman could be excluded from our society; that our leaders might serve but never govern; that each group was to be autonomous and there was to be no professional class of therapy. There were to be no fees or dues; our expenses were to be met by our own voluntary contributions. There was to be the least possible organization, even in our service centers. Our public relations were to be based upon attraction rather than promotion. It was decided that all members ought to be anonymous at the level of press, radio, TV and films. And in no circumstances should we give endorsements, make alliances or enter public controversies. (Cited from *Alcoholics Anonymous*.)[1]

The alcoholics anonymous did not invent the concept "therapeutic community," but they were the first ones to apply it in real life, and through the force of their movement, hundreds of thousands of people have been relieved of their irresistible urge to drink.

Maxwell Jones

Maxwell Jones is an English psychiatrist who started a new movement within psychiatry, generally known as "social psychiatry."

The name of Maxwell Jones is probably better known throughout the world than that of any other British psychiatrist. This is because both by his example at the Henderson Hospital, near London, and at Dingleton Hospital, Melrose, and by his eloquent expositions he has come to be identified with one of the most valuable contributions of social psychiatry: the concept of the therapeutic community. In his own terms, this means the employment to the fullest advantage of the therapeutic potential which resides in all members of a multidisciplinary treatment team and in the patients with whom they happen to work. To translate the concept into a working reality is far from easy.

Many hundreds of mental-health workers have made the pilgrimage to Henderson or Dingleton Hospital and scores from all of the "helping professions" have elected to work with Dr. Jones to learn his techniques. Many others imitated his example in their own daily work. (Cited from G. M. Carstairs.)[2]

Dr. Jones himself has described his early experience with psychiatry as disheartening, and claims that the war years were his "salvation." At that time he was a doctor at the Maudsley Hospital, part of which was evacuated to Mill Hill School, and he was put in charge of a unit of 100 beds occupied by armed forces personnel.

All presented similar symptoms, including pain over the region of the heart, breathlessness, palpitation, postural giddiness and fatigue, arising fundamentally from psychological rather than physical causes. We carried out extensive physiological studies which gave us a reasonably clear understanding of how these symptoms were produced. We wished to pass on this knowledge to our patients and, as they all had very similar symptoms, it seemed appropriate to meet with them as a body. This was my first experience of large group therapy involving a population of about 100 patients to six staff. We started in 1941 with a very didactic series of talks, but rapidly my colleagues and I realized that the patients learnt a great deal more about their condition if they were fully involved in a two-way interaction and discussion with us. And so, almost imperceptibly, we moved from the idea of teaching with a passive, captive audience, to one of social learning as a process of interaction between the staff and the patients. By the end of the war we were convinced that people living together in hospital, whether patients or staff, derived great benefit from examining, in daily community meetings, what they were doing and why they were doing it. (Cited from Maxwell Jones.)[3]

So far, it was more a group therapy experience than a therapeutic community. Dr. Jones's observations resemble those of several others from the same period. Dr. Lloyd W. McCorkle told the writer of his own experience with group therapy for recalcitrant and criminal American soldiers at Fort Knox. "I had about a hundred men in barracks. One day I showed up in officer's uniform and ordered them to line up on the ground floor. After a thorough inspection, during which I made numerous remarks about their dress, I sent them all to correct it in their rooms. They had hardly arrived there before I ordered them to line up again, this time raising my voice and reprimanding them for being slow. They were then dismissed, but I called them back again a third and a fourth time, criticizing them more sharply each time. The fifth time I ordered them to line up they were all enraged and ready to murder me. I ordered 'attention' and then 'at ease' and then said quietly: 'This is life in the army, isn't it?' " When the soldiers had recovered from their surprise, McCorkle held his first group therapy session with them.

At the end of the war, Dr. Jones and his colleagues were asked to organize a treatment unit for British ex-prisoners of war who had just returned from the prison camps in Europe and the Far East. This "presented an ideal opportunity for us to extend our interests from a predominantly psychosomatic field to a predominantly social one."[4] Daily meetings were organized with groups of approximately 50 patients and the appropriate staff. The success of this venture, according to Dr. Jones, prompted the Ministries of Health, Labor and Pensions to initiate a treatment unit for social misfits. This unit, initially known as the Industrial Neurosis Unit, Belmont Hospital, later changed its name to the Social Rehabilitation Unit and then, in 1959, became a separate hospital known as *Henderson Hospital*. Since its establishment in 1946, this unit has changed its function from a rehabilitation unit primarily concerned with unemployed "drifters" to a treatment unit for character disorders.

The essence of the therapeutic community idea, according to Dr. Jones, is the change in the usual status of the patient. In collaboration with the staff, he now becomes an active participant in his own therapy and that of other patients and in many aspects of the unit's general activities. This is in marked contrast to the relatively more passive, recipient role in conventional treatment situations.[5] The entire community of staff, patients, and their relatives is involved in varying degrees in treatment and administration. "The emphasis on free communication both within and between staff and patient groups and on permissive attitudes which encourage free expression of feeling implies a democratic, egalitarian rather than a traditional hierarchical social organization."[6] In Dr. Jones's opinion, an essential feature of the organization of a therapeutic community is the daily community meeting, which means a meeting of the entire patient and staff population of a particular unit or section. He has found it practical to hold meetings of this kind with as many as 80 patients and up to a staff of 30. The upper limit, he believes, should be about 100 patients. In larger institutions, a division into sub-units is advisable. Dr. Jones shares the opinion that administrative units in hospitals and prisons should not exceed between four and five hundred individuals. On the other hand, Dr. Jones believes on the basis of his own experience that:

> . . . Patients with non-psychotic character disorders, undergoing intensive group treatment both in small groups and daily meetings of the entire community, are best catered for in a population of between sixty to one hundred individuals. This ensures a comfortable degree of anonymity and yet offers a sufficient variety of identifications for the patients to choose among. Closed living groups of a smaller size, say twenty people, undergoing intensive group treatment for, perhaps, six to twelve months seem much more likely to us to develop difficulties in the personal relationships between members outside the actual treatment meetings. Such a relatively small number of people living together have little opportunity to develop congenial cliques, or subgroups, so that interaction in the treatment groups tend to overflow into ordinary lively situations." (Cited from *Maxwell Jones*.)[7]

Here is an account of life at Henderson Hospital written in 1969 by a visiting Swedish psychiatrist:

> There were about 40 patients, men and women, most of whom were rather young, all suffering from character disorders. Several of them were criminal, some were alcoholics, and a few were drug addicts.
> The staff comprised four psychiatrists, one psychologist, two psychiatric social workers, a number of male and female nurses, and work foremen, in addition to a category called 'social therapists,' who were generally young students sharing the daily life of the patients and thus furnishing a kind of comradely contact. Patients as well as staff wore civilian clothes and called each other by first names. The staff roles were rather flexible, everyone did almost everything.
> The most striking feature of the clinic was the inmate participation

in the government of the institution. A chairman, as well as two vice-chairmen, plus other leading functionaries such as the treasurer and some foremen, were nominated by the patients for one or several months at a stretch. All important decisions were taken at the general meeting at eight-thirty in the morning, at which all patients and staff assembled, under the one-man-one-vote principle. . . . Admittance and discharge were decided upon at Henderson by the patients. A person who wanted to be admitted had to present himself and explain his or her problems to a special admissions committee, composed of patients and staff, who decided upon the request. Discharge, on the other hand, could be decided upon only by the general meeting, on request of the patient himself, his fellow inmates, or the staff, either because a patient had been found sufficiently treated, or non-treatable (for example, as when he could not follow the few rules that were laid down). Discharge for not being treatable was, in fact, the only "sanction" that existed, but at the same time it was always hanging over the patients' heads as a threat for such misbehaviour as continuous absence from group meetings in spite of warnings, the use of violence instead of discussion, or the use of drugs.[8]

The only type of treatment consisted of group psychotherapy. Individual therapy did not exist, nor was medication used. All problems, common as well as individual, were openly discussed at group meetings, and there were several kinds of groups—the general morning meeting, the ward meeting, workshop meetings, the psychiatric groups, etc. All the groups were relatively large, from ten to twelve in the psychiatric group sessions to over fifty at the general meetings. This gave the meetings their special character, as some of them were rather unconcentrated and disorderly, even if open violence was not tolerated. Everything that happened at the small meetings was reported to the general meeting, including the discussions at the special staff meetings. This way, most incidents became known to everybody. When relatives came on visits they also were drawn into these group meetings.

The open structure of the "therapeutic community" caused a great deal of anxiety among the staff, and it was therefore necessary to have frequent staff meetings in order to neutralize this anxiety. The treatment time was generally rather extensive, lasting from nine to twelve months. The idea was that the patients should learn to analyze their own behavior, to understand other people's problems, and to know how to associate with others in order to be better prepared for a life in ordinary society. There was also an "ex-patients club" in London, where they could keep in contact with each other if they so wanted. (Cited from *Lisbet Palmgren*.)[9]

Maxwell Jones' therapeutic community methods have been copied in many places. As with group therapy, the interpretation of the idea has been manifold. One version, in a penal setting, is to be seen at the Grendon Underwood Prison in England, where about 160 male inmates, divided in four wards, are treated along the same lines as at Henderson, with the limitations imposed by the fact that the patients are prisoners and that the law requires certain rules to be enforced.

Another version is the *H. van der Hoeven Kliniek* at Utrecht. The Netherlands. The chief psychiatrist and director of the institution, Dr. Anna Marie Roosenberg, has created a special treatment system in this old, rather dilapidated institution which has made it known all over the world, making it a place of interest to penologists and treatment specialists. The inmate population consists of about 80 ex-prisoners, sentenced under the Netherlands' penal law to undergo treatment at a special institution after having served a prison sentence. The patients are generally difficult recidivists, many of whom have committed crimes of violence or sexual crimes. The number of staff corresponds to the number of inmates, about 80 staff to 80 inmates. The core of the staff is composed of "sociotherapists," about 30 persons divided up to serve the eight to nine groups of inmates. Each group consists of from seven to twelve patients and three or four therapists. There is regular, organized participation on the part of the inmates in the affairs of the institution, although it is not as far-reaching as at Henderson. Individual therapy is very much relied on, and some patients are on ordinary medication treatment.

A very modern institution is the *W.P.J. Pompe-kliniek* at Nijmegen, The Netherlands. It is built for about 100 patients of the same type as those found in the van der Hoeven Kliniek, but the staff is more numerous—about 150 persons. In principle, it is an open institution, but there is also a small closed section. The leader and chief psychiatrist, Dr. J.R.M. Maas, who has experience from his work at the van der Hoeven-Klinick, has modified to a certain extent the treatment program of the latter institution. The core of the treatment team consists of about 80 socio-therapists, and the inmates are divided up into groups of seven to nine persons who are looked after by about as many socio-therapists. Group therapy plays no major role, but the daily conferences among the staff, and between staff and patients, are numerous and varied in size and scope.

Both of these two Dutch institutions have, of course, experienced difficulties with the seriously disturbed type of inmates among their clientele and the open type of treatment employed as part of the program. Eruptions of inmate aggression can cause serious difficulties for the staff, and escapes are numerous. During the first two years of the existence of the Pompe-Kliniek there were about 200 escapes, most of which fortunately were not combined with new crimes. The feasibility of a treatment program for criminals as it is conceived in these two Dutch institutions depends highly upon the tolerance and understanding of public opinion.[10]

Chuck Dederich and Synanon

Although the term "therapeutic community" is seldom used about the Synanon institutions—never by its founder Dederich—still they furnish the best example in existence of the real therapeutic community.

Charles E. (Chuck) Dederich has been called many things: "a madman with delusions of grandeur, a saint, an opportunist, a brilliant executive, a latter-day Socrates, a loud and arrogant egotist, a hilarious comic, an earthquake, a herd of one elephant."[11] Nobody can deny that he is an extraordinary person. But, at the age of 45, he was regarded as a social misfit. At that time he had a ruined business career and two broken marriages behind him. His father was an alcoholic, as was he himself. He turned to Alcoholics Anonymous for help, participated in their meetings, went back to the use of alcohol, succeeded in recovering, and started to help other alcoholics. He let them share his own poor lodging (he lived mainly on welfare), organized daily meetings in his room at which everything was discussed from politics to the participants' own miserable lives, and one day decided what he wanted to do and set out to accomplish his idea.[12]

Drug addicts had begun to appear on the scene, until finally they outnumbered the alcoholics in Dederich's group. The American nation was even more worried about drug addiction than about alcoholism, which after all was more or less part of the American way of life. Americans are used to "social" drinking. But, drugs were new, horrifying, Oriental, unacceptable. More interest was soon focused on drugs than on alcohol, although the latter was definitely more dangerous to the health and welfare of the nation. Dederich became aware of this interest and decided to start "curing" drug addicts.

He found an empty store in Pacific Ocean Park, California, in July, 1958. This was the heart of a beach slum area, with drug traffic all around. The store, which rented for one hundred dollars a month, served both as a club house and a meeting place, but people also moved in to live there, as many had no place else to go, and slept on mattresses on the floor. Dederich held his daily meetings, mostly following the AA model, but generally dominated by himself, more or less in the role of teacher.

When the addicts began to come along and two or three of them started *not* to use drugs, I became aware of how unusual this was. I know there are periodic drunks who occasionally stay on the wagon, but—I gathered this right out of the mouths of the addicts—there are no periodic addicts. They had never, never known anyone who had voluntarily quit drugs. I started to think that the addicts perhaps knew more about addiction than the specialists—doctors and criminologists—who had tried to examine them. Almost no addict actually quits using drugs accidentally, and very few of them by design. Every addict that I've met has been to group and individual therapy on the couch—in private treatment and in prison. In that storefront, they all said: "None of it works, and yet we are not using drugs today." And they stayed free for three weeks, four, five and even seven weeks, and then one would go out and get lost—that is, take a "fix."

When they went out and fixed, I became very emotional. It was a challenge to me. I would get mad. "Who do you think you are?" I would really give them hell about it. And, believe it or not, they wouldn't fix for a while.

Psychologically, I knew the addict was emotionally immature—a child. I assumed they were like children and treated them as such. (Cited from *Daniel Casriel*.)[13]

There existed great permissiveness in this pre-Synanon house. "Sex was all over the place," Dederich admitted, but he felt he simply had to allow them to have something quickly that they could understand and stay with. "I tried to allow them to have fun in any manner as long as they didn't get drunk, shoot dope, or hurt anybody." By the end of July, 1958, he knew he had something that would work on addicts. Asked by Dr. Daniel Casriel who wrote the first book on Synanon, what his motivation was, Dederich simply stated: "I wanted to be a big man. I wanted to make history." He certainly did achieve his goal![14]

Synanon

Of course many people laughed at Dederich when on September 18, 1958, he turned his little enterprise into a foundation, duly incorporated and with a bank account of fifty dollars! He had to face an attempted "palace revolt" staged by the alcoholics who felt that the AA principles were being violated, but Dederich had the addicts on his side, and the opponents were literally thrown out. Dederich also had great problems with those who continued using drugs. But worst of all, he had to defend himself and his enterprise against a neighborhood full of mounting suspicion and overt hostility. The police came, as did representatives of the fire and sanitation authorities, and the building was condemned as a place of residence. Synanon had to move.

Dederich started looking for another place, and miraculously managed to lease a big building at Santa Monica on the Pacific Beach front, which had once served as a club house for millionaires, later taken over as an American Legion hall, and finally used as a National Guard armory. In August, 1959, 40 ex-addicts moved into the house as residents. More and more arrived, until they soon filled the house, and Dederich had to lease other buildings nearby. Then he opened new Synanons in Oakland, San Francisco, and smaller branches in New York, Detroit, Puerto Rico, and Tomales Bay (California). The last-mentioned one is now the residence of Dederich, where Foundation policy and plans are formulated, and where Synanon is designing and building its own city. At the beginning of 1972, Synanon had about 1700 people living in its various quarters, while nearly twice as many were active non-residents.

Synanon has become a large organization, but what is the derivation of the name itself? It stems from the difficulties which an addict had with the foreign terms used in the early discussions at the Ocean Park store. He tried in vain to remember "symposium" and "seminar," and finally amalgamated them into "synanon," which Dederich gratefully adopted as the name for his whole enterprise. The present-day philosophy and organization of Synanon has been described by Dederich himself:

> . . . a climate consisting of a family structure similar in some areas to a primitive tribal structure, which seems to affect individuals on a subconscious level. The structure also contains overtones of a 19th century family set-up of the type which produced inner-directed personalities. It is the feeling of the Synanon Foundation that an undetermined percentage of narcotic addicts are potentially inner-directed people as differentiated from tradition-directed people. A more or less autocratic family structure appears to be necessary as a pre-conditioning environ-

ment to buy time for the recovering addict. . . . The autocratic over-tone of the family structure demands that the patients or members of the family perform tasks as part of the group. As a member is able to take direction in small tasks such as helping in the preparation of meals, house-cleaning and so forth, regardless of his rebellion at being "told what to do," his activity seems to provide exercise of emotions of giving or creating which have lain dormant. As these muscles strengthen, it seems that the resistance to cooperating with the group tends to dissipate. (Cited from *the Narcotic Drug Study Commission of the New Jersey Legislature.*)[15]

It seems clear that the emphasis at Synanon is on formal and informal group interactions, where individuals express their true feelings about one another and about their life situations.

The Synanon has been described as a form of group therapy. The literature about Synanon would suggest that it is in a tradition of re-pressive, inspirational group therapy, where addicts reinforce one another's wish to remain "clean" and, in the terms of Synanon's resi-dents, "grow up."[16]

The "tools" for making the Synanon members "grow up" are the following:

1. All members are divided into "tribes" of from seventy to one hundred people, who provide each other with individual support. Within each tribe are members whose Synanon experience ranges from zero to three years. During an addict's first 90 days, a highly precarious period in which he alternately trusts and fears and persistently looks for injustices, he is provided comfort, friendship, new opportunities for communication, and new viewpoints. He participates three times weekly in "tribal games" where he seeks new understanding and vents frustrations. After two or three months, his behavior is scrutinized more intensely during games, and he in-creases his constructive use and enjoyment of them. Members with a year's experience who are seeking responsibility or rewards are often selected to head dormitories of 10 to 15 newer residents. A few tribe members with two to three years of experience take disciplinary action for repeated unacceptable behavior. Each tribe has a comfortable meeting area, and in some older tribe members maintain "eternal vigilance" for those seeking company, assurance, or help with immediate problems. These problems can be chan-neled to the tribe leader, who intervenes in situations ranging from uncomfortable beds to job changes and who is ultimately responsi-ble for the tribe membership.

2. The "game," once called the "synanon," which is more or less regarded as a sort of intellectual sport, an enjoyable, often demanding, pastime pitting a person against opponents. About a dozen people play the game, acting as mirrors for each other in which the individual glimpses himself as others see him. The intense, free expression of feelings which allows this new perception usually receives its impetus from an experienced player who has learned techniques of attack and defense to increase involvement and enjoyment of the contest for everyone. Synanon games are fast-paced and exciting, with frequent wild accusations, screams of rage, and peals of laughter.
3. Other treatment methods are named "the stew," where newcomers in particular discuss and learn; "the haircut," a meeting between older experienced Synanon members and the "little gangster type" who has to be "taken down" and made ashamed of his attitudes; and the "Synanon trip," which is regarded as a sort of ersatz for the drug trip and organized as a special 48 hour play, during which the participants, clothed alike in long white robes, stay awake together for the duration, talking, listening to music, and so forth.[17]

Dederich himself is the Chairman of the Board of the Synanon Foundation. His closest collaborators are all former addicts, who once "had crawled into Synanon on their hands and knees."[18] It is a paternalistic, autocratic organization where the members can earn promotion to responsible posts by proving their capacity. Everyone is requested to work and contribute what he can. He has to deposit his money and belongings with Synanon, from which he gets a small daily sum of money for incidental expenses. Food and clothing are provided by the organization, and previously cigarettes, but for some time smoking tobacco has also been outlawed. The latter decision caused an exodus of a great many synanists who had been living for a long time without drugs and alcohol, but refused to give up tobacco. The leaders of the organization receive better pay and are also better accomodated than the other members. Married couples usually are provided with their own apartments. One-fourth of the members are women.

The money needed for this costly operation comes almost entirely from private donations. The new facility at San Francisco, for example, was funded by a donation from a big company in New York. However, Synanon has not managed to receive the blessing and support of state governments, and only partly from local city councils. The Santa Monica authorities even had Dederich jailed for a short time on minor charges. Criticism is often based on accusations that Synanon demands donations from relatives before they agree to admit an addict, taking advantage of a desperate situation in which relatives are likely to do their utmost to produce any sum requested. But above all, Synanon is criticized for not obtaining the curative results that it claims. The New Jersey Commission on Narcotic Drugs tried to arrive at some sound statistical knowledge by examining the names and figures they could obtain from Synanon, along with the information in the possession of the Santa Monica police department. On this basis it concluded that Synanon is in no way more effective than more conventional and less controversial treatment methods. The Commission added:

> Sponsors of the Synanon Foundation and others supporting this organization speak favorably of the results of this endeavor which operates on the principle of group therapy and self-help. However, the lack of supervisory personnel with formal educational background and training and the lack of validated and reliable statistics are such that the success or lack of success of this method of treatment in this particular establishment was unable to be properly evaluated.[19]

Success or failure, statistically seen, probably does not render a fair judgement of Synanon. Even if many come to be cured, but leave uncured, it remains a fact that a considerable number of addicts have been cured at Synanon. This is what is of primary importance, not whether Synanon does better or worse than other treatment facilities. In any case, Dederich has shown an ability for leadership in a present-day context that might place him on the same level as Wichern with his Rauhes Haus. Like Wichern, Dederich has fought a one-man war, and like him he has succeeded in obtaining interest and support from the general public. It remains to be seen if Dederich's creation—Synanon—will become as long-lived as Rauhes Haus.

Synanon imitations have also come into being. The best known is probably the *Daytop Lodge* in Tottenville, Staten Island, New York.[20] It is, however, a rather small operation, maintained and supervised by the Probation Department of the New York Supreme Court and organized for the treatment of heroin addicts convicted of felonies. The resident manager is an ex-addict, and the treatment program is essentially the same as that of Synanon.[21]

[22] INTERNATIONAL CO-OPERATION

Enoch C. Wines

As demonstrated in this book, the great reformers in the treatment of criminals often made a profound impression on contemporary society. One result of their efforts to reform and rehabilitate concurrently with the penalty, or instead of it, was that individuals dedicated to the cause sought contact with one another. John Howard's book on the state of prisons inspired others involved in penal problems to visit institutions in different countries. This was particularly true of the experiments in the United States, which attracted numerous European visitors. During the nineteenth century, many periodicals concerned primarily or exclusively with the treatment of criminals were started, gaining international readership. One that had a great influence in Europe was *Jahrbücher der Gefängniskunde*, founded by three Germans, Nicolaus Heinrich Julius (a physician), Georg Varrentrapp (a physician), and Friedrich Noellner (a lawyer). The three, together with the prominent professor of law at Heidelberg, Karl Joseph Anton von Mittermaier, took the initiative for the first international congress, which opened in Frankfurt-am-Main on September 28, 1846, attended by 75 persons who represented the United States and 12 European countries. The participants comprised lawyers, physicians, prison chaplains, wardens, and heads of correctional administrations. The meeting lasted three days, and discussions were concentrated on solitary or separate confinement as a method of treatment. The majority resolved that individual deprivation of liberty, the usual term for separate confinement in a cell in those days, was the only acceptable foundation on which to build a modern correctional system.[1]

The congress in Frankfurt was an appetizer, followed by other meetings. At this point, governments began to be interested and became involved in an international exchange of ideas. Gradually we see how the official delegates push the idealists and experts into the background. One who unwittingly contributed to this trend was the great American prison reformer, Enoch C. Wines. After the first big American penological congress in Cincinnati in 1870, and, with its support, Wines was able to give a new lease on life to international co-operation in correctional policy, which had been terminated by the wars in Europe.[2]

In Wines's opinion, the new type of international consultation in questions pertaining to correctional policy, which was intended to have a wider scope than the actual treatment of prisoners and thus also to include the prevention of crime, should be founded on inter-governmental collaboration. Wines believed this would enhance the prestige and influence of the congresses, provide them with a solid financial base, and also clear the way for true international co-operation. He further envisaged that the governmental delegates at these congresses would come under the influence of the real pioneers in criminology. He himself had observed the eye-opening effect of Zebulon R. Brockway's speech at the Cincinnati congress.

The outcome of Wines's efforts was a world congress, which opened in London on July 3, 1872, with 400 delegates, one-fourth of whom represented government. The entire congress was planned to be inspirational, to cause people to think, not to draw up resolutions on the ninety-odd topics that Wines had put on the agenda. That the congress actually was an inspiration to all the participating countries was reflected in the events of the next few years, when a veritable wave of reform swept over the prisons of the United States and Europe. Wines succeeded in achieving a decision to try to organize a permanent organization for inter-governmental co-operation. First, this body came to be known as the International Penitentiary Commission (IPC), later as the International Penal and Penitentiary Commission (IPPC).

The next world congress was held in Stockholm in 1878. By now, the number of official delegates had reached 300. Wines was unable to attend because of old age and poor health; he died shortly thereafter. That he no longer had influence on the choice of topics that were discussed is obvious from the transactions. Beginning with this congress, the governmental delegates dominated the discussions and ran the resolution machinery. The rest of the delegates were kept in the background, whether they represent international associations or themselves. They were not allowed a voice until after the official delegates had expressed themselves.

Nevertheless, the member nations collaborated within IPPC, which maintained a secretariat in Bern, Switzerland. A world congress was held every five years in different capitals. The two world wars broke the continuity, but IPPC renewed its activities when they ended. A careful examination of the detailed minutes of the congresses, which reproduce all the speeches verbatim, does not reveal anything particularly constructive. In fact, it can be said that the progress that was made in the United States and Europe came about despite the recommendations of the congresses rather than because of them. Open prisons are a good example of this. They were introduced in several countries, even though the IPPC congress in Prague in 1930 preferred not to take a stand on the matter. It is fair to say that these congresses reflected primarily the prevailing official attitude to the prevention of crime and the treatment of criminals. There was little room for innovations in the discussions.[3]

The United Nations

After World War II, the United Nations entered the arena with claims that it could perform better than IPPC. The last Secretary General of IPPC was Thorsten Sellin, the American criminologist, whose onerous task it was to liquidate the organization and, even more difficult, to keep an eye on the United Nations to make sure that it fulfilled the obligations it assumed when it took over the responsibility for international co-operation in criminal policy. At first, the outlook was promising, as nobody anticipated military conflicts in the foreseeable future after World War II. The organizations created within (in close co-operation with the United Nations) were almost exclusively devoted to the improvement of the economic and social conditions of all peoples. Faith in fundamental human rights, in the dignity and worth of the human person, in the equal rights of men and women and of nations was affirmed in the United Nations Charter, the first article of which states that the United Nations shall endeavor to bring about co-operation between all peoples and promote and strengthen respect for human rights and the fundamental freedom of all, regardless of race, sex, language, and religion.

The United Nations had pledged to IPPC that it would not only continue its program but also considerably expand it. In 1952, the United Nations founded a journal called the *International Review of Criminal Policy*, which appeared in English, French, and Spanish. It built up a worldwide network of "correspondents" with whom the Secretariat could communicate directly, thereby bypassing the red tape involved in working through the national United Nations delegations. International associations in the area of criminal policy were affiliated with the United Nations with consultative status. The United Nations published studies and sponsored seminars in various parts of the world on such topics as probation, parole, juvenile delinquency, the medical, psychological, and social examination of delinquents, and so on. The member countries were divided into regional groups, which were expected to hold meetings of experts every second year. The United Nations was to continue the IPPC practice of sponsoring world congresses every five years.

It soon became clear, however, that the United Nations had promised more than it could deliver. The world was not the peaceful place the founders had hoped for, and the focus of the new organization did not remain as envisaged. New issues of the journal became increasingly rare with less interesting contents. There was no money to publish it in the three working languages, and all that remained was the English edition with summaries in French and Spanish. The journal soon lost its impact, with fewer and fewer readers. The seminars diminished in number, as did the publications on special topics. The section with eight officials set up in the Social Development Division of the Secretariat to handle matters dealing with criminal policy (first called the Section for Social Defence and later the Section for Crime Prevention and Criminal Justice) found it increasingly difficult to keep abreast with developments in the rest of the world, mainly because of cuts in travel funds for staff members.

One notable achievement was the founding of a regional center in Fuchu, Japan, the Asia and Far East Institute for the Prevention of Crime and the Treatment of Offenders (UNAFEI). Due to the skillful program planning by its first director, Norval Morris, law professor and criminologist, and to the strong support of the then Japanese Attorney General, Yoshitsugu Baba, UNAFEI was a great success in its part of the world. Meanwhile, since it is now financed solely by the Japanese Government (the United Nations has no real influence on its activity), it is a United Nations organization in name only. If the Institute wishes to be inspected by the United Nations, the Japanese Government must defray the travel expenses of a representative of the United Nations.

In recent years, two new regional institutes have been founded: one in Cairo, Egypt, and one in San José, Costa Rica. The former is intended primarily for the Arab countries (although it aspires to cover all Africa), but in reality it is an appendage to the Egyptian national institute for the same questions. The latter is meant to serve all Latin America. It is problematic as to how long the United Nations will be able to support these two institutes financially.

Finally, it should be noted that the United Nations, in cooperation with the Italian Government, initiated a special research center in Rome, the United Nations Social Defence Research Institute (UNSDRI), which began with great style, inaugurated by Secretary General U. Thant. But UNSDRI, too, appears to be destined to have an increasingly humble existance. For a couple of years the United Nations maintained two so-called inter-regional advisers, who visited countries that sought their counsel at no cost to the host governments. Many governments showed great interest in the program and many requests for the services of the advisers were submitted. Eventually United Nations interest, as well as financial support, gave out, and that ended the advisers' jobs. Unfortunately, this happened at exactly the moment when this form of counselling service was most urgently needed, namely, when the time had come for the implementation throughout the world of the Standard Minimum Rules for the Treatment of Prisoners.

Hitherto, the world congresses have been held more or less according to the original plan to maintain the IPPC tradition of a congress every five years. The first one was held in Geneva in 1955, followed by one in London in 1960, Stockholm in 1965, Tokyo in 1970, and Geneva in 1975.[4] In principle, these congresses have been open not only to governmental delegations but also to a few inter-governmental and a large number of nongovernmental organizations, as well as to qualified private individuals. In reality, however, they have been dominated by the governmental delegates to an even greater extent than under IPPC. Consequently, researchers, administrators, and others with practical correctional backgrounds have usually found themselves deprived of any real influence, particularly since they are only permitted a few words at the end of a debate after all the governmental delegates have finished. Wines's old dream of a dialogue between governmental representatives, innovators, and critics with practical experience has faded away.

Another form of international co-operation is now beginning to flourish under the auspices of various private organizations, primarily the International Association of Penal Law (founded in 1924), the International Society of Criminology (founded in 1937), and the International Society of Social Defence (founded in 1949). These three organizations, which sponsor well-attended international meetings at which all participants have an equal chance to express their views, collaborate with the International Penal and Penitentiary Foundation, a body formed to administer the funds belonging to IPPC at its dissolution. Thus, the Foundation has the financial means to sponsor activities that otherwise could not be undertaken. One of its projects has been to organize meetings between the heads of correctional administrations from different countries.

It is obvious that governmental delegations at congresses, sponsored by the United Nations, never criticize conditions in their own countries. No one will admit that the treatment of criminals in his country is other than tolerant and humane. For example: torture was on the agenda of the Geneva meeting in 1975. One might ask why this was so, since every governmental representative present testified that torture did not exist in his country. A different story was told at a special meeting of Amnesty International, held in Geneva concurrently with the U.N. Congress. The reports submitted were horrendous.

An unending stream of well-meaning statements and resolutions have been adopted by the United Nations. But, no state seems bound by them. This applies in the highest degree to the serious efforts made under authority of the United Nations to achieve general adherence to the humanitarian principles for the treatment of prisoners, the Standard Minimum Rules, mentioned earlier.

The Standard Minimum Rules for the Treatment of Prisoners

The idea of formulating a series of rules for the treatment of prisoners that would be valid internationally emerged from the interminable discussions that went on in IPPC regarding the most successful methods of treating persons deprived of their liberty for criminal offenses. Finally, in 1926, IPPC made a formal resolution to take on this task. In 1933, it produced a draft, which was approved by the League of Nations.[5] Nothing happened until after World War II, when the rules were revised and included in the dossier of unfinished business handed over to the United Nations by Thorsten Sellin, IPPC's last Secretary General.

This was a project that was particularly appropriate for an international organization such as the United Nations and credit should be given to it for the vigor with which it prepared a document that would be acceptable to the organization's political bodies. It called meetings of correctional experts and governmental delegates in Europe, Latin America, the Middle East, and Asia. Paul Amor, former head of the correctional administration in France, and, after him, the Bolivian, Manuel Lopez-Rey, former head of the Spanish correctional system, were at that time in charge of the United Nations Social Defence Section, and it was due to their enthusiasm for the task that it was handled so expeditiously that the rules were ready for presentation to the first United Nations Congress for the Prevention of Crime and the Treatment of Offenders in Geneva in 1955.

The 94 rules, reproduced *in extenso* as an appendix to this book, listed the principles that, at the time they were approved, appeared to be self-evident to their drafters as minimum requirements in a civilized world. These rules do not set up any guidelines for an "ideal" treatment of prisoners. They were approved by the United Nations Economic and Social Council (ECOSOC) in 1957. They were printed in English, French, and Spanish, and sent to all member nations. After that, nothing more was done about them by the United Nations. Lopez-Rey was succeeded as chief of the Social Defence Section by the American, Edward Galway. He was succeeded by the Englishman, William Clifford who, in turn, was replaced by the American, Gerhard Mueller. These people belonged to the elite in the area of criminal policy, but the funds at their disposal continued to shrink, and it grew increasingly difficult to maintain U.N.'s position of leadership in criminal policy both within the Secretariat and in the world.

The question of a revision of the rules was raised at the United Nations Congress in Tokyo in 1970, but the consensus was that efforts should be concentrated on making them known and having them implemented as they stood; at least, it appeared so.

In 1967, the United Nations Secretariat sent a questionnaire to the 135 member-countries, requesting detailed information concerning the extent to which the Minimum Rules had been implemented. Only 44 responses were received. A second questionnaire was circulated in 1974, and 62 countries replied, including the United States, Canada, and 26 European countries. No response was received from the majority of the developing countries. Even if we confine ourselves to the replies that did come in and that presumably emated from countries with the least to conceal, the results are depressing. The U.N. Secretariat's report to the Geneva Congress in 1975 states dejectedly that "some of the perhaps most important rules are among those least effectively implemented". The rules have not had the role designed for them.

The governmental delegates at the last Geneva Congress willingly signed the proposals drafted by the United Nations Secretariat and thereby agreed, among other things, that the rules should be reprinted and annotated and that all member nations should be "both persuaded to implement the rules and, if need be, assisted in doing it". The General Assembly of the United Nations had already made a helpful move when on December 20, 1971, it invited "the attention of the Member States to the rules, recommended their effective implementation and requested that favorable consideration be given to their incorporation in national legislations".

Of course, the extent to which these well-meaning resolutions will yield practical results is an open question.

Must Humanity pay off?

Through the years, Sweden has acquired a reputation (relatively underserved, as it happens) as a pioneer in the treatment of offenders. Consequently, while I was Director General of the Swedish Correctional Administration, I was invited to a number of other countries to report on the treatment of prisoners in Sweden. In 1968, for example, I was invited to New York by the Vera Institute of Justice; both Mayor John V. Lindsay and Commissioner George F. McGrath asked me to lecture on "Prison Reforms and Innovations in Sweden" at the Rikers Island Prison. Most of the audience were interested in prison reform either as professionals or for idealistic reasons. (Some prisoners were present.)

I tried to give as accurate an account as possible of the Swedish situation without gilding the lily, often difficult when speaking about one's country. Even so, what I had to tell struck many of my listeners as an approximation of Utopia. In sum, I reported that more than one-third of Sweden's prisoners were in completely open institutions. Every inmate in open, as well as maximum security institutions, had a cell or a room of his own. Inmates in all open institutions and all new maximum security institutions had keys to their rooms or cells, while the personnel had access to a master key, as in a hotel. Most rooms in open institutions and cells in maximum security institutions were equipped with washing facilities and radios. There was a television set for every group of 20 prisoners. Jobs were available for all inmates in up-to-date workshops, in some of which the prisoner could earn the same or almost the same wage as a worker in the civilian market. Furthermore, assuming that he was not dangerous, a prisoner was allowed regular furloughs several times a year to visit his family. Approximately 90 per cent of the inmates with sentences exceeding six months could count on these furloughs; short-termers were also eligible for furlough in special circumstances. Inmates of open institutions were usually allowed to take their visitors, including women, to their room, locking the door if they wanted privacy. I pointed out that this more lenient attitude had saved the Swedish correctional system from homosexual problems often found in other countries.

One member of the audience asked me how the prisoners had responded to these privileges, which did not exist in the New York State prisons at that time. Were they grateful? Not at all, I replied. Perhaps at first, when the privilege was a novelty. (Privilege soon becomes a right.) I pointed out that Sweden held the world's record in prison escapes. Prisoners ran away from open as well as maximum security institutions, as a rule simply because they disliked being deprived of their liberty and usually without committing new offenses during the generally brief period before they were apprehended by the police and returned to their institution. Since institutional personnel were always unarmed, the escapee ran no risk of being shot in connection with an escape and the punishment usually consisted merely of a few weeks' extension of the time to be served. If the escapee committed a new crime, he would, of course, get a new sentence.

This information elicited a question whether the mild form of treatment practiced in Sweden was effective. Had we a lower rate of recidivism than before we had open institutions, furloughs, and so on? I replied that the rate of recidivism had increased, but that this could be explained. It had now become relatively difficult to be sentenced to prison. The courts began with probation, often several times in succession, at least if the offense was not particularly serious. In this way, most of the "mild" cases were eliminated. What remained were the most hardened offenders with psychological and social problems that defied solution. The increased use of probation had a negative effect on the results of probation, as well as of prison sentences. At first, probation was only used in guaranteed promising cases. The results were good, as anticipated. But, when we began to experiment with probation in less promising cases, the rate of recidivism naturally rose. Likewise, the prisons showed poorer results, probation having gradually deprived them of their most promising clientele.

This line of reasoning seemed logical to my questioner. But, he went on, if you add probation to prison and measure the two forms of treatment, can one claim that the results in Sweden were better than prior to these humanitarian reforms? I admitted that I did not know. In any case, in my opinion the question was of secondary importance. My reply upset the individual who had raised the point. Did I really mean that the taxpayers should spend money on what might be meaningless reforms aimed at making life in prison more agreeable for offenders? If a reform paid dividends, then there was reason to consider its introduction. If not, we had better adhere to the principle that a criminal should atone through a punishment that fits the crime.

The argument was not new; it was to be expected. Every penal reformer through the ages, regardless of national origin, has heard it and has countered it in essentially the same way. Replies differ slightly on the conditions prevailing at the time, but their substance does not vary. As an example, I cited Swedish Minister of Justice Herman Kling's opening address at the United Nations Congress for the Prevention of Crime and the Treatment of Offenders in Stockholm in 1965. Mr. Kling brought up the question of the results of different methods of treatment. He said that humane and costly methods do not yield appreciably better results than inhumane and inexpensive ones. The rate of recidivism is approximately the same. Consequently, there is resistance to the humanization of penal treatment on the grounds that it does not pay. Mr. Kling then sharply attacked this attitude to the problem:

> We must practice humanity without expecting anything in return. Humanitarianism should be regarded as a fundamental obligation to mankind, no matter where it leads. It is particularly important that we be steadfast in our allegiance to this principle in criminal policy, a prejudice-riddled area in which vengeful feelings are so easily aroused. The treatment of a criminal should not be designed according to what appears to be worthy of the individual in question. It should be worthy of society itself. I fear that we in Sweden, as in all other parts of the world, have to admit that our methods in this field are still not entirely worthy of society.

However, even if we adhere to the principle of humanity as the lode-star in the treatment of offenders, whether or not it pays off in terms of lower rates of recidivism, everyone nevertheless hopes that it will have a positive impact. Is there any justification for this hope so far?

Research in Relation to Treatment

The Gluecks exploded the myth of the successful results of the American reformatories.[1] A long line of researchers in various countries have followed in their wake and investigated the results of different kinds of sanctions. It is distressing to find that it really makes little difference what kind of treatment offenders are given; the results are the same, statistically.

The European Committee on Crime Problems, the official European joint agency for criminal policy with headquarters in Strasbourg, France, tried on one occasion to compare the results of three different methods of handling juvenile offenders: England's detention center, Germany's *Jugendarrest*, and Sweden's system of giving the child welfare boards the responsibility for supporting and supervising the young offender at liberty. All three countries were reasonably satisfied with the results. The English were the first to hand in a report, according to which two-thirds of the juveniles treated in a detention center did not become recidivists. Next, the Germans came with precisely the same outcome for their entirely different *Jugendarrest*. Finally, the Swedes turned up with essentially the same figures for their non-institutional method. Sir Lionel Fox, Chairman of the English Prison Commission, who led the discussion on these results of treatment, remarked drily in his summing up that it did not seem to make much difference what one did with young offenders: submit them to military-like discipline as in England, put them alone in a cell as in Germany, or help and support them in a probation-like setting as in Sweden. One-third would relapse, regardless of treatment.[2]

A Swedish criminologist made a comparison of juvenile delinquents whose offenses, personal qualities, and life situations appeared to be approximately the same, but, who were given different types of treatment. He found that the chances of recidivism were less in those sentenced to probation than in those sentenced to some form of institutional care, for example, imprisonment. However, a prominent professor of statistics analyzed the figures and came to the conclusion that the claim was not valid.[3]

All studies have not yielded such depressing results. Lipton, Martinson, and Wilk's investigation, published in 1975, suggests that treatment could, in fact, "pay off". They write that "intensive probation supervision is associated with lower recidivism rates for males and females under eighteen", and that "in general, good behaviour in prison (few institutional infractions) is associated with good behavior on parole". The accuracy of the first-mentioned observation has been challenged as inapplicable outside the cultural environment in which the study was conducted. The second claim has been received with skepticism, particularly among the treatment personnel themselves, who have found that the recidivist with a background of several prison sentences has a better understanding of how to control his temper while in an institution, and, therefore, gives the impression of being a better prisoner than the novice, who rebels at being deprived of his liberty. In reality, the unruly prisoner may have a better prognosis. So, they claim.

The circumstance that criminological research has not yet revealed which, if any, forms of treatment yield good results has led to a mounting wave of pessimism. What is the point of trying when nothing seems to help. This attitude, prevalent among contemporary criminologists, has naturally spread to the national agencies that administer institutions for offenders. What is worse, it has made governments wary of allocating funds for new approaches to the treatment of criminals. The earlier interest in improving treatment methods (of which this book has given so many examples) has been replaced by total indifference in many quarters. A reaction to this negativism was registered in a meeting held by the International Society for Criminology for its members during the United Nations Congress in Geneva in 1975. A number of participants expressed their doubts about the efficacy of any kind of treatment, when finally the American criminologist, Peter P. Lejins, and the Canadian criminologist, Denis Szabo, made impassioned pleas to their collegues not to be outdone by the cancer researchers. All over the world, they said, thousands of scientists have been working for years to solve the mystery of cancer. They still have made only small advances on the way to methods that can prevent and cure this scourge of mankind. Yet, they do not despair. Nor should we, even though the problems facing us may be equally difficult to unravel.

Dr. Kerstin Elmhorn, a researcher attached to UNSDRI, added that the gravest problem besetting criminology is the abundance of poor research. Criminologists have agreed to the kind of working conditions that result in projects being poorly planned, badly executed, and, unfortunately, completely misleading in many cases.[4]

The many discouraging results of criminological research do not absolve those responsible for treatment in institutions and outside them from their duty to persist in their efforts to rehabilitate offenders. Fortunately, however, the will to help is a widespread human quality regardless of how impossible the task may seem. This quality will always withstand even the most negative findings of research.

In this book we have met some of the pioneers in the more effective treatment of criminals. Many of them are tragic figures. They struggled with the indifference of their contemporaries; they suffered reverses; they ended their days in destitution. Worse, many of them lived to see their methods go awry, leading to misfortune rather than to happiness. What united them was an indomitable will to help their erring brother, he who had yielded to temptation, who was driven to crime by poverty or personality defects that were beyond his control. These pioneers are beacons in the history of mankind, the part that deals with compassion with one's fellowmen.

May these pioneers have innumerable successors.

NOTES AND REFERENCES

[1] BACKGROUND

1. The writer's notes on Joseph Goebbels's speech at the *Krolloper*, Berlin, 1935.
2. Thorsten Sellin, *Pioneering in Penology, the Amsterdam Houses of Correction in the Sixteenth and Seventeenth Centuries* (Philadelphia: University of Pennsylvania Press, 1944), p. 15.
3. Richard R. Korn and Lloyd W. McCorkle, *Criminology and Penology* (New York: Henry Holt, 1959), pp. 395–6.
4. *The Dialogues of Plato*, translated into English by B. Jowett (New York: Random House, 1937), vol. II, p. 600; Grellet-Wammy, *Manuel des Prisons* (Paris: Cherbuliez, 1838), Tome I, p. 3.
5. Sellin, *op. cit.*, p. 14.
6. Nikolaus Heinrich Julius, *Vorlesungen über die Gefängniskunde* (Berlin: Stuhr, 1928), p. 14.
7. D. Carlo Ilarione Petitti di Roreto, *Della condizione attuale delle Carceri e dei Mezzi di Migliorarla* (Torino: 1840), pp. 62–3.
8. Grellet-Wammy, *op. cit.*, p. 9; J. Iturrioz, "Fundamentos Sociologicos en Las Partidas de Alfonso X El Sabio", in *Estudios de Historia de Espana*, Part III, published by Departamento de Historia Social de Espana, del Instituto "Balmes" de Sociologia (Madrid: 1955), p. 8; Harald Livermore, *A History of Spain* (London: Allen and Unwin, 1958), p. 138.
9. Johan Hagströmer, *Om frihetsstraffen* (Uppsala: E. Edquist, 1875), pp. 2–3.
10. Max Grünhut, *Penal Reform* (Oxford: The Clarendon Press, 1948), p. 12.
11. Hugo von Hoegel, *Freiheitsstrafe und Gefängniswesen in Österreich von der Theresiana bis zur Gegenwart* (Graz: U. Moser, 1916), p. 1. See Thorsten Sellin, "Penal Servitude: Origin and Survival" in *Proceedings of the American Philosophical Society*, vol. 109, no. 5, October 1965, pp. 277–81. Here Sellin points out that penal servitude is a direct descendant of *opus publicum*, hard labor, in its ancient and medieval forms, including galley slavery. See also Franz von Holtzendorff and Eugen von Jagemann, *Handbuch des Gefängiswesens* (Hamburg: J.F. Richter, 1888), pp. 79–83.
12. Grünhut, *op. cit.*, pp. 21–2.
13. Hagströmer, *op. cit.*, pp. 3–4.
14. George Ives, *A History of Penal Methods, Criminals, Witches, Lunatics* (London: S. Paul and co., 1914), pp. 32–43.

[2] BRIDEWELL, THE LONDON HOUSE OF CORRECTION

1. Primary sources: Edward Geoffrey O'Donoghue, *Bridewell Hospital, Palace, Prison, Schools, from the Earliest Times to the End of the Reign of Elizabeth* (London: John Lane, 1923); Austin van der Slice, "Elizabethan Houses of Correction", *Journal of Criminal Law and Criminology*, vol. XXVII, 1937, pp. 45–67; R. von Hippel, "Beiträge zur Geschichte der Freiheitsstrafe",

Zeitschrift für die gesamte Strafrechtswissenschaft, vol. XVIII, 1898, pp. 419–94, 608–66; Wilhelm Traphagen, *Die ersten Arbeitshäuser und Ihre pädagogische Funktion* (Berlin: C. Heymann, 1935); Sidney and Beatrice Webb, *English Prisons under Local Government* (London: F. Cass, 1963), pp. 12–7.

2. Ridley played a theological as well as a political role. Edward VI died at the age of fifteen years, in the same year that he donated Bridewell to the City of London, and that Ridley was thrown into the Tower prison. Ridley was executed two years later for heresy *(Encyclopedia Britannica)*. For information of Luther's influence in England, see O'Donoghue, *op. cit.*, pp. 193–4.

3. Hippel, *op. cit.*, p. 425; Webb, *op. cit.*, p. 12, writes cautiously, "between 1552 and 1557".

4. Van der Slice, *op. cit.*, p. 52.

5. Max Grünhut, *Penal Reform* (Oxford: The Clarendon Press, 1948), p. 18.

6. *Ibid.*, p. 18.

7. Webb, *op. cit.*, p. 12.

[3] AMSTERDAM'S RASPHUIS AND SPINHUIS

1. Primary sources: Robert v. Hippel, *Die Entstehung der modernen Freiheitsstrafe und des Erziehungsstrafvollzugs* (Eisenach: Thüringer Gefängnisges., 1931); Thorsten Sellin, *Pioneering in Penology* (Philadelphia: University of Pennsylvania Press, 1944); Wilhelm Traphagen, *Die ersten Arbeitshäuser und Ihre pädagogische Funktion* (Berlin: C. Heymann, 1935).

2. Sellin, *op. cit.*, pp. 23–5. Biographies of Dirck Volckertszoon Coornhert: Bruno Becker, *Bronnen tot de kennis van het leven en de werken van D.V. Coornhert*, R.G.P. kl. series No. 25 (S'Gravenhage: M. Nijhoff, 1928); H. Bonger, *Dirck Volckertszoon Coornhert* (Lochem: De Tijdstroom, 1942). The date of *Boeventucht* according to A. Hallema, "Zeldzame Bajes-boekjes uit de 16de en 17de Eeuw", *Folium librorum vitae deditum*, vol. III nos. 3–4, 1954, p. 98. Sellin gives the year 1567.

3. Hippel, *op. cit.*, pp. 3–4.

4. Sellin, *op. cit.*, p. 27.

5. *Ibid.*, pp. 26–30.

6. Simon van der Aa, "The Early History of Prison Reforms in Holland" in *Actes du congrès pénitentiaire international de Washington, Octobre 1910*, vol. I. (Groningen: 1913), p. 487.

7. Sellin, *op. cit.*, pp. 69–72. "The historians persistently ignored it", according to Sellin, "but to the numerous visitors to the house it was a constant source of astonishment".

8. Hippel, *op. cit.*, p. 8.

9. *Ibid.*, pp. 19–20, Traphagen, *op. cit.*, pp. 74–75.

10. Sellin, *op. cit.*, p. 77.

11. *Ibid.*, pp. 87–101; Hippel, *op. cit.*, pp. 6–7.

12. John Howard, *The State of the Prisons in England and Wales with Preliminary Observations, and an Account of Some Foreign Prisons* (Warrington: W. Eyres, 1777), pp. 125–8; id., *Appendix to the State of the Prisons, etc.* (Warrington: W. Eyres, 1780), pp. 13–20; id., *The State of the Prisons*, Everyman's Library, new edition, abbreviated (London: J.M. Dent and Sons, 1929), pp. 55–9.

13. Hippel, *op. cit.*, p. 47.
14. Van der Aa, *op. cit.*, p. 493.
15. Information supplied by the Dutch Penal Administration.

[4] THE OCTAGON IN GHENT

1. Primary sources: P. Lenders, "La première tentative faite par J.J.P. Vilain XIIII pour la construction d'une maison de correction" (1749–51), *Bulletin de l'Administration Pénitentiaire No. 6*, Bruxelles, 1959, pp. 291–312; Charles Lucas, *Du Système Pénitentiaire en Europe et aux États-Unis*, vol. II (Paris: Bossange, 1830), pp. 241–66; Ministère de la Justice, Bruxelles, *Prison centrale de Gand*, notice historique 1772–1935; Jules Simon, "Trois grandes figures de la Science pénitentiaire belge", *Bulletin de l'Administration des Établissements pénitentiaire*, Bruxelles, no. 9, 1956, pp. 194–213; Louis Stroobant, *Le Rasphuis de Gand* (Gand: 1900); le Vicomte Vilain XIIII, *Mémoire sur les moyens de corriger les Malfaiteurs et Fainéans à leur propre avantage et de les rendre utiles à l'État* (Gand: Pierre de Goesin, 1775); Ch. Hippolyte Vilain XIIII, *Mémoire etc., précédé, d'un Premier Mémoire inédit, augmenté d'une notice historique sur la vie et les ouvrages de l'auteur* (Bruxelles: Méline, Cans et Cie, 1841). *Author's Comment*. Vilain XIIII is a family name and should not be written XIV, a privilege reserved for princes! This has caused misunderstandings: Lucas, for example, interpreted it as XIII. Philippe was the great-grandfather of Hippolyte. Due to his book, the latter is often confused with the former.
2. Lenders, *op. cit.*, pp. 292–310.
3. Hippolyte Vilain, *op. cit.*, pp. 3–5.
4. Stroobant, *op. cit.*, pp. 34–6.
5. Hippolyte Vilain, *op. cit.*, pp. 62–94.
6. *Ibid.*, pp. 26–30.
7. *Ibid.*, p. 33; Stroobant, *op. cit.*, p. 41.
8. John Howard, *The State of the Prisons in England and Wales, with Preliminary Observations, and an Account of Some Foreign Prisons* (Warrington: W. Eyres, 1777), pp. 140–5; id., *Appendix to the State of the Prisons in England and Wales, etc.* (Warrington: W. Eyres, 1780), p. 79, id., *The State of the Prisons* (Everyman's Library Edition, London: J.M. Dent and Sons, 1929), pp. 114–8. See also Lucas, *op. cit.*, p. 262. The measurements of the cells according to Everyman's, which is based on the third edition of Howards book. In the first edition (1777), Howard gave them as 6′9″ × 4′10″ × 8′8″. Also, in this edition, he does not mention the disciplinary cells, but it is most likely that he saw them, as his inspections were thorough. The third edition says that he "always" found these cells empty.
9. C.A.L. (Carl Axel Löwenhielm), *Tankar om corrections-systemet och Fångvården* (Stockholm: 1826), pp. 5–7.
10. Werner Hebebrand, "Sind die alten Stadtkerne zu retten?", *Die Welt*, no. 213 III, September 12, 1964.
11. Stroobant, *op. cit.*, pp. 5, 35.
12. Lenders, *op. cit.*, p. 300.

[5] ISOLATION IN CASA PIA

1. Thorsten Sellin, "Dom Jean Mabillon—a prisoner reformer of the Seventeenth Century", *Journal of the American Institute of Criminal Law and Criminology*, vol. XVII, p. 592; also see a German translation in Nicolaus Heinrich Julius, *Nord Amerikas Sittliche Zustände, nach eigenen Anschauungen in den Jahren 1834, 1835 und 1836*, vol. II (Leipzig: F.A. Brockhaus, 1839), p. 421.
2. M.G. Ferrus, *Über Gefangene, Gefangenschaft und Gefängnisse* (Ratibor: Jacobsohn, 1853), p. 199.
3. Sellin, *op. cit.*, p. 592; A.F. de la Rochefoucauld-Liancourt, *Examen de la Théorie et de la Pratique du Système Pénitentiaire* (Paris: Delaunay, 1840), p. 5.
4. Ottavio Andreucci, *Gli Orfanotrofi* (Firenze: Giuseppe Mariani, 1855), pp. 245–58; Serafino Biffi, *Opere Complete*, vol. quarto: Riformatori pei giovani, edited by Ulrico Hocpli (Milano: Ulrico Hoepli, 1902), pp. 255–6; Thorsten Sellin, "Filippo Franci—a Precursor of Modern Penology", *Journal of the American Institute of Criminal Law and Criminology*, vol. XVII, pp. 104–112.
5. Thorsten Sellin, "The House of Correction for Boys in the Hospice of Saint Michael in Rome," *Journal of the American Institute of Criminal Law and Criminology*, vol. XX (1929–30), translation of Motu proprio by Clemens XI, pp. 539–40; for the original text see also *Rivista di Diritto Penitenziario* (Rome: 1934), pp. 786–7.
6. Primary sources: Biffi, *op. cit.*, pp. 278–81; Thorsten Sellin, *ibid.*, pp. 533–53; Filippo Volpicella, *Proposita di una compiuta riforma delle Prigioni*, vol. I (Naples: Stamperia e Cartiere del Fibreno, 1845), pp. 293–7.
7. The Romans soon came to speak of two St. Michaels, S.M. *dei buoni* and S.M. *dei cattivi*, the St. Michael for the good and for the bad. See Biffi, *op. cit.*, p. 278.
8. Sellin, *op. cit.*, p. 542.
9. Howard, *The State of Prisons*, 1777, pp. 98–9 (see Chapter 6, note 1).
10. Max Grünhut, *Penal Reform* (Oxford: The Clarendon Press, 1948), p. 31.
11. The prisons in Milan and Horsham were described by Howard, among others; see, for example, *État des Prisons et des Hopitaux et des Maisons de Force*, translated from English (Paris: Lagrange, 1791), vol. I, pp. 296–301, vol. II, pp. 203–6. Date cited from Stroobant (see Ch. 4, note 1), p. 79.
12. Sidney and Beatrice Webb, *English Prisons under Local Government* (London: F. Cass, 1963), pp. 54, 90.

[6] JOHN HOWARD—TRAILBLAZER

1. Primary sources: H.W. Bellows, "John Howard, his Life, Character, and Services", a lecture reproduced in Edwin Pears, *Prisons and Reformatories, being the Transactions of the International Penitentiary Congress held in London, July 3–13, 1872* (London: Longmans, Green and Co., 1872), pp. 739–96; James Baldwin Brown, *Memories of the Public and Private Life of John Howard, the Philanthropist, compiled from his own Diary, in the posses-*

sion of his family, his confidential letters; the communications of his surviving relatives and friends; and other authentic sources of information (London: R. Fenner, 1818 and 1823); Hepworth Dixon, John Howard and the Prison-World (London: Jackson and Walford, 1854); J. Field (a), The Life of John Howard with Comments on his Character and Philanthropic Labours (London: Longman, Brown, Green and Longmans, 1850); id. (b), Correspondence of John Howard, the Philanthropist, not before published with a brief Memoir and Illustrative Anecdotes (London: Longman, Brown, Green and Longmans, 1855); D.L. Howard (a), The English Prisons, Their Past and Their Future (London: Methuen, 1960); id. (b), John Howard; Prison Reformer (London: C. Johnson, 1958); John Howard (a), The State of the Prisons in England and Wales with Preliminary Observations, and an Account of Some Foreign Prisons (Warrington: W. Eyres, 1777), id. (b), Appendix to the State of the Prisons, etc. (Warrington: W. Eyres, 1780); id. (c), État des Prisons, des Hôpitaux et des Maisons de Force (Paris: Lagrange, 1791); id. (d), The State of the Prisons (Everyman's Library, London: J.M. Dent and Sons, 1929); id. (e), An Account of the Principal Lazarettos in Europe with various papers relative to the Plague, together with further observations o some Foreign Prisons and Hospitals and additional Remarks on the present state of those in Great Britain and Ireland (London: W. Eyres, 1789); J. Stoughton, Howard the Philanthropist and His Friends (London: Hodder and Stoughton, 1884).

2. Bellows, op. cit., p. 757.
3. Ibid., pp. 758–62.
4. J. Howard (a), op. cit., p. 288.
5. Ibid., p. 344.
6. Ibid., p. 380.
7. Ibid., p. 372.
8. Ibid., pp. 16–20.
9. Bellows, op. cit., pp. 765–9.
10. J. Howard (a), op. cit., pp. 78–146.
11. Cesare Beccaria, Über Verbrechen und Strafen. Übersetzt mit biographischen Einleitung und Anmerkungen versehen. Translated by Dr. Jur. Karl Esselborn (Leipzig: W. Engelmann, 1905).
12. Regarding the Calas affair, see Voltaire, Sur la tolérance, à cause de la mort de Jean Calas (Paris: 1818); Raoul Allier, Voltaire et Calas, une erreur juridique au XVIIIe siècle (Paris: Stock, 1898); and F.H. Maugham, The Case of Jean Calas (London: W. Heinemann, 1928).
13. D.L. Howard (a) accuses Howard of uncooperativeness (p. 16). He always wanted to dominate; When the other committee members did not accept his suggestion for the site of the new prison, Howard resigned, "thereby allowing the scheme for a national penitentiary to slumber for over twenty years".
14. Brown (1818), op. cit., p. 356, wrote that Howard had great problems with his diet in Sweden. He lived mainly on sour bread and sour milk. Fruit and vegetables were unavailable; he mostly drank tea and ate "Sweden's unhealthy bread", and it was with true relief that he continued his voyage to Russia.
15. Dixon, op. cit., p. 223.
16. Field (a), op. cit., pp. 373–4.
17. J. Howard (e), op. cit., p. 227.
18. Stroughton, op. cit., p. 110. Howard had refused on an earlier occasion to approve of a collection for a statue of himself. The money that was not

expended for the support of freed criminals had to be returned to the donors. See Field (b), *op. cit.*, pp. 136–40 on this point.

19. Nicolaus Heinrich Julius, *Vorlesungen über die Gefängniskunde* (Berlin: Stuhr, 1828) contains a list (p. 358), though not entirely accurate, of Howard's writings.
20. Brown, *op. cit.*, p. 651, "42,033 miles".
21. Bellows, *op. cit.*, p. 792.
22. D.L. Howard (b), *op. cit.*, pp. 15, 166.

[7] PENANCE IN SOLITARY CONFINEMENT

1. Primary sources: Joseph Adshead (a), *Prisons and Prisoners* (London: Longman, Brown, Green and Longmans, 1845); id. (b), *Our Present Goal System Deeply Depraving to the Prisoner and a Positive Evil to the Community. Some Remedies Proposed* (Manchester: G. and A. Falkner, 1847); John T. Burt, *Results of the System of Separate Confinement, as Administered at the Pentonville Prison* (London: Longman, Brown, Green and Longmans, 1852); L.A. Gosse, *Das Pönitentiärsystem, medizinisch, rechtlich und philosophisch geprüft* (Weimar: Voigt, 1839); Fred E. Haynes, *The American Prison System* (New York: McGraw Hill book comp. 1939), pp. 20–6; J. Jebb, *Second Report of the Surveyor General of Prisons* (London: Govt. print. off., 1847), pp. 61–5; William Tallack, *Penological and Preventive Principles, with a Special Reference to Europe and America; and to the Diminution of Crime, Pauperism and Intemperance, to Prisons and Their Substitutes, Habitual Offenders, Sentences, Neglected Youth, Education, Police, Statistics, etc.* (London: Wertheimer, Lea and Co., 1889), pp. 146–76; Sidney and Beatrice Webb, *English Prisons under Local Government* (London: F. Cass, 1963); E.C. Wines, *Transactions of the Fourth National Prison Congress held in New York, June 6–9, 1876, being the Report of the National Prison Association of the United States, in the Years 1874 and 1875* (New York: Office of the Association, 1877), pp. 107–12.
2. Adshead (b), *op. cit.*, p. 64. Somewhat varying data is given about Gloucester. In Nicolaus Heinrich Julius's *Nord Amerikas Sittliche Zustände nach eigenen Anschauungen in den Jahren 1834, 1835 und 1836*, vol. II (Leipzig: F.A. Brockhaus, 1839), pp. 132–4; it is stated that the prison, when completed, contained 180 sleeping cells and the same number of work cells arranged so that each sleeping cell was connected by a door with a work cell.
3. Harry Elmer Barnes and Negley K. Teeters, *New Horizons in Criminology* (New York: Prentice-Hall, 1946), pp. 486–503; Thorsten Sellin, "Philadelphia Prisons of the Eighteenth Century" in *Transactions of the American Philosophical Society*, New Series, vol. 43, part 1, March 1953, pp. 326–30; Negley K. Teeters, (a) *The Cradle of the Penitentiary* (Philadelphia: Temple University, 1955); id., (b) *They Were in Prison* (Philadelphia: Winston, 1937), pp. 440–51.
4. Teeters (b), *op. cit.*, p. 447.
5. Teeters (a), *op. cit.*, p. 40.
6. Sellin, *op. cit.*; Julius, *op. cit.*, pp. 124–7.
7. Joseph Adshead (a), pp. 221–5; Margery Fry, "Bentham and English Penal Reform" in *Jeremy Bentham and the Law*, A Symposium edition on behalf of

University College, London, by George Keeton and George Schwarzenberger (London: Stevens and Sons, 1948), pp. 49–51; Coleman Phillipson, *Three Criminal Law Reformers, Beccaria, Bentham, Romilly* (London: E.P. Dutton and Co., 1923), pp. 210–4; Nikolaus Heinrich Julius, *Vorlesungen über die Gefängniskunde* (Berlin: Stuhr, 1828), pp. 314–7, 332–4; Mary P. Mack, *Jeremy Bentham, An Odyssey of Ideas 1748–1792* (London: Heinemann, 1962), p. 367. Bentham had a younger brother Sam, who actually designed the first plan for the Panopticon. "This was a building designed like a wheel, with management offices at the central hub and corridors radiating from it like spokes. To Bentham this architectural plan seemed endlessly adaptable—to factories, schools, poorhouses, and above all to prisons. It seemed the perfect Utilitarian building, where theory could be applied and knowing translated into doing. He borrowed Sam's plans and made them his own".

8. Gilbert Geis, "Jeremy Bentham" in *Pioneers in Criminology*, edited by Hermann Mannheim (London: Stevens, 1960), p. 63; D.L. Howard, *The En-English Prisons, Their Past and Their Future* (London: Methuen, 1960), p. 17.

9. Barnes and Teeters, *op. cit.*, pp. 506–7; G. de Beaumont and A. de queville, *Du Système pénitentiaire aux Etats-Unis, et de son Application en France; suivis d'un Appendice sur les Colonies pénales et de Notes statistique* (Paris: Fournier, 1833), p. 16. This book was translated to German by Julius with the title *Amerikas Besserungssystem und dessen Anwendung auf Europa* (Berlin: Th. Enslin, 1833); O.F. Lewis, *The Development of American Prisons and Prison Customs 1776–1845 with Special Reference to Early Institutions in the State of New York* (Albany: The Prison Ass. of New York, 1922), pp. 119–20; Varrentrapp, "Das westliche Staatsgefängnis Pennsylvaniens in Allegheny (Pittsburgh)" in *Jahrbücher der Gefängniskunde*, fifth volume (Darmstadt: 1844), pp. 70–84. Measurements of the cells according to Lewis's figures. Varrentrapp stated that they were $8' \times 12'$. Frederick Howard Wines, *Punishment and Reformation. An Historical Sketch of the Rise of the Penitentiary System* (New York: T.Y. Crowell and Co., 1895), p. 159, gives what is perhaps the first printed description of the "rapping alphabet", which was as follows in its original form:

	1	2	3	4	5
1	A	B	C	D	E
2	F	G	H	I	J
3	K	L	M	N	O
4	P	Q	R	S	T
5	U	V	W	X	Y
6	Z				

For example, two sharp raps (with the knuckles) and two dull (with the wrists) signified "G." This mode of communication quickly spread all over the world, with some highly refined variations.

10. G. de Beaumont and A. de Tocqueville, *op. cit.*, pp. 8–11. This book was also translated into English in 1833, and the translation was reproduced in 1964 by the Southern Illinois University Press with an introduction by Thorsten Sellin and a foreword by Herman R. Lantz under the title, *On the Penitentiary System in the United States and Its Application in France.*

[8] AUBURN AND THE SILENT COMMUNITY SYSTEM

1. Orlando F. Lewis, *The Development of American Prisons and Prison Customs 1776–1845 with Special Reference to Early Institutions in the State of New York* (Montclair, NJ: P. Smith, 1967), pp. 77–106; W. David Lewis, *From Newgate to Dannemora, the Rise of the Penitentiary in New York, 1776–1848* (Ithaca, NY: Cornell Univ. Press, 1965), p. 85. The "lock-step" is not an American invention. It can be seen on a relief, dated 2,500 B.C., at the Iraq's State Museum in Baghdad.
2. G. de Beaumont and A. de Tocqueville, *Du Système pénitentiaire aux États-Unis, et de son Application en France, suivis d'un Appendice sur les colonies pénales et de Notes statistiques* (Paris: Fournier, 1833), pp. 281–5, contains an interview with Lynds in which he made the comment cited.
3. See also Frederick Howard Wines, *Punishment and Reformation. An Historical Sketch of the Rise of the Penitentiary System* (New York: Crowell, 1895), p. 149; Harry Elmer Barnes and Negley K. Teeters, *New Horizons in Criminology* (New York: Prentice-Hall, 1946), pp. 522–3, reports that a similar story was told about Amos Pilsbury.
4. Barnes and Teeters, *op. cit.*, p. 523.
5. Nicolaus Heinrich Julius, *Nord Amerikas Sittliche Zustände nach eigenen Anschauugen in den Jahren 1834, 1835 und 1836*, vol. II (Leipzig: F.A. Brockhaus, 1839), pp. 470–1.
6. Barnes and Teeters, *op. cit.*, p. 524; Orlando F. Lewis, *op. cit.*, pp. 107–17.
7. For the earliest history of Sing Sing, see also Lewis E. Lawes, *Twenty Thousand Years in Sing Sing* (New York: Long and Smith, 1932), pp. 78–92.
8. Frédérick A. Demetz and Abel Blouet, *Rapports à M. le Comte de Montalivet sur les Pénitenciers des États-Unis* (Paris: Imprimerie Royale, 1837), pp. 10–14.
9. *Ibid.*, pp. 15–6. (Julius, *op. cit.*, pp. 428–59, also describes in detail the institutional routine at Sing Sing.)
10. *Ibid.*, pp. 16–8. Warden Andrews described conditions at Sing Sing as follows in the *Fifth Annual Report of the Inspectors of State Prisons of the State of New York* (Albany: 1853), pp. 78–9: The prisoners came from every part of the globe and spoke every imaginable language. There were homocides, pirates, armed robbers, patricides, burglars, all of them sent to Sing Sing to protect society from acts of violence. According to the law, they were to be kept at work in shops and quarries. Due to their jobs, they were spread over the entire prison area in groups of 50 to 100 men. They were equipped with implements that could be used in riots and to massacre prison officials. The unwalled prison was open to the river on one side and to the inland on the other, and a railway bisected the property through the middle. Officials were necessarily unarmed, but 30 armed guards were stationed at some distance from the institution to prevent attempted escapes. Auburn had the same number of outside guards, but also a wall too high to be scaled, and its clientele was smaller and less dangerous. Under these circumstances, Andrews questioned how the Sing Sing prisoners could be kept on the premises for even an hour. The answer he gave was strict discipline, according to which any form of communication between the prisoners was forbidden, each man was kept in a specified place, all orders must be obeyed instantly and all breaches of rules punished immediately.

11. *Report of W. Crawford Esq. on the Penitentiaries of the United States, ordered by the House of Commons to be printed* (London: 1834); Ed. Ducpetiaux, in *Des Progrès et de l'État Actuel de la Réforme Pénitentiaire et des Institutions Préventives, aux États-Unis, en France, en Suisse, en Angleterre et en Belgique,* Tome I (Bruxelles: Hauman, Cattoir et comp., 1837), pp. 30–5, discusses a view expressed by Crawford concerning the possibilities of taking action in cases of abuse of the personnel's disciplinary authority. Crawford pointed out in his report that not only officials but also the general public had access to Auburn for a fee of 25 cents. But neither he nor Ducpetiaux believed that this kind of open policy was a guarantee against abuses. If a visitor passed by, all the guard would have to do would be to postpone chastisement until the stranger was out of sight.

12. Demetz and Blouet, *op. cit.,* pp. 19–22; Zebulon Reed Brockway, *Fifty Years of Prison Service, An Autobiography* (New York: Charities publication committee, 1912), pp. 26–28. Brockway, who had been a guard at Wethersfield and had served for a time under Amos Pilsbury when Pilsbury was warden of the prison in Albany, claims that Moses Pilsbury was the first person in the United States to assert that convicts should work to earn "their keep" and the first to introduce daily readings of selected passages in the Bible to the inmates.

[9] CHERRY HILL AND THE SEPARATE SYSTEM

1. Negley K. Teeters and John D. Shearer, *The Prison at Philadelphia Cherry Hill* (New York: Columbia University Press, 1957), pp. 19–20.
2. *Ibid.,* pp. 22–3.
3. *Ibid.,* p. 59.
4. Theodore Dreiser, *The Financier* (New York: The New American Library, Inc. 1967), p. 381.
5. Teeters and Shearer, *op. cit.,* p. 62; see also Norman B. Johnston, "John Haviland," in *Pioneers in Criminology,* edited by Hermann Mannheim (London: Stevens, 1960), pp. 91–112.
6. Teeters and Shearer, *op. cit.,* p. 67.
7. Frédrick A. Demetz and Abel Blouet, *Rapports sur les Pénitenciers des États-Unis* (Paris: Imprimerie Royale, 1837), pp. 55–64.
8. Teeters and Shearer, *op. cit.,* p. 69.
9. Demetz and Blouet, *op. cit.,* p. 56.
10. *Ibid.,* p. 28.
11. *Ibid.,* pp. 27–30.
12. *Ibid.,* pp. 35–7.
13. *Ibid.,* p. 37.
14. Teeters and Shearer, *op. cit.,* pp. 76–7.
15. *Ibid.,* p. 166.
16. *Ibid.,* p. 144.
17. Charles Dickens, *American Notes for General Circulation* (London: Chapman and Hall, 1842), pp. 119–20; also cited by James J. Barclay, *The Pennsylvania System of Separate Confinement, Explained and Defended* (Philadelphia: 1867), pp. 97–106, and subsequently by many other authors.

Dickens was most severely criticized by Joseph Adshead, *Prisons and Prisoners* (London: Longman, Brown, Green and Longmans, 1845), pp. 95–121.

18. William Tallack, *Penological and Preventive Principles with Special Reference to Europe and America; and to the Diminution of Crime, Pauperism, and Their Substitutes, Habitual Offenders, Sentences, Neglected Youth, Education, Police, Statistics, etc.* (London: Wertheimer, Lea and Co., 1889). About Dickens and Cherry Hill, see also Teeters and Shearer, *op, cit.*, pp. 113–32, and Philip Collins, *Dickens and Crime* (London: Macmillan, 1962), pp. 117–39. The last-mentioned book strongly substantiates Dickens's serious interest in penal reforms and attempts to prove that Dickens's opinion of Cherry Hill was negative from the outset. His complimentary words at the time of his visit, according to Collins, were merely uttered out of courtesy to his hosts at the dinner table!

19. William Roscoe, *A Brief Statement of the Causes which have led to the Abandonement of the Celebrated System of Penitentiary Discipline in some of the United States of America* (Liverpool: 1827). Roscoe first relates a conversation he had with Lafayette and quotes a letter from Lafayette before he left the U.S. In the letter Lafayette expresses approval of the system of solitary cell during the night and group work during the day (pp. 28–30). Later Roscoe refers to a letter from an American published in the *Daily National Intelligencer*, a Washington newspaper, in which the author relates a conversation he had with Lafayette in Paris. The quotation comes from this letter. The collection of Lafayette's own letters in French do not refer in any case to his feelings about American prisons. Cf. Teeters and Shearer, *op. cit.*, pp. 27–8. Contrary to what Teeters and Shearer appear to believe, Lafayette was never imprisoned in the Bastille.

20. Fredrika Bremer, *Hemmen i den nya världen*, Tidens Svenska Klassiker (Stockholm: Tiden, 1961), del II, p. 47, originally published in Stockholm 1853–4.

21. Teeters and Shearer, *op. cit.* pp. 93–112.

22. *Ibid.*, p. 217.

23. G. de Beaumont and A. de Tocqueville, *Du Système pénitentiaire aux États-Unis, et de son Application en France; suivis d'un Appendice sur les Colonies pénales et de Notes statistiques* (Paris: Fournier, 1833, second edition in 1836), translated to German by N.H. Julius under the title *Amerikas Besserungs-Systeme, und dessen Anwendung auf Europa* (Berlin: Th. Enslin, 1833), and to English, also in 1833, with the title *On the Penitentiary System in the United States and Its Application in France*, reproduced in 1964 by the Southern Illinois University Press with an introduction by Thorsten Sellin and a foreword by Herman R. Lantz. See also Georg Wilson Pierson, *Tocqueville and Beaumont in America* (New York: Oxford University Press, 1938). Regarding Tocqueville's preference for the Pennsylvania system, see Fernand Desportes, *La Réforme des Prisons* (Paris: 1862), p. 45.

24. *Report of W. Crawford, Esq. on the Penitentiaries of the United States, ordered by the House of Commons to be printed* (London: 1834).

25. Dr. N.H. Julius, *Die Amerikanischen Besserungs-Systeme, erörtet in einem Sendschreiben an Herrn W. Crawford, General-Inspektor der Grossbritannischen Gefängnisse* (Leipzig: F.A. Brockhaus, 1827); id., *Nord Amerikas Sittliche Zustände nach eigenen Anschauungen in den Jahren 1834, 1835 und 1836*, vol. II (Leipzig: F.A. Brockhaus, 1839), pp. 254–328.

26. Ed. Ducpetiaux, *Des Progrés et de l'État Actuel de la Réforme Pénitentiaire*, 3. vols., (Brussels: Hauman, Cattoir et comp., 1837–8).

27. *Ibid.*, vol. II, pp. 28–9.
28. Lieut. Col. Jebb, *Observations on the Separate System of Discipline submitted to the Congress Assembled at Brussels on the Subject of Prison Reform* (London: 1847).
29. Among the descriptions of Pentonville, see Adshead, pp. 225–53, and John T. Burt, *Results of the System of Separate Confinement as Administered at the Pentonville Prison* (London: Longman, Brown, Green and Longmans, 1852). See also Collins (note 18), pp. 140–63.
30. M. Coindet, *Mémoire sur l'hygiène des condamnés détenus dans la prison penitentiaire de Genève* (Paris: Guillaumin, 1838); L.A. Gosse, *Examen médical et philosophique du système pénitentiaire* (Genève: Ladoret-Ramboz, 1837), translated to German by A. Martiny under the title "Das Pönitentiärsystem medizinisch, rechtlich und philosophisch geprüft" (Weimar: Voigt, 1839). Cf. Noellner, "Påminnelser òver några anmärkningar emot pennsylvaniska systemet till straffångars förbättring", *Schmidts arkiv*, II bdt. (Christianstad: 1841), pp. 236–41.
31. Noellner, *op. cit.*, pp. 249, 250.
32. Johnston, *op. cit.*, p. 100 (See Note 5).
33. With his books, *Du système pénal et du système répressif en général, de la peine de mort en particulier* (Paris: C. Béchet, 1827) and *Du système pénitentiaire en Europe et aux États-Unis* (Paris: Bossange, 1830) Charles Lucas started a discussion on the subject of congregate *versus* solitary confinement, which lasted for decades. He himself favored the separate system for petty criminals with short sentences and detainees awaiting trial, but adhered to the Auburn system for criminals with longer sentences. (He particularly developed his ideas in the books *De la Réforme des Prisons ou de la Théorie de l'Emprisonnement*, 3 vols. (Paris: J. Bérgounioux, 1836–8), and *Des moyens et des conditions d'une Réforme Pénitentiaire en France* (Paris: Jean Marie, 1840). As we have seen, he had more or less enthusiastic allies in Beaumont and Tocqueville—the latter, however, defected to the other camp—and in Crawford. Furthermore, Lucas wanted prison treatment to be "character-building". In his own country he was in agreement with Léon Faucher (*De la Réforme des Prisons*, Paris: Angé, 1838) and Larochefoucauld-Liancourt (*Examen du Système Pénitentiaire* Paris: Delaunay, 1840). The latter, however, held his own views, was primarily in favor of eliminating the death penalty but of retaining the galleys, and for the rest of permitting convicts to be together during the day and even of allowing them wine and tobacco. Faucher, on the other hand, was closer to Lucas in that he recommended classification of prisoners according to whether they were from the city or the country, a maximum of six months of isolation and thereafter the Auburn system. At the same time, all three attacked a French Government proposal under the influence of Demetz and Blouet, according to which a separate system patterned on a modification of the Pennsylvania system would be adopted. However, increasingly strong opposition developed, principally perhaps from L.M. Moreau-Christophe, former Inspector-General of Prisons in the Seine Département. He had written a book, *De l'État Actuel des Prisons en France* (Paris: A. Desrez, 1837), in which he ridiculed American claims to have invented something new in the treatment of prisoners, and went to the attack with a publication, *Défense du Projet de Lois sur les Prisons contre les Attaques de ses adversaires* (Paris: E. Marc-Aurel, 1844). Support came from the German physician Georg Varrentrapp in his book *De l'Emprisonnement Individuel sous le Rapport Sanitaire et des Attaques dirigées contre lui par MM. Charles Lucas et Léon*

Faucher (Paris: Guillaumin, 1844). Varrentrapp was Julius's co-editor of "Jahrbücher der Gefängniskunde" and continued the debate with several articles in the same periodical. Also, in his book *Über Pönitentiärsysteme, insbesondere über die vorgeschlagene Einführung des pennsylvanischen Systems in Frankfurt* (Frankfurt-am-Main: Varrentrapps Verl., 1841) he had already chosen his side in the struggle, as had the Dutchman, W.H. Suringar (*Gedachten over de eensame opsluiting der Gevangenen* (Leeuw: G.T. Suringar, 1843), translated to French by Moreau-Christophe under the title *Considérations sur la Réclusion Individuelle des Détenus* (Paris Bouchard-Huzard, 1843). International meetings in Frankfurt, 1846, and in Brussels, 1847, gave further support to the protagonists of the separate system. All these publications were highly important to the discussion in Sweden at the time. King Oscar I had the publications and many others in his library, as did the Swedish Prisons Administration. Special mention should perhaps be made of the report of a German committee, *Gehorsamster Bericht der Gefängnis-Commission, den Bau eines allgemeinen Gefängnisgebäudes betreffend* (Frankfurt-am-Main: 1840), since it contained architectural plans for a medium-sized cell prison. These drawings are highly reminiscent of those of Swedish cell prisons.

34. Shane Leslie, *Sir Evelyn Ruggles-Brise, a Memory of the Founder of Borstal* (London: J. Murray, 1938), p. 150. Randolph S. Churchill, *Winston S. Churchill*, vol. II, (London: Heinemann, 1969), pp. 1148–53, 1190–1, accounts for an interesting correspondence on penal matters between Galsworthy and Churchill.
35. Teeters and Shearer, *op. cit.*, p. 222.
36. Sidney and Beatrice Webb, *English Prisons under Local Government* (London: F. Cass, 1922).
37. Stephen Hobhouse and A. Fenner Brockway, *English Prisons Today, being the Report of the Prison System Enquiry Committee* (London: Longmans, Green and Co., 1922). This was not a Government committee, and it encountered great difficulties in collecting material due to official opposition. Regarding separate treatment, see pp. 570–3.
38. S.K. Ruck, *Paterson on Prisons* (London: Frederick Muller Ltd., 1951), pp. 77–81.
39. "The Ballad of Reading Gaol," by C.3.3. (Oscar Wilde's pseudonym). (London: Leonard Smithers, 1898). See also H. Montgomery Hyder, *Oscar Wilde: the Aftermath* (London: Methuen, 1963), p. 42.

[10]   NORFOLK ISLAND AND THE TASK SENTENCE

1. Primary sources: John Vincent Barry (a) *Alexander Maconochie of Norfolk Island* (London: Oxford University Press, 1958); id. (b) "Alexander Maconochie" in *Pioneers in Criminology*, edited by Hermann Mannheim (London: Stevens, 1960), pp. 68–90, this is a summary of the above-mentioned biography; R.S.E. Hinde, *The British Penal System 1773–1950* (London: G. Ducksworth, 1951), pp. 84–90; D.L. Howard, *The English Prisons, Their Past and Their Future* (London: Methuen, 1960), pp. 91–3, and Captain Maconochie (a), *Australiana, Thoughts on Convict Management and Other Subjects Connected with the Australian Penal Colonies*

(London: Parker and Son, 1839); id. (b), *On the Management of Transported Criminals* (London: C. Whiting, 1845); id. (c), *Crime and Punishment, the Mark System, Framed to Mix Persuasion with Punishment and Make Their Effect Improving, Yet Their Operation Severe* (London: Hatchard, 1846); id. (d), *Norfolk Island* (London: J. Hatchard and Son, 1847); id. (e), *Secondary Punishment, the Mark System* (London: John Ollivier, 1848); id. (f) *On National Education as Bearing on Crime* (London: 1855); id. (g) *On the Mark System of Prison Discipline* (London: 1855); id. (h) *Prison Discipline* (London: T. Harrison, 1856).

2. Barry (a), *op. cit.*, pp. 8–9.
3. *Ibid.*, pp. 9–21.
4. Quoted by Barry (a), *op. cit.*, pp. 243–61.
5. Maconochie (e), *op. cit.*, p. 3.
6. Barry (a), *op. cit.*, p. 102. See also Hinde, *op. cit.* p. 84.
7. *Ibid.*, p. 105.
8. *Ibid.*, pp. 146–67.
9. Only one year after Maconochie was relieved of his post, rumors circulated that his successor was guilty of brutality. The Government appointed a commission which, after its investigation, sharply criticized the successor and absolved Maconochie. See Barry (a), *op. cit.*, pp. 201–8, and D.L. Howard, *op. cit.*, p. 93. Encouraged by this, Maconochie wrote works (f), (g) and (h). This last-mentioned contains a description of the mark system, including tables, and a description of the prison officials' functions in calculating marks.
10. Barry (a), *op. cit.*, p. 241.
11. Maconochie (a), *op. cit.*, p. iv.

[11]   THE IRISH PROGRESSIVE SYSTEM

1. Primary sources for the English deportation system, and penal servitude: P. F. Aschrott, *Strafensystem und Gefänoniswesen in* England (Leipzig: Guttentag, 1887), pp. 36–70; Fr. J. Behrend, *Geschichte der Gefängnisreform. Vereinigte Staaten, Grossbritannien, Irland* (Berlin: Brigl, 1859), pp. 138–44, this volume dwells at length on the "perils of masturbation" when men in their "most potent years" are incarcerated in cell prisons; R.S.E. Hinde, *The British Penal System 1773–1950* (London: G. Duckworth, 1951), pp. 84ff; Lieut.-Col. Jebb, *Report on the Discipline and Construction of Portland Prison and Its Connection with the System of Convict Discipline Now in Operation* (London: William Clowes and Sons, 1850).

2. Matthew Davenport Hill, *A paper on the Irish Convict Prisons, read at the first meeting of the National Association for the Promotion of Social Science, held at Birmingham* (London: J.W. Parker and Son, 1857). Cf. Carpenter, p. xiii (see note 7).

3. About Obermaier, see Sheldon and Eleanor Glueck, *500 Criminal Careers* (New York: Alfred A. Knopf, 1930), pp. 14–5; Friedrich Hofer, "Georg Michael von Obermaier—A Pioneer in Reformatory Procedure", *Journal of Criminal Law and Criminology*, May–June 1937, pp. 13–51; G.M. Obermaier, *Anleitung zur vollkommenen Besserung der Verbrecher in den Strafenanstalten* (Kaiserslautern: Tascher, 1835). Obermaier was opposed to

the death penalty, which he regarded merely as a "horrible public festival" that was quickly forgotten, while a protracted prison sentence long remains a "vivid memory" (p. 15).

4. Harry Elmer Barnes and Negley K. Teeters, *New Horizons in Criminology* (New York: Prentice-Hall, 1946), p. 819; *Revista de Estudios Penitenciarios*, No. 159, published by Dirección General de Prisiones (Madrid). The entire issue is entitled "Homenaje al Coronel Montesinos".

5. Walter Frederick Crofton (a), *A Brief Description of the Irish Convict System* (London: 1862).

6. Other of Crofton's publications reviewed: (b) *Memoranda Relative to the Intermediate Convict Prisons in Ireland from Their Establishment in January 1856 to September 30, 1857* (Dublin: 1857); (c) *A Few Remarks on the Convict Question* (Dublin: 1857); (d) *The Immunity of "Habitual Criminals" with a Proposition for Reducing Their Number by means of Longer Sentences of Penal Servitude, Intermediate Convict Prisons, Conditional Liberation and Police Supervision* (Dublin: Bell and Daldy, 1861); (e) *Convict Systems and Transportation, A Lecture Delivered at the Philosophical Institution, Bristol, on 22 December 1862* (London: William Ridgway, 1863); (f) *A Few Observations on a Pamphlet Recently Published by the Rev. John Burt on the Irish Convict System* (London: William Ridgway, 1863).

7. Mary Carpenter, *Reformatory Prison Discipline as Developed by the Rt. Hon. Sir Walter Crofton in the Irish Convict Prison* (London: Longman, Longman, Green, Longman, 1872); Franz von Holtzendorff, *Das Irische Gefängnissystem, insbesondere die Zwischenanstalten vor der Entlassung* (Leipzig: J.A. Barth, 1859), translated to English under the title *Reflections and Observations on the Present Condition of the Irish Convict System* (Dublin: J.M. O'Toole and Son, 1863).

8. See Crofton (e), *op. cit.*

9. Carpenter, *op. cit.*, p. 52.

10. Hill, *op. cit.*; Carpenter, *op. cit.*, pp. 67–89.

11. *The Intermediate Prisons, a Mistake*, by an Irish Prison Chaplain in the Convict Service (Dublin: McGlashan and Gill, 1863). Another pamphlet in the same vein was *Irish Fancies and English Facts, being an Appeal to the Common Sense of the British Public on the Subject of the Irish Convict System*, by Scrutator—Charles Pennell (London: William Ridgway 1863).

12. Jebb officially submitted to the Government a critical work by John T. Burt, *Irish Facts and Wakefield Figures in Relation to Convict Discipline in Ireland* (London: Longman, Green, Longman and Roberts, 1863), which elicited a sharp protest from Crofton (see Crofton (f)). On the other hand, the latter was able to derive satisfaction from a very favorable, detailed report made by a group of visiting judges, namely, *Observations on the Treatment of Convicts in Ireland, by Four Visiting Judges of the West Riding Prison at Wakefield* (London: Simpkin, Marshall and Co., 1862). About the Lord Chief Justice, see Sir Evelyn Ruggles-Brise, *The English Prison System* (London: Macmillan, 1921), p. 33.

13. In addition to Holtzendorff and Olivecrona, J.J.L. van der Brugghen also wrote *Études sur le Système Pénitentiaire Irlandais. Revue après la mort de l'auteur et accompagné d'une Préface et d'une Appendice par Fr. von Holtzendorff* (Berlin: Lüderitz, 1865). A major survey appeared in the United States in E.C. Wines's *Transactions of the Fourth National Prison Congress, held in New York, June 6–9, 1876, being the Report of the National Prison Association of the United States for the Years 1874 and 1875* (New York: Office of the Association, 1877), pp. 77–91.

14. Biographic data on Crofton also found in *Thom's Official Directory,* 1897 and 1898.
15. Ruggles-Brise, *op. cit.,* p. 34.
16. Holtzendorff, *op. cit.,* p. 129.
17. Van der Brugghen, *op. cit.,* p. 302.

[12] ELMIRA AND THE REFORMATORIES

1. August Zeller, *Grundriss der Strafanstalt die als Erziehungsanstalt bessern will. Mit einer Einleitung über die Ausscheidung sowohl der leichten als Schweren Verbrecher* (Stuttgart: 1824), p. 46.
2. Z.R. Brockway, "The Ideal of a True Prison System for a State" in *Transactions of the National Congress on Penitentiary and Reformatory Discipline, held at Cincinnati, Ohio, October 12–18, 1870,* edited by E.C. Wines (Albany: 1871), pp. 38–65.
3. Literature consulted concerning Elmira: Zebulon Reed Brockway (a), "The Reformatory System" in S.J. Barrows, *The Reformatory System in the United States, Reports prepared for the International Prison Commission* (Washington: Govt. print. off., 1900), pp. 17–27; id. (b), *Fifty Years of Prison Service, An Autobiography* (New York: Charities publication committee, 1912); Pierre Cannat, *La Prison-École* (Paris: Recueil Sirey, 1955); Paul Herr, *Das Moderne Amerikanische Besserungs-System* (Berlin: W. Kohlhammer, 1907), pp. 44–64; F.B. Sanborn, "The Elmira Reformatory" in Barrows, *The Reformatory System,* pp. 28–47; Alexander Winter (a), *The New York Reformatory in Elmira* (London: Swan and Sonnenstein and Co., 1891); id. (b) "Fortschritte in der New Yorker Besserungsanstalt zu Elmira", *Blätter für Gefängniskunde,* vol. 27 (Heidelberg: 1893), pp. 4–10; Fred E. Haynes, *Criminology,* 2nd ed. (London: McGraw-Hill, 1935), pp. 314–34.
4. Sanborn, *op. cit.,* pp. 34–5.
5. *Ibid.,* p. 36.
6. Cannat, *op. cit.,* p. 14.
7. Winter (b), *op. cit.,* pp. 7–8.
8. Harry Elmer Barnes and Negley K. Teeters, *New Horizons in Criminology* (New York: Prentice-Hall, 1946), p. 555.
9. William Tallack, *Penological and Preventive Principles, etc.* (London: Wertheimer, Lea and Co., 1889), p. 101.
10. Barnes and Teeters, *op. cit.,* p. 556.
11. Note is made in the above-mentioned autobiography of a number of newspaper attacks on Elmira. Brockway was able to counter most of them, but, nevertheless, he observed sadly that even entirely unjustified criticism usually causes harm, and when it is exploited in the press "it bears bitter fruit in any institution" (p. 328).
12. At the turn of the century there were 10 in existence, see Herr, *op. cit.,* p. 64.
13. Source materials concerning Borstal: S. Barman, *The English Borstal System* (London: P.S. King and son, 1934); Sir Lionel W. Fox, *The English Prison and Borstal Systems* (London: Routledge and K. Paul, 1952); William Healy and Benedict S. Alper, *Criminal Youth and the Borstal System* (New York: The Commonwealth fund, 1941); Stephen Hobhouse and A. Fenner

Brockway, *English Prisons To-Day etc.* (London: Longmans, Green and Co., 1922), pp. 410–40; Roger Hood, *Borstal Re-assessed* (London: Heinemann, 1965), the last-mentioned an excellent survey of the history and therapeutic results.
14. Barman, *op. cit.*, pp. 192, 195.
15. Brockway (b), *op. cit.*, p. 374.

[13] RAUHES HAUS AND THE FAMILY SUBSTITUTES

1. Wehrli, Johann Jakob, in A *Cyclopedia of Education* (New York: MacMillan, 1914); and Clara Maria Liepmann, *Die Selbstverwaltung von Gefangenen* (Mannheim: J. Bensheimer, 1928), pp. 2–18.
2. Primary sources concerning Wichern and das Rauhe Haus: Max Busch, *Johann Hinrich Wichern als Sozialpädagoge* (Berlin: Beltz, 1957); Martin Gerhardt, *Johann Hinrich Wichern, Ein Lebensbild*, vols. I–III (Hamburg: Rauhes Haus, 1927–31); Richard Grunow, *Wichern, Ruf und Antwort* (Gütersloh: Rufer, 1958); Nicolaus Heinrich Julius, "Das Hamburgische Rettungshaus", *Jahrbücher der Gefängniskunde*, vol. V (Darmstadt: Leske, 1844), pp. 319–43; Helga Lemke, *Wicherns Bedeutung für die Bekämpfung der Jugendverwahrlosung* (Hamburg: Wittig, 1964); D.J. Wichern, *Zur Erziehungs- und Rettungsarbeit von Johann Hinrich Wichern, Bd. V: Das Rauhe Haus* (Hamburg: Rauhes Haus, 1908); *Johann Hinrich Wichern, Bd. IV, Teil I*, "Schriften zur Sozialpädagogik" (Berlin: Luth. Verlagshaus, 1958); *Johann Hinrich Wichern, Ausgewählte Schriften*, vol. III, "Schriften zur Gefängnisreform, Die Denkschrift", edited by Karl Janssen and Rudolf Sieverts (Gütersloh: C. Bertelsmann, 1962); the foreword of the last mentioned volume pp. 9–24, is entitled "J.H. Wichern als Gefängnisreformer".
3. Rauhes Haus archives: Speech by and letter from Heuss in 1953.
4. Busch, *op. cit.*, p. 9.
5. Gerhardt, *op. cit.*, pp. 132–3; D.J. Wichern, *op. cit.*, pp. 21–49.
6. Gerhardt, *op. cit.*, p. 147; D.J. Wichern, *op. cit.*, pp. 21–49 (Speech on September 12); Nicolaus Heinrich Julius, *Jahrbücher der Straf- und Besserungsanstalten, Erziehungshäuser, Armenfürsorge und anderen Werke der Christlichen Liebe*, vol. 9 (Berlin: Th. Enslin, 1833), pp. 253–9, contains a description of "Die Strafklasse" in the Hamburg "Werk und Armenhaus". From the beginning (1828) until 1833, altogether 107 boys and 73 girls had been taken in. Of these, 8 boys and 5 girls had died in the institution. At the end of the report, it is stated in about 20 lines that, thanks to the support of "benevolent" citizens, a home was established outside Hamburg with Wichern as superintendent. The next year's report includes (pp. 65–9) excerpts from the first annual report from Rauhes Haus.
7. Grunow, *op. cit.*, p. 68; D.J. Wichern, *op. cit.*, p. 39.
8. Gerhardt, *op. cit.*, p. 148; D.J. Wichern, *op. cit.*, pp. 191–2.
9. Grunow, *op. cit.*, pp. 63–4; Gerhardt, *op. cit.* pp. 168–9.
10. D.J. Wichern, *op. cit.*, p. 235.
11. Gerhardt, *op. cit.*, p. 155.
12. Busch, *op. cit.*, p. 10.

13. Sieverts, *op. cit.*, pp. 11–22.
14. Gerhardt, *op. cit.*, pp. 214–18. The German text reads as follows:

Hört, ihr Herrn, und lasst euch sagen:
Unsre Glock hat zwölf geschlagen;
Zwölf, das is das Ziel der Zeit;
Mensch, denk' an die Ewigkeit!

Translation into English by Judy Moffett.
15. D.J. Wichern, *op. cit.*, pp. 102–3.
16. Elizabeth Gurney, *Elizabeth Fry's Journeys on the Continent 1840–41. From a Diary kept by her niece* (London: John Lane, 1931), p. 149.
17. D.J. Wichern, *op. cit.*, p. 170.
18. Lemke, *op. cit.*, p. 34.
19. Oskar Ekelin, *Råby Räddningsinstitut (skyddshemmet i Råby), dess stiftande samt kort historik över dess verksamhet under åren 1838–1928* (Lund: Gleerup, 1928), pp. 25–30. In J. Holmgren's *Kort Beskrifning öfver de förnämsta Räddnings-Institut för vilseförda och moraliskt vårdslösade barn i Norra Tyskland och på Seland* (Lund: Berlingska boktryckeriet, 1840), an official report, the author avoids any form of criticism.
20. D.J. Wichern, *op. cit.*, p. 170.
21. Lemke, *op. cit.*, p. 57.
22. From the institution's annual report and following the author's interview with the Reverend Prehn.
23. Primary sources: G. Fr. Almquist, *Om räddningsanstalter för värnlösa och fallna*, published by Föreningen till Minne af Konung Oscar I och Drottning Josephina (Stockholm, 1874); M. Bertin, *Colonie Agricole et Maison Paternelle de Mettray* (Paris: Rue Cherubini, undated); Ed. Ducpetiaux, "Die Ländliche Ansiedelung jugendlicher Missetäter in Mettray", *Jahrbücher der Gefängniskunde*, vol. III (Frankfurt-am-Main: 1843); M. Duflos, *Exposé de l'État actuel du système d'éducation pénitentiaire pour les mineurs* (Melun: 1901; Benjamin Duprat, *Fondation d'une Colonie Agricole de Jeunes Détenues à Mettray* (Paris: Libraire de la Société Asiatique de Londres, 1839); M.G. Ferrus, *Über Gefangene, Gefangenschaft und Gefängnisse* (translated from French, Ratibor: Jacobsohn, 1853); René Luaire, *Le rôle de l'initiative privée dans la protection de l'enfance délinquante en France et en Belgique* (Lyon: Libr. générale de droit et de jurisprudence, 1936); E. Robin, *Les Prisons de France et le Patronage des Libérés* (Paris: Meyrueis, 1869); K. Olivecrona, *Åkerbrukskolonien i Mettray* (Stockholm: Norstedt och Söner, 1873).
24. Bertin, *op. cit.*, p. 39.
25. Almquist, *op. cit.*, pp. 45–6.
26. Olivecrona, *op. cit.*, pp. 43–8.
27. Duflos, *op. cit.*, p. 41.
28. K. Olivecrona, "Om förbättringsanstalten Val d'Yèvre", *Naumanns Tidskrift för Lagstiftning, Lagskipning och Förvaltning*, 5 årg., 1868 (Stockholm: 1868), pp. 781–7.
29. D.J. Wichern, *op. cit.*, p. 237.
30. Henri Danjou, *Enfants du Malheur, Les Bagnes d'Enfants* (Paris: A. Michel, 1932), pp. 227–41, shocked French readers with assertions of torture at Mettray and claims that la Maison Paternelle was used by rich parents to

prevent their sons from marrying "beneath their station", among other purposes.

31. Torsten Eriksson, "Bellefaire Home. En amerikansk mönsteranstalt", *Tidskrift för Barnavård och Ungdomsskydd*, vol. 2, 1951, pp. 54–6.

[14] SELF-GOVERNMENT IN INSTITUTIONS

1. Sources consulted on the Boston House of Reformation: G. de Beaumont and A. de Tocqueville, *Du Système pénitentiaire aux États-Unis, et de son Application en France; suivis d'un Appendice sur les Colonies pénales et de Notes statistiques* (Paris: Charles Gosselin, 1833), pp. 178–200, 298–303, the latter dealing with Well's routine; Nicolaus Heinrich Julius, *Nord Amerikas Sittliche Zustände nach eigenen Anschauungen in den Jahren 1834, 1835 und 1836, Bd. II* (Leipzig: F.A. Brockhaus, 1839), pp. 361–3 and 475–7; Orlando F. Lewis, *The Development of American Prisons and Prison Customs, 1776–1845* (Montclair, NJ: P. Smith, 1967), pp. 302–9; Clara Maria Liepmann, *Die Selbstverwaltung der Gefangenen* (Mannheim: J. Bensheimer, 1928), pp. 18–25. Forerunners in the United States to the Boston House of Reformation were generally known as "Houses of Refuge". See Lewis, *op. cit.*, Chap. XXIV.
2. Sources consulted on George Junior Republic: William R. George, *The Junior Republic, Its History and Ideals* (New York: Appleton and Co., 1910); Frederick Almy, "The George Junior Republic" in Hastings H. Hart, *Preventive Treatment of Neglected Children* (New York: Charities publication committee 1910), pp. 42–9; Liepmann, *op. cit.*, 29–41.
3. George, *op. cit.*, p. 323.
4. Almy, *op. cit.*, p. 49.
5. Torsten Eriksson, "Två amerikanska experimentanstalter", *Tidskrift för kriminalvård*, no. 1, 1950, pp. 2–4.
6. Sources consulted on Osborne and the Mutual Welfare League: Rudolph W. Chamberlain, *There Is No Truce, A Life of Thomas Mott Osborne* (New York: Macmillan, 1935), Paul Cornil, "Un essai de self-government à la prison de Sing Sing," in *Revue de Droit Pénal et de Criminologie*, (Louvain: 1929), pp. 537–41; Edgar M. Foltin, *Amerikanisches Gefängniswesen* (Reichenberg: Gebr. Stiepel, 1930), pp. 171–232; Fred E. Haynes, *Criminology* (London: McGraw-Hill, 1935), pp. 335–56; Stephen Hobhouse and A. Fenner Brockway, *English Prisons To-Day, etc.* (London: Longmans, Green and Co., 1922), pp. 675–92; Liepmann, *op. cit.*, pp. 49–83; Arne Omsted, *Traekk av strafferetspleien i de forenede stater i Nordamerika* (Kristiania; Steenske boktryckeri, 1922); Thomas Mott Osborne (a), *Society and Prisons, Some Suggestions for a New Penology* (Oxford: Yale Univ. Press, 1916); id. (b), *Within Prison Walls, Being a Narrative of Personal Experiences during a Week of Voluntary Confinement in the State Prison at Auburn, N.Y.* (New York: D. Appleton and Co., 1914) id. (c), *Prisons and Common Sense* (Philadelphia: J.B. Lippincott, 1924); The Osborne Association, *Handbook of American Prisons and Reformatories* (Eaton, U.S.: 1933), pp. XXXVI–VII, p. 623; Frank Tannenbaum, *Osborne of Sing Sing* (Chapel Hill: University of North Carolina Press, 1933).

7. Chamberlain, *op. cit.*, p. 241.
8. Osborne (b), *op. cit.*
9. Cornil, *op. cit.*, pp. 538–9.
10. Chamberlain, *op. cit.*, pp. 304–64.
11. *Ibid.*, pp. 365–82.
12. Omsted, *op. cit.*, pp. 26–9.
13. Alexander Paterson, *The Prison Problem of America* (printed in the Maidstone Prison, England, for private circulation; undated), p. 92.
14. *Handbook*, p. 623.
15. Cornil, *op. cit.*, p. 540.
16. Makarenko (born 1888, died 1939), whose collected writings were published in Russian in 1950–52 (seven volumes), treated his experiences of institutions in *Pedagogitieskaia poema* (Pedagogic Poem) and *Flagi na baschniach* (Flags on the Roof). Leila Kalling-Kant has reported in detail on Makarenko's institutional experiments in *Makarenko och hans metod* (Stockholm: H. Geber, 1948).
17. Henryka Veillard- Cybulska, "Aspects of Child Welfare in the USSR", *International Child Welfare Review*, no. 3, 1965, p. 115.
18. The information about Bolchevo was obtained by the writer on a visit to the head of the Soviet Union's prisons administration, Alexander Senatov. An account by Paul Cornil in the article, "Deux tendances contradictoire de la répression pénale en URSS", *Revue de Droit Pénal et de Criminologie*, 1935 (Louvain, Belgium), pp. 702–12, is not entirely accurate, according to Senatov, probably due to a misunderstanding in interpretation. Cornil was under the impression that three previous convictions were required for admission to the colony and that the colony had a population of about 3000 inmates, which Senatov stated was not correct.

[15] PROBATION

1. Franz von Liszt, *Vergleichende Darstellung des Deutschen und Ausländischen Strafrechts, Allg. Teil, Vol. III, Bedingte Verurteilung und Bedingte Begnadigung* (Berlin: O. Liebmann, 1908), p. 6. See also, A. Löffler, "Bedingte Verurteilung im Mittelalter", *Bulletin de l'Union International de Droit Pénal*, vol. IV (1894), pp. 92–4.
2. von Liszt, *op. cit.*, pp. 8–10.
3. David Dressler, *Practice and Theory of Probation and Parole* (New York: Columbia University Press, 1959), pp. 7–11; also *Probation and Related Matters* (New York, 1951), published by the United Nations and hereafter called *U.N. Probation*, pp. 17–23.
4. *U.N. Probation*, pp. 19–20.
5. *Ibid.*, p. 20.
6. *John Augustus, First Probation Officer*, published by the National Probation Association of America (New York, 1939) with foreword by Sheldon Glueck, in a new edition of Augustus's own book, which was printed in Boston in 1852, pp. 4–5.
7. *Ibid.*, pp. 32–46.
8. *Ibid.*, p. 34.
9. *Ibid.*, p. 19.

10. *Ibid.*, p. 34.
11. See also N.S. Timasheff, *One Hundred Years of Probation 1841–1951*, Part I (New York: Fordham University Press, 1941), pp. 7–11.
12. U.N. *Probation, op. cit.*, pp. 32–41.
13. Matthew Davenport Hill, *Suggestions for the Repression of Crime, contained in Charges delivered to Grand Juries of Birmingham, supported by Additional Facts and Arguments* (London: J.W. Parker and Son, 1857), pp. 350–2.
14. On the history of probation in England, see K. Ignatius, "Bedingte Verurteilung in England", *Zeitschrift für die gesamte Strafrechtswissenschaft*, vol. 21 (1901), pp. 743–802; Timasheff, *op. cit.*, pp. 12–26; U.N. *Probation, op. cit.*, pp. 42–50.
15. U.N. *Probation*, pp. 65–67; see also L. George, *Du Sursis Conditionnel a l'Exécution de la Peine et de la Libération Conditionnelle* (Paris: A. Rousseau, 1895).
16. von Liszt, *op. cit.*, p. 7.
17. Of interest is "Förhandlinger ved den Norske kriminalistførcnings forste møde i oktober 1892" (Kristiania: Aschehoug, 1893), p. 140ff, which reports on the change in opinion as a result of the bill.
18. Knud Waaben, *Betingede Straffedomme, en kritisk vurdering av dansk rets regler* (Copenhagen: Gyldenaal, 1948), p. 17.

[16]   THE NORWEGIAN GUARDIANSHIP COUNCIL

1. Negley K. Teeters & John Otto Reinemann, *The Challenge of Delinquency* (New York: Prentice-Hall, 1950), pp. 285–6. See also Ola Nyquist, *Juvenile Justice* (Doctoral Thesis, London: Macmillan, 1960), pp. 139–40, Note 8.
2. *Udkast til Lov om saedelig forkomne og vanvyrdede Børns Behandling*, pared by Dr. B. Getz (Kristiania: Gröndahl, 1892), pp. 24–5.
3. *Udkast til Lov om Tvangsopdragelse samt til Lov om Forandring i Bestemmelserne om Fulbyrdelse af Strafarbeide*, afgivet av den ved kongelig Resolution af 14de November 1885 nedsatte Straffelovkommission (Kristiania: Gröndahl, 1892).
4. *Aktstykker vedkommende Forslag til Lov om Behandling af forsømte Børn* (Kristiania: Gröndahl, 1895), containing the Justice Department's opinion of April 19, 1895, a report on the propositions of 1893, 1894, and 1895, as well as excerpts from Getz's draft and the Penal Law Commission's proposals, the proceedings of the meeting of criminalists in 1892 and the judicial committee's proposal of 1895.
5. Negotiations in Odelstinget, March 11–26, 1896. Quotations from March 23, pp. 162, 163 and 174.
6. Negotiations in Odelstinget, March 19, 1912, pp. 366–7.
7. Quoted by permission of Tove Stang Dahl from a memorandum she wrote to assist the writer. Guidance in finding the pertinent documents was provided by Professor Knut Sveri and Ms. Dahl.
8. U.N. Probation, pp. 95–311, *European Seminar on Probation, London 20–30 October 1952*, published by UN; Joan F.S. King, *The Probation Service* (London: Butterworth, 1958); Nikolai Hoff, *Ubestemte Dommer* (Oslo: Det Norske Videnskabsakademi, 1932); Charles L. Newman, *Sourcebook on Probation, Parole and Pardons* (Springfield, Ill.: Thomas, 1958).

Concerning juvenile courts see *inter alia* Sophia M. Robison, *Juvenile Delinquency* (New York: Holt, 1960), pp. 227–68; Paul W. Tappan, *Juvenile Delinquency* (New York: McGraw-Hill, 1949), pp. 167–286; Negley K. Teeters & John Otto Reinemann, pp. 277–383, these three books mainly treat American conditions; F.T. Giles, *The Juvenile Courts, Their Work and Problems* (London: G. Allen & Unwin, 1946), which concerns England.

[17] THE SHORT, SHARP SHOCK

1. von Liszt was one of the active proponents of the conditional sentence. His international reputation as a specialist in criminal law was extremely important to the subsequent explosive development of conditional sentence. As early as 1890, von Liszt recommended in an article in *Preussische Jahrbücher* (Berlin: S. Reimer, 1890) that short prison sentences, which he considered harmful, be replaced by conditional sentences. (See Franz von Liszt, *Strafrechtliche Aufsätze und Vorträge. Erster Band, 1875 bis 1891* (Berlin: J. Guttentag 1905); *Mitteilungen der Internationalen Kriminalistischen Vereinigung*, Bd. 21, Heft 1. "Festband anlässlich des 25 jährigen Bestehens der Internationalen Kriminalistischen Vereinigung, redigiert von Ernst Rosenfeld" (Berlin: J. Guttentag, 1914); Friedrich Kitzinger, *Die Internationale Kriminalistische Vereinigung* (Munich: C.H. Beck, 1905).

2. William Tallack, *Penological and Preventive Principles, with Special Reference to Europe and America*, etc. (London: Wertheimer, Lea & Co., 1889), p. 149.

3. Tallack, *op. cit.*, pp. 145–7.

4. *Ibid.*, p. 149.

5. *Ibid.*, pp. 366–7.

6. *Ibid.*, pp. 368–9.

7. F.W. Foerster, *Schuld und Sühne*, 2nd ed. (München: C.H. Beck, 1912), p. 109.

8. *Ibid.*

9. Rudolf Sieverts, "Till ungdomsarrestens problematik i den västtyska ungdomsstraffrätten," in *Nordisk kriminalistisk årsbok 1959* (Stockholm: Ivar Häggström, 1961), p. 37, based on a lecture delivered to the Swedish Society of Criminalists.

10. Sources: Sievert's lecture; *Walter Becker, Jugendgerichtsgesetz vom 4. August 1953. Textausgabe mit ergänzenden Gesetzen Vorschriften und Materialien*, in Aschendorff's "Juristische Handbücher," vol. 35 (Münster: undated); Council of Europe, European Committee on Crime Problems, *Report on Short-Term Methods of Treatment for Young Offenders*, August 2, 1965 (stencil); *Neue Wege zur Bekämpfung der Jugendkriminalität. Beiträge zur Durchführung des Jugendgerichtsgesetzes vom 4. August 1953. Wiedergabe der Verhandlungen des 9. Deutschen Jugendgerichtstages in München am 8. und 9. Oktober 1953, nebst einem kurzen Bericht über den 8. Deutschen Jugendgerichtstag in Bad Godesberg v. 20–22. April 1950. Herausgegeben von der Deutschen Vereinigung für Jugendgerichte und Jugendgerichtshilfen e. V.* (Cologne-Berlin: Heymann, 1955).

11. Günther Augustin, "Bland ungdomsfängelseeleverna i Tyskland," in the journal *Kriminalvården* no. 1 (1963), pp. 13–4.

12. T. Eriksson, "International Experiences and Trends of Development in the Treatment of Offenders" in *Crime, Punishment and Correction, Criminological Journal*, vol. 3, no. 3, (Cape Town: October 1974), pp. 69–70.
13. Sievert's lecture, p. 42.
14. Above mentioned *Report.*
15. Sources on Detention Centre: Above mentioned *Report*; Anne B. Dunlop & Sarah McCabe, *Young Men in Detention Centres* (London: Routledge and K. Paul, 1965); on Attendance Centers, F.H. McClintock, et al., *Attendance Centres* (London: Macmillan, 1961); on Remand Homes, The Cambridge Department of Criminal Science, *Detention in Remand Homes* (London: 1952); on Approved Schools, The Cambridge Department of Criminal Science, *Penal Reform in England* (London: Macmillan, 1946), pp. 128–42. See also Gordon Rose, *The Struggle for Penal Reform* (London: Stevens, 1961), pp. 227–32.
16. Vilhelm Karlström, "Behandlingen av unga lagöverträdare i England," *Kriminalvården,* Journal of the Correctional Administration in Sweden, no. 1 (1963), pp. 8–10.
17. Above mentioned *Report.*
18. The writer's notes.

[18] WITZWIL AND THE OPEN INSTITUTIONS

1. Sources consulted about Witzwil: John Lewis Gillin, *Taming the Criminal*, Adventures in Penology (New York: Macmillan, 1931), pp. 165–89; Otto Kellerhals, *Die bernischen Straf- und Arbeitskolonien im Gebiete der obern Jura-Gewässerkorrektion* (Biel: 1895); Hans Kellerhals, " 'Le Système Witzwil' et ses Applications en Suisse-Romande," in *Informations pénitentiaires suisses*, no. 4, 1955; Ernst Mischler, *Aus Wissen und Glauben. Otto Kellerhals in Witzwil, Zum 70. Geburtstag* (Bern: Rolli, undated).
2. Named for a man called Witzwil, a high executive in a company which tried to exploit the property as a building site (Mischler, *ibid.*, p. 11).
3. The title of the brochure was "Die Domäne und Strafkolonie Witzwil, eigene Gedanken über die Verbindung von Strafvollzug und Landwirtschaft oder mit anderen Worten, der Urbarmachung von Oedland durch Strafgefangene," quoted here from Mischler, *ibid.*, p. 12.
4. Francois Clerc, in a rapport to the U.N. Congress in Geneva 1960 on the Prevention of Crime and the Treatment of Offenders.
5. Adolf Goos, "Nogle Optegnelser fra et Besøg i svejtsiske Strafanstalter," in *Nordisk Tidsskrift for Faengselsvaesen og Praktisk Straffert*, vol. 23 (Copenhagen: 1900), pp. 49–51. Goos was assistant inspector at the Vridsløselille Reformatory.
6. The writer's own notes.
7. "Jahresbericht der Anstalten in Witzwil über das Jahr 1962," p. 17.
8. *ibid.*, p. 20.
9. *Ibid.*, p. 21.
10. "California Institution for Men, Chino, California," in *Handbook of American Prisons and Reformatories*, 5th ed. vol. II, "Pacific Coast States," the Osborne Association 1942, pp. 318–26.
11. *Ibid.*, p. 321.

12. Torsten Eriksson, in *Vårdorganisation för förvarade och internerade* Sveriges Officiella Utredningar 1953, report no. 32), pp. 62–5.
13. Id., "Amerikanska experimentanstalter," in *En anstalt för svårbehandlade* Sveriges Officiella Utredningar 1950, report no. 47), pp. 145–6.
14. John A.F. Watson, *Meet the Prisoner* (London: J. Cape, 1939), pp. 93–4.
15. Sir Lionel W. Fox, *The English Prison and Borstal Systems* (London: Routledge and K. Paul, 1952), p. 153.
16. A. Hallema, *Geschiedenis van het gevangeniswezen, hoofdzakelijk in Nederland* ('-Gravenhage: Staatsdrukkerij-en Uitgeverijbedrijf, 1958), p. 287 ff; id., "Drentse gevangenissen in verleden en heden," in *Nieuwe Drentse Volksalmanak*, 75e jaar-1957, pp. 105–40, (Assen.: Van Gorcum, 1957).
17. *Twelfth International Penal and Penitentiary Congress, the Hague*, 14–19 August 1950. Proceedings, vol. IV (Bern: Staempfli, 1951), pp. 1–168.
18. *First United Nations Congress on the Prevention of Crime and the Treatment of Offenders, Geneva, 22 August–3 September 1955, Report prepared by the Secretariat* (United Nations, New York: 1956).
19. Quoted from "Vankeinhoito" (Penal Care), nos. 7–8(1960) and 3–4(1964), translated to Swedish by Lennart Wälivaara, edited by Torsten Eriksson.

[19] HERSTEDVESTER AND THE PSYCHIATRIC CORRECTIONAL INSTITUTIONS

1. *The Digest of Justinian*, vol. I, translated by Charles Henry Monro, M.A. (Cambridge at the University Press: 1904).
2. Torsten Sondén, "De sinnesjukas straffrättsliga ställning i Sverige," published as a supplement to *Nordisk Tidskrift for Strafferet* Årg. 19 (Copenhagen: 1931), p. 5.
3. Bogdan Zlataric, "Le Statut juridique des délinquants anormaux," in *Les délinquants anormaux mentaux*, Colloquium organized in Bellagio April 21–25, 1963, in collaboration with Centro nazionale di prevenzione e difesa sociale, (Paris: Ed. Cujas, 1963) pp. 84–117. The imputability concept was introduced by Pufendorff in 1660.
4. Sondén, *op. cit.*, pp. 98–9.
5. Naumann's "Tidskrift för lagstiftning, lagskipning och förvaltning," 1866, pp. 70–1.
6. Cesare Lombroso, *Die Ursachen und Bekämpfung des Verbrechens*, translated to German by Hans Kurella and E. Jentsch (Berlin: H. Bermüller, 1902), pp. 354–5; Knut Pontopiddan, "Om behandlingen av sindssyge forbrydere," in *Nordisk Tidskrift for Faengelsvaesen*, vol. IV (Copenhagen: 1881), pp. 209–37. Cf. also Cesare Lombroso, *Crime, Its Causes and Remedies*, a translation into English, made by Henry P. Horton, and appearing in "The Modern Criminal Science Series" (Boston; Little, Brown & Co., 1918), pp. 397–8. This translation was made, not from Lombroso's original Italian text (*L'uomo delinquente*, 3 vol. (Torino: Bocca, 1896–97), the third volume containing the text here referred to), but from the abovementioned German as well as from a French translation.
7. Pontopiddan, *ibid.*, p. 227.
8. *Ibid.*, p. 228.
9. Livingstone Hall & Sheldon Glueck, *Cases and Materials on Criminal Law* (St. Paul, Minn.: West Publishing Co., 1940), pp. 379–81. M'Naghten is

also spelt McNaughten, which is said to be the bearer's own spelling of his name. Concerning unimputability in English Law, see Glanville L. Williams, *Criminal Law, the General Part* (London: Stevens, 1953), p. 290ff, and F.A. Whitlock, *Criminal Responsibility and Mental Illness* (London: Butterworths, 1963), pp. 20–53 (on the M'Naghten Rules).

10. L. Vernon Briggs, *The Manner of Man that Kills* (Boston: R.G. Badger, 1921), p. 12. Briggs raises the question whether a scientific study of the character, environment and development of an individual who has committed a crime of violence would not provide an explanation and a possibility of preventing such behavior in the future. "When we find a germ that kills people we do not annihilate it so that it is impossible to learn more about it. No, we put it under glass, nurse and study it under different conditions, find out its characteristics, its source and how it develops, so that we may be able to combat other germs of the same kind and render them at least harmless."

See also Winfred Overholser, "Psychiatry and the Law," in *Encyclopedia of Criminology*, edited by Vernon C. Branham and Samuel B. Kutasch (New York: Philosophical Library, 1949), pp. 394–8; Simon E. Soboloff, "From McNaghten to Durham and Beyond," in *Crime and Insanity*, edited by Richard W. Nice (New York: Philosophical Library, 1958), pp. 136–64.

11. Sir Lionel W. Fox, *The English Prison and Borstal Systems* (London: Routledge and K. Paul, 1952), pp. 242–52, and F.A. Whitlock, *op. cit.*

12. Paul Cornil, "Le traitement pénitentiaire des délinquants anormaux," in *Les délinquants anormaux* (*cf.*, note 3 above), p. 156.

13. Georg K. Stürup, *Forvaringsanstalten i Herstedvester, Beretning om arbejdet 1935–1951* (Copenhagen: 1959), p. 11.

14. *Ibid.*

15. Torsten Eriksson, *Kriminalvård, Idéer och experiment* (Stockholm: P.A. Norstedt och Söner, 1967), pp. 189–90.

16. Georg Stürup, "Danske erfaringer," in *Vårdorganisation för förvarade och internerade* (Sveriges Officiella Utredningar, 1953, report no. 32), pp. 46–7. About Herstedvester, see further Georg K. Stürup, *Krogede Skaebner* (Copenhagen: 1951), limited circulation, and *Herstedvesteriana*, a tribute to Stürup on his sixtieth birthday; also Georg K. Stürup, *Treating the "Untreatable"* (Baltimore: The Johns Hopkins Press, 1968).

17. Since the writer of this book was deeply involved in the creation of the institution and was long a target for criticism, he prefers not to go into this stormy period in Roxtuna's early history in detail.

18. *Cf.*, the periodical *Kriminalvården*, no. 1 (1962).

19. *Cf.*, p. 275.

20. Torsten Eriksson, "Två amerikanska experimentanstalter," in *Tidskrift för Kriminalvård*, no. 1 (1950), pp. 5–9.

[20]   HIGHFIELDS AND THE PSYCHOLOGICAL INSTITUTIONS

1. August Aichborn, *Verwahrloste Jugend, Die Psychoanalyse in der Fürsorgeerziehung. Zehn Vorträge zur ersten Einführung. Mit einem Geleitwort von Prof. Dr. Sigmund Freud.* Internationale Psychoanalytische Bibliotek No. XIX (Leipzig: Internationaler Psychoanalytischer Verl, 1925).

2. David Wills, *The Hawkspur Experiment. An Informal Account of the Training of Wayward Adolescence* (London: Allen and Unwin, 1941); id., *The Barn's Experiment* (London: Allen and Unwin, 1945).
3. J.H. Pratt, "The Class Method of Treating Consumption in the Home of the Poor," in *The Journal of the American Medical Association*, no. 49, pp. 755–9. Concerning the history of group therapy, see Raymond J. Corsini, *Methods of Group Psychotherapy* (New York: Blakistone Division, 1957), which also claims that the Austrian physician and "magnetizer" Anton Mesmer and the Marquis de Sade (!) were pioneers in the field.
4. See Torsten Eriksson, Kriminalvård, Idéer och experiment (Stockholm: Norstedt och Söner, 1967), pp. 199–201; see also Lloyd W. McCorkle, Albert Elias, F. Lovell Bixby, *The Highfields Story* (New York: Henry Holt and company, 1958); A. Elias, "The Highfields Program for Juvenile Delinquents" in *New Psychological Methods for the Treatment of Prisoners*. Proceedings of the International Colloquium of Brussels, 26–31 March 1962, published by the International Penal and Penitentiary Foundation (Nivelles: R. Marée, 1963), pp. 141–55.
5. H. Ashley Weeks, *Youthful Offenders at Highfields. An Evaluation of the Effects of the Short-Term Treatment of Delinquent Boys* (Ann Arbor: University of Michigan Press, 1958); Albert F. Axelrod, Highfields—A Short-Term Correctional Program for Youthful Offenders, in *UNAFEI Resource Material Series*, no. 9 (March 1975) (Fuchu, Tokyo), pp. 83–92.
6. T. Empey & Jerome Rabow, "The Provo Experiment in Delinquency Rehabilitation," *the American Sociological Review*, vol. 26, no. 5 (October 1961); Lamar T. Empey and Maynard L. Erickson, *The Provo Experiment* (Lexington, Mass: D.L. Heath, 1973). The experiment was closed in 1965 because of lack of public support and funds.
7. Norman D. Fenton, *An Introduction to Group Counseling in State Correctional Service* (Sacramento; Calif.: Dept. of Corrections, 1957), pp. 14–16; see also Joseph W. Eaton, "Group Counseling in Theory and Practice," in *New Psychological Methods for the Treatment of Prisoners*, etc. (4), pp. 53–69; Id., *A Handbook on the Use of Group Counseling in Correctional Institutions* (Sacramento, Calif.: 1965).
8. Joseph W. Eaton, *Stone Walls Not a Prison Make* (Springfield, Ill.: C.C. Thomas, 1962), pp. 163–4.
9. *Ibid.*, p. 168.
10. International Penal and Penitentiary Foundation, *New Psychological Methods for the Treatment of Prisoners*, see note 4.

[21] THE THERAPEUTIC COMMUNITY

1. *Alcoholics Anonymous*, Alcoholics Anonymous World Services, Inc., (New York: Alcoholics Anonymous Publ. Co., 1955), 5th printing in 1962, a new and revised edition, p. XIX.
2. Maxwell Jones, (a) *Social Psychiatry in Practice. The Idea of the Therapeutic Community.* (Harmondsworth: Penguin Books, 1968), foreword by G.M. Carstairs entitled Social Psychiatry in Practice, p. 9; (b) *Social Psychiatry, A Study of Therapeutic Communities* (London: Tavistock, 1952); (c) *Social Psychiatry in the Community, in Hospitals, and in Prisons* (Thomas, Springfield, Ill: C.C. Thomas, 1962).

3. Jones (a), *ibid.*, pp. 16–17.
4. *Ibid.*, p. 17.
5. *Ibid.*, p. 86.
6. *Ibid.*, p. 86.
7. *Ibid.*, pp. 137–138. *Cf.*, World Health Organization Technical Report Series No. 73, Geneva, 1953.
8. All this strongly resembles the educational philosophy put into practice by Anton Semjonovitj Makarenko, the great Russian reformer of the treatment of juvenile offenders. *See* pp. 147–9.
9. Dr. Lisbet Palmgren, *Vård av asociala i England*, in KRIMA, Magazine of the Swedish Correctional Administration, September, 1969, pp. 36–38.
10. The information about the two Dutch institutions comes from a report made by Dr. Karl-Erik Törnqvist, Chief Psychiatrist at the Hall Internment Institution in Sweden, *Där man satsar på behandling av kriminella recidivister*, in KRIMA Magazine of the Swedish Correctional Administration, February, 1969; and on a visit made by the writer to the Pompe Kliniek. The writer has also visited Grendon and Henderson.
11. Quoted from an article written by Sally O'Quin in *Life*, January 31, 1969.
12. The account of the early days of Synanon and of Dederich's own life is based upon two books, Daniel Casriel, *So Fair a House*, (Englewood Cliffs: Prentice-Hall, 1963), and Lewis Yablonsky, *Synanon, the Tunnel Back*. (New York: Macmillan, Penguin Books, 1965).
13. Casriel, *op. cit.*, pp. 23–24.
14. Quotations from Casriel, *op. cit.* pp. 24–25.
15. Interim Report 1964, published in Trenton, N.J., March, 1965, by the *Narcotic Drug Study Commission of the New Jersey Legislature*, p. 32.
16. *Ibid.*, p. 32.
17. The writer visited the Santa Monica establishment in 1969 and the San Francisco establishment in 1971. The descriptions under points 1 and 2 follow a stencilled statement given to him by Dave Fagel, "resident" (Leader) of the San Francisco establishment, while Mr. Jack Hurst, resident at Santa Monica, described orally the methods summarized under point 3.
18. Casriel, *op. cit.*, p. 33.
19. Narcotic Drug Commission, *op. cit.*, pp. 52 and 62.
20. The name "Daytop" is derived from "*D*rug *a*ddicts *y*ield *to* *p*ersuasion."
21. The writer visited Daytop Lodge in 1970.

[22] INTERNATIONAL CO-OPERATION

1. *Verhandlungen der ersten Versammlung für Gefängnisreform, zusammengetreten 1846 in Frankfurt a.M.* (Frankfurt-am-Main: Hermann Johann Kessler, 1847).
2. E.C. Wines, *Transactions of the National Congress on Penitentiary and Reformatory Discipline held at Cincinnati, Ohio, October 12–18, 1870* (Albany: Office of the Association, 1871).
3. For the history of the International Penal and Penitentiary Commission see *Recueil de Documents en Matière Pénale et Pénitentiaire, Bulletin de la Commission Internationale Pénale et Pénitentiaire*, vol. X (Bern: Staempfli, 1942/43), which contains an article by the then Secretary General Ernest Delaquis, "L'Oeuvre de la Commission internationale pénale et pénitentiaire

1872–1942", also translated into German, English and Italian; see also Negley K. Teeters, *Deliberations of the International Penal and Penitentiary
Congresses, Questions and Answers, 1872–1950* (Philadelphia: Temple University Book Store, 1949), and Benedict S. Alper and Jerry F. Boren, *Crime,
International Agenda, Concern and Action in the Prevention of Crime and
Treatment of Offenders, 1846–1972* (Lexington: Lexington Books, 1972).
4. In the United Nations Publication series there are separate reports of all the
congresses.
5. See *Rules for the treatment of prisoners drawn up in 1929 and revised in 1933
by the International Penal and Penitentiary Commission* (Geneva: 1933).

[23] THE HEART OF THE MATTER

1. For example, in the book *Unraveling Juvenile Delinquency* (New York: The
Commonwealth Fund, 1950).
2. The writer was at that time a member of the European Committee on Crime
Problems and bases his comments on notes taken during the discussion.
3. Bengt Börjesson, *Om påföljders verkningar* (On the Effects of Punishment)
(Stockholm: Almqvist och Wiksells, 1966). The English summary (p. 211)
states: "This is the main result of the study, a distinct and statistically demonstrated difference between the individual preventive effects in favour of
non-imprisonment." However, in *Statistisk tidskrift—Statistical Review*
(Stockholm: 1966), pp. 446–64 and 498–500 (English summary), Professor of
Statistics Carl-Erik Quensel wrote: "The analysis fails to take account, however, of all the sources of error that may exist in such an analysis, and it
seems in my opinion that the sources of error might very easily have effects of
such a kind as to render the difference demonstrated by the author merely
apparent."
4. Douglas Lipton, Robert Martinson and Judith Wilks, *The Effectiveness of
Correctional Treatment, A Survey of Treatment Evaluation Studies* (New
York: Praeger, 1975). This volume names over one thousand studies (pp.
633–724). Other noteworthy studies include: Donald Cressey, *The Prison,
Studies in Institutional Organization and Change* (New York: Holt, Rinehart
and Winston, 1961), Daniel Glaser, *The Effectiveness of a Prison and Parole
System* (New York: Bobbs-Merrill, 1964), Johs Andenaes, "Does Punishment
Deter Crime," *The Criminal Law Quarterly*, vol 11 (1968), pp. 76–93,
Roger Hood and Richard Sparks, *Key Issues in Criminology* (London: World
University Library, 1970).
5. From the writer's notes made at the meeting.

STANDARD MINIMUM RULES FOR THE TREATMENT OF PRISONERS

Resolution adopted on 30 August 1955

The First United Nations Congress on the Prevention of Crime and the Treatment of Offenders,

Having adopted the Standard Minimum Rules for the Treatment of Prisoners annexed to the present Resolution,

1. *Requests* the Secretary-General, in accordance with paragraph (*d*) of the annex to resolution 415(V) of the General Assembly of the United Nations, to submit these rules to the Social Commission of the Economic and Social Council for approval;

2. *Expresses* the hope that these rules be approved by the Economic and Social Council and, if deemed appropriate by the Council, by the General Assembly, and that they be transmitted to governments with the recommendation (*a*) that favourable consideration be given to their adoption and application in the administration of penal institutions, and (*b*) that the Secretary-General be informed every three years of the progress made with regard to their application;

3. *Expresses* the wish that, in order to allow governments to keep themselves informed of the progress made in this respect, the Secretary-General be requested to publish in the International Review of Criminal Policy the information sent by governments in pursuance of paragraph 2, and that he be authorized to ask for supplementary information if necessary;

4. *Expresses* also the wish that the Secretary-General be requested to arrange that the widest possible publicity be given to these rules.

Annex

STANDARD MINIMUM RULES FOR THE TREATMENT OF PRISONERS

PRELIMINARY OBSERVATIONS

1. The following rules are not intended to describe in detail a model system of penal institutions. They seek only, on the basis of the general consensus of contemporary thought and the

essential elements of the most adequate systems of today, to set out what is generally accepted as being good principle and practice in the treatment of prisoners and the management of institutions.

2. In view of the great variety of legal, social, economic and geographical conditions of the world, it is evident that not all of the rules are capable of application in all places and at all times. They should, however, serve to stimulate a constant endeavour to overcome practical difficulties in the way of their application, in the knowledge that they represent, as a whole, the minimum conditions which are accepted as suitable by the United Nations.

3. On the other hand, the rules cover a field in which thought is constantly developing. They are not intended to preclude experiment and practices, provided these are in harmony with the principles and seek to further the purposes which derive from the text of the rules as a whole. It will always be justifiable for the central prison administration to authorize departures from the rules in this spirit.

4. (1) Part I of the rules covers the general management of institutions, and is applicable to all categories of prisoners, criminal or civil, untried or convicted, including prisoners subject to " security measures " or corrective measures ordered by the judge.

(2) Part II contains rules applicable only to the special categories dealt with in each section. Nevertheless, the rules under section A, applicable to prisoners under sentence, shall be equally applicable to categories of prisoners dealt with in sections B, C and D, provided they do not conflict with the rules governing those categories and are for their benefit.

5. (1) The rules do not seek to regulate the management of institutions set aside for young persons such as Borstal institutions or correctional schools, but in general part I would be equally applicable in such institutions.

(2) The category of young prisoners should include at least all young persons who come within the jurisdiction of juvenile courts. As a rule, such young persons should not be sentenced to imprisonment.

PART I. RULES OF GENERAL APPLICATION

Basic principle

6. (1) The following rules shall be applied impartially. There shall be no discrimination on grounds of race, colour, sex, language,

religion, political or other opinion, national or social origin, property, birth or other status.

(2) On the other hand, it is necessary to respect the religious beliefs and moral precepts of the group to which a prisoner belongs.

Register

7. (1) In every place where persons are imprisoned there shall be kept a bound registration book with numbered pages in which shall be entered in respect of each prisoner received:

(a) Information concerning his identity;

(b) The reasons for his commitment and the authority therefor;

(c) The day and hour of his admission and release.

(2) No person shall be received in an institution without a valid commitment order of which the details shall have been previously entered in the register.

Separation of categories

8. The different categories of prisoners shall be kept in separate institutions or parts of institutions taking account of their sex, age, criminal record, the legal reason for their detention and the necessities of their treatment. Thus,

(a) Men and women shall so far as possible be detained in separate institutions; in an institution which receives both men and women the whole of the premises allocated to women shall be entirely separate;

(b) Untried prisoners shall be kept separate from convicted prisoners;

(c) Persons imprisoned for debt and other civil prisoners shall be kept separate from persons imprisoned by reason of a criminal offence;

(d) Young prisoners shall be kept separate from adults.

Accommodation

9. (1) Where sleeping accommodation is in individual cells or rooms, each prisoner shall occupy by night a cell or room by himself. If for special reasons, such as temporary overcrowding, it becomes necessary for the central prison administration to make an exception to this rule, it is not desirable to have two prisoners in a cell or room.

(2) Where dormitories are used, they shall be occupied by prisoners carefully selected as being suitable to associate with one

another in those conditions. There shall be regular supervision by night, in keeping with the nature of the institution.

10. All accommodation provided for the use of prisoners and in particular all sleeping accommodation shall meet all requirements of health, due regard being paid to climatic conditions and particularly to cubic content of air, minimum floor space, lighting, heating and ventilation.

11. In all places where prisoners are required to live or work,

(a) The windows shall be large enough to enable the prisoners to read or work by natural light, and shall be so constructed that they can allow the entrance of fresh air whether or not there is artificial ventilation;

(b) Artificial light shall be provided sufficient for the prisoners to read or work without injury to eyesight.

12. The sanitary installations shall be adequate to enable every prisoner to comply with the needs of nature when necessary and in a clean and decent manner.

13. Adequate bathing and shower installations shall be provided so that every prisoner may be enabled and required to have a bath or shower, at a temperature suitable to the climate, as frequently as necessary for general hygiene according to season and geographical region, but at least once a week in a temperate climate.

14. All parts of an institution regularly used by prisoners shall be properly maintained and kept scrupulously clean at all times.

Personal hygiene

15. Prisoners shall be required to keep their persons clean, and to this end they shall be provided with water and with such toilet articles as are necessary for health and cleanliness.

16. In order that prisoners may maintain a good appearance compatible with their self-respect, facilities shall be provided for the proper care of the hair and beard, and men shall be enabled to shave regularly.

Clothing and bedding

17. (1) Every prisoner who is not allowed to wear his own clothing shall be provided with an outfit of clothing suitable for the climate and adequate to keep him in good health. Such clothing shall in no manner be degrading or humiliating.

(2) All clothing shall be clean and kept in proper condition.

Underclothing shall be changed and washed as often as necessary for the maintenance of hygiene.

(3) In exceptional circumstances, whenever a prisoner is removed outside the institution for an authorized purpose, he shall be allowed to wear his own clothing or other inconspicuous clothing.

18. If prisoners are allowed to wear their own clothing, arrangements shall be made on their admission to the institution to ensure that it shall be clean and fit for use.

19. Every prisoner shall, in accordance with local or national standards, be provided with a separate bed, and with separate and sufficient bedding which shall be clean when issued, kept in good order and changed often enough to ensure its cleanliness.

Food

20. (1) Every prisoner shall be provided by the administration at the usual hours with food of nutritional value adequate for health and strength, of wholesome quality and well prepared and served.

(2) Drinking water shall be available to every prisoner whenever he needs it.

Exercise and sport

21. (1) Every prisoner who is not employed in out-door work shall have at least one hour of suitable exercise in the open air daily if the weather permits.

(2) Young prisoners, and others of suitable age and physique, shall receive physical and recreational training during the period of exercise. To this end space, installations and equipment should be provided.

Medical services

22. (1) At every institution there shall be available the services of at least one qualified medical officer who should have some knowledge of psychiatry. The medical services should be organized in close relationship to the general health administration of the community or nation. They shall include a psychiatric service for the diagnosis and, in proper cases, the treatment of states of mental abnormality.

(2) Sick prisoners who require specialist treatment shall be transferred to specialized institutions or to civil hospitals. Where

hospital facilities are provided in an institution, their equipment, furnishings and pharmaceutical supplies shall be proper for the medical care and treatment of sick prisoners, and there shall be a staff of suitably trained officers.

(3) The services of a qualified dental officer shall be available to every prisoner.

23. (1) In women's institutions there shall be special accommodation for all necessary pre-natal and post-natal care and treatment. Arrangements shall be made wherever practicable for children to be born in a hospital outside the institution. If a child is born in prison, this fact shall not be mentioned in the birth certificate.

(2) Where nursing infants are allowed to remain in the institution with their mothers, provision shall be made for a nursery staffed by qualified persons, where the infants shall be placed when they are not in the care of their mothers.

24. The medical officer shall see and examine every prisoner as soon as possible after his admission and thereafter as necessary, with a view particularly to the discovery of physical or mental illness and the taking of all necessary measures; the segregation of prisoners suspected of infectious or contagious conditions; the noting of physical or mental defects which might hamper rehabilitation, and the determination of the physical capacity of every prisoner for work.

25. (1) The medical officer shall have the care of the physical and mental health of the prisoners and should daily see all sick prisoners, all who complain of illness, and any prisoner to whom his attention is specially directed.

(2) The medical officer shall report to the director whenever he considers that a prisoner's physical or mental health has been or will be injuriously affected by continued imprisonment or by any condition of imprisonment.

26. (1) The medical officer shall regularly inspect and advise the director upon:

(a) The quantity, quality, preparation and service of food;

(b) The hygiene and cleanliness of the institution and the prisoners;

(c) The sanitation, heating, lighting and ventilation of the institution;

(d) The suitability and cleanliness of the prisoners' clothing and bedding;

(e) The observance of the rules concerning physical education and sports, in cases where there is no technical personnel in charge of these activities.

(2) The director shall take into consideration the reports and advice that the medical officer submits according to rules 25 (2) and 26 and, in case he concurs with the recommendations made, shall take immediate steps to give effect to those recommendations; if they are not within his competence or if he does not concur with them, he shall immediately submit his own report and the advice of the medical officer to higher authority.

Discipline and punishment

27. Discipline and order shall be maintained with firmness, but with no more restriction than is necessary for safe custody and well-ordered community life.

28. (1) No prisoner shall be employed, in the service of the institution, in any disciplinary capacity.

(2) This rule shall not, however, impede the proper functioning of systems based on self-government, under which specified social, educational or sports activities or responsibilities are entrusted, under supervision, to prisoners who are formed into groups for the purposes of treatment.

29. The following shall always be determined by the law or by the regulation of the competent administrative authority:

(a) Conduct constituting a disciplinary offence;

(b) The types and duration of punishment which may be inflicted;

(c) The authority competent to impose such punishment.

30. (1) No prisoner shall be punished except in accordance with the terms of such law or regulation, and never twice for the same offence.

(2) No prisoner shall be punished unless he has been informed of the offence alleged against him and given a proper opportunity of presenting his defence. The competent authority shall conduct a thorough examination of the case.

(3) Where necessary and practicable the prisoner shall be allowed to make his defence through an interpreter.

31. Corporal punishment, punishment by placing in a dark cell, and all cruel, inhuman or degrading punishments shall be completely prohibited as punishments for disciplinary offences.

32. (1) Punishment by close confinement or reduction of diet shall never be inflicted unless the medical officer has examined the prisoner and certified in writing that he is fit to sustain it.

(2) The same shall apply to any other punishment that may be prejudicial to the physical or mental health of a prisoner. In no case may such punishment be contrary to or depart from the principle stated in rule 31.

(3) The medical officer shall visit daily prisoners undergoing such punishments and shall advise the director if he considers the termination or alteration of the punishment necessary on grounds of physical or mental health.

Instruments of restraint

33. Instruments of restraint, such as handcuffs, chains, irons and strait-jackets, shall never be applied as a punishment. Furthermore, chains or irons shall not be used as restraints. Other instruments of restraint shall not be used except in the following circumstances:

(a) As a precaution against escape during a transfer, provided that they shall be removed when the prisoner appears before a judicial or administrative authority;

(b) On medical grounds by direction of the medical officer;

(c) By order of the director, if other methods of control fail, in order to prevent a prisoner from injuring himself or others or from damaging property; in such instances the director shall at once consult the medical officer and report to the higher administrative authority.

34. The patterns and manner of use of instruments of restraint shall be decided by the central prison administration. Such instruments must not be applied for any longer time than is strictly necessary.

Information to and complaints by prisoners

35. (1) Every prisoner on admission shall be provided with written information about the regulations governing the treatment of prisoners of his category, the disciplinary requirements of the institution, the authorized methods of seeking information and making complaints, and all such other matters as are necessary to enable him to understand both his rights and his obligations and to adapt himself to the life of the institution.

(2) If a prisoner is illiterate, the aforesaid information shall be conveyed to him orally.

36. (1) Every prisoner shall have the opportunity each week day of making requests or complaints to the director of the institution or the officer authorized to represent him.

(2) It shall be possible to make requests or complaints to the inspector of prisons during his inspection. The prisoner shall have the opportunity to talk to the inspector or to any other inspecting officer without the director or other members of the staff being present.

(3) Every prisoner shall be allowed to make a request or complaint, without censorship as to substance but in proper form, to the central prison administration, the judicial authority or other proper authorities through approved channels.

(4) Unless it is evidently frivolous or groundless, every request or complaint shall be promptly dealt with and replied to without undue delay.

Contact with the outside world

37. Prisoners shall be allowed under necessary supervision to communicate with their family and reputable friends at regular intervals, both by correspondence and by receiving visits.

38. (1) Prisoners who are foreign nationals shall be allowed reasonable facilities to communicate with the diplomatic and consular representatives of the State to which they belong.

(2) Prisoners who are nationals of States without diplomatic or consular representation in the country and refugees or stateless persons shall be allowed similar facilities to communicate with the diplomatic representative of the State which takes charge of their interests or any national or international authority whose task it is to protect such persons.

39. Prisoners shall be kept informed regularly of the more important items of news by the reading of newspapers, periodicals or special institutional publications, by hearing wireless transmissions, by lectures or by any similar means as authorized or controlled by the administration.

Books

40. Every institution shall have a library for the use of all categories of prisoners, adequately stocked with both recreational and instructional books, and prisoners shall be encouraged to make full use of it.

Religion

41. (1) If the institution contains a sufficient number of prisoners of the same religion, a qualified representative of that religion shall be appointed or approved. If the number of prisoners justifies it and conditions permit, the arrangement should be on a full-time basis.

(2) A qualified representative appointed or approved under paragraph (1) shall be allowed to hold regular services and to pay pastoral visits in private to prisoners of his religion at proper times.

(3) Access to a qualified representative of any religion shall not be refused to any prisoner. On the other hand, if any prisoner should object to a visit of any religious representative, his attitude shall be fully respected.

42. So far as practicable, every prisoner shall be allowed to satisfy the needs of his religious life by attending the services provided in the institution and having in his possession the books of religious observance and instruction of his denomination.

Retention of prisoners' property

43. (1) All money, valuables, clothing and other effects belonging to a prisoner which under the regulations of the institution he is not allowed to retain shall on his admission to the institution be placed in safe custody. An inventory thereof shall be signed by the prisoner. Steps shall be taken to keep them in good condition.

(2) On the release of the prisoner all such articles and money shall be returned to him except in so far as he has been authorized to spend money or send any such property out of the institution, or it has been found necessary on hygienic grounds to destroy any article of clothing. The prisoner shall sign a receipt for the articles and money returned to him.

(3) Any money or effects received for a prisoner from outside shall be treated in the same way.

(4) If a prisoner brings in any drugs or medicine, the medical officer shall decide what use shall be made of them.

Notification of death, illness, transfer, etc.

44. (1) Upon the death or serious illness of, or serious injury to a prisoner, or his removal to an institution for the treatment

of mental affections, the director shall at once inform the spouse, if the prisoner is married, or the nearest relative and shall in any event inform any other person previously designated by the prisoner.

(2) A prisoner shall be informed at once of the death or serious illness of any near relative. In case of the critical illness of a near relative, the prisoner should be authorized, whenever circumstances allow, to go to his bedside either under escort or alone.

(3) Every prisoner shall have the right to inform at once his family of his imprisonment or his transfer to another institution.

Removal of prisoners

45. (1) When prisoners are being removed to or from an institution, they shall be exposed to public view as little as possible, and proper safeguards shall be adopted to protect them from insult, curiosity and publicity in any form.

(2) The transport of prisoners in conveyances with inadequate ventilation or light, or in any way which would subject them to unnecessary physical hardship, shall be prohibited.

(3) The transport of prisoners shall be carried out at the expense of the administration and equal conditions shall obtain for all of them.

Institutional personnel

46. (1) The prison administration, shall provide for the careful selection of every grade of the personnel, since it is on their integrity, humanity, professional capacity and personal suitability for the work that the proper administration of the institutions depends.

(2) The prison administration shall constantly seek to awaken and maintain in the minds both of the personnel and of the public the conviction that this work is a social service of great importance, and to this end all appropriate means of informing the public should be used.

(3) To secure the foregoing ends, personnel shall be appointed on a full-time basis as professional prison officers and have civil service status with security of tenure subject only to good conduct, efficiency and physical fitness. Salaries shall be adequate to attract and retain suitable men and women; employment benefits and conditions of service shall be favourable in view of the exacting nature of the work.

47. (1) The personnel shall possess an adequate standard of education and intelligence.

(2)   Before entering on duty, the personnel shall be given a course of training in their general and specific duties and be required to pass theoretical and practical tests.

(3)   After entering on duty and during their career, the personnel shall maintain and improve their knowledge and professional capacity by attending courses of in-service training to be organized at suitable intervals.

48.   All members of the personnel shall at all times so conduct themselves and perform their duties as to influence the prisoners for good by their examples and to command their respect.

49.   (1)   So far as possible, the personnel shall include a sufficient number of specialists such as psychiatrists, psychologists, social workers, teachers and trade instructors.

(2)   The services of social workers, teachers and trade instructors shall be secured on a permanent basis, without thereby excluding part-time or voluntary workers.

50.   (1)   The director of an institution should be adequately qualified for his task by character, administrative ability, suitable training and experience.

(2)   He shall devote his entire time to his official duties and shall not be appointed on a part-time basis.

(3)   He shall reside on the premises of the institution or in its immediate vicinity.

(4)   When two or more institutions are under the authority of one director, he shall visit each of them at frequent intervals. A responsible resident official shall be in charge of each of these institutions.

51.   (1)   The director, his deputy, and the majority of the other personnel of the institution shall be able to speak the language of the greatest number of prisoners, or a language understood by the greatest number of them.

(2)   Whenever necessary, the services of an interpreter shall be used.

52.   (1)   In institutions which are large enough to require the services of one or more full-time medical officers, at least one of them shall reside on the premises of the institution or in its immediate vicinity.

(2)   In other institutions the medical officer shall visit daily and shall reside near enough to be able to attend without delay in cases of urgency.

53.   (1)   In an institution for both men and women, the part

of the institution set aside for women shall be under the authority of a responsible woman officer who shall have the custody of the keys of all that part of the institution.

(2) No male member of the staff shall enter the part of the institution set aside for women unless accompanied by a woman officer.

(3) Women prisoners shall be attended and supervised only by women officers. This does not, however, preclude male members of the staff, particularly doctors and teachers, from carrying out their professional duties in institutions or parts of institutions set aside for women.

54. (1) Officers of the institutions shall not, in their relations with the prisoners, use force except in self-defence or in cases of attempted escape, or active or passive physical resistance to an order based on law or regulations. Officers who have recourse to force must use no more than is strictly necessary and must report the incident immediately to the director of the institution.

(2) Prison officers shall be given special physical training to enable them to restrain aggressive prisoners.

(3) Except in special circumstances, staff performing duties which bring them into direct contact with prisoners should not be armed. Furthermore, staff should in no circumstances be provided with arms unless they have been trained in their use.

Inspection

55. There shall be a regular inspection of penal institutions and services by qualified and experienced inspectors appointed by a competent authority. Their task shall be in particular to ensure that these institutions are administered in accordance with existing laws and regulations and with a view to bringing about the objectives of penal and correctional services.

PART II. RULES APPLICABLE TO SPECIAL CATEGORIES

A. PRISONERS UNDER SENTENCE

Guiding principles

56. The guiding principles hereafter are intended to show the spirit in which penal institutions should be administered and the purposes at which they should aim, in accordance with the declaration made under Preliminary Observation 1 of the present text.

57. Imprisonment and other measures which result in cutting off an offender from the outside world are afflictive by the very fact of taking from the person the right of self-determination by depriving him of his liberty. Therefore the prison system shall not, except as incidental to justifiable segregation or the maintenance of discipline, aggravate the suffering inherent in such a situation.

58. The purpose and justification of a sentence of imprisonment or a similar measure deprivative of liberty is ultimately to protect society against crime. This end can only be achieved if the period of imprisonment is used to ensure, so far as possible, that upon his return to society the offender is not only willing but able to lead a law-abiding and self-supporting life.

59. To this end, the institution should utilize all the remedial, educational, moral, spiritual and other forces and forms of assistance which are appropriate and available, and should seek to apply them according to the individual treatment needs of the prisoners.

60. (1) Tne régime of the institution should seek to minimize any differences between prison life and life at liberty which tend to lessen the responsibility of the prisoners or the respect due to their dignity as human beings.

(2) Before the completion of the sentence, it is desirable that the necessary steps be taken to ensure for the prisoner a gradual return to life in society. This aim may be achieved, depending on the case, by a pre-release régime organized in the same institution or in another appropriate institution, or by release on trial under some kind of supervision which must not be entrusted to the police but should be combined with effective social aid.

61. The treatment of prisoners should emphasize not their exclusion from the community, but their continuing part in it. Community agencies should, therefore, be enlisted wherever possible to assist the staff of the institution in the task of social rehabilitation of the prisoners. There should be in connexion with every institution social workers charged with the duty of maintaining and improving all desirable relations of a prisoner with his family and with valuable social agencies. Steps should be taken to safeguard, to the maximum extent compatible with the law and the sentence, the rights relating to civil interests, social security rights and other social benefits of prisoners.

62. The medical services of the institution shall seek to detect and shall treat any physical or mental illnesses or defects which may hamper a prisoner's rehabilitation. All necessary medical, surgical and psychiatric services shall be provided to that end.

63. (1) The fulfilment of these principles requires individualiza-

tion of treatment and for this purpose a flexible system of classifying prisoners in groups; it is therefore desirable that such groups should be distributed in separate institutions suitable for the treatment of each group.

(2) These institutions need not provide the same degree of security for every group. It is desirable to provide varying degrees of security according to the needs of different groups. Open institutions, by the very fact that they provide no physical security against escape but rely on the self-discipline of the inmates, provide the conditions most favourable to rehabilitation for carefully selected prisoners.

(3) It is desirable that the number of prisoners in closed institutions should not be so large that the individualization of treatment is hindered. In some countries it is considered that the population of such institutions should not exceed five hundred. In open institutions the population should be as small as possible.

(4) On the other hand, it is undesirable to maintain prisons which are so small that proper facilities cannot be provided.

64. The duty of society does not end with a prisoner's release. There should, therefore, be governmental or private agencies capable of lending the released prisoner efficient after-care directed towards the lessening of prejudice against him and towards his social rehabilitation.

Treatment

65. The treatment of persons sentenced to imprisonment or a similar measure shall have as its purpose, so far as the length of the sentence permits, to establish in them the will to lead law-abiding and self-supporting lives after their release and to fit them to do so. The treatment shall be such as will encourage their self-respect and develop their sense of responsibility.

66. (1) To these ends, all appropriate means shall be used, including religious care in the countries where this is possible, education, vocational guidance and training, social casework, employment counselling, physical development and strengthening of moral character, in accordance with the individual needs of each prisoner, taking account of his social and criminal history, his physical and mental capacities and aptitudes, his personal temperament, the length of his sentence and his prospects after release.

(2) For every prisoner with a sentence of suitable length, the director shall receive, as soon as possible after his admission,

full reports on all the matters referred to in the foregoing paragraph. Such reports shall always include a report by a medical officer, wherever possible qualified in psychiatry, on the physical and mental condition of the prisoner.

(3) The reports and other relevant documents shall be placed in an individual file. This file shall be kept up to date and classified in such a way that it can be consulted by the responsible personnel whenever the need arises.

Classification and individualization

67. The purposes of classification shall be:

(a) To separate from others those prisoners who, by reason of their criminal records or bad characters, are likely to exercise a bad. influence;

(b) To divide the prisoners into classes in order to facilitate their treatment with a view to their social rehabilitation.

68. So far as possible separate institutions or separate sections of an institution shall be used for the treatment of the different classes of prisoners.

69. As soon as possible after admission and after a study of the personality of each prisoner with a sentence of suitable length, a programme of treatment shall be prepared for him in the light of the knowledge obtained about his individual needs, his capacities and dispositions.

Privileges

70. Systems of privileges appropriate for the different classes of prisoners and the different methods of treatment shall be established at every institution, in order to encourage good conduct, develop a sense of responsibility and secure the interest and co-operation of the prisoners in their treatment.

Work

71. (1) Prison labour must not be of an afflictive nature.

(2) All prisoners under sentence shall be required to work, subject to their physical and mental fitness as determined by the medical officer.

(3) Sufficient work of a useful nature shall be provided to keep prisoners actively employed for a normal working day.

(4) So far as possible the work provided shall be such as will maintain or increase the prisoners' ability to earn an honest living after release.

(5) Vocational training in useful trades shall be provided for prisoners able to profit thereby and especially for young prisoners.

(6) Within the limits compatible with proper vocational selection and with the requirements of institutional administration and discipline, the prisoners shall be able to choose the type of work they wish to perform.

72. (1) The organization and methods of work in the institutions shall resemble as closely as possible those of similar work outside institutions, so as to prepare prisoners for the conditions of normal occupational life.

(2) The interests of the prisoners and of their vocational training, however, must not be subordinated to the purpose of making a financial profit from an industry in the institution.

73. (1) Preferably institutional industries and farms should be operated directly by the administration and not by private contractors.

(2) Where prisoners are employed in work not controlled by the administration, they shall always be under the supervision of the institution's personnel. Unless the work is for other departments of the government the full normal wages for such work shall be paid to the administration by the persons to whom the labour is supplied, account being taken of the output of the prisoners.

74. (1) The precautions laid down to protect the safety and health of free workmen shall be equally observed in institutions.

(2) Provision shall be made to indemnify prisoners against industrial injury, including occupational disease, on terms not less favourable than those extended by law to free workmen.

75. (1) The maximum daily and weekly working hours of the prisoners shall be fixed by law or by administrative regulation, taking into account local rules or custom in regard to the employment of free workmen.

(2) The hours so fixed shall leave one rest day a week and sufficient time for education and other activities required as part of the treatment and rehabilitation of the prisoners.

76. (1) There shall be a system of equitable remuneration of the work of prisoners.

(2)   Under the system prisoners shall be allowed to spend at least a part of their earnings on approved articles for their own use and to send a part of their earnings to their family.

(3)   The system should also provide that a part of the earnings should be set aside by the administration so as to constitute a savings fund to be handed over to the prisoner on his release.

Education and recreation

77.   (1)   Provision shall be made for the further education of all prisoners capable of profiting thereby, including religious instruction in the countries where this is possible.   The education of illiterates and young prisoners shall be compulsory and special attention shall be paid to it by the administration.

(2)   So far as practicable, the education of prisoners shall be integrated with the educational system of the country so that after their release they may continue their education without difficulty.

78.   Recreational and cultural activities shall be provided in all institutions for the benefit of the mental and physical health of prisoners.

Social relations and after-care

79.   Special attention shall be paid to the maintenance and improvement of such relations between a prisoner and his family as are desirable in the best interests of both.

80.   From the beginning of a prisoner's sentence consideration shall be given to his future after release and he shall be encouraged and assisted to maintain or establish such relations with persons or agencies outside the institution as may promote the best interests of his family and his own social rehabilitation.

81.   (1)   Services and agencies. governmental or otherwise, which assist released prisoners to re-establish themselves in society shall ensure, so far as is possible and necessary, that released prisoners be provided with appropriate documents and identification papers, have suitable homes and work to go to, are suitably and adequately clothed having regard to the climate and season, and have sufficient means to reach their destination and maintain themselves in the period immediately following their release.

(2)   The approved representatives of such agencies shall have all necessary access to the institution and to prisoners and shall be taken into consultation as to the future of a prisoner from the beginning of his sentence.

(3) It is desirable that the activities of such agencies shall be centralized or co-ordinated as far as possible in order to secure the best use of their efforts.

B. Insane and Mentally Abnormal Prisoners

82. (1) Persons who are found to be insane shall not be detained in prisons and arrangements shall be made to remove them to mental institutions as soon as possible.

(2) Prisoners who suffer from other mental diseases or abnormalities shall be observed and treated in specialized institutions under medical management.

(3) During their stay in a prison, such prisoners shall be placed under the special supervision of a medical officer.

(4) The medical or psychiatric service of the penal institutions shall provide for the psychiatric treatment of all other prisoners who are in need of such treatment.

83. It is desirable that steps should be taken, by arrangement with the appropriate agencies, to ensure if necessary the continuation of psychiatric treatment after release and the provision of social-psychiatric after-care.

C. Prisoners under Arrest or Awaiting Trial

84. (1) Persons arrested or imprisoned by reason of a criminal charge against them, who are detained either in police custody or in prison custody (jail) but have not yet been tried and sentenced, will be referred to as " untried prisoners " hereinafter in these rules.

(2) Unconvicted prisoners are presumed to be innocent and shall be treated as such.

(3) Without prejudice to legal rules for the protection of individual liberty or prescribing the procedure to be observed in respect of untried prisoners, these prisoners shall benefit by a special régime which is described in the following rules in its essential requirements only.

85. (1) Untried prisoners shall be kept separate from convicted prisoners.

(2) Young untried prisoners shall be kept separate from adults and shall in principle be detained in separate institutions.

86. Untried prisoners shall sleep singly in separate rooms,

with the reservation of different local custom in respect of the climate.

87. Within the limits compatible with the good order of the institution, untried prisoners may, if they so desire, have their food procured at their own expense from the outside, either through the administration or through their family or friends. Otherwise, the administration shall provide their food.

88. (1) An untried prisoner shall be allowed to wear his own clothing if it is clean and suitable.

(2) If he wears prison dress, it shall be different from that supplied to convicted prisoners.

89. An untried prisoner shall always be offered opportunity to work, but shall not be required to work. If he chooses to work, he shall be paid for it.

90. An untried prisoner shall be allowed to procure at his own expense or at the expense of a third party such books, newspapers, writing materials and other means of occupation as are compatible with the interests of the administration of justice and the security and good order of the institution.

91. An untried prisoner shall be allowed to be visited and treated by his own doctor or dentist if there is reasonable ground for his application and he is able to pay any expenses incurred.

92. An untried prisoner shall be allowed to inform immediately his family of his detention and shall be given all reasonable facilities for communicating with his family and friends, and for receiving visits from them, subject only to such restrictions and supervision as are necessary in the interests of the administration of justice and of the security and good order of the institution.

93. For the purposes of his defence, an untried prisoner shall be allowed to apply for free legal aid where such aid is available, and to receive visits from his legal adviser with a view to his defence and to prepare and hand to him confidential instructions. For these purposes, he shall if he so desires be supplied with writing material. Interviews between the prisoner and his legal adviser may be within sight but not within the hearing of a police or institution official.

D. CIVIL PRISONERS

94. In countries where the law permits imprisonment for debt or by order of a court under any other non-criminal process,

persons so imprisoned shall not be subjected to any greater restriction or severity than is necessary to ensure safe custody and good order. Their treatment shall be not less favourable than that of untried prisoners, with the reservation, however, that they may possibly be required to work.

INDEX

Discipline of prisoners (cont'd)
  Norfolk Island, 84; at Saint Michael,
  30; at Wethersfield, 59–60
Disease in prisons, 34–35, 65, 67, 75
Dreiser, Theodore, quoted 63
Drug addiction, 141, 233–38
Ducpetiaux, Edouard, quoted 74
Dwight, Reverend Louis, quoted 51

Eastern penitentiary, 62–72, 74, 77
Eaton, Joseph W., quoted 224
Eden, Sir William, 43
Education, 89, 98; at Auburn, 55; at
  Bellefaire Home, 129; at Boston
  House of Reformation, 132, 134; at
  Chino, 188; at Eastern penitentiary,
  71; at Elmira, 100; at La Maison
  Paternelle, 122–23; at Mountjoy,
  93; at Norfolk Island, 86; at Rauhes
  Haus, 109; at Wehrli, 108
Edward VI, 8
Elizabeth I, 33, 89
Elmhorn, Dr. Kerstin, 251
Elmira prison, 99–104
Employment, 91, 96, 155, 168–69;
  and juveniles, 157; and recidivism,
  95–96; at Witzwil, 183, 184
Enlightenment, The, 38
Eriksen, Alfred, quoted 165
Escape, 11, 20, 34, 233, 248; at Au-
  burn, 48; at Eastern penitentiary, 65;
  at Lusk, 95; at Natural Bridge, 191;
  at Roxtuna, 209; at Sing Sing, 56; at
  Wethersfield, 60; at Witzwil, 183
Exercise, 48, 80; at Eastern peniten-
  tiary, 63–65, 71; at Elmira, 100; at
  Pentonville, 74–75
Expenses, institutional 59, 60–61, 73,
  76, 78; at Bellefaire Home, 131; at
  Eastern penitentiary, 69; at George
  Junior Republic, 134; at La Colonie
  du Val d'Yèvre, 124; at La Maison
  Paternelle, 123; at Mettray, 124,
  127; at Norfolk Island, 86; at Rauhes

Haus, 124, 127; at Roxtuna, 208; at
  Synanon, 237; at Witzwil, 182

Family substitutes: for juveniles, 107–
  31; at Mettray, 120–23; at Rauhes
  Haus, 109–12, 114–16; at Wehrli
  Institution, 107–8
Fenton, Dr. Norman, 221, 223
Fielding, Henry, 35
Fling, 152–53
Foerster, F.W., 169, quoted 170
Fontana, Carlo, 28
Franci, Filippo, 27–28, 30

Galsworthy, John, 77
Gambling, 23
Gaol fever. See Disease in prison.
Geis, Gilbert, quoted 47
George Junior Republic, 134–46
George, William R., 134, 135, 136
Getz, General Bernhard, 160–61
Ghent prison, 18–25, 37, 39–40, 43,
  46, 48, 62–63
Gipps, Sir George, 86–87
Gloucester prison, 47, 168
Glueck, Eleanor, 101
Göebbles, Dr. Joseph, 1
Golden Rule Brotherhood, 142–43
Gosse, Dr. L.A., 75
Grendon Underwood prison, 231–32
Grievance court, 142
Griffiths, Major Arthur, quoted 103
Grünhut, Max, quoted 10
Guardianship Council, 161, 162,
  164–66
Gyllenkrok, Baron Gustaf, quoted
  117–18

Hagerup, Francis, 162
Hagstömer, Jonas, 5
Hamburg Society for Visiting the Poor,
  108–9
Hanway, Jonas, quoted 31, 35
Haviland, John, 48, 62–64, 74, 76

Hawthorne Cedar Knolls School, 211–15
Helsinki Work Camp, 192–97
Henderson Hospital, 229–32
Heretics, 10
Herstedvester institution, 204–7
Heuss, Theodor, *quoted* 120
Heytesbury Street Refuge, 96
Highfields, 217–20
Hill, Matthew Davenport, 88, 92, 156–7
Hitler, Adolf, 119
Homosexuality, 141, 143–44, 185, 248
Hospitals, 40, 41, 47
Howard, D.L., *quoted* 42
Howard, John, 11, 15–16, 23, 27, *quoted* 30–31, 32–34, 45, 47, 84, 239, 258 (nn. 13, 14, 18)
Howard League for Penal Reform, 104, 158, 168

Indeterminate sentences, 13, 83–84, 99, 100; in California, 189; at Elmira, 102
Insanity, 77–78, 207–15; at Auburn, 49; and classification, 201, 204; at Eastern penitentiary, 72–73; and medical evidence, 202; at Pentonville, 75–76; psychiatric examination for, 202–3; and Roman law, 198–99; and solitary confinement, 200
International Association of Penal Law, 244
International Penal and Penitentiary Commission, 240–41, 243–45
International Penal and Penitentiary Congress, 191
International Society for Criminology, 251
International Society of Social Defense, 244
International Union of Penal Law, 168
Irish Progressive System, 91–97

Isolation, 26, 31, 37, 43–49, 74; at Auburn, 141; at Bolcheva, 151; at Casa Pia, 28; at Eastern penitentiary, 62, 68, 70; and Jugendarrest, 171–72; at Mettray 121–23; at Pentonville, 75–76; at Roxtuna, 209; at Saint Michael, 20

Jail fever. *See* Disease in prison.
Jebb, Sir Joshua, 74, 91–92, 97
Jewish Agency, the, 128
Jones, Maxwell, 227–33
Joseph II, 23
Judicial reprieve, 152
Jugendarrest, 170–76
Julius, Dr. Nicholas Heinrich, *quoted* 52, 73, 109, 134, 239
Justinian I, 4–5
Juvenile court, 156, 157, 160, 166–67, 171
Juvenile crime, 14, 27–28, 169, 250; at Bellefaire Home, 128; at Bolchevo, 149–51, 154–56; at Borstal, 104–6; at Casa Pia, 27–28; at Detention Centres, 176–80; at Djershinski Commune, 149; at George Junior Republic, 134; and Guardianship Councils, 160–61; at Hawthorne Cedar Knolls School, 211–15; at Highfields, 217–20; and Jugendarrest, 170–76; at Maxim Gorki Work Colony, 147–48; at Rauhes Haus, 108–12, 114–16; at Roxtuna, 207–11; at Saint Michael, 28–30; at Wehrli, 107–8

Kellerhals, Otto, 181–82, 184–86
Kling, Herman, *quoted* 249
Klukman, Jesuit, 21

Labor in prison, 10, 18–19, 31, 37, 45–46, 71, 75, 84, 86, 93, 99, 247; at Auburn, 62, 65–67; at Bolchevo, 150; at Boston House of Reforma-

Panopticon, 46–47, 255 (n.7)
Pardons: at Auburn, 58; at Eastern penitentiary, 67–68; and transportation, 89–90;
    see also Ticket of leave
Paterson, Alexander, 72, quoted 77–80 and 147
Paul, Sir George Onesiphorus, quoted 43, 44
Penal laws, 4, 5, 30–31, 40
Penal Servitude Act (England), 90–91
Penitentiary Act (England), 43
Penn, William, 44
Pennsylvania system, (see also Western penitentiary), 73, 76
Pentonville prison, 74, 90
Personnel of prisons, 33, 34, 60; accommodations for, 95; at Auburn, 56; at Bellefaire Home, 129–30; at Boston House of Reformation, 132; conduct of, 4, 37, 54, 72, 86, 94, 195; at Eastern penitentiary, 66–67; at La Colonie du Val d'Yèvre, 124; at Mettray, 120–21; payment of, 37, 112; at the Rasphuis, 4–15; at Sing Sing, 57; training of, 111–13, 179, 190–91, 208
Petri, Olaus, 2–3
Philadelphia Society for Alleviating the Miseries of Public Prisons, 45, 69, 73
Photography: for crime prevention, 95
Pilsbury, Amos, 60
Pilsbury, Moses, 60, 262 (n. 12)
Plato, 3
Police Court Mission, 157
Political prisoners, 10
Pompe-kliniek, W.P.J., 232
Pope Boniface VIII, 5
Pope Clement XI, 28
Pope Innocent VIII, 4, 27
Psychopaths, 202; in Herstedvester, 204–7; juvenile, 207–15
Psychotherapy, 217, 219, 220–24, 231;

at Bellefaire Home, 130; at Boys Republic, 139; at Chino, 188; at Natural Bridge, 191
Pratt, J.H., 217
Prehn, Reverend Wolfgang, 119
Prevention of Crime and Treatment of Offenders, 1
Prevention of Crime Act of 1908 (England), 105
Prince, Dr. Richard, 36
Prisoners aid societies (see also individual listings), 45, 51
Probation, 90, 106, 152–59, 201; for Boys Republic, 139; for insanity, 203, 218; in Sweden, 248
Probation of First Offenders Act (U.S.), 158
Property in service, 89
Public punishment, 2
Public Works prisons, 91
Punishment, philosophy of, 25–27, 44, 51, 57–58, 80, 82–83, 88, 249; and Brockway, 98–99; and Crofton, 92; and Howard, 37; and Jugendarrest, 173–76; and Tallack, 168–69

Quakers, 44, 45
Qvam, Ole Anton, 161, quoted 163–64

Rapping, 65; alphabet for, 260 (n. 9)
Rasphuis, the, 13–17, 20, 39
Rauhes Haus, 108–19, 238
Recidivism, 190, 249–51; at Bolchevo, 149–51; at Detention Centres, 178; at Elmira, 100; at Helsinki Work Camp, 194; at Highfields, 220; at Lusk, 95–96; at Rauhes Haus, 119; in Sweden, 248; at van der Hover Kliniek, 232
Recognizance, 152, 153, 157
Recreation: at Auburn, 43, 145–46; at Bellefaire Home, 130; at Bolchevo, 151; at Chino, 189; at Elmira, 100;

Recreation *(cont'd)*
  at George Junior Republic, 136; at
  Helsinki Work Camp, 195–6; and
  Jugendarrest, 173; at Natural Bridge,
  191; at Norfolk Island, 87; at Rauhes
  Haus, 118; at Roxtuna, 210
Reformation, the, 6, 26
Reformatories, 98–99, 101, 104,
  120–23
Register, 29, 57, 101, 157
Rehabilitation, 12, 16–17, 26, 43, 44,
  79; of alcoholics, 157; at Auburn,
  50; at Chino, 186–90; at Detention
  Centres, 176–80, 250; at Eastern
  penitentiary, 68–69; at Elmira, 100;
  at Ghent, 22; and Juggendarrest,
  173–74, 250; at La Maison Paternelle, 121–23; at Natural Bridge,
  190–92; at Norfolk Island, 83–84,
  88; at Pentonville, 74; at Saint
  Michael, 28–30; at Witzwil, 182
Religion: at Auburn 51, 55, 58; at Bellefaire Home, 128; at Boston House
  of Reformation, 134; at Chino, 189;
  at Eastern penitentiary, 66, 68, 69,
  71; at Elmira, 101; at Ghent, 23, 26;
  at Helsinki Work Camp, 196; at La
  Colonie du Val D'Yèvre, 126; at
  Mettray, 120–21; at Mountjoy, 93;
  at Norfolk Island, 86; at Rauhes
  Haus, 110, 114–18; at Saint
  Michael, 28–29; at Sing Sing, 57
Ridley, Bishop Nicolas, 8, 255 (n. 3)
Right or wrong test, 201
Riots, 85, 88
Roosenberg, Dr. Anna Marie, 232
Roxtuna, 207–11
Royal Serafimer Order Society, 201
Ruck, S.K., 77
Ruggles-Brise, Sir Evelyn, 104–5
Rules for Judges, The, 2–3
Rush, Benjamin, 44

Safety, 37, 54, 65

Saint Bruno of Cologne, 27
Saint Cyprian, Bishop of Carthage,
  3–4
Saint Michael House of Correction,
  28–30, 39, 43, 48, 63, 176, 257
  (n.7)
Sanitation, 34–35, 37, 49, 51, 53–54,
  65
San Michele, Ospizio di. *See* Saint
  Michael House of Correction.
San Quentin, 187–89
Savage, E.H., 156
Scudder, Kenyon J., 187–88
Security, 47, 95; at Auburn, 53–55; at
  Detention Centres, 179; at Ghent,
  24; at Helsinki Work Camp, 193; at
  Saint Michael, 29–30
Self-government, 132–51; at Auburn,
  139–47; at Boston House of Refor-
  mation, 132–34; at Boys Republic,
  136–39; at Djershinski Commune,
  149; at George Junior Republic,
  134–36; at Maxim Gorki Work Col-
  ony, 148; at Sing Sing, 142
Sellin, Thorsten, 1, 3, 11, 17, *quoted*
  27, 30, 46, 241
Seneca, 3
Sentences, conditional, 157, 158,
  273–74 (n. 1)
Separate system, 62–66, 74, 76–77,
  97, 102, 104
Separation of sexes, 35, 43–44, 71–72,
  149–150, 211–13, 219
Shock treatment, 177–180
Sieveking, Johann Peter, 109
Silence, 26, 37; at Auburn, 48–49,
  51–61; at Eastern penitentiary, 65; at
  Ghent, 23; at Pentonville, 75; at
  Philadelphia, 45; at Sing Sing,
  56–57
Simula, Arvo, 192–96
Sing Sing, 51–52, 56–59, 99, 142,
  261 (n. 10)
Slavery, 5, 254 (n. 11)

Walnut Street prison, 44–45, 62, 72, 76

Wehrli institution, 107–8

Wehrli, Johann Jakob, 107–8

Wells, Reverend E.M.P., 132–34

Wesley, John, *quoted* 41

West, John, *quoted* 85

Western Penitentiary, 47, 59

Wethersfield, 59–60, 73

Wichern, Johann Hinrich, 108–119, 122, 238

Wigram, Judge Knox, *quoted* 169

Wilhelm I, 113

Wilhelm IV of Prussia, Friedrich, 112–13

Wilste, Robert, 58, *quoted* 59

Wines, Enoch C., 239–40, 244

Winter, Alenxander, *quoted* 103

Wistar, Richard, 45

Witzwil prison, 181–86

Yoshitsuju Baba, 242

Zeller, August, 98

Zetterberg, Herman, 208